More praise for *The Black Sheep*

"Cuts through the brag of 'Pappy' Boyington to the unvarnished realities of the remarkable Black Sheep."

—Stanley Weintraub
Author of *Long Day's Journey into War*

"Any scrupulously fair squadron history would take some of the gloss off the Boyington myth. . . . But enough of the myth remains—enough to serve as a reminder of the swashbuckling Black Sheep, their screwball commander, and the planes they flew with such consummate skill."

—*Naval Institute Proceedings*

"Takes us to the Solomon Islands in the shoes of young hotshot pilots, and nudges us to experience the squalid conditions of islands so newly liberated."

—*ForeWord Magazine*

THE BLACK SHEEP

The Definitive Account of Marine Fighting Squadron 214 in World War II

Bruce Gamble

BALLANTINE BOOKS • NEW YORK

A Presidio Press Book
Published by The Random House Publishing Group
 Published in the United States by The Random House Publishing Group, a division of Random House, Inc., New York and simultaneously in Canada by Random House of Canada Limited, Toronto. Originally published by Presidio Press, an imprint of The Random House Publishing Group, a division of Random House, Inc., in 1998.

Presidio Press and colophon are trademarks of Random House, Inc.

www.presidiopress.com

ISBN 0-89141-825-3

Manufactured in the United States of America

First Mass Market Edition: October 2003

OPM 10 9 8 7 6 5 4 3 2 1

For Ace, whose many gifts to me include the love of books, history, and flying

CONTENTS

ACKNOWLEDGMENTS

I would be remiss if I did not thank God first for the unusual, rewarding series of events that have shaped my life. Without them I would not have met the people who made this book possible. That includes above all my wife, Margaret, who unselfishly devoted innumerable hours above and beyond the call of duty to occupy our two young children while I wrote in peace, then provided many helpful queries regarding the manuscript's content.

I relied heavily on many others, of course. Hill Goodspeed performed many hours of manuscript review at the world-class National Museum of Naval Aviation and cheerfully answered my numerous questions; Jim Curry duplicated dozens of photographs; Bill Hardman and others among the volunteer staff were indispensable. My earlier work with the museum's nonprofit foundation provided the impetus for this book, and I am especially grateful to Capt. E. Earle Rogers, USN (Ret.), and Nancy Lichtman for their support.

Thanks also to Bernard Cavalcante and his staff at the Navy History Center, Naval Aviation History Branch, along with Joyce Conyers-Hudson, head of the Official Papers Unit at the Marine Corps History Center, both at the Washington Navy Yard. Other research assistants were Amy Elizabeth Stuart and Nikia Breedlove at the Still Photographs department of the National Archives Annex, and Thérèsa Angelo at the Royal New Zealand Air Force Museum in Christchurch. I owe a special debt to energetic

Henry Sakaida, who responded with enthusiasm and speed in sharing the results of his many years of research into Japanese records. First-class help also came from Roger Seybel at the Northrop-Grumman history center and Phil Spalla at the Igor Sikorsky archives; they provided information on F4Fs and F4Us, respectively. Corsair expert and writer Jim Sullivan donated copies from his personal archive of photographs, and Dr. Robert Mitchell assisted with aviation physiology details.

I must also acknowledge authors Paul Stillwell, Dr. Stanley Weintraub, and Barrett Tillman, who were not too busy to field questions, send encouraging letters, and help polish a first-timer's manuscript. Thank you, gentlemen. Finally, two pilots who participated in the events described herein scrutinized the manuscript, then offered critical commentary: I am grateful to Col. Bruce J. Matheson, USMC (Ret.), and Col. George F. Britt, USMC (Ret.), for their priceless insight and authentication.

PREFACE

Marine Corps aviation grew by an astonishing total of ten thousand pilots during World War II, a population explosion that yielded some sixty new fighter squadrons. Today only a handful of those outfits still exists. The wartime exploits of a few pilots have been recorded by historians and aviation buffs, and their fighter planes are universally known, but the squadrons themselves and their fanciful names—the Fighting Corsairs, the Hellhawks, the Wolfpack, the Fighting Falcons—have largely been forgotten.

All, that is, except VMF-214, the Black Sheep.

They are far and away the most famous fighter squadron in American aviation history for one simple reason: No other can claim the distinction of its own network television series. Fans of the Flying Tigers might argue that they are the more famous pilots, but that nonmilitary bunch was actually *three* squadrons in the American Volunteer Group. In addition, no single member of a fighter squadron—Claire Chennault included—has more name recognition than the Black Sheep's famous leader, "Pappy" Boyington.

When *Baa Baa Black Sheep* first aired on NBC in 1976, it sent a handful of beautifully restored Corsairs into the living rooms of millions of viewers around the world. The aircraft dueled in pulse-racing dogfights with plenty of stereotyped Japanese villains, many of whom fell to the Corsairs' chattering machine guns. After doing battle, the victorious young Marine pilots, troublemakers all (according to the opening credits), celebrated by drinking and getting into fistfights. The show unabashedly used the tried-and-true format of cowboy westerns, substituting airplanes for horses, machine guns for six-shooters, Japanese for Indians. The viewing public didn't seem to care.

As *Baa Baa Black Sheep*'s central character, Boyington was a living legend whose autobiography of the same name had been published eighteen years earlier. He ranked as the Marine Corps' all-time leading ace, and he could rightly claim distinction as one of the most colorful characters of World War II. His book became an instant classic and still remains in print. When it spawned the NBC television series, he was hired as a technical adviser.

As might be expected after Hollywood became involved, the real Black Sheep pilots were not enthusiastic supporters of the series. A few basked briefly in hometown attention, but most were incensed by uncomplimentary portrayals of their behavior. The opening credits identified them as misfits and screwballs, and during at least one contemporary talk show Boyington perpetuated the idea that they all faced courts-martial unless they went into combat with him.

As the first season premiered, a former member rose up to publicly oppose the series. Frank E. Walton, Jr., who had been the squadron's intelligence officer during Boyington's reign as squadron commander, was a nonflier assigned to gather information, give briefings, and type reports. Older than the others—even older than Boyington—he was devoted to the pilots and earned their loyalty. He found Hollywood's hokey portrayal of the squadron offensive and viewed Boyington's participation as salt in the wound. Through a letter-writing blitz, he learned that most former Sheep were equally distressed (several briefly entertained thoughts of a lawsuit), and he decided to launch a campaign of protest through magazine articles and other media. His efforts culminated in the 1986 publication of his own book, *Once They Were Eagles: The Men of the Black Sheep Squadron.*

For all their public recognition, the books by Boyington and Walton covered barely four months of VMF-214's three-year operational history during World War II. More problematic is the realization that Boyington's book is surprisingly inaccurate when compared with Marine Corps records. His statements have been widely accepted as factual for better than fifty years. After all, as a commanding officer and the recipient of a Medal of Honor, he was assumed to be forthright. But he once told an interviewer, "I'm a psychopathic liar," probably intending to say "pathologic," in a statement that seems justified by closely examining his book.

Boyington was perhaps less concerned with veracity than he was with drama and philosophical commentary, for the result might be considered an injustice to his Marine pilots. He misspelled several of their names and identified only five members who participated in his second combat tour. Of eleven pilots killed during his tenure with the Black Sheep, he mentions only three. Many of his stated deeds did not happen as he described them, yet over the years they have become part of the very fabric of aviation history. Black Sheep myths abound.

This book accomplishes far more than exposing myths, however. Nine chapters discuss VMF-214's first year of service, including two combat tours before the Black Sheep even materialized. A great many men contributed to the squadron—several with their lives—before the now-famous name was adopted, but they have scarcely been recognized before now. Nor has the story of the late-war Black Sheep, who trained for an entire year only to operate in combat for barely twenty-four terribly costly hours, been evaluated in detail prior to this account.

Many new names are introduced in this complete chronological history of VMF-214's operations in World

War II. The roster was filled with brave men, some of them legitimate heroes, others who unquestioningly performed their assigned duties. It is for their recognition, long deserved, that this book was written.

INTRODUCTION

The Adversary: Japan's Legendary Zero

Marine Fighting Squadron 214 was credited with 126 Japanese aircraft destroyed and 34 others probably destroyed in aerial combat during World War II. Among the credits were nine Aichi D3A "Val" dive-bombers, three Mitsubishi G3M "Nell" medium bombers, three Aichi E13A "Jake" floatplanes, and eight Kawasaki *Ki*-61 "Tony" fighters; combined they represented 15 percent of the total. The other 137 aircraft were variants of the renowned Mitsubishi A6M Zero, flown by land-based units of the Imperial Japanese Navy (IJN). Except for a few operations when IJN carrier-based Zeros were used to augment their forces, the vast majority of A6Ms encountered by VMF-214 belonged to elements of the 11th Air Fleet, headquartered at Rabaul.

Beginning in late 1942, Allied intelligence assigned male nicknames to Japanese fighters and female names to bombers in an effort to simplify identification. "Zero" was not one of the nicknames (as has often been construed), but the anglicized version of the Japanese word *rei,* a digit. Following Japanese military custom, the Mitsubishi fighter received its designation based upon the year it was to enter service, in this case 1940.* Thus the A6M1 became the

*The military derived type numbers from the last two digits of the ancient *koki* calendar, which was based on the founding of the Japanese dynasty. For example, the Mitsubishi A5M "Claude" entered service in the year 2596 (1936), becoming the type 96 fighter. The A6M was introduced in the calendar year 2600 (1940), but only the last digit was used.

Type 0 carrier-borne fighter, or *Rei Shiki Sento Ki,* soon shortened to *Rei-sen.* Even among the Japanese, the English word for zero sometimes supplanted their own, and over the years the aircraft has been popularized as *Zero-sen.*

The Zero wore several Allied nicknames during its wartime service, including "Zeke" for the first widely used production version, the A6M2. The second variant, identified by its clipped, square wingtips, was initially called "Hap" to compliment Henry H. "Hap" Arnold, commanding general of the U.S. Army Air Force. But Arnold was thunderously opposed to having an enemy plane named for him, and the A6M3's nickname was quickly changed to "Hamp." Even so, "Zero" prevailed among Marine Corps fliers until late summer 1943, when the Allied nicknames began to see limited use. Afterward "Hap" and "Hamp" were both found in VMF-214's war diaries to describe the A6M3. Pilots often reported encounters with "Zekes," "Haps/Hamps," and "Zeros" interchangeably, the latter being a catchall and certainly accurate at that.

The A6M3 was not well received by its pilots, which resulted in the introduction of the improved A6M5 in the summer of 1943. With its clipped but rounded wingtips, the A6M5 was difficult to distinguish in the heat of combat from the earlier A6M2. Both versions were therefore identified as "Zekes," although the A6M5 was by far the more common model; more than six thousand were produced in various configurations. Several examples of the unique floatplane version of the Zero, the A6M2-N "Rufe," were encountered and one was claimed by a Black Sheep pilot.

In the hands of a skilled flier, any Zero was extraordinary in its performance. The little A6M2, weighing barely 5,300 pounds fully loaded, offered tremendous range, which permitted a careful pilot to cover distances approaching 2,000 miles. It was well armed with two machine guns and two Oerlikon-licensed 20mm cannon, the same package used in the other major variants. The Zero's weight jumped by 300 pounds in the A6M3 Model 32 (horsepower and top speed also increased), whereas the A6M5 Model 52 topped 6,000 pounds and was the fastest, at 351 knots. By comparison, the F4U Corsair was approximately 3 tons heavier and 50 knots faster.

The Zero's light weight came at the expense of survivability, for it utterly lacked armor protection, long a source of scorn from the Western viewpoint. It was true that the Zero had a reputation for burning easily, but the conventional wisdom in the East was based upon an unfamiliar principle, as Japanese author Shigeru Nohara explained.

> Japanese military philosophy and tradition honored only the attack[;] the additional weight for armored defense even to protect the life of a very expensively trained pilot was abhorrent to a military tradition of 100 years. Some Rei-sen pilots regularly flew combat missions without a parachute to further reduce weight.

During the South Pacific war, as many as thirteen VMF-214 fighters were shot down by Zeros. Several more were damaged, some so severely that they were subsequently scrapped. There was no arrogance among the Marine pilots, who found the small, lightweight Japanese fighter a worthy adversary.

Aerial Victories: Credits Versus Losses

Receiving credit for aircraft downed in battle has been a source of controversy since the advent of aerial combat. Captain Edward V. Rickenbacker, idolized as the leading American ace of World War I, once dodged artillery fire at the front lines in order to take statements from eyewitnesses. In those days, protocol demanded detailed confirmation. But during World War II such verification became virtually impossible, mostly due to the sheer numbers of aircraft involved and the tremendous distances across which they fought. Confusion and exaggeration were common. Today it is widely accepted that overall claims in World War II exceeded actual losses by roughly a three-to-one margin, higher in some combat theaters, with equal complicity among all participants.

The same was true in the small part of the globe where the Marines of VMF-214 fought. All but one of the squadron's aerial encounters occurred in a narrow, linear zone between the Santa Cruz Islands and the Bismarck Archipelago, and with few exceptions the destroyed planes fell into the sea. Marine fighter planes were not equipped with operable gun cameras, nor were eyewitnesses generally available (except other pilots) for independent confirmation, so the onus for determining the validity of claims was on the shoulders of the squadron's air combat intelligence officer (ACIO). His task was to record the accounts of adrenaline-charged fliers after a shooting engagement and then, if possible, compare them with supporting statements from other sources.

The ACIOs were influenced by certain pressures, not the least of which was the knowledge that America's public hungered for good news from overseas. By the time VMF-214 entered combat, the war was well into its second year with no end in sight to severe rationing at home or the rising death toll abroad. Citizens sorely needed heroes. Among the accounts by war correspondents and radio announcers doing their melodramatic best to report good news, none could match in excitement the tales of a daring pilot's exploits in aerial combat. Most pilots were thrilled to have their actions recognized back home, and ACIOs were inclined to be generous with victory credits.

This tendency was acknowleged by intelligence officer Frank E. Walton, Jr., one of the Black Sheep's most influential members.

> The records were way, way inflated; all of our claims were inflated. We shot down about four times as many planes as the Japanese ever produced according to the

records. We never had any verification on a lot of the claims. We trusted, in many cases, just the guy's word: "Yes, I did this and I did that." The way he detailed it was what we put down. Sometimes his wingman could see enough to verify it.

More than half a century after those encounters took place, it is possible to compare American claims with actual Japanese losses (and vice versa). The records of VMF-214's most frequent aerial opponents, the naval air groups of the 11th Air Fleet, have been reconstituted by Henry Sakaida, who provided the author with copies of the 201, 204, and 253 Kokutai casualty lists and other documents. Similarly, Dr. Frank J. Olynyk compiled exhaustive lists of victory credits by reviewing American claims for enemy aircraft destroyed, probably destroyed, or damaged in the Pacific theater. As expected, Olynyk's record of credits is much larger than Sakaida's record of Japanese losses. In the preface of his Marine Corps list, Olynyk acknowledged that his findings told only half the story: "From the historian's point of view, one should not say that a pilot shot down a plane without finding a corresponding loss in the enemy records."

The available Japanese records provide a measure for the validity of American claims, but neither side's records contain enough information to match specific victories with specific losses on an aircraft-for-aircraft basis. Japanese documents have not been located to verify the few occasions when VMF-214 claimed enemy fighters from Rabaul-based Japanese Army Air Force (JAAF) Sentais, or level bombers and dive-bombers from nonfighter Kokutais. Many records were destroyed at Rabaul. In their place, transcripts from postwar interviews with Japanese officers conducted during the U.S. Strategic Bombing Survey proved helpful but provided few concrete details.

Likewise the available Kokutai casualty lists are not all-inclusive. Some documents contain only the names of pilots killed in action but do not account for pilots who were shot down and lived to fight again (as happened on several occasions when VMF-214 pilots witnessed successful bailouts over what was friendly territory for the Japanese). Therefore the Marines shot down a few more Japanese aircraft than the casualty lists would suggest.

Ultimately, to strike a balance between what is considered reliable documentation and the veracity of victory claims, it must be sufficient to present the facts as they are best known. Readers will then decide for themselves.

1

DARK DAYS

America's journey into World War II has always been symbolized by the flames and wreckage of Pearl Harbor. Repetitive scenes of the carnage at Battleship Row have become so indelibly printed on the nation's collective memory that the history of what happened elsewhere in the Territory of Hawaii and across the Pacific on that fateful morning has been largely forgotten. On the island of Oahu alone, three army airfields, two naval air stations, and a Marine air station were devastated by Japanese bombs and bullets.

The surprise attack shocked America, but it should not have. It was the inevitable result of a slow descent into war that had started long before, when throttling budget cuts and years of isolationism during the Depression led to neglect among the military services. America's deteriorated fighting capability led the Japanese to anticipate a hasty capitulation. They were not far wrong. The havoc at Pearl Harbor was due as much to American leadership's lack of vision as to the Japanese quest for domination.

Nowhere was the eroded condition of readiness more apparent than in Marine Corps aviation. Already saddled with an image as the Navy's poor stepchild, the Marine Corps was a minor force equipped with mostly inferior aircraft and struggling for respect. On the day prior to the attack on Pearl Harbor, the Marines had seventy-one fighter planes in operation among four squadrons. About a fifth of the fighters were Brewster F2A Buffaloes, oft-maligned little planes already being cast off by the Navy after barely a year of service. The remaining inventory boasted only fifty-seven frontline fighters: Grumman F4F-3 and F4F-3A Wildcats.

When the shooting started on December 7, two Marine air groups (MAGs) controlled this tiny force. One was MAG-11, conducting maneuvers far from the war zone along coastal North Carolina with thirty-five of the Wildcats. The remaining twenty-two Grummans and all of the Brewsters were assigned to MAG-21, headquartered at Ewa (pronounced EH·va), a windblown, backwater air station a few miles west of Pearl Harbor.

Not surprisingly in those hardscrabble days, Marine Corps Air Station (MCAS) Ewa was itself a naval hand-me-down. A mooring mast erected in the early 1930s for the giant airships had never been used. *Shenandoah* had crashed in 1925, *Akron* plunged into the Atlantic in 1932, then *Macon* went down off the California coast three years later. Never having served its intended purpose, Ewa Mooring Mast Field and its accompanying airstrip were eventually handed over to the Marines by default.

As the sun rose that first day of the war, Ewa's commander, Lt. Col. Claude A. Larkin, could count forty-eight aircraft of all types parked at his field. By the time the last Japanese attacker departed, all but one parked plane had been destroyed without having left the ground. In a stroke of luck for Larkin, the Japanese found only ten of his assigned fighters lined up at the field. Of the two fighter squadrons in MAG-21, one was deployed on a carrier and the other had split its forces in half, leaving only a rear echelon at Ewa. Aboard *Saratoga* at San Diego, VMF-221 was picking up more Brewsters to reinforce its sister squadron on Wake atoll. Although VMF-211 was already garrisoned at Wake with twelve Grummans, its rear echelon remained at Ewa with ten fighters and suffered the consequence of the surprise attack.

The forward echelon was almost simultaneously engaged, although it was actually Monday morning on the other side of the international date line when Wake was raided. Only four of the Wildcats were airborne when the Japanese air strike arrived from Kwajalein, but because they lacked radar support the Marines were patrolling miles to the north while the Japanese attacked from the opposite direction. They bombed and strafed the eight Wildcats on the ground with impunity. When the airborne patrol returned afterward, they found that seven of the Wildcats had been reduced to smoking hulks. The eighth was repairable, but one of the returning pilots struck scattered debris on the runway and ruined an irreplaceable propeller. Without firing a shot, VMF-211 had lost two-thirds of its meager air force.

For the next two weeks, the pilots and ground crews slaved to keep their four remaining fighters operational. They cannibalized parts from wrecks, even moved engines to the most usable airframes, but despite these ingenious measures the relentless Japanese air raids chewed up the F4Fs one by one. On the morning of December 22, while the squadron was defending against a large raid of Japanese carrier planes, the last Wildcat was shot up thoroughly and crash-landed on the runway. Having never flown more than four of its fighters in combat, VMF-211 lost every plane.

The surviving pilots became infantrymen and took up small arms to defend their island on foot, but they soon faced an overwhelming Japanese landing force. By the morning of December 23 only a handful of pilots were still alive to surrender. The eighteen Brewsters that had been headed toward Wake with VMF-221 were never delivered; *Saratoga* had turned away the night before due to controversial staff decisions aboard the carrier. The F2As were delivered instead to Midway on Christmas Day.

To replace the losses suffered at Pearl Harbor and Wake a major expansion of Marine aviation occurred on March 1, using the training pipeline's steady flow of brand-new pilots. Almost overnight, several new MAGs and their squadrons were created, built upon a nucleus of experienced pilots from MAG-11 who had been on the East Coast when the war began. Much of the reorganization began on paper, with pilots shuffling back and forth in seemingly unfathomable transfers among units. Frequently pilots reported to a new squadron only to receive orders to another outfit within a few weeks, sometimes just days.

Even the Marines' grip on their own aircraft was sometimes tenuous during this time of expansion and confusion. VMF-121, based at Quantico when the war started, hurried out to San Diego hoping to get into the fight. Among the first Marine squadrons equipped with F4F-3s some six months earlier, it was eager to pit its fighters against the Japanese. Soon after arriving in San Diego, VMF-121 received orders to Naval Air Station (NAS) North Island to install armor plate and self-sealing fuel cells in the aircraft. It was a promising sign. As Navy engineers watched in amazement, the Marines ripped apart twenty planes and installed the internal equipment in just three weeks. But as soon as the job was finished, the Navy took the planes. It was a simple matter of priority—the planes were needed aboard the carriers.

VMF-121's executive officer, Maj. John P. Condon, later recalled that insult was heaped upon injury:

> It didn't sit too well when they gave us six Brewster Buffaloes, and half of them wouldn't fly most of the time. We used to call them "flying gas leaks." You could smell fuel all the time you were in that cockpit. It made us nervous and we cut back on smoking. That was a junk-heap airplane if there ever was one, but it was the only thing we had to fly.

After the big expansion in Marine aviation on March 1, most of Condon's fellow pilots departed to create new air groups. Condon became operations officer for a brand-new MAG-12, although initially the ready rooms of the old

VMF-121 and the newly commissioned VMF-122 were empty. Soon dozens of new graduates began arriving from the flight training bases at Corpus Christi, Texas, and at Pensacola, Jacksonville, and Miami, Florida, to fill the vacancies. A handful of F4Fs trickled in. The newcomers barely got a taste of flying real fighters before MAG-12 was turned upside down by an urgent order. Forty experienced pilots were needed at a little-known outpost called Midway. "We had only about half a dozen of those," said Condon. "If we'd sent *everybody,* we couldn't have made forty. We sent what we could—that was the order we received."

By spring 1942, the evidence was clear to everyone on Midway (and the high command in Hawaii) that the Japanese were planning an invasion. Enemy destroyers had shelled Midway on December 7, then submarines returned from time to time to lob rounds from their deck guns. Since Christmas the Marines had been operating the Buffaloes delivered by *Saratoga,* but they were growing bored after weeks of local patrols. On March 8, a large four-engine Kawanishi H6K "Mavis" flying boat attempted a reconnaissance mission, and a division of F2As sailed in to make certain the intruder would not return to its home base. All four Marines—one of whom would later figure in the creation of VMF-214—made firing passes at the seaplane until it finally tumbled into the ocean.

The attempted surveillance and enemy message traffic (cryptologists had broken the Japanese code) indicated that an invasion was imminent. Midway forwarded the request for pilots and aircraft to MAG-12 in May. Ultimately VMF-221 accumulated twenty-one F2A-3s and seven F4F-3s for aerial defense of the island, and Maj. Floyd B. Parks welcomed almost two dozen new pilots (many just out of flight school) to his roster by the end of the month. Although fewer than half of his pilots had any real fighter time in their logbooks, they were given less than a week to prepare for the fight of their lives.

Early on the morning of June 4, Midway's radar detected an incoming raid by more than a hundred aircraft. Major Parks was immediately airborne with nineteen F2As and six F4Fs, all soon engaged in heavy aerial combat. In a matter of minutes, his valiant little defense force was practically annihilated. Only ten Marines flew back from the encounter, eight in aircraft too damaged to ever fly again. Parks was not among them. With shocking ease the Japanese had virtually eliminated the squadron as a fighting unit, although the blame was not laid at the pilots' feet. The Zeros that knocked them down had been flown by experienced Japanese naval aviators who held an unbeatable upper hand with their superior numbers and the all-important advantage of altitude.

Despite their mauling, the Marines could savor one small consolation. The sacrifice of Major Parks and his fighter pilots had played an influential role in the battle's outcome, for in shooting down eleven aircraft (plus claiming a probable and four damaged), the Marines had carved away enough attackers to convince the Japanese carrier commander that a follow-up raid on Midway's facilities was needed. Admiral Chuichi Nagumo made that decision before he was aware of the approaching American fleet, thereby crowding the flight decks of his carriers with aircraft while they rearmed for land targets. At this fateful moment, the U.S. Navy's torpedo bombers and dive-bombers appeared overhead to write their glorious page in history. Ultimately all four of Nagumo's carriers were sunk.

Midway will be forever remembered as the battle that destroyed the heart of the Japanese fleet, the naval victory that brought carrier aviation into a new era. But for the Marine pilots it was a shattering loss. They took little comfort in the final outcome, not out of resentment for the accolades showered on their Navy brethren but from the distress of knowing how badly outclassed their aircraft had been.

Measured against the loss of every F4F positioned at

Ewa and Wake, and at least twenty-three of the Brewsters and Grummans garrisoned at Midway, the Marines could claim only a few enemy fighters and a handful of bombers shot down. Complaints about the obsolete aircraft they had been compelled to fly were vociferous; it was their lowest point in the war.

At Ewa, base commander Claude Larkin had been busy picking up the pieces after the Japanese attack six months earlier. Combat-ready aircraft were still scarce, but he had some well-trained fighter pilots from the rear echelon of VMF-211 (whose airplanes had been blasted on the ground), and Midway's survivors had begun to arrive. East Coast veterans and freshly trained replacements were reporting almost daily from the States, and Navy units began combing their inventories to provide aircraft. To accommodate this influx, Larkin began enlarging and improving Ewa, including plans to commission several new squadrons.

As a cornerstone, VMF-211 was reconstituted under the command of Maj. Luther S. "Sam" Moore, whose first assignment was relatively harmless—base defense duty on the tiny island of Palmyra. From there his melting pot of pilots would provide core personnel for new squadrons when the time came. Larkin could also divert several fighter pilots who had survived Midway and were awaiting orders to the mainland; he would use them to temporarily staff these newly created outfits.

In this fashion, two new fighter squadrons were commissioned at dusty Ewa on July 1, less than a month after the battle of Midway. They simply came into existence on paper, without fanfare, as Marine Fighting Squadrons 213 and 214, joining VMF-221 as sister units in MAG-21. A couple of Buffalo pilots from Midway and several enlisted men were told to organize VMF-214, unaware that it would one day become the most famous squadron in Marine Corps history. Such insight probably would have mattered little to the small group of men who christened the squadron on that otherwise insignificant Wednesday. Still stunned by the battle of Midway, they were more concerned with the frustrating outlook of a long and bitter struggle ahead. History could wait.

2

STARTING FROM SCRATCH

On the day of its commissioning, VMF-214 would hardly have passed for a fighting squadron. It consisted of two officers, twenty enlisted men, and no aircraft. Furthermore both officers were assigned as temporary caretakers, nominally holding the titles of commanding officer and executive officer while knowing that others would soon take over. Both were captains. Command of a squadron was usually a major's billet, but after six months of war there were precious few of those left. Besides, their duties were mostly supervisory, and most of their time would be devoted to the tedium of organizing spaces, seeing to the men's needs, and procuring supplies and essentials.

Charles W. Somers and Philip R. White carried disturbing memories of the one-sided air battle at Midway. Somers, the interim commanding officer, had flown in the division of F2As that successfully downed the Mavis flying boat in March. Phil White was credited with shooting down one Aichi D3A dive-bomber and damaging another during the vicious fight in June.

Both men were dismayed at the F2A's awful performance against Zeros, but White was particularly vehement if not grammatically neat. Two days after the battle he wrote:

> The F2A-3 is not a combat aeroplane. It is inferior to the planes we were fighting in every respect . . . The Japanese Zero can run circles around the F2A-3.

It is my belief that any commander that orders pilots out for combat in a F2A-3 should consider that pilot as lost before he leaves the ground.

Considering White's comment, it no doubt disturbed him that VMF-214's first aircraft were seven F2A-3s, which arrived on July 6 courtesy of MAG-21. The same day, 2d Lt. R. A. Jefferies joined, giving the squadron almost half as many pilots as aircraft. Somers directed the men to form an assembly and repair shop and prepare the Buffaloes for flight. Just as they were getting the aircraft ready, however, orders arrived to return the planes to the Navy. Phil White was vindicated. The Buffaloes were flown less than ten miles to the supply department at NAS Ford Island on July 15 and Jefferies was transferred to MAG-23 the following day.

After enjoying temporary ownership of a few planes, even if they were Brewsters, the squadron was now back where it began with just two pilots and no planes. The lack of activity was frustrating. The only entry they could think up for the squadron diary on July 18 was, "This would be a good time for a week's leave."

But there was no immediate relief, and idleness bred trouble. A sergeant was brought up on unrecorded charges serious enough to warrant summary punishment; he was court-martialed and the next day reduced in rank to corporal. Thirty minutes after the results of his court-martial were published, he committed the same offense. This time, following another summary court-martial, he was booted all the way to private.

The lull was temporary, however, because a seasoned Marine soon arrived to take permanent command. He was George F. Britt, a twenty-seven-year-old captain and the son of a dreadnought-era naval officer. After spending most of his life around shipyards up and down the East Coast, he graduated from Georgia Tech with an ROTC commission into the regular Marine Corps and completed obligatory ground service before reporting to Pensacola for flight training. Trained as a dive-bomber pilot, Britt was assigned to VMB-1, the first Marine outfit to receive SBDs. The squadron, on maneuvers along the North Carolina coast when the war started, rushed out to San Diego, only to while away the next several months in a tent city at Kearny Mesa. VMB-1 was broken up in the reorganization of March 1, and Britt was reassigned to another bombing outfit until a fortunate opportunity came his way. He received orders to evaluate a new lead-computing gunsight under production by Bendix, a job requiring flight proficiency in F2A-3s. Just like that, he became a fighter pilot.

When the job was complete he was sent to Hawaii as a replacement pilot. He soon joined Sam Moore's VMF-211 down on Palmyra, nine hundred miles south of Hawaii, where the F2As were equipped with the Bendix gunsight. Despite Britt's relatively few hours in fighters, he was senior enough to come aboard as executive officer. He understood the unusual turn of events, realizing that qualified regular officers were in demand. "The Marine Corps expanded so fast it was mind boggling," he recalled. "You found yourself thrust into positions of responsibility that you never dreamed you would encounter."

Along with Moore and the other Buffalo pilots, Britt spent a few months on Palmyra flying plenty of lonely patrols as part of the long defensive perimeter established by the Pacific high command. Between patrols there was little else to do but fly, and the pilots soon became gunnery experts. It was a perfect place for learning the fighter business, and the former SBD pilot began to outshoot his own mentor. Moore was quick to recognize Britt's leadership and flying talent. When word came that two new squadrons were being formed up at Ewa, he wrote to Claude Larkin, recommending that one of the squadrons should be given to Britt. Larkin agreed; VMF-214 had only two transient officers assigned, both on temporary orders.

In mid-July, Captain Britt departed Palmyra with orders

to report to VMF-214 at Ewa. His arrival on the twenty-first increased the number of officers by 50 percent—to three—and gave the fledgling squadron a measure of continuity. Although still without airplanes, it now had a senior officer (Britt's promotion to major was imminent) who could provide the necessary leverage to oversee months of acquisition, training, and eventually combat.

For the first week after Britt took command, there was little outward change. Not much could be accomplished with only three pilots and no planes. But training commenced on July 30 when they borrowed planes to conduct dummy gunnery runs. "Having trouble finding pilots for the target plane," someone neatly penned that day. Apparently, acting as the target was hazardous, unpopular, or both.

In early August, Charlie Somers was transferred to Palmyra as the Marines continued their perplexing rotation of officers. Once again VMF-214 was reduced to just two officers, who grabbed whatever flights they could in borrowed planes. Two improvements toward the end of the month brightened their outlook. Britt was "frocked" to major, permitting him to pin the oak leaf insignia on his uniform while awaiting the meager raise in pay. And eleven new fighters were received; ten F4F-3s arrived on August 27 from VMF-222, and another was acquired from Ford Island.

For the first time, outnumbered as they were by the aircraft in their inventory, Britt and White had some legitimate machines to fly. A newer version of the Wildcat was currently in frontline service (the folding-wing, six-gun F4F-4), but the pilots were hardly concerned with minor variations. They were grateful for airplanes, which ended their reliance on other squadrons for flight time.

The Dash-3 Wildcats had fought well for the Navy at Coral Sea and were nearly identical to the newer Dash-4s. All F4Fs showed a thick belly when viewed from the side—continuing the lineage of earlier Grumman designs built around a common retractable landing gear system—and were invariably described as "stubby." The Wildcat's predecessor was a biplane, as the Wildcat was originally designed to be, but in the late 1930s Grumman revised the design to a monoplane to compete with Brewster's new Buffalo. The Dash-3 was mated to a supercharged Pratt & Whitney fourteen-cylinder engine of 1,200 horsepower, giving it an advertised top speed of approximately 330 knots. The Wildcat's handling characteristics made it a relatively nimble dogfighter, considering its heritage.

But the Wildcats were also known for unpredictable behavior on the ground. Their tall, narrow-tracked landing gear placed the main wing high above the ground, challenging inexperienced pilots during crosswind takeoffs and landings. The wing had a tendency to tip, causing one side to stick up like a barn door. In such situations, recalled Britt, "It was almost impossible to keep from ground looping." Indeed, VMF-214's first operational loss came only one day after receiving the new planes when a pilot from another squadron borrowed one and wrecked it. Three more Wildcats were soon damaged beyond repair during routine operations, all in a six-day span in early September.

Another of the Wildcat's quirks was a direct result of its simplicity. Except for a small system to power the wheel brakes, it lacked conventional hydraulics, so the landing gear had to be raised or lowered manually by a chain mechanism turned by the pilot. The hand crank was located on the cockpit's right side, requiring the pilot to transfer the control stick to his left hand in order to turn the wheel crank with his right hand. It took approximately twenty-seven turns to fully raise the gear, and inexperienced pilots often transmitted the rotating motion subconsciously into their stick hand. Newcomers were easy to spot as they took off and climbed away from the runway, their aircraft porpoising up and down for half a mile or more.

New pilots finally began arriving in mid-September. Two young replacement pilots, reservists fresh from the training command, checked in first. They were followed on September 28 by an experienced fighter pilot, Capt. Henry A. Ellis, Jr., a University of California graduate. Ellis had earlier served in VMF-211 with George Britt, who requested Ellis as his executive officer. Phil White stepped down from that capacity, although he would remain with the squadron for two more months while awaiting reassignment. The squadron, which now boasted five pilots, often joined with other outfits to conduct training exercises.

A two-seat North American SNJ-4 trainer had been acquired on September 15 for instrument flying. A movable hood could be drawn inside the rear canopy, compelling the backseat occupant to fly and navigate by the gauges—useful skills for poor weather conditions and night flying. A safety pilot in the front seat kept a watchful eye outside while the backseater flew blind.

Pilot acquisition began in earnest with the arrival of nine reserve second lieutenants from San Diego on Thursday, October 8. They averaged fewer than three hundred flight hours apiece, and not a single man had conducted live aerial gunnery training. They were boys almost, not far removed from elite universities—Yale, Harvard, Princeton—or public institutions such as Oregon and Louisiana State. By virtue of their educational status they were qualified for cadet training after meeting the physical requirements. Most had signed up immediately after Pearl Harbor. Exchanging fraternity parties and tree-shaded lawns for sand fleas and sweat, they learned to fly at Corpus Christi or Pensacola or Jacksonville. Some, such as John L. Fidler, had prior flight instruction thanks to the civilian pilot training (CPT) program offered at colleges across the country. Others, as one newcomer succinctly put it, came "off the farm, into the airplane and overseas."

During cadet training, each of the new arrivals had been given the option of remaining in the Navy or receiving Marine commissions. Each had selected the latter for different reasons. Some liked the Marine Corps aviators' dark green uniforms; others were lured by the mystique of the Leathernecks. Many figured correctly that after Midway, Marine pilots would see action sooner than their Navy contemporaries.

Several new pilots had shown prowess on the playing fields of their alma maters. One standout was Vincent W. Carpenter, twenty-two, a native of Minneapolis. A world-class hammer thrower at Yale, he captained the track team during his junior year before departing New Haven for aviation training. In addition to athletic ability he was an accomplished student in physics and music. Though he had no prior aviation experience, he was a natural pilot and excelled at flight training; he became cadet commanding officer in his class at Corpus Christi. Soon after arriving at Ewa, he caught George Britt's attention with his smooth touch on the controls.

Another twenty-two-year-old found his first assignment to a legitimate fighter squadron eye-opening. "Flight school was one thing," recalled Howard L. Cavanagh, "this was a *real* squadron." To the California native, Major Britt was hard boiled, a strict disciplinarian. Considering the youngster's flight training, there had been little to prepare him for the business end of a fighter plane. All he had learned as a student were methods of gunnery without an opportunity to try them. At Corpus Christi the only serviceable fighter was a weary F3F biplane, restricted from the high g's that were a necessary part of gunnery training. "If you'd been a good boy you got to fly that thing," he added, "but they wouldn't let us do any aerobatics in it. We just got the little honor of flying it around."

On October 9, the day after the new lieutenants' arrival, two enlisted pilots added their considerable savvy to the roster. Technical Sergeants Alvin J. Jensen and James G. G. Taylor had earned their wings of gold the hard way. Enlisted pilots were integrated with commissioned officers in significant numbers after the Five-Year Air Program Act of 1926 established a 30 percent quota of enlisted pilots in naval aviation, Marines included. Their number peaked in 1942, with more than 130 "flying sergeants" in the Marine Corps alone.

Jim Taylor's circuitous route to assignment in a fighter squadron was fairly typical. He enlisted in the Marines right out of high school in 1936 and completed a four-year hitch before returning home to Cape May, New Jersey, as a corporal in the reserves. After training as a mechanic at Hemphill Diesel, he landed a job with the transit authority, a real gem in those economically tough times. But in 1940, just as he was getting his life started with a solid career, the Marines recalled inactive reservists and he was posted to the elimination base at the Philadelphia Navy Yard. Taylor was "mad as hell" in his new job, teaching young aviation cadets the rudiments of military life, but his disappointment was erased when a captain nominated him for a rare slot in the Naval Aviation Pilot (NAP) program. Taylor happily reported to Pensacola, where he met Alvin Jensen.

At Pensacola, NAP students received flight instruction virtually identical to aviation cadet training. After completing the primary and intermediate courses, Jensen and Taylor moved to Opa-Locka, near Miami, for the advanced fighter syllabus. They logged a few more hours in actual fighters than Howard Cavanagh had received—perhaps ten hours in F2As—but they had no live gunnery training either. The two sergeants received orders to the same squadron and were soon en route to Hawaii. They were the first of five enlisted pilots to join VMF-214 and the only ones to make it home.

Soon after the new pilots' arrival, George Britt gathered them in the ready room. He went out of his way to smooth the integration of enlisted and commissioned pilots. Remembered Taylor:

> Britt made it abundantly clear that we were all, first and foremost, pilots. There were social differences but not professional differences between us. We were all of

the same cloth, even though we were from different pay grades. In his welcoming address he made sure that nobody felt left out, and nobody could possibly assume that they would have an elevated position.

Several of VMF-214's fighters had been turned over to other squadrons, making for quite a few more pilots than aircraft, so a handful of pilots were rotated through Link trainer class for instrument basics while others checked out in the available F4Fs. Training continued to be restricted by a shortage of planes even though the SNJ-4 was pressed into use; one day it was nearly lost, and two of the new lieutenants with it.

One of the lieutenants was "Big John" Fidler, who had enlisted as a Naval Aviation Cadet following his junior year at Monmouth College in Illinois. In the middle of flight school he requested a transfer to the Coast Guard, but the Navy denied his request, considering him too valuable because he already had some fifty CPT hours in his logbook. Upon his arrival at Ewa, he had been assigned the job of scheduling instrument flights; he penciled himself in for a training flight on October 12 and added Carol D. C. Bernard as safety pilot. "Bernie" was a fun-loving Cajun who had been raised on a plantation in New Iberia, Louisiana. His father owned land and was president of a bank, but Bernie remained modest and made friends fast.

Bernard and "Big John" Fidler shared boyish adventurism in their new roles as fighter pilots. Shortly after Fidler went under the hood, he tired of the instrument training. Ready for something more exciting, he pulled back the hood and said, "Let's go for a ride!" Bernard needed no further prompting. Taking over the controls, he dropped the SNJ down to treetop level above the rugged terrain north of Ewa. Soon they were roaring up one of Oahu's canyons, laughing like schoolboys. Bernard was watching the walls to maintain clearance and did not see a series of high tension wires strung across the canyon until it was too late. He yanked back on the stick, but the trainer struck the lowest wire with an explosion "like a bolt of lightning" right at the base of the windscreen and the vertical radio antenna. The cable sheared the antenna from the fuselage and smashed the J-bird's windscreen, sending shards of Plexiglas into Bernard's face. He turned around yelling, "John, I can't see!" Fidler was shocked to see the pilot's face—a mass of little cuts, with Plexiglas in one eye despite protection from goggles.

Fidler took over and flew back to Ewa, made a hot landing, and taxied rapidly to the ready hut. The men jumped from the trainer, grabbed a jeep, and raced to the sick bay, where a flight surgeon cleaned out Bernard's eyes.

The two shaken Marines, who knew they had come within an eyelash of killing themselves, were sitting quietly on a sick bay cot when Major Britt walked in. Fidler went to bat for his friend: "I guess we hit a big bird . . ." Britt was satisfied to let it go at that, realizing that their huge scare was lesson enough. But the truth surfaced anyway when word flashed around Ewa that a massive power failure had blacked out the Army's Schofield Barracks. It was no coincidence, and the downed power cable created a major headache for the facility. Consequently Bernard was called on the carpet in front of a general who threatened to take away his wings. The threat might have been acted upon were it not for greater needs in the South Pacific. The Marines had a good chuckle over knocking out the Army's electricity, but the damage to the J-bird was a setback the squadron could ill afford. "More aircraft would certainly come in handy," wrote an adjutant in the diary. "We have five assigned with usually three in commission."

But there would be no new aircraft for at least two months or much change in routine for the pilots. Nevertheless during those quiescent days the squadron continued to grow as dozens of enlisted personnel arrived to fill technical positions. In clusters they came: engine mechanics, truck drivers, ordnance specialists, plane captains, parachute riggers, clerks, and cooks. It took dozens of people to operate a squadron independently. Personnel had to be paid, transported, accounted for, and fed. The F4Fs required numerous man-hours of maintenance for each hour in the air, and when something on the aircraft broke someone had to fix it. In a Marine fighter squadron circa 1942, each aviator had nine enlisted men backing him up. The pilots grabbed the public's attention, of course, leaving no one to praise the blue-collar men and boys toiling behind the scenes. VMF-214 was fortunate to have veteran master sergeants running the technical side: Jack J. Downs as noncommissioned officer in charge, Oscar A. Knopf as leading chief.

On November 27, a break from the daily routine of training and flying came in the person of none other than the commander-in-chief of the Pacific Fleet, Adm. Chester Nimitz. In a ceremony recognizing pilots who had fought at Midway, Nimitz personally awarded Phil White a Navy Cross for his part in the battle.

Although the award gave White a measure of recognition, it could not alleviate the disenchantment he felt afterward. George Britt described him as bitter.

> Those who were required to enter the battle flying F2A-3s didn't have a chance. They lost so many of their squadron mates. It was a hastily thrown-together affair . . . and they were lucky to survive.

White departed later that day with three of the squadron's lieutenants to join VMF-121 in Samoa. The reduction of four pilots was partially offset by the arrival of a nonflying officer, Capt. Arthur W. Little, a reservist who joined as squadron adjutant. The thirty-eight-year-old New Yorker was single and wealthy, with a Park Avenue address, and the pilots considered him a playboy. He would serve the most continuous duty of any ground officer in VMF-214, remaining with the squadron until at least 1944. His duties as an administrative officer were hidden in the background, but later in the Solomons he commanded the ground echelon of enlisted maintenance personnel and transient replacement pilots. Turned down for training as an air combat intelligence officer—the hot job for Marine ground officers—he compensated by writing accounts of action with melodramatic journalism.

Following the Navy Cross ceremony, the squadron settled into an intense training phase. Britt drilled the pilots in proficiency and tactics and filled their days with training flights. His young lieutenants had never flown anything as powerful as the F4F, and it took several hours to get them acquainted with the Grumman's peculiarities. One F4F-3 was lost on December 2 when Adolph R. Vetter overstressed the airplane during a gunnery run and snapped the right landing gear chain. In this situation the chain often wrapped itself around the other wheel, preventing it from lowering. Runway landings were deemed too hazardous, and pilots were generally given the option to bail out or make a water landing. Vetter chose the latter after the right wheel dropped loose, then he made a smooth water landing in the Pearl City Channel and extracted himself from the sinking plane.* Two more Wildcats were damaged ten days later when unidentified pilots ground-looped them; the pilots were unhurt but both planes needed new wings.

Aside from the reduction in aircraft, the regimen of training flights continued at a breathless pace. Weekends were workdays just like any other—the only breaks came from occasional cloudbursts that precluded flying. On the first anniversary of the Pearl Harbor attack, the squadron began a stretch of twenty-seven flying days in a row; not even for Christmas or New Year's Day were the pilots exempted from the rigorous schedule. "You fly every day you can get the wheels in the well," Britt told them.

*Vetter was transferred before the squadron deployed and was killed in January 1944 during a mission in the Solomon Islands.

More second lieutenants began to check in from the States. They came in random bunches, some staying, others rotating to different squadrons. One who stayed was recently married David W. Rankin, who joined Vince Carpenter on the list of notable athletes. Tall and muscular, Rankin was an All-American end at Purdue and became a cadet before the war began; he took the oath at a rousing halftime ceremony during the 1941 college All-Star game. Maintaining an orderly diary, he documented his arrival at Pearl Harbor aboard the seaplane tender *Pokomoke*. Like so many thousands of his fellow servicemen, he was greatly impressed by the blackened battleships still resting on the harbor's muddy bottom.

Along with the influx of pilots, a marked improvement in the squadron's readiness occurred on December 17, as noted by this enthusiastic log entry.

> Great day! After having only four F4F-3s, we are assigned eight new F4F-4s and another SNJ-4. Total planes in the squadron is now 14! . . . We are beginning to look more like a squadron every day.

With the arrival of Dash-4 Wildcats, the squadron now owned the latest operational version of Grumman's famous design, but a newer fighter owned bragging rights as the hottest airplane in the Marine Corps. Major William E. Gise's VMF-124 began flying F4U-1 Corsairs in September and was now well into a history-making training program. The new planes were declared fit for combat on December 28, though they still suffered from mechanical ills that would take time to correct.

Meanwhile Britt and his pilots were generally pleased with their own capable little F4F-4s, which had proven themselves with the Navy at Midway and were even now meeting Zeros in the skies over Guadalcanal. The latest version's primary changes were the installation of a wing-fold mechanism and an increase in armament to six .50-caliber machine guns, alterations not widely popular with combat veterans after exchanging their Dash-3s. The new Wildcat had extra punch but was burdened with additional weight, which affected its overall climb performance and speed. Furthermore, to offset the weight of the two additional guns, Grumman was forced to compromise with less ammunition. The Dash-3 carried 450 rounds for each of its four guns, totaling 1,800 bullets for approximately thirty-four seconds of firing time, but the F4F-4 was limited to 240 rounds per gun—a total of only 1,440 bullets. Firing time was cut nearly in half, a sixteen-second reduction that some said was tantamount to eternity.

There was one advantage, however. The reliable Colt-Browning M2 machine guns discharged half-inch-wide slugs that weighed more than an ounce apiece at a muzzle velocity of 2,840 feet per second, and the battery of six guns equated to an extra thirty slugs for each one-second burst. More than five *pounds* of metal came blitzing out of the barrels of an F4F-4 every second, a veritable buzz saw against unarmored Japanese planes. The effect of the new gun arrangement was devastating to the enemy, but the reduction in total rounds did force pilots to shoot conservatively.

Major Britt and his pilots soon learned for themselves, wringing out their new Wildcats on gunnery hops after boresighting the guns. To accomplish the latter, the planes were towed to a large excavated pit off the end of Ewa's runway, where the wheels were chocked in place to prevent them from rolling backward. Next the tails were elevated and placed on cradles to level the guns. Pilots climbed aboard to trigger the guns while ordnancemen adjusted their aim to converge at the specified distance—usually 150 to 300 yards. Such a seemingly innocuous task was not without its hazards, as John Fidler discovered. "It was hotter 'n hell down there," he lamented. "We'd had a big party the night before, and I was throwing up all over the place."

Once the guns were boresighted, the serious business of gunnery training began. Because the lieutenants and enlisted pilots had arrived with virtually no live gunnery experience, Britt had only a few weeks to teach them everything he knew about hitting a moving target from a moving airplane. He began by diagramming the basics: Airplanes move relative to one another in three spherical dimensions, and minor flight control changes have dramatic effects. Next he demonstrated how to manuever a fighter into the proper position to acquire, track, lead, and hit another fast-moving airplane.

After the rudiments were displayed on a chalkboard, the fledglings were sent to an aerial gunnery range to practice. Most gunnery hops were conducted at six thousand feet over the water, just west of Barbers Point in a rectangle of airspace fifty miles long by ten miles wide. Later, after refresher training with oxygen masks, occasional forays were made to twenty thousand feet for high-altitude gunnery.

Day after day, the pilots flew out to the range and fired paint-tipped bullets at a white target sleeve towed behind another aircraft. To keep score and measure performance, each pilot began the flight with a load of one hundred paint-tipped bullets, one load coated with blue paint, another with red, and so on, enabling hits to be counted by the smears of color. As expected, some pilots were naturals whereas others struggled to hit the sleeve. Big John Fidler felt that he belonged in the latter category as he recalled, "There were some guys who would practically destroy that sock with all their blue or red bullets."

Britt was one of those, having learned so well under Sam Moore's tutelage on the island of Palmyra. A few days before Christmas, while testing one of the brand-new F4F-4s, Britt scored forty-six hits out of one hundred; on Christmas Day he punched forty-seven holes in the sleeve, a score then unmatched by any pilot at Ewa. His secret was instinctive and simple.

> Most of my gunnery scoring was made doing overhead runs, coming down to the sleeve. I found that if I put the pipper on the tow line and put the sleeve at the proper mark on the illuminated sight ring, I couldn't miss. There was that one sweet moment where everything came together, and the sleeve appeared to not be moving at all.

On December 26 the pilots moved into unit D of the bachelor officers' quarters (BOQ), newly constructed as part of Colonel Larkin's expansion of Ewa Field. Junior officers each had a small private room in a tropical-style wooden building where they shared a communal bath; the major moved into a duplex structure and enjoyed a private bath. Beyond that improvement, there were few diversions in their busy routine. Entertainment for officers and enlisted men consisted primarily of open-air movies due to Ewa's remote location. They rarely made trips to off-base watering holes. The island remained blacked out at night, so ventures into Honolulu by car were downright hazardous. Nevertheless three young lieutenants jointly funded the purchase of an old car for sixty dollars and used it mainly for trips to a local laundry, although they did risk a few night runs into the city. Dave Rankin wrote of the dances held every full moon. Popular band leader Artie Shaw and his orchestra played for three of the affairs at the air station, which turned into "drunken brawls with liquor free."

But the main activity at Ewa was flying, and VMF-214's training agenda continued almost nonstop. When a twenty-seven-day stretch of flying was interrupted by foul weather on January 3, the pilots simply started again the next day and flew for forty days straight. In addition to improving their shooting skills on gunnery hops, they practiced the discipline needed to keep two-plane sections and four-plane divisions intact during combat maneuvering. Britt assigned his pilots according to rank, meaning that he and

Henry Ellis led divisions while observing the second lieutenants carefully to see who showed the most promise. Those not selected as division or section leaders would have no easy task either. As wingmen they were challenged to stick close to their leaders, which required plenty of throttle jockeying during hard turns while keeping their necks constantly on a swivel.

During the first week of January 1943, the squadron approached full operational strength with the arrival of seven more F4F-4s. Five new pilots checked in, all having switched to fighters from SBDs. Among them was another enlisted pilot, Gunnery Sergeant Bateman, who passed his first aerial test on January 10 by nursing home a Wildcat crippled by a broken oil line. He succeeded in saving the plane, but the episode marked the beginning of a troubling string of bad luck.

Two days later George Britt took a division of four Grummans to the range west of Barbers Point for a morning gunnery flight. After completing routine firing runs about five miles out to sea, the pilots began joining on Britt's wing for the return trip to Ewa. Using standard rendezvous procedures, Britt held a steady left turn into the approaching pilots while they closed the gap, each judging his own speed and rate of closure, then throttling back before sliding into assigned positions. It was a routine they had practiced many times since cadet training. Lieutenant Hartwell V. Scarborough, Jr., was the first to join the major's left wing, followed by John Fidler leading the second section. With three planes now in formation, Britt looked over his left shoulder just as something went terribly wrong.

Lieutenant Jeremiah J. Reinburg had misjudged his high rate of closure and swooped in too fast beside Fidler, who was stunned to see a whirling propeller in front of his left wing. An instant later came a jarring collision as Reinburg's plane slammed into Fidler's. Airframe parts flew in all directions. From his position up forward, Britt was relieved to see two parachutes blossom as both pilots jumped from their stricken fighters. He keyed his mike and shouted a Mayday over the radio, then instructed Vic Scarborough to circle one of the descending chutes while he followed the other down to the ocean.

Britt's relief at seeing two parachutes was short-lived.

> After no more than thirty seconds I noticed that something odd was going on. The chute I was circling was not descending at anywhere near the rate the other was. I circled in for a closer look and saw, to my horror, that the chute harness was empty.

Unable to determine whose harness was empty, Britt continued to circle the drifting canopy until the other one landed in the water.

Big John was the fortunate one. Never having jumped from an airplane before, he followed the procedures learned in training with remarkable composure. He was poised to bail out when he felt a tug on his head; the radio cord was still plugged into the console. He sat back down, disconnected the plug, stood again, and jumped, brushing against a crumpled wing. During the parachute descent he carefully stored the ripcord in a pocket of his flight suit for safekeeping and had time to remove one shoe before splashing down. After freeing himself of the shroud lines, he kicked off the other shoe and toggled his Mae West; only one half worked. Fidler started swimming as he squinted into the bright morning sun toward the mountains of Oahu in the distance. He was getting his bearings when he spotted Reinburg's empty harness floating down, and knew it meant the end of his squadron mate.

George Britt's Mayday had alerted a submarine running on the surface nearby. Fidler, blinded by the sun's glare on the water, never saw it approaching until he smacked into its side. "It was just amazing. Bang, and there it was." His troubles were not quite over. A couple of sailors hauled him aboard, but his near blindness caused a wrong step and he tumbled painfully down the sub's conning tower. After resting on the captain's bunk while his clothing dried, he arose to find a pool of blood from an undiscovered injury. His buttocks had been sliced open by a jagged piece of metal on the Wildcat's crumpled wing. When the sub tied up at Pearl Harbor, Fidler caught a ride back to Ewa, unfazed by his second brush with disaster.

There was no trace of Jerry Reinburg. Britt's interview with the enlisted plane captain who assisted Reinburg into his aircraft revealed Reinburg had a habit of taxiing away from the flight line without securing the leg straps of his parachute harness. The straps crossed below the crotch and were uncomfortable, but they absorbed much of a parachute's opening shock. Reinburg had bailed out after the collision, but the unsecured harness was torn from his body when the chute opened. As with most fatal accidents, the pilot's mistakes caused his own demise. It was a harsh lesson for the others, who then began to cinch their own straps a little tighter.

Misfortune continued to plague the squadron. On January 16, only four days after the fatal collision, the wheels on Scarborough's Wildcat folded during landing, causing extensive damage to the airplane. Three days later TSgt. Al Jensen bent a wing, a wheel, and the prop on another fighter during a ground loop; he ground-looped again the following day, this time crunching the Wildcat sufficiently to scrap it. If Jensen's inauspicious beginning raised any questions about his ability, the flying sergeant overcame them later by earning numerous accolades in combat. In any case, one of the lieutenants took the heat off Jensen the day after his second ground loop. Robert T. Hoover did the same thing after letting a Wildcat get away from him during takeoff, and the resulting ground loop sent another plane to the scrapyard.

The bottom line was that in a nine-day span, the squadron lost four Wildcats and damaged three others, with one aviator dead. "Bad luck seems to be upon us," wrote the adjutant. Yet the setbacks barely caused a ripple in the frenzy of wartime training. The losses were deemed acceptable, even anticipated, and the pace hardly allowed anyone time to reflect. Gunnery training did stop for a short time beginning January 23, but only because the fighter pilots had shot up so much target ammunition that it took the ordnance shop two days to rebelt more. As soon as they finished, Britt used the new ammo to good effect, plastering a sleeve towed at 130 knots with forty hits.

With the arrival of eight new pilots on the last day of January, the roster was finally complete. Gunnery Sergeant Bateman was transferred to another unit, but two more enlisted pilots, TSgt. Harrell Steed and TSgt. Wilbur H. Blakeslee, took his place. If the names Harrell and Wilbur were somewhat distinctive (both quickly became "Bill"), they were not alone among a roster that included Ledyard Hazelwood, Drury McCall, Lincoln Deetz, Carol Bernard, Otto Williams, and Hartwell Scarborough. Nicknames were natural substitutes and practical on the radio. Hazelwood, a tanned, happy-go-lucky Princeton man, became "Ledge." The obvious handle for McCall was "Mac," who loved Broadway show tunes. "Link" Deetz, one of the more diminutive pilots, had a feisty spirit that later earned him the alternate call sign of "Scrappy." Bernard's continental first name was dropped in favor of "Bernie," and Otto's middle name of Keith led invariably to "OK." Finally there was Scarborough, a North Carolinian so tall and lanky that he appeared gaunt; his shortened middle name was "Vic."

Among the most recent group of incoming pilots were two captains with extensive flight experience, one with a regular commission. William H. Pace, of La Jolla, California, was an Annapolis graduate whose promotion to major was imminent. Britt made him the flight officer, responsible for scheduling daily operations.

The second captain was Henry S. Miller, a reservist

who fit none of the typical profiles. With a degree from Harvard Law School, he was an attorney in a Philadelphia suburb before the war started. He tried to join as an aviation cadet in 1940 when he realized that the United States could not remain isolated from the conflict. Too old for the current age limits set by the Army and Navy for flight training, he completed the civilian pilot training program at nearby Boulevard airport and took his enthusiasm north of the border, where he joined the Royal Canadian Air Force (RCAF) in early 1941. There, he said, "They were delighted to have me."

Miller earned his pilot officer wings in November and the Canadians liked what they saw. They made him an instructor but five months later an American recruiting team arrived by train from the States and offered Miller a transfer to the Navy. The Canadians did not simply hand over their skilled pilot; they had provided night flying, low-level training, and instrument flight training superior to that available in the U.S. programs. In the end the Navy paid $25,000 to the British Commonwealth air training program for Miller's transfer, and got a bargain in the process.

Curiously, once Miller was back in the States the Navy couldn't decide what to do with him or the other RCAF-trained pilots they had picked up. Just to be sure that the pilots had not missed something, they were sent back through an abbreviated naval flight training syllabus, which allowed Miller to benefit from the RCAF pilot training course, a complete instructor's course, five months' experience as a flight instructor, and naval aviation training. After finishing the basic course, he opted for a commission in the Marines, then sailed through the fighter training syllabus at Corpus Christi as a first lieutenant. Now a captain at the age of twenty-nine, he was more than a year older than Britt, who made him a division leader on the spot.

Despite Miller's rank and experience, his first flight with VMF-214 proved humbling. He had accumulated only a few hours of fighter time during his accelerated

Navy training and was unfamiliar with Wildcats. Launching in complete darkness for a predawn patrol around Hawaii, he did not notice that his radio switch was mistakenly set to make carrier wave transmissions instead of voice calls, and he was unable to talk to his division while trying to lead them through the darkness. In frustration he signaled his wingman to lead the formation, so Sgt. Jim Taylor took over and completed the patrol, saying nothing and earning Miller's gratitude. After that beginning, Miller became a natural teacher. His skill at instrument flying was a rare commodity in those days, and he freely imparted his knowledge among the younger pilots. The one point he constantly hammered into them was the most important issue of flying blind. "Do you know where you are? You damn well better find out."

The arrival of Pace and Miller rounded out the list of captains at four. John R. Burnett, short to the point of appearing tiny alongside some of the long-legged fliers, had arrived in mid-December. He was personable enough and had a pleasant visage, but his compact stature and occasional erratic flying would later become a source of contention.

The squadron reached its total strength of 249 officers and men only a few weeks before deployment. In addition to Marines, VMF-214's working roster included seven Navy men. Having no medical personnel of its own, the Marine Corps relied on the parent service to provide them. Each squadron had its own flight surgeon, for instance, based on a sound rationale: Pilots were compared after a fashion to thoroughbred horses, and the watchful eye of a trainer was necessary to maintain peak performance. VMF-214's doctor, Lt. George L. Kraft, USNR, brought a small staff of corpsmen to assist (especially with the everyday needs of the ground echelon) while he looked after the pilots. As a qualified flight surgeon he was knowledgeable about the idiosyncrasies of pilot mentality, having completed a modified flight training syllabus in Pensacola with enough hours to safely solo. He was authorized to dole out liquor for medicinal purposes—to ease the stress of aerial combat—a duty that virtually guaranteed his popularity. As was customary in every squadron, only one nickname was suitable for the Chicagoan, "Doc."

By early February a few of the original pilots who had been with the squadron for several months were showing signs of fatigue. Knowing that the grueling pace could easily result in further mishaps, Doc Kraft arranged for those with at least three months in the outfit to have some time away from the field. They were rewarded with a few days at the Holmes Estate, a private mansion near Diamond Head that the pilots dubbed the "Rest Palace." It had been deeded to the United Service Organization (USO) for the duration of the war. The pilots arrived in groups of two or three to relax on the beach, dance with USO girls in a picturesque setting, or partake of the well-stocked bar. "Plenty of liquor," wrote Dave Rankin, "and a fine show anytime we wanted one."

The recovery period did not prevent accidents, however, as two mishaps involved new lieutenants who had arrived in late January. The first was Carl O. Dunbar, Jr., from New Haven, Connecticut, who was practicing slow rolls at an altitude of 4,500 feet on February 3 when he entered a roll, crossed the controls, and put his Wildcat into a spin from which he was unable to recover. He bailed out and incurred only mild injuries, but another F4F-4 was destroyed. A week later, Sgt. Bill Blakeslee was landing his Wildcat when the wheels folded, causing damage to the prop and landing gear.

Blakeslee's accident proved to be the squadron's last mishap at Ewa, bringing the squadron's total to ten airplanes destroyed outright or wrecked beyond repair, with six others damaged to varying degrees during six months of flying. The cost to taxpayers, approximately half a million dollars, was justifiable for the Marine Corps in their haste to get pilots to the combat zone.* Arguably the new pilots had arrived with little experience in fighters, yet they mastered the F4F while learning gunnery and tactics as well. With a war to fight, there was little time to dwell on the costs.

As the time for deployment drew near, George Britt continued to push his pilots hard, scheduling them at every opportunity to practice gunnery, instrument flying, and oxygen familiarization. Rumors began circulating that the squadron would move within a week, loading their airplanes on a carrier (as yet unidentified) to sail for the war zone. Britt directed the maintenance crews to give the airplanes special attention, and they began final checks on February 10. Guns were boresighted, compasses swung for accuracy, engines fine-tuned. Once checked, the fighters were grounded until the day they would be ferried to Ford Island.

The excitement became palpable. Other than a voyage to Hawaii on crowded troopships or seaplane tenders, few of the men had ever experienced life aboard a naval vessel at sea. Fueling their anticipation of an ocean voyage were the mysteries of the South Pacific and its tropical islands, coupled with the realization that they would soon face the enemy. Combat veterans returning from Guadalcanal would occasionally stop by Ewa on their way to the States, giving reports on the Japanese pilots. Said one, "You're not going to be facing amateurs. These people know what they're doing. They're among the very best the Japanese have, and you'd better be prepared."

After the combat-ready Wildcats were grounded, Britt made use of a few F4F-3s and an F4F-7 to squeeze in two more days of gunnery training, but he finally called a halt

*The "flyaway" cost of a single Wildcat—including government-furnished equipment such as engine, guns, and instrumentation—was roughly thirty thousand dollars.

on February 12. Everyone gathered personal belongings and packed the miscellaneous gear needed for deployment, then settled down to wait. Although the baby flattop *Nassau* (ACV-16) soon tied up at the Navy yard, days dragged by with no orders to report. To pass the time, swimming parties, softball games, and a beer bust were organized. Another F4F-4 was acquired on Valentine's Day, bringing the squadron's total to twenty-four. Mechanics tinkering with engines determined that several were troublesome enough to warrant replacement, which gave them something to focus their attention on.

Finally, after a week of waiting, deployment orders arrived. Work spaces were buttoned up and the Wildcats were ferried to NAS Ford Island on February 20, although one plane remained at Ewa due to a history of landing gear malfunctions. As if in protest, the wheels folded while it sat in the revetment; the mechanics simply left it squatting on its belly.

At 0745 on the morning of February 21, all hands were transported from Ewa to Pearl Harbor's West Loch, where they boarded a ferry for the trip to Ford Island. *Nassau* got under way at about the same time, shifting from berth 16 at the Navy yard to berth F1 at Ford Island. Once in place, fifty-four Wildcats from MAG-21's three fighter squadrons were craned onto her flight deck, a task lasting several hours. Finally at 1600, after hundreds of Marines had also boarded, *Nassau* slipped her moorings and headed out of the harbor. In the channel the destroyer *Sterett* (DD-407), a one-stacker with a low, sleek fantail that had fought at Guadalcanal the previous November, maneuvered off *Nassau*'s stern. The tiny convoy, if it could properly be called that, headed out of the channel and turned west.

Watching from the carrier's flight deck were some of the best-prepared fighter pilots the Marine Corps could muster. George Britt's pilots and ground personnel had labored intensely for months to prepare for this moment, and Britt was pleased with what he saw. Individuals had jelled into a cohesive unit, with genuine camaraderie and good morale. Just as important, the pilots had become proficient at shooting target sleeves full of holes.

Pacific means peaceful, but the Marines looking beyond *Nassau*'s bow to where the afternoon sun dipped toward an endless horizon knew that a fight was waiting. Their next targets would be shooting back.

3

SHELLBACKS AND SUBMARINES

To get to the fight, the Marines first had to traverse several thousand miles of submarine-infested ocean, and *Nassau* was hardly a sea-going fortress. Commissioned only six months earlier, she had been converted into a baby flattop from a C-3 cargo hull. Displacing all of 9,800 tons, she was puny compared to the hefty new 27,000-ton *Essex*-class flattops being raised in the shipyards. And she was slow. The big carriers could cut the waves at speeds approaching thirty-five knots, but *Nassau* with her single screw was hard pressed to reach eighteen in an emergency.

The little carrier's commander was Capt. Austin K. Doyle, USN, an acclaimed fighter pilot during the golden age of naval aviation. Because his ship's company was small—only fifty-five officers and about six hundred men—Doyle was known to stand a watch or two himself, helping his inexperienced crew maintain a vigil for submarines. In the event they were encountered, the destroyer *Sterett* carried detection equipment and depth charges, but *Nassau* could do little to protect herself aside from defensive zigzagging. The Wildcats lashed to her deck were simply cargo, of no practical use against submarines. On this particular voyage, *Nassau* was a transport, not a fighting ship.

Not a soul aboard either ship doubted that their destination was the South Pacific, but until *Nassau* and *Sterett* sailed from Pearl Harbor their exact objective remained secret. Soon after they cleared the channel, a secret dispatch from the Commander, Air Forces Pacific (ComAirPac), confirmed their hunches. As *Nassau* neared the New Hebrides, its load of airplanes would be catapulted and flown to the island of Espiritu Santo, code named Buttons. This was no surprise to the Marines, who had guessed they would pause at Espiritu before restaging to the legendary island of Guadalcanal, otherwise known as Cactus.

Meanwhile the men faced long days and nights of ocean transit under extremely cramped conditions. With three squadrons including ground echelons and the air group staff embarked, it was a major undertaking merely to find space for hundreds of men to sleep, then tasks enough to keep them occupied. Living quarters for the original ship's company were none too spacious. Many Marines settled on the hangar deck and slung hammocks or bedrolls wherever they found room to lie down. Plane captains slept on the open flight deck near their aircraft, appreciating the extra breeze created by the carrier's progress, as did at least one of the flying sergeants. "The weather was so warm," remembered Jim Taylor, "it was not uncomfortable sleeping in that fashion." Officers were afforded the relative comfort of bunking in staterooms, spartan by civilian standards but roomy compared to the crowded troop transports that ferried many others to the South Pacific.

The Marines passed the time in the fashions learned from their dungareed shipmates. When not tinkering with airplanes or otherwise employed, the enlisted men indulged in card games or acey-deucey tournaments. So did the pilots, who also attended classes and lectures every morning where they practiced navigation, engineering, and enemy ship and aircraft recognition drills. Junior lieutenants were pressed into service to stand watches as duty officers.

Vince Carpenter discovered one free-time diversion that served both himself and his squadron mates well in the months to come. One of the ship's officers in the next stateroom had a Victrola and was fond of playing a vocal arrangement of "Old Black Magic." The song was also a favorite of Carpenter's, whose extraordinary interest in music included a fine voice inherited from his mother, a professional singer, plus an affinity for composing. Honing those talents, he played the recording repeatedly until he knew the chords and "every one of those harmonies down cold," then transposed his own arrangement using some of the blank music paper he had brought in his belongings. Other pilots wanted to sing their favorite Ivy League songs, so Carpenter formed a quartet. There was no shortage of Ivy Leaguers to choose from, with six on the roster from Harvard, Yale, or Princeton.

For *Nassau*'s crew and passengers, the crossing never had the opportunity to become monotonous. The little convoy encountered its first sub scare at 1136 on February 24, when *Sterett* reported a sonar contact as a possible submarine. General quarters (GQ) sounded and *Nassau* increased to her top speed of eighteen knots, then began a series of twisting, rolling evasive maneuvers that could be felt by all hands. As if the clamor had not raised enough adrenaline, *Sterett* dropped three depth charges, their detonations reverberating through *Nassau*'s hull. After the underwater concussions subsided, *Sterett* was unable to regain sonar contact, and both ships secured from general quarters shortly past noon. Already disquieted, the Marines found themselves disturbed by a new problem that day when *Nassau*'s crew began preparations for the most boisterous ceremony encountered in naval service. They were going to cross the Line.

The ceremonial rituals associated with crossing the equator are at once mysterious and ludicrous. Evolved from British naval tradition more than two hundred years old—a time when ships of the fleet sometimes spent years away from home—the honored occasion permitted the crew to temporarily drop many of the conventional protocols of rank. From the most senior flag officer embarked down to the lowest seaman apprentice, all hands enjoyed a brief period of equal status.

The essence of *Nassau*'s observance was that each man on board belonged in one of two categories. He was either a Pollywog, a sorry soul unfamiliar with the mysteries of the deep, or a Shellback, already initiated on a previous passage. Despite the atmosphere of silliness, woe befell Pollywogs who did not take their lowly position seriously, thus incurring the wrath of Shellbacks. Being a Pollywog was not considered a good thing; being a Shellback was, provided a man could prove indisputably that he had already received initiation. The names of new Shellbacks were carefully documented when a vessel crossed the Line, and certificates were awarded each new membership of the Realm of Neptune. Those who claimed Shellback status but could not substantiate it were duly demoted to the rank of Pollywog and could expect an extra ration of hazing.

Unfortunately for *Nassau*'s Marine passengers, she had just completed a Pacific crossing from the Fiji Islands and virtually the entire ship's company was Shellbacks. They waited eagerly for the opportunity to administer the rites. Because only a handful were needed to run the ship and maintain precautionary watches, more than plenty would get the chance.

As with most naval traditions, a proper crossing of the Line was accomplished only by following a prescribed, orderly process. At the moment *Nassau* crossed the equator, the lowly Pollywogs would be allowed to genuflect on their knees before King Neptune and his royal court (played by costumed Shellback representatives). Before that could take place, a ritual of hazing activities was organized on the eve of the crossing. In scattered groups throughout the ship, the uninitiated were brought before hostile-looking panels of inquisitors, who accused them of trumped-up transgressions. "Wog!" they would shout, "worthless scum!" as the confused Marines performed small acts of contrition—buying rounds of refreshments or clowning in silly costumes—all deviously planned to guarantee discomfort without causing real harm.

At approximately 1000 on the morning of February 25, the hapless Pollywogs were shepherded up to the flight deck for the main event. The ceremony was neither as lengthy nor elaborate as it might have been in peacetime, but *Nassau*'s Shellbacks made the most of their opportunity for fun as they dragged each crawling, kowtowing Wog before the royal court. Paying homage included kissing the sweaty, greased belly of the royal baby, played by the most obese Shellback aboard. Wogs were annointed with all manner of obnoxious, foul-smelling concoctions mixed in the ship's galleys, then they ran a long gauntlet of rowdy Shellbacks armed with shillelaghs, made from wetted lengths of canvas fire hose. Meant to connect with Wog posteriors, the shillelaghs delivered intimidating smacks that left smarting, rosy welts.

To a man, VMF-214 suffered the indignities. Major Britt, a veteran of service aboard *Wasp* in the Atlantic, had never made a crossing and took his turn with the others. The Shellbacks showed particular enthusiasm with Marine officers by administering "a couple of extra whacks."

After the last Pollywog stumbled through the gauntlet, the ceremony ended, and in an about-face the newly initiated were warmly congratulated by their former tormentors. All traces of animosity were suddenly gone, although the welts and soreness took longer to fade. In keeping with tradition, *Nassau*'s captain distributed exquisite, personally signed certificates that officially proclaimed each individual a Trusty Shellback. Britt's reminder of the day he crossed the equator bears Artie Doyle's signature and still occupies a place of honor on his study wall.

The diversion over, *Nassau* returned to the business of transporting fighter planes across the Pacific. She still faced another five days of steaming to reach her launch position off the New Hebrides. After enduring the antics of crossing the Line, the Marine officers extracted a measure of revenge the next day by beating the ship's officers at volleyball on the hangar deck. The remainder of February 26 was peaceful, but the following day brought excitement anew.

With *Nassau* sailing farther away from the relative safety of Pacific Fleet headquarters, anticipation of encounters with enemy submarines heightened. Holding a steady speed of seventeen knots, *Nassau* plodded along while *Sterett* sniffed about for underwater contacts. At 1050 on the morning of February 27—close to the same hour as the scare three days earlier—*Sterett* again reported a sonar contact as a possible submarine astern of *Nassau*. The baby flattop went to general quarters and *Sterett* screened astern while the carrier rumbled up to eighteen knots and began radical course changes. *Nassau*'s crew and Marine passengers held their collective breath, not knowing if a torpedo was already on its way. But after twenty minutes with no further contact, both ships secured from the alert.

It happened again the next morning—this time at 1127—when *Sterett* had another sonar hit astern of *Nassau*. The carrier went to GQ again, *Sterett* searched again, and once more the sound contact was lost. Wrote a *Nassau* officer, "This procedure was not exactly conducive to quiet nerves on the part of the crew of either ship. It seemed the task unit was being shadowed by a submarine, but a miraculously elusive one."

That afternoon *Sterett* regained the sound contacts on two more occasions. The destroyer prosecuted them while *Nassau* responded with general quarters and evasive maneuvering. *Sterett* dropped four depth charges at 1520 but nothing was found. *Nassau*'s occupants, increasingly frustrated by the disconcerting alarms and explosions, began wishing that something, anything, would happen. Crossing the international date line provided a distraction as the last hours of February 28 were exchanged somewhat magically for the first day of March. The following afternoon the disturbances were renewed. *Nassau* went to GQ twice more in response to mysteriously similar sound contacts by *Sterett,* but each time the results were the same. Whatever was stalking the carrier failed to reveal itself.

Finally at dawn on March 3, Pentecost Island, in the New Hebrides, hove into view off the starboard bow. Captain Doyle brought *Nassau* to a spot northeast of Espiritu Santo for launching aircraft, and plane captains began warming up the Pratt & Whitney engines in preparation. Some of VMF-214's pilots would have to remain aboard *Nassau* as she steamed into Segond Channel, but the rest manned aircraft with a sigh of relief, anxious to be off the slow-moving target that for days had seemed to be in a submarine's crosshairs.

The excitement wasn't quite over, however. Among the pilots in VMF-214, only George Britt had experienced a carrier launch, and all grew concerned when things went wrong almost from the beginning. Because of *Nassau*'s short and thoroughly crowded flight deck, a catapult was used to fling the Wildcats on their way. The first plane airborne was piloted by Lt. Col. Raymond E. Hopper, commanding officer of MAG-21. Next was an NAP from VMF-213 for whom things did not turn out so well. Just after clearing the catapult, Sgt. Gordon Hodde's Wildcat stalled and spun in. The plane sank immediately, but Hodde managed to swim free and was picked up by *Sterett,* now acting as plane guard for just such a purpose.

Promptly the remaining pilots were signaled to shut down their engines and report to the ready room. When they shuffled in, the Navy lieutenant commander in charge of *Nassau*'s catapult appeared and gave a finger-wagging "I told you so." He blamed Hodde's steep, climbing turn and premature flap retraction for the accident, not his own catapult. Thus rebuked, the pilots returned to their planes and resumed launching without further mishap.

But the flight to Espiritu Santo was hardly better for

some. A group led by Henry Ellis drifted too far north and east among a cluster of islands he could not identify, then bounced into turbulent squalls. The situation began to unravel. Fortunately for Ellis, Henry Miller was alongside, quietly applying his considerable instrument navigation skill. Miller alone recognized their approximate position and radioed Ellis with a suggested heading that finally got them to Espiritu. By the time they landed ("pancaked" was the code used in the combat zone), Ellis's group was more than an hour overdue, nearly out of gas, and soaked with perspiration.

A few of the Marines landed on the white coral surface of the fighter strip at Turtle Bay, but the rest pancaked at Bomber One, where they were to stay as a transient unit. In so doing they suffered a few flat tires, experiencing firsthand the main drawback of a runway paved with steel Marston matting. Designed to be a durable landing surface that could be built in a hurry, the individual Marston mats were perforated rectangular steel plates that locked together. Simple to install—a Navy construction battalion could bulldoze a strip and pave it with steel in short order—the finished product demanded some precaution. Aircraft touching down with damaged or malfunctioning gear could go out of control if a protrusion caught in the plates. The surface was slick when wet (which was often), and the fighter strips in particular were narrow. A pilot who let a wheel drift off one side of the matting and into the graded shoulder faced a violent ground loop or even a flip. And as some of the Marines already learned, sharp edges were a frequent source of shredded tires.

Around noon that day, *Nassau* reached her own haven at Espiritu and passed quietly through the antisubmarine nets at the entrance to Segond Channel. At last, the mysterious underwater contact that had caused so many alarms would threaten them no more, and "great sighs of relief were heard on all sides."

Even so, *Nassau*'s young aerology officer was most unhappy and approached the executive officer with a complaint. First he explained that an aerological laboratory on Hawaii had loaned him a bathythermograph, designed for measuring water temperature as a function of ocean depth, so he could take readings during the crossing. But each time he extended the device on its long cable behind *Nassau,* his tests were interrupted by the general quarters alarm. He had to abandon his tests, reel in the bathythermograph, and hurry to his battle station.

More than suspicious, the exec began asking questions. It required little sleuthing to determine that the tenderfoot's underwater tests coincided precisely with the deck log's record of sonar contacts. Unable to realize that his own bathythermograph was the "enemy" submarine, even after six incidents, the aerology officer was now hugely embarrassed. The exec was not amused. In time, however, the tale of "The Submarine Plague" became one of Adm. Artie Doyle's favorite sea stories.

4

THE STORM BEFORE THE CALM

Espiritu Santo, largest of the New Hebrides Islands and four hours by air from Guadalcanal, had been developed over the past eight months into one of the most vital Allied bases in the Pacific. Code named Buttons in message traffic, it offered two bomber strips, a fighter strip, a seaplane base, and a deepwater anchorage. Each of those areas had become crowded as men and material flowed in from the States, but the strain was offset by amenities not found in combat areas. There were substantial clubs to serve officers and enlisted men, even a separate mess facililty for transient personnel.

The squadron was glad to be back on dry land after enduring *Nassau*'s numerous "submarine" scares and cramped quarters, but its arrival did not result in days of repose. There was much to accomplish while awaiting combat orders to Guadalcanal, during which the men remained at Bomber One without a place to call their own. They passed the first night in temporary quarters with Navy patrol squadron VP-51, then searched for something more permanent. On an island in the middle of the South Pacific there was but one option: building an encampment.

Exploring the tropical environment was a new experience. Picturesque beaches were lined with enormous palms, and lagoons beckoned invitingly for a relaxing dip. Inland stood stately groves of coconut palms, swaying in the sea breeze amid lush grasses. VMF-214 staked a claim in one such grove and began building its temporary home, but the men soon found that the tall grass was deceiving. After eight months of American presence, the once attractive groves had become littered with junk. Wartime expansion and environmental preservation were mutually exclusive, and the squadron's coconut grove had to be cleaned up first.

During construction the Marines learned to endure another fact of island life—rain. Day upon day the downpours soaked them as a frontal system settled in. Dave Rankin described the growing tent city as a "mud hole." During their battle with the elements to raise tents, they also fought the rain and mud to dig latrines, or "heads" in naval jargon. Until their own mess tent was erected, they ate meals with VMD-154, a Marine PB4Y squadron that had been on the island for several months. Eventually their efforts resulted in an independent camp.

While waiting for the weather to improve, Henry Miller busied himself by preparing the Wildcats for combat duty. Major Britt, having realized that the deliberate, inquisitive former attorney could absorb more information about Wildcats and how to maintain them than any other officer in the squadron, had selected Miller as the engineering officer. To that end, Miller relied on the mechanical experience of MTSgt. Oscar Knopf and signed on several lieutenants to assist him. His team dodged frequent squalls on the flight line, laboring with the maintenance personnel to warm engines, check batteries, and rub down prop blades.

Meanwhile Britt and Bill Pace continued to finalize the roster into seven divisions of four planes each. Although there were four captains to lead divisions, among the junior officers there had been no promotions, so two leaders would have to come from the long list of second lieutenants. Vince Carpenter, the Olympic-class athlete, had already established himself, as had Dave Rankin, the award-winning football player. Another pilot with credentials was Charles C. Lanphier, who graduated from Stanford two years before the war began and at twenty-six was older than the other lieutenants. His father was a West Pointer, now at the Pentagon serving on Gen. George Marshall's staff as air intelligence officer. His brother Thomas was a P-38 pilot in the 339th Fighter Squadron based on Guadalcanal. Charlie proved a popular leader, although Tom thought him somewhat straightlaced. "He wasn't much of a drinker (may his Irish forebears forgive). He didn't smoke and didn't gamble—at dice and cards, that is."

Britt weighed the choices carefully, for the responsibilities facing division leaders would be heavy. Besides operating their own planes smartly, they had to make rapid decisions affecting the lives of at least three other pilots.

In addition to division leaders, Britt needed to name section leaders who displayed responsibility and quick reflexes. Maintaining division integrity was the objective, but if the two-plane sections did become separated, each unit tried to remain intact and utilize strength in numbers. It was sound philosophy on the chalkboard, though not always practical when the fur began to fly.

At last the weather cleared enough to resume flying on Wednesday, March 10, but by then the pilots who had ridden *Nassau* into the Segond Channel had been earthbound for a month and those who catapulted off the deck had logged only a couple of hours. All of them were rusty. On that first day back in the saddle, five divisions took off at various intervals to shake out the cobwebs. The Wildcats rolled down Bomber One individually, then joined into divisions while the leaders throttled back in an easy turn. Not normally difficult in clear weather, the rendezvous would become interesting in predawn blackness or when dodging rain squalls. Radio silence would be strictly enforced on combat missions, further compounding the challenge. Successfully joined, the divisions rehearsed tactics such as defensive weaving, navigation, and patrol techniques, throwing in a little tail chasing at the finish. When it was time to return, leaders brought their flights in echelon over the field, where they peeled off individually to join other traffic circling the strip, then found their intervals to enter the landing pattern.

Additional training flights were planned for Thursday, but early in the morning Colonel Hopper informed George Britt that VMF-214's flight echelon would move to Guadalcanal the next day. The day's flights were canceled amid tremendous excitement, and the Wildcats were made ready for the long trip. It was more than 550 miles to Fighter One on the island they would come to know as Cactus, so the planes were fitted with two external fuel tanks. The fifty-gallon drop tanks, constructed of doped hemp fiber, were a relatively new modification that greatly extended the Wildcat's range, and Fighter Command wanted them hung on Britt's planes. Only one was necessary for the trip, but the tanks were in big demand on Guadalcanal and the Wildcats could deliver the extras. The only drawback was the Wildcat's speed limit. A redline of three hundred knots was imposed when the tanks were mounted, but they could be released by a sharp tug on a T handle in the cockpit.

The pilots scurried about their preparations, thrilled at the prospect of heading to the island where so many legendary battles and acts of heroism had been played out. The ground war had ended there only a month before when the Japanese withdrew more than eleven thousand starved and diseased troops. The air battle was far from over, although it was not as critical as those desperate months of late 1942 when the Leathernecks had written history in their Wildcats, clawing almost four hundred Japanese aircraft out of the sky. Those heroes—Harold Bauer, Marion Carl, Joe Foss, Bob Galer, and John Smith—were already legendary, having accounted for some eighty-seven victories. Each had been shot down at least once (a fighter pilot's chances were infinitely better if he came down over friendly territory), and all but Bauer lived to fight another day. Carl was the first ace in the Marine Corps but the only member of that elite handful not to receive a Medal of

Honor. Now VMF-214 was eager to test its own mettle, and the sky above Cactus was the place to find enemy aircraft.

Instead of leaving the following morning, however, an unwelcome change in plans was announced. The squadron would fly only nine Wildcats, fitted with one external tank apiece, to Cactus a day later than planned while most of the pilots rode in a transport. For Henry Miller this was a real blow, because more than half of the squadron's brand-new F4F-4s would be left behind. "I was too discouraged even to inquire the numbers," he wrote, referring to the identification stenciled on fuselages. "Our squadron, so carefully organized in many respects, seems to be under the knife."

In addition to forfeiting aircraft, another surprise came when the squadron itself was carved up. Two of the squadron's pilots and the entire 220-man ground echelon were stripped away to serve with a new headquarters for MAG-21 on Banika, in the Russell Islands. Bill Pace and David R. Moak were ordered to temporary duty on Colonel Hopper's MAG staff, as was the intelligence officer. Lieutenant Walter E. Teich, the air combat intelligence officer (ACIO), would be replaced by another once the flight echelon reached Cactus.

The pilots further learned that their MAG-21 sister squadrons would remain on Buttons for the time being. VMF-221 would bring its Wildcats to Guadalcanal in a few weeks, but VMF-213 was in for a long delay, having been selected to transition into F4U Corsairs. It was only the second Marine squadron so equipped. Its skipper, by great coincidence, was also a major named Britt (Wade H., Jr.), a graduate of the Citadel. The two were not related but had been close friends since their training days at Quantico and Pensacola.

Thus informed, VMF-214's flight echelon continued packing while George Britt selected eight other pilots to fly the Wildcats. Remembering the NAPs, he named Jim Taylor to the short list to fly at the rear with Henry Ellis as tail-end

Charlie. Those not in fighters would ride up to Cactus on a Douglas twin-engine transport operated by the South Pacific Combat Air Transport Command, SCAT for short. For all of them, the prospect of flying to their new combat duty on Cactus made sleep elusive.

At dawn on Saturday, March 13, they were greeted by the dismaying news that bad weather would cause another delay. A huge front had settled between Espiritu and Guadalcanal. The Wildcats were denied clearance to depart, but an R4D—the Navy's designation for the venerable Douglas DC-3 transport version—received the okay to airlift Doc Kraft and the remaining seventeen pilots. When the Skytrain landed at Henderson Field at noon and rolled clear of the strip, the passengers were treated to a huge surprise. They gaped out the windows at hundreds of wildly cheering soldiers lining the sides of the runway. OK Williams, unsure what to make of it, decided the soldiers were "tickled to death to see a bunch of fighter pilots show up." But soon the real reason for the crowd's enthusiasm appeared in the form of another transport, this one with nurses aboard. A roar went up from the waiting crowd as the females stood in the open cargo door and waved. All too soon, however, the second transport took on a load of patients and "got the hell out of there."

Doc Kraft and the advance pilots made their way from Henderson Field to Fighter One and spent the rest of the day exploring. They were filled with curiosity, and there was much to see around the airfield, including scattered evidence of the recent fighting. They further discovered that they would share the fighter strip with the history-making VMF-124, the first outfit to make a combat tour with the gull-wing Corsair. The Wildcat pilots looked over the new fighters with fascination; compared to their boxy F4Fs, the Corsairs were *huge*.

Down on Buttons, George Britt was chafing. In addition to being held up by the weather, he objected to a new doctrine from Commander Aircraft, Solomons (ComAirSols) requiring a navigational lead plane for fighters being ferried to Guadalcanal. Having flown plenty of overwater flights off *Wasp* in the Atlantic and knowing how to navigate, he particularly disliked the idea of having a junior transport pilot herd the flight. The policy left him no choice. Perhaps more troubling was the ever-increasing size of the overall formation: Thirteen Grumman TBF Avengers from VMSB-143 were joining his nine Wildcats. Now there would be almost two dozen mismatched aircraft on the flight, crossing a long stretch of open ocean on the wing of an Army lieutenant.

At 0610 on Sunday morning Britt released the brakes on his F4F and in short order eight more Wildcats followed him down the bomber strip. They soon completed the rendezvous with the C-47 (the Army's designation for the Skytrain), and Britt tucked under its right wing as the other fighters slid into a loose echelon behind him. Captain Wilfred L. Park, executive officer of VMSB-143, formed his thirteen big Grumman "Turkeys" on the other side.

Unknown to them, the ugly weather that had interrupted their original departure still sat squarely between Buttons and Cactus, but within an hour of their departure it was obvious. The gaggle of planes approached a huge wall of menacing clouds—a major storm labeled "real mean" by one pilot. Instead of trying to skirt it or turning back altogether, the C-47 pilot decided to lead the formation over the top. As he began to climb, he spied a low valley among the towering ridges of clouds that he thought they could squeeze through; with a little luck, he thought, they'd be able to pick their way through the worst of it.

At that moment, while the formation approached the cloud wall, Henry Ellis ran into serious trouble. His engine quit cold and he immediately fell behind the others, rapidly losing altitude. His position as tail-end Charlie was the worst possible—no one saw him descend—and the rest of the flight droned ahead, oblivious to his plight.

Too busy for a radio call, Ellis worked furiously to restart the engine, but when every trick failed he realized that the fuel pump was out. Gliding down through three thousand feet with a dead engine, heading into a storm, his only option was to hit the silk. Ellis slid back the canopy, jumped from the stricken Wildcat into a blast of humid air, and pulled the ripcord. Hours would pass before he was missed.

Up ahead, Jim Taylor encountered a fuel problem of his own just before entering the clouds. The pilots had been instructed to use the fuel in the new drop tank first, but there was no gauge for monitoring its quantity. They could monitor the engine's consumption rate or watch for a momentary drop in pressure as the tank emptied, then switch to internal tanks, but Taylor didn't catch his in time. His engine quit when the external tank ran dry, and he had difficulty restarting it. After long, disconcerting moments the engine finally coughed to life, but Taylor had already dropped several thousand feet and was far behind the formation. Soon the others disappeared into the clouds and Taylor was forced to continue alone. He would draw heavily on Henry Miller's valuable lessons about situational awareness.

Alongside the C-47, George Britt signaled for his remaining pilots to close the formation. Seeing that the Skytrain pilot had misjudged the altitude of the gap he was aiming for, Britt realized they were in for a rough ride. Vic Scarborough tucked in as close as he dared, so near that "his left wingtip was in my ear," recalled Britt. The rest of the echelon followed suit.

The lumbering Skytrain, straining for altitude, began losing airspeed. At just ninety knots, barely above stall speed, the Army pilot plunged them into the dark, turbulent mass of clouds. Britt could scarcely believe the pilot's judgment but tried to stay alongside, flying dangerously close to keep the aircraft in sight. Inside the storm, visibility dropped to almost nil as sheets of rain rattled against the Plexiglas windscreens. Unstable air seethed within the blackness, alternately lifting the small fighters as though they were on invisible elevators, then slamming them down hard without warning. Controlled flight became virtually impossible, and Britt soon lost sight of the C-47. The difficulty of trying to maintain formation was amplified for each pilot behind him, and near the back of the formation the situation turned dire. John Fidler saw fleeting images of planes flying past his canopy two or three different times, "guys completely out of control."

The formation's integrity was gone. Doctrine or no doctrine, Britt realized that staying with the C-47 was suicidal. He needed to make a quick decision in the interest of self-preservation, with no time for radio calls. He spotted an opening in the clouds off to the right, what wary pilots called a sucker hole. The gap might lead to clear air below or could tempt them into a disastrous plunge to the sea. Britt made his choice and steered for the hole, breaking to the right as he dived through the clouds with five of the Wildcats still behind. Keeping one eye on the compass to maintain a northwest heading, he led what was left of his group on a corkscrewing, roller-coaster ride down through the storm, dodging and weaving his way around the worst storm cells. They spiraled down a funnel of churning gray walls, bumping hard against pockets of updrafting air that jarred their tailbones and shook their little planes.

Britt's Wildcat rapidly accelerated to the external tank's three-hundred-knot redline, and he yanked the T handle to release it, precious or not. As he chanced a quick look back to make sure the jettisoned tank had not struck someone, he saw five more tanks flutter down. The boys were following his every lead.

At last they sighted the surface of the Coral Sea. To get below the storm clouds, they leveled out just seventy-five feet above the water. The air was calmer, but suddenly Britt realized that they had exchanged one problem for another.

The new threat was rain. It positively thundered down, so heavily that they seemed to be flying through a wall of water while horrific swells churned the surface only a few feet below. As rain and hail pelted them, Britt grew concerned that their Pratt & Whitneys would virtually suffocate for lack of air. "Good Lord," he wondered aloud, "how long are these engines going to keep running? If they even cough, that's it."

For more than two hundred miles the little band of Wildcats hugged the surface, eventually pulling clear of the squalls to find Guadalcanal straight ahead. The weather at Cactus was still dismal, the island in shadows beneath a dark overcast, and instead of relief at reaching their destination Britt was struck with a sense of foreboding. Five grueling hours after departing Buttons, the remnants of the fighter formation entered the traffic pattern at Fighter One, banged onto the Marston mat, and taxied to meet the contingent that had flown up from Buttons the previous day.

Climbing down from their aircraft, the six pilots were greeted by a faint odor of decay that wafted out of the jungle and mingled with the vapor of hot engines. They circled the planes, stretching muscles cramped from their long ordeal, and discovered amazing evidence of the storm's power. The frontal surfaces of every Wildcat had been stripped clean by rain and hailstones. Normally painted with matte blue-gray on the upper surfaces and light gray underneath, the engine cowlings and leading edges of wings and tails now gleamed of aluminum; even the prop blades were bare.

Soon a seventh Wildcat appeared. Big John Fidler, separated from the formation in the turbulence, had paid close attention to his compass and maintained a constant airspeed while plowing through the storm. When he popped out he was completely alone, but he continued to Cactus without incident and without encountering any other planes.

There were still two fighters unaccounted for. As the time for their calculated fuel endurance came and passed, Hank

Ellis and Jim Taylor failed to appear. Britt's sense of foreboding appeared well founded. This was the squadron's first major event—supposedly a routine ferry flight to begin its first combat tour—yet it had ended disastrously. The pilots walked away from their parked planes with the sinking realization that two of their own were missing.

The two missing pilots were long since down but very much alive. Jim Taylor had made landfall. After restarting his engine, he elected to climb above the worst turbulence, using dead reckoning to estimate his position relative to Guadalcanal. When he finally broke out of the clouds, he saw what appeared to be the northern tip of an island and decided that his elapsed time had placed him over Cactus. He turned east and south, hoping to fly around the north end of the island to Fighter One, but after thirty minutes on this heading he realized he was not over Guadalcanal. Recalculating the numbers in his head, he realized he had underestimated his ground speed during the long climb through the storm. The island beneath his wings was actually San Cristobal. Now that he knew his position, he reversed course and headed north once more.

Thirty minutes on the earlier heading had burned too much fuel, so as Taylor flew back over the water toward Cactus he began a slow descent to two thousand feet. The fuel gauge hovered near the empty mark, resulting in a most uncomfortable feeling as he urged his fighter toward land. Finally he spotted the next island—this time he was certain it was the southern end of Guadalcanal—and began reviewing his options. By staying just off the shoreline, he could wait until the last minute before deciding whether to bail out or make a wheels-up landing on the beach. But after surveying the shoreline from the air, he decided to reject the beach landing idea. The beach was narrow and his airplane was likely to overturn in the water. There was another important factor to consider: In the Wildcat's belly hatch with his personal gear was a precious bottle of brandy. "People on Guadalcanal were counting on that bottle," he recalled. "Discretion was the better part of valor, and I'd better put the damn thing down where I had a chance to recover the booze."

Soon Taylor ran out of time to think it over. Just shy of the island's southeastern shore, his engine sputtered and quit. At the same moment he saw an inviting field off to his left; it looked like a perfect green lawn, freshly mowed. Cranking down the wheels, he lined up for a dead-stick landing. As Taylor neared the touchdown point, he could see a tree line approaching fast, but he judged he would be on the ground in seconds and could stop with room to spare. Suddenly he found himself flying *through* the grass and looked up to see green blades above his head—and still he had not touched down. A belly landing would stop him faster, but there was no time to crank the wheels back up. If he didn't do something soon, he would pile into the trees. The instant the wheels bumped down on solid ground, he kicked the rudder violently, sending the airplane into a sideways skid and deliberately wrecking it by tearing the landing gear free. The Wildcat slid to a halt on its belly a few feet short of the trees.

Taylor congratulated himself. "The prop was bent and the undercarriage was gone, but the rest of the airplane was in very usable condition. I thought I'd done a fair job." Best of all, the brandy was intact. He retrieved his gear and started walking in the direction of the beach, but it was a struggle. What had appeared to be a smooth green lawn from the air was really a field of swamp grass, grown to a height of more than twelve feet.

Emerging from the field, Taylor startled a couple of soldiers manning an outpost. They had watched him fly over without realizing that the engine was silent and assumed he was making a low pass. At first they did not believe him when he said he'd just crashed his Wildcat nearby.

"The hell you did," they said in surprise.

"No, it's a fact—I did it," he replied.

They gave him a lift to company headquarters, which

notified Fighter One of his safe arrival, then he spent the night with the Army before catching a ride to the fighter strip in the morning.

One of the first to greet him was Maj. John Sapp, commanding officer of VMSB-143. Had Taylor seen any of his missing TBFs?

Taylor was unaware of the previous day's tragedy. It turned out that Britt's decision to leave the Skytrain and take charge of his own airplanes was reinforced by the disaster that befell the rest of the formation. When the C-47 finally punched through the storm, only six TBFs remained on its wing. Two more reached Henderson Field later, but by the end of the day it was evident that five had been lost. The TBFs were the largest single-engine planes in the war, far less maneuverable than the Wildcats. Perhaps several had suffered a chain-reaction collision in the midst of the violent storm. It was a small consolation to the Avenger squadron that instead of the normal combat crew of three, only gunners had ridden with the pilots aboard four of the missing planes and one pilot flew solo. But the blow was still tremendous: Nine souls were gone including the executive officer.* The cause of their disappearance remains a mystery, for no trace of them has been found.

With Taylor back in the fold, only Henry Ellis remained unaccounted for, and an entire day passed without word of his whereabouts. It was widely held that a downed pilot not plucked from the sea within twenty-four hours had a dismal chance of surviving. Fliers occasionally hauled up on some tropical beach, but Ellis had disappeared over the

*Five pilots and four enlisted men were declared missing in action: Capt. Wilfred L. Park, 2d Lt. John H. Martindale, 2d Lt. Glen I. Anderson, 2d Lt. Raymond E. Eastcott, 2d Lt. Joseph H. Kurz, Cpl. Raymond J. Barrachi, Cpl. Francis Danielson, Cpl. George C. Roberts, and Cpl. Joseph A. Orszulak. Ten months later, VMF-422 lost fewer personnel (six) during a similar fiasco that received extensive publicity, probably because twenty-two Corsairs went down in the process.

Coral Sea, not within a hundred miles of anywhere and in the middle of a storm.

Ellis had beaten the odds, although by the slightest of margins. It was no small miracle that he survived the initial water entry after descending by parachute into the storm-tossed ocean. As Britt and others had witnessed, the sea was violent, and Ellis faced an exhausting battle just to extract the rubber raft from his parachute seat pack, inflate it, and climb aboard. To get into one of the tiny boats, too small for a man to sit straight legged, was challenging on a calm day, but Ellis accomplished it in rough seas. The raft was far from dry inside, and much of his body remained immersed in seawater, but it was better than swimmng.

Having survived the immediate threat of drowning, Ellis now faced the harrowing experience of drifting alone upon the sea. Among his personal effects he could list only a canteen of water, a few mouthfuls of rations, and token survival tools. For the rest of that day and throughout the night he huddled aboard the raft, his world an endless expanse of dark water and empty sky. Another full day passed, then another. Having several times spotted friendly aircraft overhead, he decided he was still in the corridor between Buttons and Cactus, but there seemed to be no dedicated search in progress and the aircraft continued past. Even the regular SCAT transports failed to notice him. "He was ignored by many," wrote Henry Miller. A fourth day at sea was endured and passed into darkness. The executive officer's chances for rescue were fading as rapidly as the setting sun.

5

CACTUS

As the days passed for Henry Ellis, drifting alone on the Coral Sea, his squadron mates flew their first sorties from Guadalcanal and had already lost a man in the process. George Britt was justifiably unhappy with the squadron's initiation after completing the nerve-racking flight through the storm. Two new Wildcats were gone, leaving them with a grand total of seven, and Ellis was still missing. Taylor's safe recovery had provided some good news on Sunday, but the situation would get even worse in a couple of days.

To start their first full day in the combat zone, the pilots gathered Monday morning for a briefing in their new "ready room"—nothing more than a few poles and a spread of canvas. A large tent was staked in the dirt near the strip, the only furnishings some rough tables and chairs built from empty crates, coconut logs for benches, and a chalkboard. The sides were rolled up for ventilation, allowing a wide view of surrounding activities. From before dawn until well after dark, the area around Fighter One was busy and noisy, dominated by the throaty rumble of reciprocating engines, their *pocketa-pocketa* sounds rising to howls at takeoff. In the background was the constant sound of aircraft passing overhead, their drone blending with the whine of jeeps and vehicles of every description, always in a hurry to get somewhere. Occasionally these sounds were punctuated by the rattle of field telephones or by the boom of black-powder cartridges as ground crews fired up engines.

The briefing this morning was given by a major from Fighter Command, John Condon, who had been the operations officer on Cactus since January and knew his business well. Standing at the front of the tent, he observed eager anticipation in the young faces before him. Here were more new pilots, plenty gung-ho and ready to take to the skies yet completely naive about the realities of combat. None had seen a Japanese aircraft or knew firsthand what the Zeros were capable of. But Condon was able to impart some wisdom. "If you go off on your own when you sight enemy aircraft, you're putting yourself at the wrong end of some pretty long odds. Stay with your unit or your leader. Do your job. Don't try to go off and do your own thing."

Their chance to do battle would come in time, he reminded them. The pilots were trained for it, their planes were built for it, and shooting down planes was their ultimate goal. But he warned against engaging the nimble enemy planes in a prolonged dogfight. He urged the Marines to take their shots when they had the advantage, then duck away and build up speed to reenter the fight. He would repeat the same lecture often in the days and weeks to come: "Don't stick around and try to turn with a Zero."

Long before the lessons of combat could be experienced, there were local instructions and ground rules to learn, and Condon tacked a map of the area onto the chalkboard. By this point in the war the airfields on Guadalcanal and the skies overhead had become crowded with aircraft. The main base at Henderson Field and the two outlying fighter strips housed a growing collection of heavy and medium bombers, patrol planes, dive-bombers, torpedo bombers, fighters, transports, and auxiliary aircraft. It was Allied airspace, shared by the U.S. Army Air Forces (USAAF), Navy, Marines, even the Royal New Zealand Air Force (RNZAF), but it was regularly challenged by the Japanese. When enemy raids approached, it was vital to intercept them as quickly as possible, but equally important to keep friendly aircraft from colliding. To that end, the airspace had been chopped into code-named segments, each with specific rendezvous and intercept points, and the airstrip had its own takeoff and landing routes in order to avoid conflicting traffic patterns.

At the conclusion of Condon's briefing, several pilots manned the available planes for their first flight. As assignments went, it would normally be routine, even dull—a local patrol over Guadalcanal. But the ones who flew first would benefit greatly from familiarization, and there was always a possibility of encountering the enemy. With only seven Wildcats left after the ferry flight from Buttons, there were not enough to put two complete divisions in the air. Fortunately VMF-123 was just wrapping up a six-week combat tour and was preparing to return to Buttons for a rest. Five of their F4F-4s, described as "beat up" by one pilot, were acquired by VMF-214.

Shortly past noon, John Burnett's division accelerated down the steel strip and climbed skyward for the squadron's first patrol in the combat zone. Throughout the afternoon three other divisions went aloft, Vince Carpenter's at dusk. For most of the pilots this was the first decent opportunity to survey the island from the air. Guadalcanal seemed dirty on the ground, largely unattractive; but as they climbed, the ugliness softened, the surrounding sea looked beautiful, and the cool air aloft comfortably ventilated their cockpits.

Through spinning blades the pilots looked upon sites of legendary battles. Fighter One and Henderson Field were just inland from Lunga Point, off which Japanese battlewagons had stood to pound the beleaguered force on "Black Tuesday" the previous October. South of the fields they could see Bloody Ridge, still nothing but raw earth and mangled trees from the withering force of explosions and bullets. Just west of Henderson Field was Fighter Two, where Tom Lanphier flew P-38s. Twenty miles along the coast Cape Esperance formed the northwest tip of the island, pointing like a finger toward the Japanese on New Georgia. Across a few miles of sparkling water sat the perfect cone of little Savo Island. And although the azure sea looked inviting, beneath the surface lay the recent ruins of many a good ship and sailor. The bottom was littered with so many hulks that the area was known collectively as Iron Bottom Sound. Now the pilots turned north and crossed Sealark Channel and the passage everyone called "the Slot," north of which lay Florida Island and the fine anchorage at Tulagi, always hectic, always a favorite target of the Japanese.

The first operational patrols were uneventful until the return of Miller's division. Ledge Hazelwood earned the distinction of the squadron's first ground loop at Guadalcanal, and his damaged Wildcat required a tow to the flight line by an Army vehicle. Aside from the temporary reduction in aircraft, it had been a fruitful outing. Sixteen pilots gained exposure to the operating environment and logged thirty-five valuable flight hours, initiating what would prove to be a record-setting tour.

Tuesday's operations provided even more interest. Four divisions were awakened at 0430 to stand strip alert duty. Eight of the pilots waited by the ready tent all day, prepared to scramble aloft if an inbound raid was detected; the other two divisions were released for local patrols. Navy destroyers steaming between Savo Island and the eastern tip of Guadalcanal requested air cover over the Slot, still considered no-man's-land even in broad daylight. The land battle for Guadalcanal may have been finished, but the Japanese could contest the airspace at any time. The Slot was within easy reach of their raiders, making it necessary to cover naval vessels whenever they moved. Vince Carpenter's division got the nod and completed the patrol without incident.

George Britt was already suffering from a minor bout of dysentery, which grounded his division, so Charlie Lanphier's division took the next hop. They launched at 1545 on a Cleanslate patrol to cover the airspace west of Guadalcanal toward the Russell Islands. The patrol was routine until a division of VMF-124's new Corsairs suddenly jumped his four Wildcats in a case of mistaken identity. It was not a playful tail chase and required some hard, defensive maneuvering and urgent radio calls before the Corsair pilots finally realized they had bounced friendlies.

Such incidents, not uncommon, were yet another thorn in Maj. Bill Gise's side. So far VMF-124 had experienced several nagging problems, and his Corsairs had made only an average impression on local observers. Teething pains were expected when introducing a brand-new model to combat, but an inordinate number of the squadron's missions had been fouled by mechanical difficulties. The distractions were causing mental mistakes.

The bugs resulted from the Corsair's relatively complex systems. The early F4U-1 version was afflicted with hydraulic leaks, oil and fuel leaks, and a troublesome ignition system. The magnetos were unpressurized and occasionally caused "mag flash" at high altitude—only one of the two spark plugs in each cylinder would fire. Compounding the mechanical headaches were three primary design flaws, collectively deemed serious enough that the Navy had refused to okay the current model for carrier service. First, visibility was poor in the taxi, takeoff, and three-point landing attitude; next, the left wing had a nasty tendency to stall without warning at low speed, sending unprepared pilots into an often-fatal roll; finally, an unpleasant bounce in the landing gear oleo struts affected rollout after landing.

That very afternoon, Henry Miller and other VMF-214 pilots watched as a Corsair driver lost directional control during landing, cartwheeled his plane down Fighter One, and washed it out completely. The crash was just one of a series of mishaps involving VMF-124 Corsairs that destroyed more planes during their first tour than did the Japanese. The design flaws were eventually overcome, but the Corsair's combat debut was painful. George Britt observed, "During the time that their tour coincided with ours at Guadalcanal, VMF-124 rarely had more than four aircraft in commission."

Britt's own physical ailment was an early symptom of the hazards of jungle living. At this stage of the war the island was not as harmful as enemy bullets once had been, but the harsh environment forced the Marines to live with invisible enemies. Any number of bacterial and viral organisms flourished, and singly or in combination they could virtually wreck a man. Diseases such as malaria, dysentery, and dengue fever had disabled thousands of soldiers and Marines during the ground battle only a few months earlier. Malaria was endemic, causing five times as many casualties as did the Japanese throughout all of the South Pacific. When the vicious fighting on Guadalcanal ended, more attention was devoted to battling the diseases—and a few improvements were made—but the scourges persisted.

In the first place, it proved nearly impossible to fight the conditions that caused them. Nothing could alter Guadalcanal's climate, of course; temperatures averaged in the nineties during the day with extreme humidity. Rain was frequent, sometimes falling in torrents, but even without precipitation the atmosphere practically dripped, enveloping everything in dampness. It was an environment that accelerated decay, whether of Japanese bodies still scattered in the jungle, the rotting vegetation surrounding them, or the khaki, canvas, and leather articles used by the living.

Not much had been done to improve general living conditions. The surroundings were an ideal breeding ground for flies, mosquitoes, parasites, and a host of viruses. Sanitation was almost nonexistent. Open-pit latrines swarmed with flies, which also buzzed through all of the open canvas structures around the fighter strip, including the mess tent.

As the saying went, the flies relieved the mosquitoes at 0530. They crawled with impunity over mess kits and canteen cups, contaminating food and water with fecal matter from latrines or bacteria from decomposing bodies. "During the day they were just horrendous," remembered Drury McCall. "It was really hard to eat without thinking that you were going to bite into a fly."

The bacteria they carried made dysentery a matter of roulette. It was not so much *if* as *when* a man would be struck. The disease caused inflammation of the lower intestines, with frequent and painful diarrhea, which in turn led to dehydration and weakness. Fortunately dysentery was readily treatable due to the recent advent of antibiotics. Most cases did not require hospitalization, but the disease caused great discomfort and was debilitating over the long haul.

Although good nourishment was known to be a requisite for health and stamina, the diet on Guadalcanal was barely adequate. Nearly everything was canned, powdered, or otherwise heavily preserved. Spam prevailed, followed by salted chipped beef mixed with a cream base of powdered milk and slopped over toast—the ubiquitous "shit on a shingle," or SOS for short. There were tasteless powdered eggs and giant tins of dry hardtack.

Vince Carpenter discovered that the food was not only bland, its very origin was suspect.

> We were opening cans of meat and looking at the labels. It was horsemeat canned in South America sometime after World War I—fifteen or twenty years before. Somebody said, "God! This is horsemeat! Look what we're eating, guys."

When the mosquitoes started in at night, the men wore long pants and kept long sleeves rolled down. They gathered whenever possible around a scrap-wood campfire, choosing smoke and heat as the lesser evil to swarms of bloodthirsty insects. Inside their four-man pyramidal tents, they slept on canvas army cots draped with mosquito netting and learned quickly to keep elbows, knees, feet, and arms from touching the sides. Those who found it hard to believe that a tiny insect could cause such misery and were lax about the precautions usually paid, but even among the vigilant it was impossible to prevent bites. The threat of malaria was not as great as it had been a few months earlier, when more than eighty-five hundred Americans had been rendered ineffective, but members of VMF-214 did get the "Old Joe." Jim Taylor would be the first pilot to contract it, barely a week after arriving, and others had mild bouts during the tour.

To ward it off, Doc Kraft and his corpsmen dispensed prophylactic Atabrine pills daily. Although the drug was effective when taken, two rumors hampered its widespread acceptance. The first, unfounded, was that it affected sexual potency. The second was more accurate: Skin and eyes took on a yellow tinge that lasted for months, even after usage was stopped. Malaria persisted despite the pills, especially harrying those already sick or tired.

Taking their medicine and learning the realities of tropical life, VMF-214 began operations on Wednesday, March 17, with some good news. Six more F4F-4s had been acquired and were being flown over from Fighter Two. These additional hand-me-downs from VMF-123 were well used but still operational. Henry Miller and Charlie Lanphier began the flight schedule with early Cleanslate and local patrols, and in the afternoon two divisions were picked for a Dumbo mission. Their assignment was to escort a Navy PBY attempting to rescue a downed pilot near Segi, some 150 miles away on the island of New Georgia. Vince Carpenter and Dave Rankin gunned their divisions down the strip at 1340, then joined with one of the ungainly looking seaplanes nicknamed for their resemblance to Disney's big-eared flying elephant.

The flight was making good progress when disaster struck. Just east of the Russell Islands the last man in the formation suddenly dropped out. Bill Steed, on his first flight since arriving in the South Pacific, inexplicably rolled over, spun in, and vanished beneath the waves. The others searched, but Dave Rankin saw simply "a hole in the water," and that was it. Carpenter gathered up his Wildcats and completed the mission, but the entire squadron was disturbed by Steed's unexplained disappearance, their feeling of loss compounded by troubling questions about what might have happened. No determination could be made, and Steed's belongings were packed for return to his next of kin. "He was a fine young man," wrote George Britt later, "and his loss was a grievous one for a squadron just starting out in combat."

Without so much as sighting an enemy plane, VMF-214 had lost three planes since leaving the New Hebrides. Taylor walked away from his mishap, but Henry Ellis was still missing and Bill Steed was obviously dead. A turbulent storm and mechanical problems had contributed to the loss of the first two Wildcats, but the third was a mystery.

There was always the threat of sudden injury or death, either by enemy action or accident, with anything as complex as a flying machine. Those chosen for the fighter community were generally regarded as having extra measures of coordination and physical ability, but they were still vulnerable to human error, let alone mechanical failure. Early in the war—and it was still early—pilots frequently found themselves in new situations they had not been trained to face. Through no fault of their own, some were simply unprepared, almost frighteningly so, and many died without knowing what killed them. Student pilots poured through the pipeline having proven that they could handle trainers, but high-performance fighters were unforgiving. The last group of pilots to join VMF-214 in late January had less than two weeks to fly F4Fs before deployment. Drury McCall, for instance, logged less than fifteen hours in F4Fs before heading into combat. Steed, who had arrived only a few days before McCall, might have logged enough hours for minimal proficiency but no more.

VMF-214 completed its third day of the combat tour without sighting a single bogey or firing a round. On the fourth day, a few pilots finally received a taste of combat when two divisions led by George Britt and Charlie Lanphier were scheduled to participate in the squadron's first strike against enemy territory. The blue-gray Marine Wildcats would join two divisions of Navy fighters, then shepherd SBD Dauntlesses to Vila, a Japanese airfield 190 nautical miles northwest on Kolombangara, in the New Georgia group.

The flight elements departed their respective strips at midafternoon on Thursday, then formed up as they headed toward the Russell Islands before proceeding up the Slot toward New Georgia. After reaching Kolombangara unopposed, the SBDs deployed their perforated dive flaps and nosed over toward Vila. Britt's eight Wildcats stayed with the bombers much of the way down, scissoring back and forth to avoid accelerating ahead. Soon they saw tracers coming up to meet them, receiving fire for the first time as glowing balls of antiaircraft fire snaked up from scattered emplacements around the field. The tracers began to peter out at three thousand feet, so Britt leveled his fighters to search for enemy aircraft while the bombers continued earthward. No hostiles were spotted, surprise apparently favoring the attackers. After pickling their bombs the Dauntlesses sped away, then regrouped over Rice Anchorage before steering southeast toward home base.

Back at Fighter One the rest of the squadron lounged in the ready tent, smoking cigarettes, chatting about what the strike might encounter, playing acey-deucey, shuffling cards, waiting. Among them was Walter Teich's replacement as air combat intelligence officer, Capt. Peter Folger, a San Franciscan who easily qualified as one of the unique personalities in the region. Not only was he a family member of Folger's coffee, *the* coffee west of the Mississippi, but he was actually serving as the company president. The eldest brother, J. A. Folger III, normally held the title but had to relinquish it due to service on the War Production Board. Pete was now acting president to avoid a conflict of interest, keeping control in the family while a trusted vice president ran daily operations. At thirty-seven Pete was the oldest officer in the flight echelon, having graduated from Yale some fourteen years earlier. When the war began he had originally been denied enlistment because of partial deafness in one ear, but his desire to serve was so strong that he threatened to join the French Foreign Legion. A sympathetic friend who happened to be a Navy doctor helped him pass the physical. Folger chose the Marine Corps, wanting nothing more than to serve as an ACIO at the squadron level, where he happily accepted his place in the hierarchy.

When George Britt and his pilots finally returned from the strike, they gave those on the ground the benefit of a high-speed pass. The Wildcats broke hard left, engines snarling as they reached the upwind end of Fighter One, then stood on their wingtips above the green jungle. The steep echelon turn was a visual morale booster for the maintenance troops and served to slow the planes for the downwind leg. After finding their intervals the pilots lowered flaps, cranked down wheels, and rolled into the groove to pancake onto the steel mat. One by one they taxied to the flight line and shut down, hot engines ticking as plane captains jumped onto wings to help pilots unstrap. Tired but satisfied, the pilots sauntered over to the ready tent. Large patches of their khaki flight suits were stained dark with sweat; later these would evaporate, leaving hardened streaks of salt. As the pilots shuffled into the tent, Pete Folger began his round of interviews to compile an accurate report of events. While the fliers waited their turn to describe what they had seen, each tossed down a small shot of brandy from Doc Kraft's locker, their reward following a combat mission. The whole thing was deemed a success.

No matter what damage the dive-bombers had actually caused at Vila, no planes had been lost, and none of Britt's fighters received so much as a scratch.

The squadron's first strike was but a hint of important things to come. A new phase of the South Pacific war was beginning, and the Marine squadrons would figure prominently. Guadalcanal had been wrested from the Japanese, but it was only a toehold. Winning the rest of the Solomons and beyond was another matter, requiring the eventual capture or complete neutralization of Japan's principal bases at Rabaul and Kavieng. It was a daunting task, and for good reason. The enemy stronghold encompassing New Britain and New Ireland was commonly referred to as "Fortress Rabaul," with 560 miles of heavily defended enemy islands standing like a row of sentinels en route. New Georgia and Bougainville, two of the largest, were themselves guarded by heavily protected airfields on small adjacent islands. In the New Georgia group, Munda was located on a western point of the main island; Vila was nearby on Kolombangara. Bougainville was even more formidable, with a ring of airfields and seaplane bases on the big island and adjacent ones surrounding it. Aerial superiority and perpetual bombing raids would be needed to knock out all of them.

The first choice of weapons for such a campaign would have been aircraft carriers, due to their ability to maneuver strike forces wherever needed, but the roster of big fleet carriers had dwindled until only *Enterprise* and *Saratoga* were left. Both were back in the South Pacific following repairs from earlier battle damage, but they were not yet capable of such an undertaking. Without carriers, the job would fall to land-based aircraft, but the round-trip from Guadalcanal to Bougainville was too great for anything except the Army's long-range bombers and twin-engine P-38 fighters. The distance would have to be reduced before employing Navy and Marine land-based aircraft, which meant capturing enemy-held islands, either for their existing airfields or as sites to build new ones.

The task of advancing up the Solomons was put in the capable hands of Adm. William F. "Bull" Halsey, who was given an untethered rein. He developed a campaign based on capturing only the strategically important islands along the chain, not taking all of them. Some islands occupied by Japanese would be bypassed, the defending troops rendered ineffective by cutting off their supplies and reinforcements. Others would have to be invaded after pounding their defenses.

Most of Halsey's offensive weapons in the Solomons fell into broad categories. The Army's 13th Air Force supplied nearly all of the level bombers—some B-25s and B-26s, a few heavy B-17s, but mostly B-24 Liberators. The Navy and Marine bombing squadrons came under the auspices of Strike Command, providing single-engine SBD and TBF bombers. All of the Allies provided fighter aircraft. The RNZAF squadrons flew the enduring P-40 Kittyhawk, although it performed anemically above ten thousand feet and was relegated to low-altitude work. So was the Army's unique P-39 Airacobra, with its car-type cockpit door and a cannon firing through the prop spinner; it used the same basic power plant as the P-40 and stayed low. The P-38s, on the other hand, had great range and were well suited to high-altitude bomber escort, although they were considered too large to be agile dogfighters.

A large share of fighter chores fell to the Navy and Marines. The brethren services already had much in common, their pilots having trained together before selecting a favored branch, and both were predominantly equipped with F4F Wildcats. In addition to assignment on area patrols (including air cover for naval vessels), those wearing wings of gold were called upon to escort the Army's medium and heavy bombers as well as Navy/Marine dive-bombers. Thus did VMF-214 quickly warm to its role in Bull Halsey's island-hopping campaign, and the routine of the first combat tour settled into a mixture of patrols and strike escort missions. Flight time began piling up.

On the morning of March 19, for instance, Henry Miller's division logged more than two and a half hours on a Cleanslate patrol, then spent another four hours with Burnett's division on a return strike to Vila in the afternoon. Once again, two divisions of Navy F4Fs joined as they escorted nine SBDs to the enemy airfield. This time the flight encountered heavy weather most of the way, causing the SBDs to reverse course to locate the target. With the ground obscured, the fighter pilots were unable to observe results of the strike, and there was even some doubt as to whether Vila or Munda had been bombed. Wherever they had gone, the flight encountered only light antiaircraft (AA) fire, and all planes returned safely.

The otherwise-successful strike was marred by a nasty landing accident at Fighter One, caused when a Navy F4F pilot landed too close behind a squadron mate who was still losing speed on the strip. The second fighter touched down practically on top of the slower plane while Henry Miller watched. "The overtaken pilot was almost instantly killed, in rather bloody fashion, as his ship continued to taxi under power." No one could let down his guard.

Over the next few days, VMF-214 narrowly escaped a few disasters of its own. On March 20, John Burnett and nine others escorted an SBD strike against Munda, where they faced heavy but mostly inaccurate AA fire. Dave Rankin picked up a small shrapnel hole in his Wildcat, the first battle damage suffered by the squadron.

When Burnett brought the flight back to Fighter One, he mimicked George Britt's hot flyby and buzzed the field, but the pilots were stepped down in echelon formation and Burnett allowed barely enough room for the last man. Al Jensen practically scraped the palm trees. When Burnett landed, MAG-21's operations officer, who was among the witnesses on the ground, telephoned the ready tent, then walked over to chew out Burnett in person. The captain took it in stride, displaying the sardonic grin that had earned him the nickname "Smiley" earlier in his career, but in this case it was not a term of endearment.

Many junior pilots were beginning to distrust Burnett's leadership, a trend that continued to fester, as Britt recalled.

> Though personable, he could not somehow earn the respect of the pilots subordinate to him, particularly those in his flight division. His occasional erratic airmanship and irrational behavior caused embarrassment and sometimes danger to those who flew with him in formation.

The following day, Britt led two divisions on another SBD escort. Dodging lousy weather all the way, the flight became separated. One half continued to Munda and the other group split off for Vila. Again there were no enemy planes, although one lieutenant did some shooting by mistake after the division landed back at Cactus. Richard A. Sigel's guns went off accidentally as he was taxiing back to the line, and the bullets hit an American plane and a truck. He had dubiously earned the squadron's first "kill." No one was hurt, but the incident was a not-so-subtle reminder to hit safe gun switches before landing.

As the tempo of flight operations increased, the pilots were often scheduled for two and sometimes three flights between dawn and sunset, and it was not uncommon for them to log six or more flying hours in a day. After missions were briefed in the ready tent, the pilots walked next door to the parachute riggers' tent where each strapped on a harness. To this was attached a heavy parachute, plus a bulky seat pack that contained an inflatable rubber boat; a third pack containing jungle survival equipment weighed as much as thirty pounds.* All three packs hung near or below the buttocks and banged into the backs of the pilots' legs as they waddled out to their planes. As the days wore on, the act of climbing into cockpits baked hot by the sun became an exercise in endurance.

Because the clothing and survival equipment were not standardized, pilots experimented with different options. The most common garment was a Navy-issue khaki cotton flight suit with a zippered front and convenient leg pockets, although many pilots wore regulation khaki slacks or even shorts with a button-down shirt. Footwear was also a matter of individual preference. Australian-made flight boots lined with sheepskin were particularly sought after for their chic appearance, with the added benefit of warmth during long patrols at altitude.

The famed cloth helmet with sewn-in earphones and worn with a pair of goggles constituted the headgear, a setup that was often hot and itchy. Just as uncomfortable but equally indispensable was the rubberized oxygen mask, required for any flight briefed to climb above ten thousand feet. The mask became sticky with sweat and smelled foul, was dirty and chafed the skin, but a pilot literally could not live without it on high-altitude missions.

In the event of going down over unfriendly territory, pilots wore sidearms, usually a .45 automatic in a shoulder holster often augmented by a knife and extra ammo strapped to their belt. Some carried a minimum of ammunition; others were armed to the teeth.

Everyone wore an inflatable yellow Mae West, universal among American fliers in World War II. After long hours of patrolling with heads on a constant swivel, the hard collar

***The contents were not standardized and depended entirely upon what an individual could stuff into the pack. See Appendix E for a representative list of Henry Miller's survival equipment.**

seams caused painful chafing. Silk scarves, once considered dashing affectations, were in demand for their soft protection. Another source of irritation was the parachute seat pack with its stowed inflatable boat. The pack fitted into the deeply dished metal aircraft seat as a sort of cushion, but after hours of heat and compression it became hard as a rock.

The cockpits themselves suffered from the harsh environment on Cactus, which continuously exposed the aircraft to a witch's brew of harmful elements. Parked on the flight line near the strip, the Wildcats were unsheltered from the corrosive effects of rain, humidity, and glaring sunlight. Dust clouded Fighter One during dry spells, invading thousands of moving parts. The planes became dirty, their paint scarred and faded. Keeping them in operating condition was challenging enough, allowing little time for housekeeping, and the cockpits became full of litter, which then showered pilots when they rolled inverted. Because maintenance facilities were primitive, the pilots learned to accept planes in less than perfect condition. If not every component or cockpit instrument functioned as advertised, minor gripes could be overlooked as long as the engine and fuel systems were performing, the flight controls were smooth, and the guns worked.

The days of exhausting patrols and long-distance strikes wore on, and feeling tired became just another fact of life. It was typical for pilots to rise before 0400, crawl into khaki flight suits still damp from yesterday's sweat bath, then eat a meager breakfast and take off into a pitch black sky. Roaring down the fighter strip to join with the division in total darkness took intense concentration, only to be followed by mind-numbing hours of boredom while patrolling an empty sector of sky. In the afternoon, having fought the flies to eat another tasteless meal, the pilots answered the call for a strike or another patrol that could last until well after dark. The flying was characterized by long hours of concentration and the realization that *something* could happen at any moment, but almost nothing ever did. Even the dangerous segments of strikes against Japanese strongholds began to seem routine. Concerns, which did not evaporate once the men were back on the ground, sometimes became active worries, as when air-raid sirens sounded or a big strike was scheduled for the following day. Fears were usually suppressed, but they were always there.

Between the oh-dark-thirty wakeups, bad food, the strain of worry, energy-sapping infections, and the sweltering tropical climate, men began to wither. Sleep became a precious commodity, but the Japanese regularly shattered even that basic need with a warfare of harassment. They sent raiders at night from their bases on Bougainville and New Georgia, the attacks often conducted by a single bomber, occasionally two or three. Each was characterized by the distinctive pulsing sound of unsynchronized engines reminiscent of the agitator in an old-fashioned washing machine, hence the bombers appearing overhead were collectively known as Washing Machine Charlie.

Although the Japanese arrived with a degree of regularity, they rarely caused much actual destruction. Even so, the chilling sound of air-raid sirens compelled men to head for nearby foxholes or bomb shelters, their slumber replaced by glaring searchlights, antiaircraft guns, a whistling stick of bombs, crunching explosions.

The shelters, such as they were, consisted of shallow excavations fortified with logs and mounded dirt and filled to varying degrees with stagnant runoff from the frequent rain showers. Entrances were narrow, and there was only enough headroom inside to kneel or sit. Unconcerned with decorum, men roused from sleep dived into the shelters wearing only their skivvy shorts and shoes, turning the air stale. Just getting to the shelters could be hazardous due to numerous obstacles that groggy men could stumble upon in the middle of the night.

The squadron's first opportunity to use the shelters did not come until the night of March 23, although the sirens had periodically sounded during their first week on Cactus.

Poor weather had prevailed for two days, leaving the men to drone along during local patrols feeling dull indeed, but on this clear evening they sat around the campfire after supper, talking quietly, half expecting a raid by one of the Bettys that the Japanese were wont to send. The men's expectations proved accurate. Through the overcast came the erratic wish-wash noise of engines out of sync, a dead giveaway, and before the warnings even sounded the men headed for the shelters.

This time, instead of the normal anticlimactic results, the raid yielded a spectacular display of fireworks over Henderson Field. Henry Miller was one of many witnesses.

> The lights and guns let go, and on Charlie's second run he was blown to bits, after getting three B-17s, two new B-24s and a PBO [Lockheed Hudson patrol bomber], along with putting shrapnel in 14 TBFs. We really thought he had hit a small ammo dump instead of the main field, and I went to bed watching several large explosions.

The aerial display was in fact a precursor of good news, for the next day Hank Ellis appeared in their camp. He had won his epic struggle for survival and had an amazing story to tell.

After bailing out of his crippled Wildcat on March 14, Ellis remained adrift in his tiny raft upon the Coral Sea for five days and four nights, constantly wet, as hour after interminable hour passed with nothing but the vastness of sea and sky surrounding him. But as he floated in the well-traveled lane between Espiritu and Guadalcanal, he never relinquished the hope that a passing ship or plane might spot him. Despite enormous odds against rescue, his perserverance paid off on the fifth day; grace appeared in the form of a Navy greyhound. From the destroyer, Ellis was a mere speck on the ocean's surface, but an alert lookout spotted his raft and the ship stopped briefly to pluck him from his watery purgatory. It continued on its way to Espiritu, where Ellis was immediately packed off to the field hospital. Amazingly, five days in a raft had caused him little harm aside from dehydration and painful overexposure, and after several days of rest he was cleared to return to his squadron. He hitched a flight on a transport and walked into camp to a rousing welcome. Even better, he brought along their first mail in six weeks.

Ellis was not entirely healed, however, as Drury McCall recalled after seeing his badly burned legs.

> The place where he hurt the most was on his shins. When he was sitting in the life raft during the day, his flight suit was higher on his calves than his socks would cover. The sunburn that he got was almost like a burn to the bone. He really had a bad time with that.

Following Ellis's return, the squadron resumed a normal existence for the rest of the month. In addition to routine local and Cleanslate patrols each day, new patrols over the Russells (call sign of "Knucklehead") had been added to the schedule. There were also a few opportunities to strike enemy locations. On March 25, intelligence provided a target for strafing—a small barge beached on a tiny island—and Smiley Burnett and seven others emptied their guns not only at the barge but over the entire island, firing more than eleven thousand rounds. Returning to Guadalcanal, Burnett once again held the formation down low, crossing the Russells at just three hundred feet and causing surprised American antiaircraft gunners to nearly open fire. In addition to whispered criticism among the pilots, Burnett received another tongue-lashing from operations. Even worse, the barge was later discovered still intact.

Two days later Burnett's and Miller's divisions escorted nine Grumman TBFs on another strike to Vila, followed by an afternoon strike with Lanphier's division covering six SBDs to Rendova, where they bombed a concentration of Japanese troops. On March 28, divisions led by Britt and Burnett joined a large Rekata Bay strike involving eighteen dive-bombers guarded by twenty-four Navy and Marine Wildcats. Finding nothing worth hitting at Rekata, the strike headed to Vila, found bad weather there, and finally triangulated to hit Munda. As before, no aerial opposition was encountered during any of these missions. The only enemy planes they encountered were the Washing Machine Charlies that attacked them in the darkness on three occasions that week. The raids impressed nobody, prompting some men to complain that even those were boring.

Life was not always grim, however. Conditions on Cactus may have been hell, but living in tents and spending time outdoors provided a camp atmosphere. Despite the island's heat and humidity, there was beauty to be found: Vividly colored birds and exotic tropical plants were abundant, and during off-duty days (about one in seven for each division), the men could explore on bicycles left behind by the Japanese. Pete Folger periodically used a bike, allowing four or five pilots to borrow his jeep for an island excursion. The ever-inquisitive Henry Miller took his division on a driving tour of areas that had received bomb damage, curious to assess what the various weapons were capable of doing.

Weather permitting, George Britt hosted a campfire every evening in front of his tent. The fires, quicky extinguishable in the event of an air raid, were an essential contribution to the men's wellness. Beginning with their training period at Ewa, Britt had noticed growing bonds among the young pilots, later writing, "A certain squadron personality began to develop, characterized by pride in the attainment of increased flight proficiency, congeniality, humor and high morale."

Among the many reasons for the success of these gatherings, the most visible was Vince Carpenter's talented quartet.

He had never let the primitive conditions prevent him from pursuing music.

> I found quite a few Ivy League guys there, so I said, "Why don't we sing some old college songs?" We didn't have any sheet music, so I got out this blank music paper and reconstructed college songs. From there we went into some jazz and popular songs. I wrote them out in four- and even five-part close harmony, when it was called for. The three other guys could hardly read music—they'd have trouble reading a hymn. So I had to walk them through. They had pretty good pitch, and we had a lot of fun.

Among the singers, only Vic Scarborough lacked Ivy League roots. Carl Dunbar and Vince Carpenter were from Yale, and Henry W. Hollmeyer, of Boston, was Harvard through and through. He was nicknamed "Harry the Horse" by McCall, a fan of Broadway musicals who matched him with the character from the hit play *Guys and Dolls*. Hollmeyer's contribution ran the gamut of bawdy pub songs, such as "Three Old Ladies in the Lavatory," "Roll Your Leg Over," "The Sexual Life of the Camel," and more, but the quartet's favorite number was a complex jazz rendition of "Old Black Magic." Carpenter had scored the arrangement during the voyage aboard *Nassau* and tutored the group until the men achieved spine-tingling harmony. The song became a campfire staple.

Because there was no daily ration of beer in the combat zone, another fundamental element of the fraternal gatherings was privately stashed liquor. Drinks did not flow freely, however, because of a minor disaster. Back at Ewa, the squadron had contributed two thousand dollars toward purchasing a large stock of duty-free liquor, which was loaded aboard *Nassau*. It arrived safely on Espiritu Santo, but when the ground echelon was ordered to the new airstrip on Banika, in the Russell Islands, most of the liquor supply went with them aboard USS *Wright*. At Banika the cargo was off-loaded into barges to go ashore. As one pilot later lamented, "The Seabees saw some of this liquor coming ashore, so they staged a fake air raid, told our guys to get into foxholes, then went out and drove off with the barge full of our liquor." Although some of the booze escaped the Seabees' cunning, most of what remained was stuck in the Russells.

Personal hordes of liquor were doled out in miserly quantities, shared, and savored. Amazingly, ice was available thanks to a small working factory built by the Japanese that had been spared in the heavy fighting. At the end of the month George Britt received a prized bonus—seven pints of Schenley—from the assistant commanding general of the 1st Marine Air Wing, Gen. Ralph J. Mitchell. One bottle was given to the Navy cooks who supplied the grateful pilots with donuts many evenings, and the remainder of what they called "Black Death" was passed around the campfire.

The cooks were generous enough to occasionally provide a few potatoes, perhaps a little bacon, to augment the mess tent's meager fare. The pilots operated a small gasoline cookstove at night, handy for making homemade specialties. Dick Sigel was known for his excellent fudge, and Vic Scarborough for his North Carolina hoecakes. Sigel and John Fidler sometimes provided fish they "caught" with dynamite. At many gatherings, entertainment was as nearby as Carpenter's quartet; during other times, talk invariably turned to news from the States, women, and the frustrating lack of combat action the squadron had endured for the past weeks.

The Japanese certainly seemed to be keeping their heads down. If the Marines had only known why, the current situation might not have seemed so peaceful. Earlier in the month, Imperial Japanese Headquarters had formulated a plan to strike a powerful blow in revenge for losing

Guadalcanal. This time they would use airpower against the Allies, hitting the anchorage at Tulagi and airfields on Guadalcanal and the Russells.

The task of retaliation was given to Adm. Isoroku Yamamoto, mastermind of the attack on Pearl Harbor but more recently defeated at Midway. Calling his plan "I" Operation, Yamamoto went to Rabaul to personally oversee details. More than 185 combat aircraft of the land-based 11th Air Fleet of the Imperial Japanese Navy were already housed there, but Yamamoto upped the ante by calling in planes from four aircraft carriers. Rabaul's airfields swelled to some 350 combat planes, more than 180 of them fighters flown by seasoned pilots. Although Japan had lost many elite naval aviators at Midway and over Guadalcanal, the combat pilots at Rabaul represented some of the best available, and they were bent on vengeance.

The Japanese buildup was impossible to disguise. The Marines sensed that things were too dull, too quiet to continue at their present level for much longer. On the last day of March, word was passed via coastwatchers that twenty Japanese aircraft were milling about over Vella Lavella. The bogeys were far to the west when VMF-214 went on scramble status at 0910 in hopes of getting aloft to mix it up, but after two hours with no further reports the alert was secured. Still, it was hard to shake the feeling that action would soon come, prompting Howard Cavanagh to write in his flight operations summary: "The calm before the storm? Could be!"

His words were prophetic. The following day a swarm of fifty-eight enemy planes, mostly A6M Zeros along with a few D3A Vals, approached from the northwest to sweep Allied fighters based on the Russells and Guadalcanal. The gaggle was detected with ample warning, and at approximately 1030 several divisions of Navy F4Fs were scrambled along with Wildcats from VMF-221 and Corsairs from VMF-124. George Britt's division followed at 1055, but it was reduced by one fighter when the blowers in

Howard Cavanagh's F4F failed and he was forced to land early. Britt's remaining Wildcats never made contact with the enemy, although they were vectored toward Tulagi by the radar director. Other Marine fighters did get into a good scrap, giving better than they got by a three-to-one ratio, but it was not to be The Big Day for VMF-214—only April Fools' Day.

The routine patrols had already been canceled, so the rest of VMF-214's pilots stood by in case they were needed. While they were waiting, several Navy F4Fs that had tangled with Zeros returned to Fighter One and made colorful landings.

Henry Miller witnessed evidence that they had been involved in battle, judging by the performance of the pilots and the condition of their planes.

> One ground-looped off the runway to their taxi strip, another landed too fast and nosed up at the west end of the strip, and a third, with controls shot away, made a crash landing just east of our tent. Some other F4Fs came over with a corner out of an elevator.

Primed by the sight of battle-damaged planes, Miller led three divisions on a scramble at 1220, but more than an hour had passed since the first action and there were no Japanese aircraft in sight. The fracas was long over by the time the squadron reached Tulagi. Adding to the frustration, the Navy claimed eight Zeros downed and four Wildcats lost (though only one pilot); another ten Zeros were felled by Marines. VMF-221 was credited with seven, including three by Lt. William N. Snider, without losing a plane. It was the squadron's first combat since the one-sided air battle at Midway the previous June, but this time they were prepared and equipped with capable airplanes. VMF-124's Lt. Kenneth A. Walsh, a Corsair pilot and former NAP, scored a hat trick to claim all but one of his squadron's four kills; one F4U went down and its pilot was safely recovered. In all, eighteen Zeros were claimed against the loss of six planes and only two pilots.*

VMF-214 seemed hexed, but Howard Cavanagh (now called "Chalky" after a comic-strip character) remained hopeful. In the small notebook he kept of squadron flight operations, he wrote: "Our squadron seems plagued with bad luck. Today was our first real opportunity to tangle with the enemy and, as luck would have it, we were never vectored in. Well, maybe tomorrow."

But tomorrow produced nothing of interest, and there was no improvement in the routine for the next few days. The endless patrols over Cactus and Knucklehead continued, with an occasional assignment for air cover over Tulagi. Three divisions on strip alert duty were scrambled over the Russells late on the morning of Saturday, April 3, but the Zeros failed to show. It appeared that the Japanese had no intention of following the April Fools' parry with another strike.

The next day was even slower. Only four divisions were scheduled for local patrols, so Henry Miller decided to take Folger's jeep to Guadalcanal's southern shoreline and search for Jim Taylor's crash-landed F4F. The plane might be recoverable, but if not there would be plenty of salvageable parts. Taylor and a mechanic occupied the front seats while Miller enjoyed the rough ride on primitive roads from the backseat. They observed colorful cockatoos and bright jungle blossoms and even stopped for lunch at a native village. Back on the trail they crossed two pontoon bridges, then swam another river in order to haul a raft back to get the jeep across. Without a reliable map of the muddy roads and trails, it took considerable experimenting to make their way south. Miller's companions lacked his

*One Army fighter and its pilot were lost. Among the land-based Japanese fighters from the 11th Air Fleet, only two Zeros from the 204 Kokutai were lost on April 1. Records for the temporarily assigned carrier units have not been located, and it is not certain what percentage participated in this attack.

endurance. Both had earlier suffered mild bouts of malaria, and by midafternoon their patience was waning. Finally, after getting stuck in a mudhole perhaps a mile from the Wildcat's resting place, they gave up. Taylor's plane remained where it sat, undiscovered.

Two long days in the saddle began on April 5 as the pilots endured dozens of collective hours providing air cover for ships moving from Tulagi. One force of six destroyers and two cruisers presented "a fine sight sailing westward," but the heavy schedule soon became a grind. VMF-214 accumulated 180 flight hours in two days, nearly all of it making lazy circles above the ships. Instead of resting, the men lost precious sleep during the night when an air-raid siren forced them into the foxholes at 0200 the morning of the sixth. It was a false alarm.

The feint was deceptive, for the Japanese raiders were actually becoming bolder. Late that afternoon, having already flown a morning "ass-buster" above the task force, Burnett and Miller led their divisions back into the air for another patrol and remained on station until well after dark. Cleared to return, Burnett's division landed without incident, but Miller's was on final approach when all the lights around the field went out and AA guns opened fire abruptly. Realizing that a raider had sneaked in behind them, Miller and his pilots cranked up their wheels and beat a hasty retreat. Ledge Hazelwood and Carol Bernard managed to stay with Miller in the night sky, but Mac McCall was caught by several searchlights and had to climb to twelve thousand feet to avoid being shot. The excitement finally quieted and they pancaked by 2030, only to learn they were scheduled to escort a strike at 0400 the next morning. Little did they know that the morrow would bring the big opportunity everyone had awaited.

After just a few hours' rest, Miller's division was airborne again at 0440 on April 7, joining those of Smiley Burnett and Vic Scarborough in utter darkness for a dive-bomber strike on Vila. Keeping up with Burnett was no easy task, as Miller later wrote: "I lost John somewhere near Rendova, after an agonizing 75 minutes during which I decided it was hardly safe to fly near him." The divisions completed their escort without incident, returning early enough for Scarborough's division to refuel and prepare for a local patrol by midmorning.

Just before their departure, however, the day took a decided turn for the better when rumors began circulating that the Japanese were assembling something big in their part of the Solomons. Round two of Yamamoto's "I" Operation was about to begin. The previous day, an F-5A (a P-38 photoreconnaissance variant) snapped damning evidence over Bougainville that the Japanese were mobilizing a large aerial force. Earlier passes had revealed forty planes at Kahili, but now there were more than a hundred. The count at Ballale, a tiny island airstrip southeast of Bougainville, had likewise mushroomed from zero to ninety-five airplanes.

Four hours dragged by while the Marines waited to see what would happen next. The local patrols already on the flight schedule went out as planned. Finally coastwatchers farther up the Solomons reported many Japanese planes headed toward Guadalcanal. The incoming raid was massive by area standards: 67 Vals escorted by a juggernaut of 110 Zeros. Shortly after 1300 came the order that VMF-214 had waited so long to hear—scramble!

6

FIRST BLOOD

Contrary to the popular image of a large-scale scramble in which dozens of pilots run to their planes and roar en masse into the skies, the squadron's sixteen participating defenders took off over a period of thirty minutes. With plenty of advance warning, the Marines had no need to scurry pell-mell from Fighter One. First to roll were the eight Wildcats of Burnett's and Miller's divisions, already gassed after flying the earlier strike to Vila. They released brakes at 1320, followed ten minutes later by Vince Carpenter's division, recently returned from a Knucklehead patrol that had lasted more than three hours. Another twenty minutes passed before a fourth division joined the fray. This was an ad hoc bunch who decided not to wait around. Charlie Lanphier, Vic Scarborough, Chalky Cavanagh, and Al Jensen simply grabbed leftover Wildcats and took off at 1350. Although Lanphier was the first off, he soon turned over the lead to Jensen, the only enlisted pilot in the bunch. Jensen had established himself as such a good pilot that rank mattered little, and the other pilots, Howard Cavanagh among them, agreed. "We just grabbed a few planes and told Al Jensen—at that time he was already considered one of our better pilots—'You take us, Al.' "

Together with Marines from VMF-213 and VMF-221 plus several dozen Army and Navy fighters, a total of seventy-six American combatants from three airfields climbed to face 177 Japanese aircraft. Radar controllers on the ground struggled to cope with the mass of blips on their primitive screens as they tried to sort friend from foe and pass intercept vectors to the nearest defenders.

It was a beautiful day, with crystal-clear visibility above scattered low cumulus clouds. From the air, the lush green jungle islands and vivid blue-green water might have resembled a travel poster were it not for the angry black blossoms of exploding AA, thrown by ships and gun emplacements below.

Aboard the fighter planes, with cloth helmets and oxygen masks strapped tight and protective goggles in place, grim-faced defenders raced to intercept the attack, stretching against harnesses, straining to see over instrument panels for a first glimpse. Adrenaline surged as headphones broadcast radio chatter, described by one Marine as "just a bunch of screaming and static." Among those about to engage in their first combat, a year and a half of training and endless hours of patrol were about to be tested. As the men activated gun switches and charged their machine guns, no one knew what to expect, what reactions their first shots in anger would evoke.

Burnett and Miller were initially directed to thirty thousand feet heading toward the Russell Islands until ground controllers reported bogeys over Cape Esperance. Spotting a large group of aircraft north of Tulagi, Miller turned his division toward them, but he soon realized they were friendlies. He was turning back to the original course when Recon radar called bogeys southeast of Tulagi. Instead he sighted the enemy over Cape Esperance. Two separate formations of Vals, the fixed-gear dive-bombers so lethal at Pearl Harbor and Midway, were heading straight for Tulagi harbor. The approaching armada was a stunning sight to the American pilots, who in their wildest dreams had never seen so many dozens of planes in the sky at one time. Burnett's division spotted them, too. "Look at the bogeys! Christ, there's a million of them," Burnett hollered on the radio, turning his division toward the northernmost formation. Miller's division went for the other group.

Miller's tail-end Charlie (twenty-one-year-old) Mac McCall, had his hands full. The external tank was malfunctioning, perhaps because of a crimp in the wing attachment, and was useless, neither feeding fuel nor releasing when McCall tugged on the T handle. He had burned internal fuel at a prodigious rate in the climb, trying to hold his position in formation while struggling with the wing tank. Gaping at the approaching group of enemy airplanes—he counted seventy in the nearest formation—he grew concerned about the exposed fuel tank. One stray incendiary round and his Wildcat would become a flaming meteor.

Reaching a position to dive on the Vals from above, Miller nosed over, followed by Ledge Hazelwood, Bernie Bernard, and McCall. Using their altitude advantage to initiate the attack, Miller eased down at first to overtake the Vals, then pushed over at twenty thousand feet in a high-side run at almost full deflection. Six or seven vees, each with three Vals, were spread before him. He drew a bead on the leader of the last vee, his Wildcat plunging through the enemy formation almost as soon as he opened fire. The next two Marines gunned for the same plane, giving the hapless Val the equivalent of an eighteen-gun broadside. The Val finally exploded under Bernard's withering barrage. Bernie was then distracted by the sight of another Val's rear gunner, who looked him right in the eyes as he banged away. Bernard nearly collided with a third Val as he dived vertically through the cluster.

McCall's turn came next. He was still yanking on the drop tank's release handle as he lined up a Val in his sights, but the momentum of his dive took care of the drop tank when his speed exceeded the redline. A loud boom signaled the tank's departure just as he was about to trigger the guns. For an instant he thought the tank might have carried back into his tail, distracting him from an otherwise perfect high-side run.

It was a pure overhead. We were tailing in behind them, with about a seventy-degree deflection. I could see the rear gunner in the Val, and could see the Zeros that were flying cover for them starting after us. I just tried to lead the Val enough to get my shots in. When he started to smoke, I saw him nose over. Then I went by, and tried to look back up as I was pulling out of my dive. I could see his smoke going all the way straight down toward the water.

Unable to get independent confirmation that the Val crashed, Mac was later given credit for a probable. Henry Miller, meanwhile, dropped beneath the enemy formation and pulled up to try for another shot from below. He remembered to check his own tail—a timely glance because the Vals' guardian Zeros were now pouncing, from over his left shoulder. He pulled into a protective cloud, then climbed again as he turned toward another group of aircraft over Tulagi. Judging that it would be impossible to get into position, he reversed direction once more and was suddenly in the midst of a dozen Zeros. Reacting instinctively, he held down the trigger and "flew through the whole pack, without hitting any to the extent of downing them." The next instant the sky around him was empty, his division scattered, the shooting over. Such was often the nature of high-speed aerial combat. One minute a pilot would be in the middle of a swirling melee, the next all alone. Miller's entire division eventually emerged unscathed, with Bernie claiming one Val destroyed and Mac receiving credit for a probable.

Smiley Burnett's division waded into their chosen formation of Vals with even better success, although he gave up his own plane in the process. Over Cape Esperance, Burnett and Jack W. Petit each singled out a Val and dropped both into the Slot on their first passes. Then the Zeros came down. One latched onto Burnett's tail, putting him on the receiving end. His F4F was hit hard in the engine, and he was forced to bail out over the channel, slightly wrenching a knee when he jumped. He floated down to the warm water, then waited only a short time before a Navy lighter was on the scene. Another member of the division, Lincoln Deetz, tipped the scales even further by exploding a Zero over Cape Esperance.

A few minutes later Vince Carpenter's division received a vector from Recon radar toward Savo Island, where several Zeros had been spotted above thirty thousand feet. The slow-climbing Wildcats clawed for altitude and began dropping their wing tanks, but John Fidler found that his tank would not release. Like McCall, he knew that a well-placed incendiary could turn him into a fireball. Soon after he turned reluctantly for Fighter One, the remaining three Marines sighted eight Zeros.

By now their F4Fs were practically staggering, they were near the limit of their performance ceiling as the fight began. Carpenter recalled:

> Four of the Zeros peeled off and came for us. Those Zeros were better at high altitude because they were lighter, and we were really at the max altitude for the F4F. We had a lot of throttle on, and were burning fuel like mad once we dropped those wing tanks. Our first pass was head-on, but we were sort of squishing through the air. When we passed each other, they went over the top of us. We threw ourselves around into a turn—they did, too—and started back after them. With that, everybody split up, and that was the beginning of the big fight. I got on the tail of a Zero. He held his altitude for a minute and I took a good long shot at him. He turned over on his back and smoked, then pulled down in a dive.

Carpenter debated whether to follow the Zero down. With his Wildcat's superior weight, staying with the damaged plane in a dive would be no problem and he could make certain of the kill. However, there were plenty of other aircraft up at altitude, not to mention his own division. Responsibility won and he chose to remain where he was, letting the Zero go. But in the time it took to make the decision, the sky had suddenly emptied of aircraft. He began descending just as Recon radioed that a large force of dive-bombers was escaping to the northwest.

Carpenter flung his Wildcat earthward, determined not to let the next target get away. He picked out a group of Vals hugging the wave tops as they fled toward the Russells. As he approached one from dead astern, he began squeezing the trigger from a long way out. The Val's rear-seat gunner returned fire. At first Carpenter "blew a lot of shots away," frustrated to see his tracers fall short of the fleeing Val, but gradually he closed the distance. Down on the deck there was no room for the dive-bomber to maneuver, no room for escape. Carpenter held in the trigger. He was still too far away to actually see rounds hitting the enemy plane, but under his fusillade it nosed over and tore itself apart against the ocean as it hit at full speed.

Next the impromptu division led by Al Jensen joined the action. Climbing over Sealark Channel, just north of Guadalcanal's coast, the division first encountered a Zero straggler. It was a favorite Japanese tactic to provide tempting bait while others waited in the sun, ready to ambush whoever went after the easy prey. But this was four against one—too good to pass up—and Jensen promptly polished off the lone duckling. Soon other Zeros were upon them, and the four Marines scattered to fend for themselves, with widely varied results.

Charlie Lanphier downed a Zero over Koli Point, then Chalky Cavanagh found himself behind a seemingly oblivious Japanese pilot whose lack of maneuvering played right into his hands. "It just happened to be there," he recalled later. "I saw him up ahead, and it was a come-from-behind shot, straight in. It was the easiest shot going." The Californian made good, claiming his first and only confirmed victory of the war.

Vic Scarborough also jumped a Zero over Koli Point and splashed it, then found himself in the middle of a daisy chain. Another A6M latched onto his own tail, boresighting his F4F and plastering it with 7.7mm bullets and 20mm shells. Al Jensen came racing to assist, but he was not yet in position, and Scarborough seemed unable to shake the nimble Zero. With his engine mortally hit and rudder severely damaged, he tried a move born of desperation that wasn't in the manual, virtually hitting the brakes by lowering his flaps. The sudden deceleration sent his surprised attacker zooming past, reversing the tables. Scarborough's plane was too riddled to pull back into the fight, but Jensen had a clear shot and flamed his second Zero.

Inside a smoking, shot-up F4F, Scarborough weighed the choices between bailing out or trying to glide to Fighter One. He was still close enough to the field to opt for the latter, but without engine power to make corrections or abort the pass and try again, his approach would have to be perfect. Dead-stick landings were among the most challenging feats a pilot could attempt. Scarborough's approach was further complicated by the fact that his damaged rudder gave him only partial lateral control. His landing gear had also been damaged, so he crash-landed on the Wildcat's plump belly, skillfully putting it down between the runway and taxiway to prevent blocking the strip. He unstrapped and climbed out, untouched by enemy bullets, but his aircraft was labeled a "sieve." Onlookers counted more than a hundred bullet holes and at least three bigger punctures from 20mm cannon shells.

Some Marines had already returned to Fighter One by the time Scarborough crash-landed, and more began to straggle in as Recon called the divisions to pancake. They landed low on fuel and ammunition but were full of jubilation as they headed for the ready tent to give Pete Folger their battle reports. While the ecstatic Marines talked and gestured all at once, Doc Kraft proudly dispensed small doses of brandy.

Some of the senior pilots were disappointed that they had missed their first opportunity. George Britt's division was not on the schedule (it was their day off), and he was in the middle of laundry chores when the battle started. When fighters began returning he grabbed Jim Taylor and they ran for the first two Wildcats that could be rearmed and refueled. They were airborne at 1545 and climbed toward Tulagi, but the Japanese were long gone.

Hank Ellis, likewise off the flight schedule, stood with OK Williams to watch from the ground as the battle progressed north of Guadalcanal. "We looked over toward Tulagi harbor," recalled Williams, "and saw two or three planes go down. God, we were upset as hell that it was our day off." At 1555, after two more Wildcats had been turned around, they took off to see what they could find, but the sky was empty of targets and they returned barely forty minutes later.

While Pete Folger sorted out the details of the air battle for his intelligence report, Smiley Burnett arrived after being dropped off by the lighter that had fished him from the drink. Burnett's sore knee and a few scratches Scarborough had sustained during his crash landing (both pilots were later awarded Purple Hearts) were the sum of the squadron's injuries. Folger determined that VMF-214 had bagged ten planes for sure, counting at least three others as probably destroyed. The usually stoic Britt turned to Doc Kraft, beaming. "See this smile, Doc—that's pride!"

Before the men had a chance to unwind, a request came for two divisions to fly air cover for Tulagi naval units. Henry Miller, although certainly due for a break, departed at 1700 for his division's third flight of the day, and Charlie Lanphier followed (with his regular division) a few minutes later. By day's end, Miller's group had logged more than 7.5 hours apiece in their Wildcats, and the squadron combined for more than 112.

VMF-214's pilots had accounted well for themselves when the opportunity to fight finally arrived, but they were slightly one-upped by their MAG-21 sister squadron based at Fighter Two. VMF-221, which had begun designing a new squadron logo featuring a fierce falcon, claimed eighteen victories and two probables. Making a few incredible gunnery passes, one lieutenant splashed seven—more than a third of his squadron's total bag—during his first aerial combat.

Scrambling from his airstrip, James E. Swett became separated and raced ahead of his division, catching up with several vees of enemy dive-bombers just as they were nosing down toward Tulagi harbor. He slid into the middle of a string of Vals, using brief bursts at point-blank range to flame three before they had completed their dives. As Swett was pulling out above the anchorage, a 40mm shell from an American ship punched a hole in his left wing, ruining his flaps and knocking the outboard machine gun askew.

Staying low to avoid more of the same, Swett crossed Florida Island and came upon another dozen Vals attempting to rejoin after their attack. They were low and slow, fish in a barrel. Kicking the rudder pedals, Swett skidded his Wildcat from one bomber to the next, burning four more in quick succession. The eighth potential victim gave him trouble. Swett approached too close, perhaps within twenty-five to thirty feet, and the Val's rear gunner couldn't miss. His bullets hammered the Wildcat's oil cooler and windshield, wounding Swett. But the plucky Marine expended the rest of his ammunition into the Val and killed the gunner, causing the plane to smoke heavily.

Swett pulled away and tried to make Guadalcanal, but his shot-up Wildcat could go no farther. The engine seized as he recrossed Tulagi harbor, forcing him to ditch in the Slot. Without time to lower the flaps, he hit fast and hard. The airplane bounced high, then plunged twenty feet below the waves with Swett still strapped inside. He was able to free his snagged harness with a mighty tug, then managed to kick away and swim to the surface.

Swett became an instant celebrity. While he recovered in a Guadalcanal field hospital, ComAirSols (RAdm. Marc A. Mitscher) quickly set in motion Medal of Honor proceedings for Swett's superlative performance. The feat was all the more astounding because of the F4F-4's limited shooting time. Swett had splashed seven aircraft, and probably killed an eighth, using just eighteen seconds' worth of bullets. Swett's behavior after the event was just as exemplary. Offered an early return to the States, he instead chose to remain in the fight. He ended the war as the ninth-highest Marine ace, with fifteen and a half victories.

When the results of the April 7 donnybrook were compiled, the three Marine squadrons involved received credit for twenty-nine enemy planes destroyed without losing a single pilot. All but one of the Japanese were shot down by Wildcats. A lone Corsair from Wade Britt's VMF-213 bagged the other for the squadron's first kill, a good start considering they had arrived on Cactus only a few days before. Their appellation as the Hellhawks seemed appropriate.

Personal deeds and squadron accomplishments aside, a remarkable chapter in aviation history had just come to a close. Never again would a Marine in an F4F shoot down an enemy aircraft, and the twenty-eight planes credited to Wildcats this day put an exclamation point on the Leathernecks' relationship with the venerable little Grumman fighter. Now the fast and heavy Corsairs, no longer novelties, were making their mark in combat as they began replacing Wildcats at a rate of about two squadrons per month. Wade Britt's Hellhawks were the second Corsair squadron in the Corps, and the remaining Wildcat units would transition when their current combat tours ended.

As for the overall score, the Japanese had sacrificed—by American claims—some fifty-eight aircraft during their two unsuccessful "I" Operation raids. Japanese records for the period are incomplete, although the loss of three Zero pilots from the 204 Kokutai can be accounted for. Those returning to Bougainville made exaggerated claims of their own, reporting widespread destruction. Some of their dive-bombers did fight past the defenders and reach Tulagi harbor to sink an American tanker, a destroyer, and a small New Zealand corvette, but their claims misled Yamamoto, whose goal for the Solomons had failed. Guadalcanal and the airspace over the southern islands still belonged firmly to the Allies, who even now were preparing an island-hopping campaign that would force the Japanese back one chunk of real estate at a time.

Yamamoto's "I" Operation phase in New Guinea fared no better, sinking one transport and damaging a few other ships. On April 16 he called it off and ordered the remaining carrier planes back to their flattops, having been convinced by his boasting pilots that the damage was much greater than it really was. As a result, no more Japanese aircraft were encountered in the skies above Guadalcanal for the remainder of VMF-214's combat tour. Only the night bombers continued their regular probes as the Marines watched from their muddy shelters.

Accordingly the remaining three weeks of April became an exercise in endurance. The Marines, anticipating repeat attacks, stepped up local patrols. Hour upon hour, day after day, they flew assigned sectors until the exhilaration of the big fight wore off. Then the boredom of endless patrols merely heightened their frustration. The mood swing was rapid, confirmed by this war diary entry only two days after the action: "Hangovers from the 7th still afflicting most of the squadron. Really let down after all that excitement."

Bill Pace rejoined the squadron on April 10, having completed a temporary assignment on the Russells with MAG-21 headquarters. After a few warm-up flights with other divisions, he was ready to lead a patrol on April 12. That same day, George Britt and Hank Ellis took their divisions back to Vila for another strike. Cleared to break off before reaching the target, they raced ahead, strafing the airfield and bivouac area heavily before the bombers arrived. Surprise was theirs. The combined effect of forty-eight heavy machine guns was devastating to personnel, vehicles, and supply dumps, igniting at least one major fire and causing widespread destruction.

Before anyone could become overconfident from the success of the preemptive strafing attack or the recent air battle, an accident at Fighter One swung the pendulum the other way.

Several events were scheduled for the early hours of April 13, making for a busy morning at the fighter strip despite total darkness. "You've never seen such predawn blackness as you could find there at Guadalcanal," George Britt remembered. "There was no light pollution. You didn't have much reference except the crude boundary lights on the Marston mat runway." At 0515 several Navy F4Fs sped down the strip heading eastward while Britt's division taxied to the opposite end of the runway for a westward departure (a time-saving procedure permitted when winds were calm). They rolled to a stop behind Wade Britt and a flight of his Corsairs from VMF-213, scheduled to take off next.

Most of the big Corsairs roared into the sky, blue flame spitting from the exhaust collectors below their cowlings, but one taxied off the strip and rolled quickly back to the flight line along the northern boundary of the strip. It was Wade Britt, whose landing light would not retract. After hastening to the line for a plane captain to push in the light, Britt wheeled his Corsair around and returned to the runway. Gaining the end of the strip, he spun to the east and lined up on what he thought were the runway boundary lights, then revved up the power and released the brakes. In his haste, he mistakenly lined up on the evenly spaced position markers atop the tails of Corsairs parked on the flight line. In addition, he did not account for the Pratt & Whitney's mighty torque. As horrified bystanders watched, his accelerating fighter veered into the parked planes, plowing through two Corsairs and igniting a chain of explosions.

Henry Miller, who had been standing in front of his tent, ran to the nearest burning Corsair, its wrecked fuselage resting on its belly. Wade Britt was still strapped in, slumped over, his clothing afire. From the ring of darkness surrounding the blaze, one of the ground crew appeared with a fire extinguisher. Miller directed him to spray its contents directly on the pilot, which temporarily snuffed the flames so Miller could reach in and release the harness. He climbed onto the cockpit sills and reached under the pilot's armpits to pull him out, but despite the good leverage his efforts were futile. Bernie Bernard joined him astride the cockpit to help, but even two men could not budge the body. The pilot's legs were hopelessly jammed in the wreckage, and flames began again in the cockpit as they continued to strain. Finally, as fire leaped from between the pilot's feet and machine-gun rounds in the Corsair's wings ignited, the two men were forced to retreat.

Later that day Miller recorded the grisly scene in his diary.

> [Britt] was unconscious when I first arrived and just alive—there are no words to describe the feeling of abandoning a man, dead or alive, in that furnace. The only other casualty was a lineman who had been sitting in another ship. He was so badly burned that he died this afternoon.* The pilot I tried to pull out was unrecognizable, his arms blown bare and his face bloated. I had no idea it was the major.

Wade Britt's death came just ten days after the Hellhawks began their first combat tour, making him the ninth squadron commander killed since the beginning of the war, the sixth on Guadalcanal alone. So many highly qualified

*Private First Class Robert M. Whitefield, a ground crewman from VMF-124, died of burns at 1408.

leaders died that a new policy soon emerged, limiting commanding officers to one combat tour. The measure would have a profound effect on George Britt and, ultimately, his successor.

As for Henry Miller and Carol Bernard, their valiant attempt to pull Wade Britt from the fiery wreckage did not go unnoticed. Miller sustained burns on his hands, arms, and one leg, "minor damage for such a catastrophe for their major," he claimed. Both received the Navy–Marine Corps Medal for their bravery.

Another example of fate's vagary occurred two days later, this time to one of VMF-214's own. An SBD strike to Rekata Bay, a floatplane base on Santa Isabel, about 130 miles west of Guadalcanal, was scheduled for early afternoon. Henry Ellis's and Charlie Lanphier's divisions provided escort, but just before departure the tail wheel on Charlie's F4F went flat and he switched to another available plane. The strike proceeded to Rekata without incident until Charlie encountered trouble just beyond the enemy base. An oil line broke and his Wildcat's engine promptly failed. Too low to hit the silk, he glided toward the water adjacent to the beach and made a clean splashdown only ten miles east of the Japanese facility. Al Jensen stayed around long enough to see Charlie climb aboard his raft, then winged back to Guadalcanal with the others. The task of getting the SBDs home was still their priority, but as soon as they returned they reported that Charlie was down on an enemy-held island.

Not much later, a pair of P-39 pilots from the 70th Fighter Squadron passed Lanphier's location after completing a reconnaissance flight over Rekata Bay. Lieutenants Darryl Cosart and James Daggit were low on the deck when they spotted a figure waving to them from a beach. Circling back for another look, they verified that the figure was a downed American pilot, then waggled their wings to acknowlege his situation. No sooner had Cosart begun filing a report of his sighting back at Fighter Two than some of Charlie's pals pulled up in a jeep and told Tom Lanphier of his brother's dilemma.

Tom immediately grabbed a friend's only bottle of bourbon, took a jeep down to the docks, and approached the pilot of a Dumbo. There were no dedicated units for air-sea rescue on Guadalcanal then, but the Navy's amphibious planes were regularly called upon to search for downed aviators. Assuring Lanphier that the offered booze was not required (though welcome), the PBY pilot said that VMF-214 had already called him to get a rescue attempt under way but that it would be necessary to wait until morning. Lanphier asked if he could accompany the pilot the next day and received an affirmative, then returned to Fighter Two. Meanwhile fighter operations scheduled two divisions from VMF-214 for the next day's rescue mission.

At 0930 on April 16, Bill Pace and Vince Carpenter took off with their divisions for the rescue. The Navy had switched amphibians, however, substituting a single-engine Grumman J2F Duck for the bigger Catalina. Worse, the Duck's pilot was thoroughly unprepared and took off without enough fuel in the main tank, so he had to turn back before reaching Santa Isabel. Pace's division peeled off to provide escort and Carpenter's flight continued in hopes of spotting Charlie. Sure enough he emerged from the tree line onto the beach, jumping and waving to catch their attention.

Fortunately, at about the same time that Pace and the inept Duck pilot returned to Cactus, the Catalina became available for another attempt. This time George Britt joined with a flight of seven Wildcats as aerial escort, accompanied voluntarily by Army lieutenants Cosart and Daggit in their P-39s. Tom Lanphier caught a ride in the Dumbo's cluttered belly, later writing, "It was still a very informal war out there, at least among the combat troops."

Guided by Vince Carpenter's recent sighting, the collection of planes reached Charlie's location and again found him jumping up and down on the sand. But as Tom looked through one of the PBY's tear-shaped blisters, he could see something Charlie did not. Just around a small promontory, six armed Japanese soldiers were walking along the beach. Spotting the PBY, they broke into a trot. The Navy pilot greased his Catalina onto the gentle surf about two hundred yards from the beach for the pickup.

The pickup was later described by Tom Lanphier in an unpublished autobiography.

> As our aircraft drifted slowly shoreward on the swells off his position, we waited for Charlie, a good swimmer, to move into the surf and swim to our flying boat. But he wouldn't move more than knee deep into the surf. In exasperation, the crewmen inflated a rescue raft, and one of them and I got in it and paddled to about twenty yards offshore.
>
> Then, finally, Charlie plunged into the water and swam out to climb aboard the raft, with what I took to be a less than grateful, "What kept you?" He hadn't come out before because he swore he'd seen shark fins in the water about 100 yards out. All our lives he and I had been afraid of snakes. I could empathize with fearing a shark, should I ever meet one in the sea. (One of the prime reasons I had welcomed the two-engine P-38 to the Canal was the added insurance it offered against becoming shark bait.)
>
> About the time the three of us scrambled aboard the PBY amidship, the Japanese patrol came into view around the head of the point. Though they popped away in frustration with their rifles, we were far out of range and suffered no damage.

Charlie was reunited with the squadron in time to recount his close call at supper, having suffered no ill effects other than a sleepless night in the jungle due to steady rain. He had been lucky, even though his brother claimed he had not inherited much of that commodity from his Irish forebears.

Ironically his rescue came on the same day that Admiral

Yamamoto scrubbed his "I" Operation. Two days later Tom Lanphier became embroiled in a controversial episode of enormous historical magnitude involving the Japanese admiral. Months earlier, cryptological specialists had cracked the Japanese code used in many of their scrambled radio messages, aiding Adm. Chester Nimitz and his planners immensely in their preparations for Midway. Now a freshly intercepted message presented a dramatic opportunity. Analysts at Pearl Harbor determined that Admiral Yamamoto planned a tour of his air bases south of Rabaul, and with luck he could be picked off en route. They determined that Yamamoto and his staff would fly from Rabaul in two transports, landing first at Ballale, off the tip of Bougainville, on the morning of April 18. The intercepted message even identified Bettys as the transports and included Yamamoto's estimated time of arrival over Ballale: 1135. ComAirSols, ordered to plan the intercept, gave the job of working out the details to Fighter Command. The exec of Fighter Command was none other than George Britt's former squadron commander, Sam Moore, who in turn gave the task of route planning to his operations officer, John Condon. He worked out a circuitous route, both to avoid radar detection and to preserve the secret that the Japanese code had been breached. The planners hoped the appearance of American fighters would seem purely coincidental rather than a deliberate ambush. The intercept assignment was given to the Army's 339th Fighter Squadron, commanded by Maj. John W. Mitchell and equipped with P-38s, the only fighters with the range to pull it off.

Tom Lanphier, considered one of the 339th's best shots, was assigned as a shooter. (Six were originally scheduled, but two suffered aborted takeoffs.) Mitchell and eleven additional Lightnings provided top cover. Condon's precise flight planning worked to perfection, placing the Lightnings at their intended point south of Empress Augusta Bay on Bougainville's coast just as the Bettys began their descent toward Ballale. Three of the escorting Zeros were shot down against the loss of one P-38, but the truly stunning blow came when Lanphier and Lt. Rex T. Barber shot down both bombers. The Betty carrying Isoroku Yamamoto crashed into the jungle, killing the mastermind of the Pearl Harbor attack.

From the moment the Lightnings landed back on Guadalcanal, the controversy began over who shot down Yamamoto. Naturally whoever bagged him owned the biggest bragging rights in the entire Pacific, but because Lanphier and Barber could not actually see the famous admiral inside his Betty, neither could state with conviction who had been in their respective bombers. The Japanese knew, of course, having recovered Yamamoto's body, but the Americans had no way to be certain. Concerned that loose talk would reveal to the Japanese that their secret code was compromised, ComAirSols wanted to keep a tight lid on the whole affair.

Tom Lanphier apparently had other ideas. He visited Charlie at the Marines' campfire and told his version while Henry Miller listened in.

> Tom Lanphier, who was claiming credit for shooting down Yamamoto himself, came down to our area that night and spilled the whole thing. As soon as the word got out that he had done this, he got in a lot of hot water. They wanted to court-martial him for blabbing so much, revealing that the U.S. had broken the code so the Japanese would get the message. They felt it was such a breach of security that the Japanese would know their transmissions weren't secure any more, they were going to cut his head off.

Before long the heat moved off Lanphier, probably because many on Guadalcanal had overheard the Lightning pilots' radio traffic. Rumors flew that somebody big had been shot down. The Japanese themselves left little doubt when they retaliated that same night, sending "every plane that could carry a rock to drop." The raids, which lasted from sundown until dawn the next morning, were by far the biggest attack endured on Guadalcanal during VMF-214's stay. By Dave Rankin's count, a total of nine raids came over. "Bastards kept up all night," he wrote in his diary.

The first raid, described colorfully by Henry Miller in his own diary, arrived even as Tom Lanphier sat at their campfire.

> On the first run last night we were all enjoying the searchlights and criticizing the antiaircraft when a stick came down. I don't know who hit the dugout first, but I was third with Pace behind me (spilling a precious drink) and Scarborough on top of him as a result of the plunge. On several of the succeeding runs, for some of which we did not bother to get out of bed, no bombs were dropped. At about 0400 we had a very rude awakening—not the gentle tinkle of an alarm clock but the whine of another stick. I think John [Burnett] made the hole first. As I was going over the major's gear cot I was concerned about getting in his way, but when I hit the bottom there he was beside John. Henry Ellis said he decided he could not make it and watched from his cot—he said there was a star shell of some sort along with the bombs. Up to this point neither the night fighters nor the antiaircraft had accomplished anything. But a moment later, out to the northwest, there was a sudden flare as a night fighter got one bomber. As the burning plane fell, the sound of the fatal machine-gun fire, or defending fire, reached us.

Britt's division never bothered to go back to bed but departed instead at 0530 for a routine Knucklehead patrol. For the remainder of the day, in fact for the rest of the tour, "routine" became the prevalent comment. After the exciting air battle followed by the drama of Charlie Lanphier's rescue a week later, then the all-night raids on April 18, life slowed drastically. Throughout the rest of April the division flew hours of local patrols punctuated by only five strike escorts. Excepting occasional notations for poor weather, the official war diary recorded each patrol simply as a "routine flight." Remarks about escort missions were equally cryptic. The phrase "no opposition encountered and no planes lost" was entered after nearly every mission.

A couple of mishaps provided the only excitement as far as flying was concerned. On April 21, a plane making an emergency landing tore up sections of steel mat on the strip, then Charlie Lanphier pancaked behind the damaged area. When one of his tires burst on jagged metal, his Wildcat pitched onto its nose. The plane skidded for more than a hundred yards at this precarious angle, balancing on two prop blades and the main gear without so much as scratching the wingtips or even the cowling. After the engine, a tire, and propeller were replaced, the Wildcat was as good as new.

A week later, Mac McCall wasn't able to save his Wildcat. Just after taking off at 0530 on April 27 he heard a bang as the engine caught fire and threw a shower of sparks. He declared an emergency and reversed direction, landing downwind without time to crank down the wheels. The impact with the Marston matting cracked the drop tank and released a trail of fuel, which ignited and chased his plane as he slid along the steel strip. The burning stream overtook the stricken Wildcat as Mac jumped free, ran, and watched from a safe distance as his airplane was consumed by fire.

Later that morning, Smiley Burnett flew to the Russells on a solo mission that restored some much-needed esteem from his fellows. After stuffing the little luggage bay of his Wildcat with mail, a Victrola, some phonograph records, and several cases of beer, he took his airplane high on the return flight. He remained in the freezing air as long as he could before dropping like a rock to Fighter One; when he landed the beer was still cold—a welcome treat.

Otherwise life on Cactus became exceedingly dull, and the first days of May brought no deliverance from the boredom. The normal period for a squadron's combat tour was six weeks—a milestone they had since surpassed—yet there was no relief in sight. Former Wildcat squadrons were transitioning to Corsairs in the rear area, extending turnaround times and forcing VMF-214 to wait for the logjam to clear. Only one other Marine squadron operated F4Fs longer, by a few weeks.

VMF-214 participated in only two strikes during May, the first notable because of its size. A total of sixty-eight aircraft, including Army, Navy, and Marine escorts, struck Rekata Bay on May 3, with eight of VMF-214's Wildcats taking part. A smaller strike on Vila the following day marked the squadron's last escort mission for the tour, after which it flew routine patrols and answered requests for shipping coverage.

Those not flying passed tedious days down at the ready tent with gaming and horseplay. Some fabricated slingshots, intending to use them against the noisy cockatoos, but plinked at unsuspecting squadron mates instead. So quiet were the early days of May that a miniature airplane became big news: "The Horse's F4U-1 model is progressing rapidly," someone wrote in the war diary. Harry Hollmeyer had decided to use his hands to pass the time. With some rough planks from an ammunition crate, he carved a pair of wings into the unmistakable gull form, then shaped a slender fuselage topped with a framework canopy and tall vertical fin. Next came elliptical horizontal stabilizers and the thin blades of a propeller. After gluing the pieces together with clear dope, he painted the whole with authentic Vought colors. His model was beautifully detailed down to the radio mast and its thin strand of antenna cable. Once everyone had admired it, he boxed the treasure carefully and mailed it to his father in Boston.*

*As a testament to Hollmeyer's thoroughness, the model is still in fine shape fifty-five years later.

While Hollmeyer labored on his miniature version, the real thing was rapidly replacing Wildcats. VMF-214's engineering and ground crews proved that the Grummans were still plenty dependable, making twenty of their twenty-two planes available on May 8. All were briefly airborne at one time. Then Hank Ellis and John Burnett attempted to locate two crippled Japanese warships in the Blackett Strait. After failing to make contact, they diverted instead to strafe Munda, where they encountered intense AA fire. That evening it began to rain as a front moved over the island, and by morning Fighter One was inundated. The standby division sloshed through rivers of water coursing through the ready tent while others awoke to find their pyramidal tents flooded. It seemed appropriate weather, considering the recent lack of flying.

One last opportunity to tangle with Zeros bore no fruit. Admiral Mineichi Koga, Yamamoto's replacement, ordered more than a hundred planes to Rabaul from Truk on May 10, then sent a reconnaissance plane escorted by twenty-five Zeros toward Guadalcanal on May 13 to determine American aerial strength. They never made it, met instead by Army and Marine fighters between the Russells and Florida Island. Majors Britt and Pace (the latter promoted in mid-April) were scrambled at 1245, but Recon never vectored them into the scrap and they saw nothing of the enemy.

On the other hand, F4Us from VMF-112 and -124 were heavily engaged. They claimed fifteen enemy fighters (the 204 Kokutai lost only two pilots) but lost five Corsairs. Three of the downed Marines were from VMF-124, recently back in action for their second combat tour. One Marine seen to bail out over Tulagi had been shot in the foot and was recovered, but the big blow was the loss of Bill Gise, the squadron's commander since its inception eight months earlier. The first Corsair squadron had suffered more than most, and the loss of yet another commanding officer bolstered ComAirSol's case for limiting commanders to one tour.

Later that day, VMF-214's relief arrived as elements of VMF-123 began to settle in at Fighter One. Ultimately the last Wildcat outfit in combat with the Marine Corps, VMF-123 was a welcome sight. In the evening, a lone Japanese bomber gave George Britt and his pilots a fitting send-off. Red flares and searchlights illuminated the night sky, and with no further warning a stick of four or five bombs suddenly detonated close to the camp. Henry Miller, driving back from MAG-12 headquarters, heard the incoming bombs and dived under his jeep, then drove into camp to find his squadron mates "quite shaken up."

May 14 was VMF-214's last full day on Cactus. Suitably it included flying, beginning at 0530 with routine patrols recorded as "dull and uneventful save for the thought that we knew it was all about to end." Henry Miller was the last to land, having flown to Banika to collect mail. At 1500 the logbooks were secured and operations were turned over to VMF-123. By nightfall a tremendous party was under way as the Horse, Ledge, Big John, and Mac built a raging bonfire. The Navy protested but their complaints were ignored. Link Deetz managed to find some ice cream, and Sam Moore dropped by from Fighter Command. The remaining bottles of liquor were unstopped and the quartet was in full voice. As one man put it, "All possible songs were sung that night."

There was good reason. In its first eight weeks of combat (a new record for a single tour) VMF-214 had claimed ten Japanese aircraft while losing only two planes and no pilots to the enemy. Operationally its losses were somewhat heavier. Bill Steed was officially listed as missing but had obviously died on the third day of the tour, and a half-dozen aircraft had been lost to mishaps. Hank Ellis, Jim Taylor, Charlie Lanphier, and Mac McCall each walked away from crash landings or ditchings. Accidents were expected in war and VMF-214 suffered considerably fewer than many outfits. When the squadron next returned to combat, its members would not find their fortunes so favorable.

But for now their thoughts went no farther than getting their bags packed for a well-deserved rest. Anticipation soared as they talked of a week's leave that was promised to take place in a civilized paradise compared to their current surroundings. They were going to Sydney.

7

RESTING UP, DOWN UNDER

Payback for the late-night party came within hours as the Marines were ousted from their cots at 0300. Most awoke with thick tongues, blurred vision, throbbing headaches, their earlier jubilation all but forgotten. After gathering their belongings, the listless group rode trucks to Henderson Field and crowded aboard two SCAT transports. Doc Kraft and Pete Folger came along, the latter getting a grudging okay from the good doctor even though a nasty infection from an accidental leg wound had sickened him.

At 0610 on Saturday, May 15, the transports departed Guadalcanal and turned south for the five-hour flight to Buttons. It was not a pleasant ride. No one was physically airsick, but all were sagging from hangovers and lack of sleep. During the last portion of the flight, an F4F out of Buttons used the pair of R4Ds for target practice, initiating repeated dummy firing runs. Finally the Skytrains landed and rolled to a stop in front of the SCAT facility.

When the squadron disembarked they discovered another irritation. Pay accounts were missing, and back pay was due for the weeks they had spent in combat (where money was useless). After voicing their concerns, the fighter pilots headed to the transient officers' mess for lunch, then hiked to the storage compound and checked the nonessential gear they had stowed almost nine weeks earlier. Other than a few broken pieces of luggage, their belongings were in better shape than anyone expected. The men recovered items needed in Australia—"greens" (stylish winter uniforms), dress shoes, casual clothing, accessories—then retired to their new quarters. These were plywood structures called Dallas huts, some of which had been joined together to create larger bunk rooms. Before long the coconut grove surrounding the huts was festooned with bedrolls and laundry airing in the sunlight.

The next day was vastly different from those on Cactus. "It is greatly relieving to have no duties but to swim, eat good food, etc.," wrote Henry Miller. Gone were the horrid flies, the SOS, the predawn wake-ups. The men eased tensions in the warm waters of a nearby lagoon, where a deep crevice in the coral dubbed the "Imperial Tub" held an array of colorful fish. After supper on Sunday, the men watched a double feature in the open-air theater, enjoying the movies without the threat of a Japanese raider overhead. They found Hollywood's depiction of air combat laughable in *Flying Fortress,* now that they had tasted the real thing. After the show, many headed to Club Buttons, supposedly a Navy-only officers' club, but the Marines crashed it after linking up with Navy friends and doctoring their khaki uniforms.

Refreshing as the days of rest on Buttons proved to be, they were not to last for long. At midday on Monday, Hank Ellis and about half the pilots—mostly junior lieutenants—boarded another SCAT transport for Efate. It was a short, bumpy 140-mile ride to the smaller island southeast of Espiritu, where a rest camp had been established at Quoin Hill. The second half of the echelon rode down the next day, somewhat sorry to leave behind Espiritu's peaceful luxury, but they soon discovered that Efate was even more beautiful and far less busy. Almost 700 miles south of Guadalcanal and considerably milder, the island was a palette of vivid colors. Lush palm groves and brightly flowered tropical shrubs decorated the foreground. Mountains covered with verdant jungle foliage jutted into a cobalt sky dotted with white cumulus sails. Underfoot, soft sand and grass invited a stroll to the nearby lagoon, with its splendid beach and crystal-clear water.

After a lunch of fresh bread and real butter, the Marines hastened down to the beach for a swim. In the evening, Pete Folger introduced them to Capt. Jere Tipton, an intelligence officer from Tennessee, who invited them to his camp for what Henry Miller later described as "an excellent movie—*A Yank at Eaton,* with a newsreel and a short—and all on a bench with a real back!"

In the morning, while the tide was out, a walk along the shore revealed stunning shells and a fascinating variety of creatures. Midmorning brought a scene straight from Hollywood as Melanesian natives paddled dugout canoes into the lagoon to sell trinkets and fruit. Dave Rankin befriended a native named Sam, who had learned sufficient English to do business with the obliging Americans. Rankin was intrigued by the canoes—hollowed logs as much as fourteen feet long, fitted with outriggers and sails of old canvas. "Takes about two year to make," boasted Sam. "Maybe work one day, rest two or three. Last fifteen, twenty year." The canoes were filled with goods for sale: grass skirts, beads, jewelry made from shells. Fifty cents bought a small bunch of bananas; a dozen oranges could be had for a dollar. A few pilots sat and talked with the natives, listening while children who had attended missionary school spelled the words of their language. Rankin carefully copied more than twenty words into his diary along with their translations. The natives had acquired some business savvy after learning the hard way from a squadron encamped earlier at Quoin Hill, who "sold" Dallas huts to the natives. When the fliers left, the natives tried unsuccessfully to collect.

VMF-214 lounged for a week in tropical bliss. The days were spent swimming, hiking to native villages and copra plantations, laundering clothes and darning socks, enjoying good meals and siestas, and talking of Sydney. The pending trip Down Under was not necessarily guaranteed. The Aussies did not want disease-infested visitors so on Wednesday morning everyone lined up for a Schneider test. Doc Kraft used a cuff to check each pilot's blood pressure and his fingers to measure pulse, then checked the results against a chart to determine cardiovascular fitness. The higher the Schneider index, the better.* Next he drew a drop of blood and placed it on a glass slide, added a chemical agent, then viewed each smear under a microscope. Any malaria organisms present would be surprisingly easy to detect. A collective sigh of relief followed the results, all negative; everyone had a green light for the trip.

On May 20 and again two days later, Smiley Burnett and Harry Hollmeyer borrowed an SBD and flew over to Havana Harbor, a former French plantation now serving as a Navy club. The drinks were cold and strong, so their return flights to Quoin Hill were not nearly as smooth. Henry Miller and Pete Folger made the trip overland one day, hiking nearly all of the twenty-eight miles, but they accepted a ride for the last few miles to relieve Folger's still-infected leg.

The less adventurous enjoyed their ration of two tepid bottles of beer every evening, usually augmented with drinks at the private clubs run by other squadrons. One night they listened to graphic stories about Sydney from a dive-bomber pilot named Taylor. As the week progressed, the recuperative effects of life on Efate began to show. "Life is beautiful, not grim, for a change" was an anonymous entry in the war diary. Later the writer included his anticipation of their trip to Australia: "Ah, Sydney, beware! Mothers, draw in your daughters."

The flight to Australia required two transports and an intermediate layover, because the R4Ds did not have the range to make it nonstop. On May 25 the first delegation

*Dr. Robert Mitchell, a World War II flight surgeon and pioneer in aviation physiology, called the Schneider test "the most useless cuss ever devised." The index had an essential flaw—pilots with significant hangovers often yielded the highest scores—and Mitchell eventually succeeded in getting it dropped from the Navy manual for physicals.

from VMF-214 flew to Tontouta, New Caledonia, and stayed overnight. The second planeload followed the next afternoon, although not before hearing some grim news. Dive-bomber pilot Taylor had collided with another pilot in a practice dive over Efate; there were no survivors. The island's idyllic setting had not provided an exemption from cold reality that the man you are drinking with tonight might be dead tomorrow.

But Sydney beckoned and the distraction was brief. The SCAT transports were scheduled to depart as soon after midnight as possible to give the Marines every hour's worth of precious leave, which commenced at 0001 on any given date. While waiting at Tontouta for their late departure, the fliers dined, slept, pitched horseshoes, and explored the facilities of the transport squadron (VMJ-253), including its swank club.

The first half of the group was finally rounded up to board a Douglas late on the evening of May 26. It was a tight squeeze. The R4D had been fitted with two internal fuel tanks in the cabin and was dangerously overloaded by the time passengers and baggage were crammed aboard. But at 0056 the aircraft lumbered down Tontouta's runway with the passengers crowded as far forward as possible, even lying on top of the fuel tanks and luggage in an attempt to shift the aircraft's center of gravity and get her tail up. After several hair-raising moments the R4D staggered into the air. That the heavy takeoffs were fraught with risk was tragically realized only two weeks later when a transport crashed, killing twenty-four passengers and crew.

VMF-214's crossing was uneventful save for the bitter chill in the unpressurized cabin as the plane climbed above turbulent weather. Several of the men decided that SCAT actually stood for "severe cold air transport." When the squadron arrived at Sydney's Mascot airport it was still early morning. As the men disembarked in a steady rain, their teeth chattered. The month of May marked the onset of winter in Australia, just the opposite of the seasons in the Northern Hemisphere, and the Marines' bodies were accustomed to the Tropics. Nothing, however, could dampen their exhilaration at touching Australian soil. As soon as they could unload their baggage and find a flatbed truck, they proceeded to their first destination, the Red Cross hotel at Kings Cross. An identical scene was repeated the next day with the second echelon's arrival, also in a light rain.

From the Red Cross hotel, which served as unofficial headquarters, the festivities began. Almost universally the top priority was a hot shower, a luxury not enjoyed since the men's arrival in the South Pacific nearly three months earlier. The place to get the works was the Hotel Australia in downtown Sydney, where their greens were pressed while the pilots pampered themselves with steam baths, massages, and facials. Invigorated, they donned clean uniforms and descended to the lobby, soon identified as *the* place to meet. By afternoon the bar had become crowded with civilians, Australian soldiers, and "a siege of beautiful women." All were full of bonhomie and ready to drink with the Yanks. Stories were exchanged frequently, empty glasses even more so.

A well-pickled barrister named Arthur Paton delighted the Marines with impassioned renditions of Shakespeare and his knowledge of where to meet the eligible women of the city. He seemed positively old, perhaps in his fifties, but he was all too happy to be adopted by a squadron of fighter pilots. He was soon nicknamed "Walter Mitty," and guided the men to the city's best establishments. Sydney, with its million-plus inhabitants, had fine restaurants, clubs, and theaters, and Paton proved indispensable as he steered them through the monetary exchange of pennies, shillings, and pounds, then educated them about Aussie slang and customs. Other Australians were equally accommodating, from cabbies who refused to accept fares to doting Red Cross volunteers.

Although the Red Cross hotel offered hot showers,

excellent food, beds with springs, and clean sheets, several of the more independent minded decided to rent an apartment. Mac McCall and Carl Dunbar located a large frame house and initiated what they later called "the Campaign of 11 Carlisle Road." The house had a kitchen they never used and five bedrooms that they did, but its greatest appeal was the enormous living room. Late in the evening after the rounds of dinner and barhopping, a regular crowd of young ladies and assorted guests filled the room to overflowing during spontaneous parties that lasted until the wee hours. The company sat around the hearth to fight off winter's chill and share songs and drinks. The crackling blaze was first fueled with broken Coke and beer cases, but when those were gone the men tore siding off a corner of the house that was hidden from the street. An enormous supply of liquor was accumulated, such that twenty-nine quarts of beer were ultimately left behind for the next inhabitants.

Daily activities went according to individual plans, whether from 11 Carlisle Road or the Red Cross hotel, and usually began with a late breakfast of steak and eggs. Beef was plentiful and consumed in great quantities in Australia, and the Marines took advantage of it. After breakfast it was time to explore Sydney's shops, perhaps swim at an athletic club such as Tattersall's where Henry Miller went looking for a pool and was made an honorary member. Lunch (another steak) was often followed by a round of golf at the Royal Sydney Club. Late afternoon meant tea—the Aussies remained true to their British heritage—and time to regroup in the Hotel Australia, where drinking evolved into the rousing camaraderie of songs and sport, including a gleeful game of flipping tuppence into the upturned globes of the chandeliers. The bar kept pub hours and closed at six, signaling a move to dining and drinking establishments such as the Millions Club, Jim the Greek's, The Roses cafe, Prince's, the Legacy Club, and Mr. Bonington's. An especially popular site was the Tivoli Ballet, where several pilots befriended the theater's attractive ladies. Later the pilots would meet at the stage door and escort the girls to restaurants or parties at 11 Carlisle Road. Romance inevitably blossomed, particularly for Charlie Lanphier. His brother later wrote, "Charlie's term of leave was but seven days, but during that week my reserved, almost shy brother found time, opportunity and gumption to get himself engaged to a lovely young Australian girl." Sadly it would not be his fortune to marry her.

Not everyone burned the midnight oil. Vince Carpenter and Link Deetz met a wealthy Australian family who graciously invited them to stay in their home. While the other Marines played hard, Carpenter and Deetz practically collapsed, sleeping long hours and otherwise relaxing in quiet elegance. Indulged by butlers and the family's warm generosity, neither pilot saw a need to venture downtown, thus keeping the luxurious arrangement to themselves.

Most did just the opposite, sacrificing sleep in the interest of maximizing their limited time to frolic. After several days of late breakfasts, shopping, drinks with lunch, golfing, drinks with tea, more drinks at dinner clubs, and late parties at 11 Carlisle Road, Henry Miller began to wonder if they weren't leading their adopted Arthur Paton to alcoholic ruin. Another pilot wrote, "Systems (ours—circulatory) are running on 50 proof alcoholic content at this point. Dangerous to smoke a cigarette."

But that didn't prevent the men from throwing a boisterous squadron party at Prince's on the night of June 1, and Paton was there. Jim Taylor had good reason to celebrate, too, having received a field commission to second lieutenant two weeks earlier. Al Jensen and Bill Blakeslee were now the only pilots without bars on their collars, but the flying sergeants—equal in the eyes of all—were warmly included in the party.

All too soon, of course, the idyllic vacation ended. The first echelon was scheduled to depart for Tontouta on June 3, and in the gray dawn the men reluctantly boarded a truck parked in front of the Red Cross hotel. They arrived at

Mascot airport to hear the best possible news: Their flight was canceled due to unfavorable weather en route. After a wild thirty minutes phoning girls, they piled back onto the truck, singing loudly as they passed back through the city for one more day and night of revelry. The next morning the weather was good, and this time both echelons departed aboard two heavily loaded transports, bidding a fond "ta-ta" to wonderful Sydney.

The men's return to Efate was met with some uncertainty as to what would happen next. It was generally held that their next destination would be the Turtle Bay fighter strip at Espiritu Santo, where they would transition into F4U Corsairs, but no one had a clue as to when that would happen. Other fighter squadrons were there ahead of them, and Corsairs were not yet available in large quantities. Efate, therefore, would remain their home until someone decided to move them to Buttons and begin their transition to Corsairs. Nobody objected to the idea of more beer and relaxation.

The squadron was joined on June 6 by a new member, Maj. William O'Neill, whose arrival was an ominous sign for George Britt. By the eighth it was official: Britt fell victim to a policy established by Maj. Gen. Ralph J. Mitchell, now commander of Marine Air, South Pacific (MASP) in addition to the 1st Marine Air Wing (MAW), who had reached the conclusion that too many valuable squadron commanders were being killed to allow second combat tours. With the war only eighteen months old, ten Marine Corps skippers had died, including Wade Britt and Bill Gise while serving alongside VMF-214. Consequently George Britt was ordered to report to MAG-21 on the Russell Islands and assume the duties of operations officer. A farewell party was held in the Dallas huts that evening and Britt departed the next day, quiet and composed as he spoke with some at the huts and others who followed him out to the plane. By lunchtime on June 9, his eleven-month association with the squadron ended, though he would continue to cross paths with VMF-214 in the months to come.

While Britt settled into his new job, ten languid days passed as the squadron enjoyed Efate's peaceful beauty. During daylight hours there was little to do but eat, sleep, and play in the water. Those not interested in fishing or swimming often returned to bed after breakfast. To maintain a minimum of flight proficiency, pilots took turns borrowing SBDs and SNJs for the four-minute hops between Quoin Hill, Havana Harbor, and Vila, the island's biggest developed town.* Dubbing their service the "VMF-214 Ferry Command," they dropped off movie reels from the previous night's showing and picked up new selections. The movies took on significant importance in the absence of other activities. The Marines were willing to sit through rain showers and generator failures to watch *That Hamilton Woman* (two nights to complete), *Gold Rush Maisie, The Maltese Falcon,* and *The Mark of Zorro*. The showings were a bit of a culture shock after their visit to Sydney, according to Dave Rankin: "One week in a soft cushioned cinema, next week on a board beneath squalls and moonlight."

The evening of June 14 was their last on Efate. Appropriately Ginger Rogers and David Niven flickered onscreen as they danced through *Free and Easy,* for a party of some notoriety developed soon after. It was a big farewell blast, a kind of hallowed ritual that defines men-at-arms sharing the kinship of imminent mortality in combat. Henry Miller got things rolling in one of the enlarged Dallas huts by concocting a punch from condensed milk and powdered eggs, sweetened at Carl Dunbar's suggestion with sugar. The main ingredient was Doc Kraft's medicinal brandy, to which was later added any other liquor that could be found. Fueled by the potent punch, the party

*Not to be confused with a Japanese airfield of the same name on the island of Kolombangara.

gained momentum. After someone slit the back of Chalky Cavanagh's shirt with a pocket knife, the Dallas hut erupted in a tremendous free-for-all.

Just as the horseplay began to subside, VMF-123 sent an invitation for the men to join them at their bar. The pilots spilled out of the hut and piled into jeeps dressed in little more than skivvy shorts. In this condition they joined their brother fighter pilots for more drinking, singing, and yelling. They lived in a strange world ten thousand miles from their loved ones, had seen other men vanish into the sea or die in a gush of brilliant flames, had just been teased with a week of civilization and pretty women, and were now peering in a new direction toward more combat, renewed risk, more destruction. The band of brothers piled together their burdens and roared loudly against the fates that placed them there.

When the hullabaloo finally ended, most of the men were faced with the daunting task of walking back to their camp. Dave Rankin later wrote of his stumbling trip home with Cavanagh, Dick Sigel, and Carl Dunbar, as he fell frequently on the sharp coral and tried to walk officerlike (although he was nearly naked) past a number of sentries: "Positively the worst drunk I've been on. Stomach still against liquor."

Somehow everyone recovered in time to board transports on June 15 for the flight north to Buttons, where they found temporary quarters in the MAG-11 area. The next day, Pete Folger arranged their pay accounts and dispersed a backlog of mail. As many as twenty letters awaited some of them, the most anticipated being the "sugar reports" from the States and Australia. Just as important as pay and mail was a sizable jump in the roster. Twelve fresh pilots, all second lieutenants, arrived on the sixteenth to bring the flight echelon's strength to thirty-eight for the time being. Seven of the new lieutenants would eventually be reassigned elsewhere, but five were retained.

On June 17, Major O'Neill was transferred to VMTB-232, and Hank Ellis assumed command of the squadron he had belonged to for almost nine months. "Today we greet our former Executive Officer, Major H. A. Ellis as Skipper," reads the war diary, "and mighty glad in our salutations and salutes."

There were other comings and goings, beginning with Doc Kraft, transferred to MAG-21 on the same day. The Marines were sorry to see him go, as George Britt echoed with a later tribute.

> Doc Kraft did more than dispense medicinal brandy, and he was pretty stingy with that. He diligently oversaw the many sanitation problems associated with life in the tropics. With their maturity, he and Pete Folger were strong right arms for many of the younger guys.

Kraft's replacement was Lt. Ralph Bookman, another flight surgeon in the Navy Medical Corps, who arrived two days later and integrated easily. Charlie Lanphier departed the same day as Doc Kraft for temporary duty on Guadalcanal. On the evening before their departure, the squadron threw a song-and-beer farewell party that was the envy of Turtle Bay. It was also a hurrah of sorts for the whole squadron, now that a refreshing month had passed since departing Cactus. The original members were ready to prepare again for combat, their turn to transition into the hottest fighter in the air, the F4U Corsair, drawing nigh. They would remain in the rear area to undergo those weeks of training, joined by new pilots who would need their guidance and leadership. The period of rest was something they would always fondly remember, but now it was time to put their fighting hats back on.

8

"THE EWE IS MIGHTY SWEET"

Under ideal circumstances, with plenty of time and adequate training facilities available, a squadron's transition into F4Us was deliberate, even painstaking. Pilots listened to lectures and studied operating manuals until they were thoroughly familiar with the aircraft's systems, then conducted cockpit orientation and familiarization flights. Once they were comfortable with handling the new plane, more demanding routines such as formation flying, division tactics, and gunnery training were introduced.

VMF-214's changeover to the new airplane was anything but normal. The first of several obstacles was a matter of supply. No rows of shiny new Corsairs awaited the squadron at Turtle Bay; F4Us would have to be borrowed.

The next hindrance, highly subjective and varying among pilots, was opinion about the airplane itself. The veteran pilots had observed the first two Corsair squadrons for two months of combat, and what they saw gave them pause. VMF-124 had suffered lackluster performance from its airplanes because of mechanical headaches, claiming only seven enemy planes while losing three Corsairs and two pilots to the Japanese. Even more damning was the loss of eight aircraft and two pilots to mishap. The second tour had barely started when Bill Gise was shot down. Likewise VMF-213 claimed just seven victories in six weeks and lost Wade Britt in a horrendous crash. During the month of April alone, the Hellhawks lost eight F4Us to all causes and three pilots dead or missing. In retrospect the F4U appeared to be an unforgiving handful.

The problems of supply and safety could be dealt with, but the final hurdle was the biggest uncertainty. The squadron had but one month to learn the new airplane.

The push was on because Bull Halsey was preparing for the next step in his island-hopping campaign, the New Georgia group, a large cluster of islands in the central Solomons that halved the distance between Guadalcanal and Bougainville. Halsey's planned road to Tokyo passed through New Georgia, then Bougainville, and finally Rabaul, and each had to be taken in sequence. The Japanese were already operating from airfields at Munda and Vila in the New Georgia group, and Allied engineers wanted sites for additional bases from which to launch attacks more effectively against Bougainville.

Munda and Vila had been bombed, strafed, and shelled for months, making them barely tenable, but the Japanese always managed to repair the runways. Munda had been reduced to serving only as a stopover for Japanese planes returning from strikes on Guadalcanal and the Russells, but regional air strength was still a major threat. The critical element was New Georgia's proximity to Bougainville. Scores of Vals, Bettys, and Zeros would be less than an hour's flight away. The invasion forces would need ample fighter protection overhead, and Halsey looked to ComAirSols to provide it.

VMF-214 pilots began their Corsair initiation on June 17 (approximately two weeks before the New Georgia landings), as engineering officers and Vought representatives lectured on F4U systems and attempted to dispel rumors.* Lessons continued the next day, accompanied by

*The Corsair entered production in 1942 as the Vought Sikorsky F4U-1, but in January 1943 United Aircraft (which also owned Boeing and Pratt & Whitney, among other aviation industries) reorganized the corporation as Chance Vought. The VMF-214 diary refers to civilian field representatives as Vought Sikorsky employees.

cockpit orientation under the watchful conduct of experienced plane captains. Here the Marines discovered the degree of physical dexterity needed simply to board the big fighter. Getting to the seat, which was located behind the wing's trailing edge, required a hefty step from a recessed toehold on the starboard side of the fuselage.

The first impression inside the cockpit was of its sheer size. Those familiar with the Wildcat's cozy simplicity found the Corsair's cockpit enormous, with dials, switches, and knobs surrounding the pilot on three sides. Magnifying the sensation of space was the lack of a deck between the pilot's feet. Aside from two steel channels there was nothing but a dark void all the way down to the belly. The earliest Corsairs were fitted with a small window that allowed pilots to look between their knees and through the belly, but rarely did pilots use it (if they were even aware of it) for the simple reason that the vast space attracted trash. "[The windows] got dirty inside real quick," OK Williams recalled, "and there was so much space inside that you couldn't get them clean. All that coral dust from our shoes just kept piling up in the cockpit."

Above the pilot's head was a latticework canopy that slid over the spine of the rear empennage, defined by an armored bulkhead behind the pilot's seat. Because of the armor plate, visibility to the rear was poor, so engineers fitted a mirror inside a raised blister at the front of the canopy. The canopy's unique, sight-restricting framework prompted pilots to nickname the F4U-1 "the birdcage."

Armed with operating manuals and plane captains' guidance, the Marines studied the location and function of each item in the cockpit. Controls for the reciprocating engine, such as the throttle, prop revolutions per minute, fuel mixture, and so forth, were much like those of the Wildcat, as were flight controls, but there ended the similarities. The Corsair used a complex hydraulic system to operate the cowl flaps, landing gear, wing fold mechanism (which was practically never used), and massive landing flaps. The ignition and electrical systems were also more elaborate and required busier control panels along the cockpit's sides.

Other comparisons to the familiar little Wildcat were inevitable. An empty Corsair was a half ton heavier than a fully loaded Wildcat, whereas a Corsair filled with fuel and ammunition had a weight advantage of two tons. And the Corsair simply *looked* more stable. The Wildcat sat on spindly, narrow-tracked landing gear; the Corsair was planted firmly on hydraulically operated gear extending from the elbows of its unique wings.

Aside from their unusual appearance, the inverted gull wings were ingeniously functional, giving extra ground clearance for the Corsair's enormous thirteen-foot propeller as well as structural strength. The wings were spacious internally, containing oil coolers just outboard of the roots, plus three .50-caliber machine guns per side and plenty of ammunition in the midwing area. The gun arrangement was the same as the Wildcat's with one significant difference: The Corsair's capacious bays held 400 rounds for the inboard guns and slightly fewer (375) for the outboard gun on each side, allowing approximately thirty seconds of firing time, a healthy improvement. A fifty-gallon unpressurized fuel tank also occupied each wing. Prior to entering combat, a CO_2 bottle was manually activiated to purge the tanks, hopefully preventing fire.

As for performance, the Corsair's superiority was evident even when it was standing still. One of its dominant features was a long cowl wrapped tightly around the most powerful radial engine currently available, the eighteen-cylinder Pratt & Whitney R-2800 Double Wasp. This was a gas-guzzling monster with a two-stage turbo supercharger and pistons the size of paint cans. At full military power, an almighty roar vented through its unrestricted exhaust stacks.

One testimony to the Double Wasp's awesome power

was provided by Lt. William N. Case, a pilot with another outfit who would later join the squadron. During a combat encounter, a round entered the side of his Corsair's cowling and penetrated the exhaust manifold, but as he later recalled:

> The engine was running so hard that it blew the round out the exhaust stack. There was no paint on the far side of the manifold. Now, I was really impressed with the power that can turn a bullet ninety degrees and blow it out the back.

The Corsair's most bothersome design flaw was the result of an early modification. Engineers located the cockpit three feet farther aft to install a huge internal fuel tank (232-gallon capacity) behind the engine, creating a cylindrical nose measuring fourteen feet from the pilot to the propeller. The long cowl blocked forward vision and earned the Corsair several nicknames, including "Hose Nose," "Hog Nose," and in VMF-214's war diary the less-than-flattering "Ewe," though the squadron's famous association with sheep was still some months in the future.

Ultimately cockpit familiarization and ready-room lectures eased negative perceptions about the Corsair, and the Marines itched to fly it. Their first opportunity apparently occurred on June 19, although a slight anomaly exists between Henry Miller's meticulous *Solomon Islands Diary* (Bill Pace and Smiley Burnett flew borrowed Corsairs on June 18 for approximately thirty minutes) and the official war diary. In any case, initial reactions to the new aircraft were more than favorable. "Red hot," reported one. Dave Rankin added that he was "looking forward to flying it with great zeal."

There was no question that the Corsair would outperform the old Wildcat in virtually every category. The pilots' first sensation was of accelerating down Turtle Bay's white coral strip and climbing into the sky with an exhilarating rush, the thirteen-foot propeller taking huge bites of air. Leveling off, they further explored the aircraft's responsive handling. Vought had devoted numerous test flights to aileron perfomance, and the Corsair enjoyed a superb roll rate despite its size and weight. For sheer speed nothing could touch it. Straight and level it was a good hundred knots faster than the Wildcat; a power dive improved the margin even more because of the Corsair's superior weight.

When it was time to land, however, the thrills turned to initial apprehension for many pilots. Newly commissioned Jim Taylor thought the old Wildcats now seemed mighty forgiving.

> We could do a lot of things in an F4F that were really dumb and manage to survive, but when we stepped from that F4F into an F4U, we had a different bear by the tail. The stall characteristics of the F4U were so vastly different from the F4F as to be unbelievable. That in itself was particularly frightening. We were from the school of thought that every landing was a three-point landing. We hadn't learned that for this airplane, it was a good idea to put it down on the main wheels first.

Landing on the mains did have its advantages. A low angle of attack gave improved visibility over the long nose, and directional control was reportedly better with the tail up.* (Many pilots claimed that the Corsair's huge flaps spoiled airflow over the rudder in the three-point attitude.) But the tail-high approach raised the landing speed, and the resulting impact on the too-stiff oleo struts caused control

*Angle of attack (AOA) describes an aircraft's nose attitude relative to its flight path. Three-point landings in a tailwheel-equipped plane require a relatively high AOA, so that all three wheels touch the ground at the same time.

problems. The planes often bounced three or four times before settling onto the runway.

Feeling their way through the Corsair's landing techniques, many came in hot the first time, either leery of stalling or mentally behind the aircraft's higher speed. OK Williams wanted to touch down early on the main wheels, "so that I could see because the damn nose was so long," but he used up every inch of runway before he got the aircraft stopped. Vince Carpenter echoed that the F4U was "a beautiful plane to fly, but it was intimidating because it was so much heavier and more powerful. Coming around for my first landing, I couldn't get the doggone plane slowed down."

Despite their colorful landings, the pilots completed the inaugural flights without incident. Gaining confidence fast, they spent every day for the next week conducting routine flight training, though not necessarily in Corsairs. Lacking their own fighters, the pilots acquired flight proficiency in whatever they could get their hands on, including SNJs and some old F4F-3s without guns or ammo. The Wildcats proved particularly useful for mock dogfighting and keeping reflexes sharp; Henry Miller and Vince Carpenter tangled in a pair of them on June 23, the elder Harvard lawyer versus the young composer from Yale, and the latter demonstrated his natural talent. Miller wrote, "He licked me, even when I had the advantage. I think I had the better ship, too."

Carpenter's skill was beyond reproach, but discord was brewing among some of the other veterans. Fueled with liquid courage during a party one night, Smiley Burnett confronted Henry Miller and stated bluntly that he did not want their divisions flying together, adding that Carpenter and Ellis commanded the most respect as division leaders. Miller quite agreed, later inserting in his diary, "Bill [Pace] is too inexperienced, Smiley is too reckless, and I think too much."

The assessment of Pace's skill level was accurate, for he

had accumulated little flight time since rejoining the squadron in April (and had logged only forty-five hours by the end of the first tour). His lack of experience would manifest itself in a few weeks when he encountered a dire emergency.

Seen objectively, the personality clashes and bickering were common in any squadron, and for the time being the conflicts remained petty and did not negatively impact training. A more immediate problem was the lack of aircraft. By June 23 there were only three Corsairs in the squadron's inventory, including a "beat up hypochondriac" that the new lieutenants used for familiarization flights. It was difficult for anyone to accumulate hours, so a plan was hatched to ferry much-needed Corsairs to Guadalcanal and benefit from the long flight. The first trip, scheduled for the twenty-fourth, would accompany the Fighting Falcons of VMF-221 as they moved up for their first combat tour in Corsairs, but poor weather settled over Espiritu Santo. Several attempts to depart were aborted over the next few days, but Bill Pace finally made it with eight Corsairs on the twenty-eighth. Hank Ellis and eight others rode a SCAT transport to Tontouta, there to collect a mixed bag of Corsairs and Wildcats. Pace's group returned to Buttons the next day with six war-weary Corsairs, followed on the thirtieth by Ellis with seven Corsairs and two Wildcats from Tontouta.

Surprisingly, considering his lack of fighter time, Bill Pace was tapped to become commanding officer of VMF-124, and he departed VMF-214 on June 30. His reassignment, addressed with few comments in the contemporary diaries, would prove to be brief.

The last day of June was also a benchmark in the central Solomons as simultaneous amphibious landings took place on Rendova Island and Wickham Anchorage on New Georgia, both vigorously opposed by Japanese aerial forces. ComAirSols' plan to have a thirty-two-plane fighter patrol constantly overhead paid off handsomely as Army, Navy, and Marine pilots had a field day, claiming 101 Japanese planes against the loss of 14 fighters and 7 pilots. With remarkable accuracy, considering that claims had not yet been finalized or all American pilots accounted for, Dave Rankin reported in his diary, "Big fight over Rendova—117 Nips shot down to 17 U.S." Four Marine squadrons claimed a staggering fifty-eight enemy aircraft, including sixteen for VMF-221 within days of beginning their new tour, but the actual results were not so one-sided. The Japanese reported a loss of thirty fighters and bombers. Among Corsair squadrons it was a particularly costly day: Eleven aircraft went down with five pilots dead or missing.

The next day, July 1, there were so many off-island ferry hops in progress from Espiritu that few pilots were around to celebrate the squadron's one-year anniversary. Chalky Cavanagh, Ledge Hazelwood, and Vic Scarborough, newly promoted to first lieutenants, flew refurbished Wildcats to Guadalcanal.* Later in the day Hank Ellis and six others made the same trip ferrying new Corsairs, riding wing on a B-17. Those remaining on Espiritu conducted routine training in Corsairs brought up from Tontouta the previous day.

In accepting new or overhauled Corsairs (almost exclusively "birdcage" models), the pilots soon experienced the same mechanical bugs that had plagued earlier Corsair outfits. At midday on July 2 the squadron had thirteen Corsairs assigned, but within an hour seven had been grounded, much to Henry Miller's frustration. As the engineering officer, he was busy acquiring planes, studying their systems, and ensuring their availability, all while relying on another squadron's ground crew because VMF-214's original ground echelon was still in the Russells. Some of the older U-birds remained especially cantankerous. "Oil leaks are

*Grumman's new replacement, the F6F Hellcat, would not appear in combat until August. Several Navy squadrons soldiered on with Wildcats for months.

the worst difficulty," Miller wrote, two days later adding, "We were limited to three planes, plus any of some others going to Cactus or requiring test hops. The whole morning was stupid, as all the last few days have been—the 124 ground crew . . . are about to give up."

Luckily it was not all work and no play. Espiritu offered some of the best recreational amenities around, and the well-stocked officers' club merited special comment in the squadron log.

> The beer at the O.C. is a godsend though often tepid and loosely rationed. A slight buzz seems to be the general effect produced by one if taken in small doses prior to a meal (breakfast usually excluded).

Evening movies were good, too, with such classics as *Casablanca* on the outdoor screen. A belated squadron anniversary party on July 3 coincided with the appearance of a USO show featuring Artie Shaw's orchestra. Festivities began with fried barracuda, tuna, and snapper caught fresh from Turtle Bay, followed by a songfest featuring the quartet. During the next few days Shaw and his band played several engagements around Espiritu. Dave Rankin, who was an old friend of the band's liaison officer, threw a party for them one night in his Dallas hut. It was evidently a success, because he "sent most of the boys home tight."

By July 5 the tempo of training improved considerably as the squadron acquired new Corsairs and worked the bugs out of old ones. Gunnery hops, division exercises, and attack tactics continued unabated for eight days until bad weather interrupted. Despite occasional mechanical problems, comments such as "the Ewe is mighty sweet," and "the F4U reacts beautifully" reflected the Corsair's increasing popularity.

Another captain joined (or, more accurately, rejoined) the squadron on July 7, having first traveled a somewhat irregular path. Harold A. "Tony" Eisele, an early member of the squadron during its formative days at Ewa, was one of the lieutenants who departed in November with Phil White after his Navy Cross ceremony. Eisele eventually came to Espiritu as a replacement pilot and was assigned to VMF-121, which was just returning to Guadalcanal after a rest period. He was privileged to fly occasionally with the squadron's famed executive officer, Capt. Joe Foss. (During Eisele's tour Foss eclipsed the long-standing American record for aerial victories held by Eddie Rickenbacker since the Great War, gaining his twenty-sixth victory on January 15.) VMF-121's tour ended in late January, and Eisele returned to Espiritu for reassignment.

After a rest period he was ordered to VMF-122, and encountered a completely different type of executive officer. Whereas the legendary Foss was reserved and officer-like, Maj. Gregory Boyington was a former Flying Tiger more inclined to "drink, fly and brawl." He had come to the South Pacific in January, and VMF-122 was his first regular squadron posting since his stint with the American Volunteer Group (AVG).* By April he had replaced Maj. Elmer E. Brackett, Jr., as commanding officer.

Tony Eisele flew with Boyington on several occasions before a jungle nemesis intervened. Normally robust at six feet two and almost 220 pounds, Eisele's weight plummeted due to malaria. After losing seventy pounds he was evacuated to the naval hospital at Auckland, New Zealand, where he was not particularly surprised to see Boyington show up in June with a broken ankle, an injury that resulted from the major's propensity to drink and fight. It had apparently taught him little. "He would get me or others to help him to the local bars," remembered Eisele. "After helping him back to MOB-4, drunk, and at least on one occasion

*Curiously, even though Boyington had command of this squadron for several weeks, he continually referred to it as VMF-222 in his autobiography. The real 222 operated out of Vella Lavella later in the war alongside Boyington's new VMF-214, and it participated in the first fighter sweep of Rabaul on December 17, 1943, which Boyington led.

with a broken cast on his leg after another friendly brawl, I stopped helping him."

Eisele was finally declared fit for duty even though he had recovered to only 149 pounds. Gaunt but game, he was a welcome addition to VMF-214 because of his experience in Corsairs. On his first flight he proved his stuff during an airborne emergency. A hydraulic line blew, soaking him and the cockpit with slippery red fluid, but he calmly brought the plane around, used the standby CO_2 bottle to blow down the landing gear, and put the aircraft down nicely without flaps or brakes.

With this kind of experience to emulate, the new lieutenants soon shaped up. They had arrived together in the South Pacific as a group of twelve, graduates of advanced training at Opa-Locka, near Miami, where their only fighter time was in old Brewster Buffaloes. Largely discounted because of their inexperience, the lieutenants had bounced from one unit to another, hearing: "What are you doing here? You don't have any training!" until they finally settled at VMF-214. As of their arrival, none had yet flown a Corsair, but Eisele and other veterans helped to break them in.

One pilot who showed particular promise was twenty-three-year-old Robert M. Hanson, born in Lucknow, India, where his parents were missionaries. The Hansons raised a solid, stocky lad, who at eighteen was the heavyweight wrestling champion of the United Provinces. He matriculated at Hamline University, in St. Paul, Minnesota, where he continued to wrestle.

Wrestling may have been Hanson's way to vent aggression. One of his fellow lieutenants, Joe Curran, described Hanson as occasionally belligerent and quick to identify people he didn't like.

> He was a real husky boy, and he was a different sort of guy. We'd be walking through the camp area, and he'd say, "Do you see that guy over there? Do you like him?"

"I don't know him."

"I don't like that SOB."

But Hanson was an excellent gunner in the training command, and continued to shoot well when he reached the South Pacific.

Meanwhile newcomers and veterans alike logged as many hours as the planes would allow, mixing gunnery hops with high-altitude training, where familiarization with the oxygen system was important. Attack tactics with TBFs and SBDs were rehearsed, and on one occasion they "beat the hell out of a lonely reef."

As Bob Hanson's flying skills were being developed, at least one of the veterans seemed in decline. Smiley Burnett's erratic airmanship prevented him from shaking his mediocre reputation. He pulled another snafu on July 8 when someone shot away the target sleeve during a gunnery run. Instead of waiting for another opportunity to fire on a fresh sleeve, Burnett made a dummy run on the tow plane itself that ended with the empty tow cable wrapped around Burnett's elevator. The consternation he caused the pilot of the tow plane went unrecorded.

On Monday, July 12, Hank Ellis received the unexpected notification that he was going home. It came as a disappointment to the squadron, whose members were eager to have their popular major lead them through the next combat tour, but at the same time they were pleased for his safe return to his wife, Retha, in California. Bill Pace was recalled from VMF-124 and took command of VMF-214 the same day, even as Ellis was transferred to the Headquarters Squadron in MAG-11 for transhipment to the States.

With Ellis's departure a few days off, the squadron threw one of its patented farewell parties Wednesday night. Some of the details were preserved in the log.

> The Quartet was the best it has ever been; Smiley Capt. gave us a mechanically perfect version of *Old*

Black Joe on Major Pace's picolo [*sic*], while the latter gave us *The Deacon and the Parson*. . . . Five quarts of brew quickly consumed. Bon Voyage, Major.

July 14 was also notable in that three pilots formed a committee to develop a squadron insignia: Dick Sigel, Mac McCall, and "Harry the Horse" Hollmeyer were given free rein to come up with an original design and took their assignment seriously, even polling the ground echelon at Banika for suggestions. The final selection, much of it the work of Hollmeyer, would take about two weeks to complete, but Hollmeyer nearly lost the opportunity to contribute because of an adventure with an unexpected ending.

Bright and early Thursday morning, Hollmeyer was section leader in Dave Rankin's division as eight Corsairs took off for a high-altitude gunnery exercise. As Hollmeyer's aircraft passed through eight thousand feet, the engine failed, not altogether unusual when switching tanks, but a hundred gallons of fuel were left in the main cell. Another bad sign was that the fuel pressure read zero. Calmly he went through the checklist for restart—electric fuel pump, mixture control, fuel selector valve, engine instruments—all to no avail. Having made one forced landing in the training command, he was familiar with the symptoms, "even to the smell of hot metal and burning paint."

With the propeller windmilling and the engine loudly backfiring, Hollmeyer spiraled downward through the clouds, seeking a place to land. Ditching seemed the best bet, so he began to undo the parachute harness, tighten his shoulder straps, and unplug the radio cord to prepare for a water landing. He was just about to jettison the hood when he glanced between his knees through the Plexiglas belly window and saw a sheet of yellow flames streaming by, accompanied by an awareness that "it was getting quite hot in the cockpit." From a plane alongside, Dave Rankin observed a thirty-foot tail of flames behind Hollmeyer's airplane.

The Horse was already descending through three thousand feet and it was time to get out. He reconnected his parachute straps, unsnapped his seat belt and safety harness, lifted the nose, and rolled the Corsair on its back. Nothing happened. The plane was inverted and settling, causing enough positive gravity to hold him fast to the seat. So he wriggled out of the cockpit and over the side, then slid under the tail. His chute opened at a thousand feet just as the crippled Corsair smashed into the sea with a mighty splash, leaving "a green and white ring on the water."

Hollmeyer drifted with the wind. Although he did not know it at the time, he was descending toward a portion of Espiritu occupied by a large plantation, and his bailout had been witnessed by Tonkinese and Melanesian natives harvesting coffee and copra. One of the natives, who had attended missionary schooling, saw Hollmeyer pumping his legs to untwist the parachute shrouds. In amazement he shouted to his supervisor, "Him walk on air! Him brother Jesus Christ!"

Hollmeyer did experience Providence of some sort, for he came down on dry land by the slimmest of margins, crashing through saplings and vines at the edge of a hundred-foot cliff below which ocean waves pounded. His first rational thought was to see if he still had his ripcord, just as Big John Fidler had done many months before (an honestly used D ring was a fine souvenir). Unhurt, Hollmeyer then moved to the edge of the cliff and waved to the Corsairs circling overhead. Dave Rankin saw him and radioed ahead to Turtle Bay, then he landed and ran to the dock where MAG-11's crash boat was moored. He jumped aboard with Doc Bookman for the coastal run to Hollmeyer's location.

An hour later Hollmeyer was still where they had left him, for the simple reason that the cliff blocked travel in one direction and impassable jungle blocked it in the other. Hollmeyer was smoking his last cigarette when the sound of an approaching plane reached him. Ledge Hazelwood buzzed overhead in an SBD with Pete Folger in the back-seat. They tried to pitch a note with a first-aid kit, but the packet landed out of Hollmeyer's reach. Then the sound of ringing machetes came from the island side, and presently two grinning natives hacked their way through the growth to the trapped Marine. After much gesturing, and with a little pidgin English and even some French thrown in, they led him back through the brush, wielding their machetes while carrying his parachute and seat pack. To them it was an honor. Two hundred yards later they emerged onto a wagon path, where Hollmeyer's day took a decided turn for the better.

An old Ford pickup driven by an even older Tonkinese bounced down the path to deliver them to the plantation. Hollmeyer was met by its gracious owners, forty-one-year-old Auguste Harbulot, who spoke reasonable English, and his pretty wife, heavy with child. Hollmeyer's Harvard education and interest in things European made him the perfect candidate for such an unexpected visit, and he accepted his hosts' hospitality with poise. Inside the large, opulent one-story masonry villa, he luxuriated in a tiled shower, dried off with scented towels, then changed into clean *planteur* clothing. It proved a bit skimpy on his six-foot-two frame, causing Madame Harbulot to giggle, "*Oooh, mon Dieu, comme il est grand!*"* It was a tonic for Hollmeyer, who years later wrote, "I privately thought she was the most attractive seven-and-a-half-months-pregnant woman ever seen."

The rest of the morning he enjoyed first brandy, then whiskey with his new friends. Monsieur Harbulot, originally from New Caledonia, had established the plantation twenty years before to process copra and plant coffee and cacao. He had contributed to the war effort by assisting with the establishment of an advance radar site, but he was best known among the military brass for his prized coffee.

*He is tall!

A number of admirals and generals on Espiritu routinely sent gifts of American goods.

The crash boat bearing Dave Rankin and Doc Bookman rumbled into the plantation's cove, and the men were welcomed into the big house with another round of drinks. Then the old pickup returned with the Harbulots' foreman, a grizzled old Aberdeen Scot and former sea dog who loved to tell stories. Robbie Robertson had them in stitches with his newest tale, about the native who saw Hollmeyer "walking on air." Soon a Navy tender arrived at the pier with two more doctors—one Army, the other Navy—for a prearranged checkup on Madame Harbulot; a third officer carried ashore a case of beer for her husband. More whiskey was poured, then port, then vermouth.

It was time for lunch. The boat crews enjoyed a buffet on the lawn while a grand spread for the officers was set up in the dining room. Servants brought courses of pâté and fresh-caught fish, millionaire's salad made with hearts of palm, and dessert of papayas and fresh cream. Wineglasses were kept full. After the table was cleared the merriment continued late into the afternoon thanks to rounds of brandy from Doc Bookman's supply.

At last the sailors and Marines bid farewell to the Harbulots and wobbled down to the boats. The breeze from the fast run back had no effect on their inebriation, making Hollmeyer's welcome upon reaching Turtle Bay after dark less than complimentary.

> The lights were on and I could see some of my squadron mates waiting, thinking they would see a charred form swathed in bandages, carried off on a stretcher. Instead I staggered off the gangplank, my arms around Dave Rankin on one side and the Doc on the other, all singing "Three Old Ladies in the Lavatory," or "Roll Your Leg Over," or both. My dear fellow pilots took another look, and walked away muttering disgustedly, "*You*

Hollmeyer . . . go *away*—go back where you came from!"

Hollmeyer's Corsair was the first one lost by the squadron but certainly not the last—not even that day. Less than an hour after his adventure began, ten more Corsairs had launched on an attack problem before conducting a mock strafing of the fighter strip. Lieutenant Thomas M. Tomlinson was starting his run when the engine of his Corsair began running roughly. Pressing on, he came over the strip just as the engine quit. He was flying too fast to set the aircraft down on the strip, and he had no power to make another circuit for an emergency landing. His only option was a water landing just off the beach. After barely making it that far, he encountered an all-too-common difficulty.

It was nearly impossible to settle a Corsair down for a soft water landing. The large propeller and engine-heavy nose invariably plowed under, jerking the plane to a rapid halt with the tail pitched high in the air. Worse, the canopy had a frightening tendency to slam shut from the sudden deceleration. Tommy Tomlinson's ditching was no different. He was further impaired when he banged into the gunsight or instrument panel and sustained minor head injuries. He struggled to jettison the hood and finally managed to kick free as the plane sank. Once more the crash boat went out; it picked him up at about 1040. The squadron had lost two Corsairs in a matter of hours, both to engine failure, a scene that was destined to repeat itself in a few weeks' time.

Two days later and two hundred miles away, a scenario developed that would give some of the pilots a different type of unexpected action. Near Vanikoro Island, in the Santa Cruz group, the seaplane tender *Chincoteague* was mauled by Japanese bombers. Dead in the water, adrift, and pleading for assistance, she endured intermittent attacks until finally taken under tow by the destroyer *Thornton*.

On the afternoon of July 17, the squadron was tagged to

provide air coverage for the stricken tender for the following day, and Bill Pace called a meeting to discuss the situation. Pete Folger and Henry Miller worked late that night with maps and plotting boards to plan strategy, including a pathfinding PV-1 Ventura, then grabbed a few hours' sleep, awoke to shave by moonlight, and started again before three in the morning.

Miller's division was scheduled for takeoff at 0415, but a heavy overcast rolled in, delaying their departure until well past seven. Miller and Ledge Hazelwood took off alone with the Ventura and flew on instruments until they broke out of the overcast. Their uneventful mission began a long day in which twenty-one other pilots, all veterans of the first tour except Tony Eisele, maintained a series of overlapping patrols above the stricken vessel. Were it not for a quirk of nature, the day might have ended just as uneventfully—at least for VMF-214, if not *Chincoteague*.

The final division to depart Buttons late Sunday afternoon was Pace's, with Jack Petit, Dick Sigel, and Mac McCall rounding out the flight. They arrived over *Chincoteague* at 1730, still dead in the water with *Thornton* alongside, and commenced an orbit at nine thousand feet as daylight began to fade. Seen from above, the darkness appeared to rise up, so that in a few minutes the two ships on the surface were shrouded by the evening while the four Corsairs remained in the golden light of sunset. Likewise anything higher than the Marines was relatively easy to see, enabling Jack Petit to call a tallyho on three aircraft approaching from the north at twelve thousand feet. Pace, thinking they were Venturas, decided to lead his flight up for visual confirmation.

To the intruders, actually Mitsubishi G3M Nells, it must have appeared that four Corsairs suddenly burst upward from the darkness. The twin-engine Nells dumped their bombs early, to the delight of *Chincoteague* and *Thornton,* and the surprised Japanese gunners opened fire at the Marines from extreme range—more than a thousand yards.

Ignoring their machine-gun fire, Pace continued to climb while Dick Sigel and Mac McCall split away and maneuvered to catch the bombers between them. The Nells turned to the right and dived, but they were no match for the Corsairs' speed as they plunged into the rising darkness. The Nell on the outside of the turn fell behind, and from fifteen thousand feet Pace selected it as his target for an overhead run. It was just like gunnery practice. He came down on the bomber with a full deflection shot, with just the very tip of its tail in the outside ring of his gunsight, and triggered his guns. Incendiaries found the Nell's fuel tanks and the bomber promptly blew, a spectacular sight in the fading dusk.

Jack Petit rolled in next, selecting the leader of what had once been the vee of three planes, but this target proved more hardy. Petit raked it with a steady stream and was rewarded with a trail of smoke. He reversed, came back for a firing pass from the front quarter, and reversed again for "a roundhouse to the left." With each successive pass, he achieved more hits, though not to the extent he had hammered it the first time. Much to his frustration, the badly wounded Nell reached the haven of a cloud.

At the same time, Sigel and McCall ganged up on the last Japanese bomber, which was losing altitude fast and was barely visible as it dived into the gloom. Sigel poured solid hits into the Nell and drew smoke, but when McCall's turn came there was a problem. It was April 7 all over again, his Irish luck deserting him in the form of his guns this time; only one was working. The whole division had tested guns after taking off, flipping individual gun switches, squeezing the trigger, then turning off the master switch, and his had been working. Now only one gun was popping away and his pass was ineffective. He was chagrined to think that "the guy in the top turret has more guns than I have!"

The other fighters came back around to finish the Nell. Dick Sigel swung in for a beam run, observing no hits but noting that his quarry's guns were silent. No doubt he had hit it hard on his first run, perhaps aided by McCall's lone gun. Finally Bill Pace made a low-side run using the last moments of twilight. He could see that the Nell was smoking, although he was unable to confirm hits in the darkness.

By now it was pitch dark. None of the four Marines had received night fighter training, making further pursuit hazardous. Pace turned on his landing lights for a visual aid and ordered the men to join up. The newly baptized Corsair pilots formed without incident and headed for home, leaving hundreds of jubilant witnesses on two vulnerable warships below.

When they returned to Turtle Bay, Pace and his three grinning lieutenants gave their full account to Pete Folger in the ready tent. The exploded Nell was witnessed by the whole division, simplifying confirmation of Pace's claim. The other two Japanese bombers were smoking when last seen headed into the clouds, so Petit and Sigel were given credit for a probable apiece. After the debriefing they walked to the evening movie to share their tale, satisfied that they had foiled the attack. Ten minutes later the movie was halted for an exciting announcement: *Thornton* had radioed that all three Nells had splashed. It would take about two weeks for official confirmation, but Sigel and Petit had their victories and an even better ending to their story.

The brief, deadly clash over *Chincoteague* and *Thornton* was a fitting conclusion to the squadron's transition into Corsairs. Major Louis B. Robertshaw, ops officer for the air group, informed them that they would return to combat in two days, even though the pilots averaged less than twenty-five hours in Corsairs. They were needed to support the New Georgia campaign now that the ground battle was taking longer than expected. ComAirSols had maintained constant bombing raids and roving air patrols, but strong resistance from the Japanese was slowly taking its toll. VMF-214's sister squadron was an example of the severe attrition. VMF-213 had started its combat tour on Banika weeks earlier with twenty-one pilots, but it now had only eleven active pilots left.

Just as the squadron began packing for its second combat tour, one of the new lieutenants encountered some difficulty. Robert W. McClurg, from New Castle, Pennsylvania, had been struggling to handle the F4U during takeoffs and landings. On the nineteenth, after McClurg ground-looped into an embankment and caused heavy damage to his plane, Pace arranged for a more experienced pilot to replace him. Despite McClurg's disappointment at being left behind, it might have been the best thing that happened. Six weeks later, thanks to the benevolence of another major, he was given a second chance, this time proving himself far more menacing to the enemy.

The pilot who took his place was 1st Lt. Stanley T. Synar, a twenty-five-year-old veteran of two tours with the Wolfpack, VMF-112. Blessed with uncanny vision, the Oklahoma native was rumored to have Cherokee bloodlines. "I didn't have a hell of a lot, if I had any," he admitted, "but they called me 'Eagle Eye' and 'Chief' because my eyesight was so very good. I could spot planes way the hell off."

He could shoot them down, too, having splashed a Val and a Zero during his first tour in Wildcats, then two floatplanes and another Zero while flying Corsairs. Although only by acquisition, VMF-214 had its first ace. His exchange with McClurg took place only a day before they were scheduled to begin their next tour. There was a twenty-four-hour delay before the squadron was finally airborne in three SCAT transports on the morning of July 21. After a brief layover on Cactus, the transports continued to the Russells and landed at the Banika strip by midafternoon. There the squadron's flight and ground echelons were reunited for the first time since March.

In addition to the welcome sight of familiar faces, it was pleasing to find a standard of living unexpected in the forward area. As the smaller of two principal islands in the

Russells (Pavuvu lay across a narrow channel to the west), Banika had been acquired five months earlier without opposition and remained largely undisturbed, its pristine coconut groves spared from violence. Flat and narrow, it was spanned by a white coral strip extending from the channel side completely across the island to the seaward beach. MAG-21 and VMF-214's ground echelon had arrived before the field was completed, then spent the ensuing months outfitting Banika to a degree described as "palatial" in the war diary. The flight echelon was quartered in hard-shell Dallas huts instead of flimsy tents and enjoyed good food in the dining mess (or snacks at Joe's South Pacific Pilot Club, a real hamburger joint). With improved sanitation facilities and preventive measures in place, the threat of malaria was almost a memory.

The Japanese were still pests, however. The Russells were a hundred miles closer to Bougainville's five airfields—particularly dreaded Kahili—and closer still for daring floatplane pilots out of Rekata Bay. Washing Machine Charlie triggered two air-raid warnings that first night. Neither produced anything except interrupted sleep as the pilots ran to their foxholes, but they hinted at what lay ahead. Each of the next six nights brought at least one raid, which caused little damage but impressed the newcomers. Joe Curran, from the small town of Yazoo City, Mississippi, spoke of the raids in a way that succinctly described war's lonely side: "[Washing Machine Charlie] would come over when the moon was full, and at that particular time the moon was very bright. It got our attention, and we were aware that we were a long way from home."

9

THE SWASHBUCKLERS

Chief Synar and Tony Eisele were the only pilots in the squadron with more than twenty-five hours in Corsairs. The others would have to learn fast, because they were handed a combat assignment on their first full day in the Russells. Kahili, the most formidable Japanese airfield on Bougainville, had been targeted for a B-24 strike, with two divisions led by Chief and Dave Rankin accompanying the Liberators on July 22. The Corsairs lifted off from Banika's dazzling white coral surface and joined up over the Russells, located the bombers that flew over from Guadalcanal, then proceeded northwest toward New Georgia and beyond, where they knew the enemy would be waiting.

It was almost a complete reversal from the previous tour, when the Marines had been called upon to defend their own island and occasionally escort comparatively small dive-bomber strikes to Munda or Vila, where they encountered not a single Japanese interceptor. Hitting the big island of Bougainville was a major offensive leap toward an enemy stronghold. In addition to Kahili, two other bases nearby, Kara and Ballale, were capable of adding a hundred or more aircraft. Ballale, situated on a tiny island off Bougainville, bristled like an armed satellite with sharpshooting AA positions, and the Marines had been warned to give it a wide berth. Kahili and Kara were well protected with their own positions, some on nearby hills that made low-level strafing attacks extremely hazardous.

As the formation flew up the Slot with New Georgia on the left and the long island of Choiseul (schwa·ZULE) on the right, the Marines could look down at the stepping-stones that Bull Halsey planned to use for neutralizing Rabaul. Had they enough fuel, Synar and Rankin could have flown straight there with nary a change in heading. The ground battle was raging even then on the first big step, New Georgia. The Allies would have to knock off Bougainville next.

Approaching Kahili with dry mouths, their thoughts to themselves because of strict radio silence, the Corsair pilots saw long plumes of dust rising from the airfield as enemy planes raced into the sky. Somehow, and perhaps just as well for their first mission, the opposing planes never met. But the mission turned fruitful when the Liberators joined a larger strike attacking Japanese shipping just east of Bougainville. Together more than fifty SBDs, TBFs, and B-24s rained bombs on the seaplane tender *Nissin,* which sank in half an hour with her cargo of tanks and troops. VMF-214's divisions returned without incident, reporting intense AA fire.

The next day several divisions conducted the squadron's first patrols over Rendova, joining the protective umbrella that had covered the embattled islands during daylight hours for more than three weeks. Throughout the rest of July, assignments came at a furious pace, especially for the pilots who remembered the long, dull days on Guadalcanal. During favorable weather, one and sometimes two strike missions against well-defended Japanese strongholds were scheduled each day in addition to regular patrols over Rendova and Munda.

As of July 23 the squadron no longer had enlisted pilots on the roster. Technical Sergeants Al Jensen and Bill Blakeslee received their field commissions to second lieutenant, based on recommendations forwarded by George Britt before his departure, but the promotions were secondary to their capabilities as pilots. This was particularly true of Jensen, already considered one of their best, who more than justified his reputation as the combat tour unfolded.

The squadron had acquired seventeen F4U-1s, enough to schedule four divisions on duty and three off every day, but the tempo of combat operations began taking its toll on the inventory. Despite the efforts of the competent mechanics, it was difficult to keep the overworked F4Us going. The first significant problems occurred on July 26, when divisions led by Miller, Burnett, and Synar escorted another B-24 strike to Kahili. Of the twelve Corsairs plus a spare that launched, only six lasted the whole trip. The rest turned back before reaching Kahili due to engines cutting out or blowers failing at altitude. Two could not even make it back to Banika and landed instead at Segi, an emergency strip on the southern end of New Georgia completed just two weeks before.

Those who continued witnessed problems among the other Corsairs participating in the strike, including some from VMF-215. Henry Miller saw one hurtle by in a vertical dive just west of Vella Lavella, its pilot an apparent victim of hypoxia. Then Vince Carpenter had a surprise encounter on the return trip from Kahili, after the remnants of his division joined with several Corsairs from VMF-215. They were at sixteen thousand feet, weaving above the formation of Liberators as they headed home to their base on Guadalcanal, when a Corsair beside Carpenter suddenly burst into flames. A Zero had sneaked up behind the unsuspecting Marine and exploded him without warning. Shouting an alarm on the radio, Carpenter instinctively wheeled around to give chase, followed by a VMF-215 wingman.

After heading toward Kahili for a few minutes, Carpenter sensed they were being followed. He remembered the oft-repeated warnings about chasing Zeros and thought, I'll bet this is one of those famous traps. Sure enough, three Zeros were high above, "waggling their wings like mad" as the pilots tried to look down and spot the lone Corsairs.

The Japanese had apparently been forewarned but could not see the blue-camouflaged F4Us.

Carpenter took the offensive and pulled up in a vertical climb, firing at one of the Zeros as he rose. His airspeed began to bleed off rapidly and he reversed direction, unable to determine whether his shots were effective.

> I didn't want to get into a stall, have these guys see me and do a wingover and nail me, so I flipped over and was diving right for the deck to scoot home. I thought I better look behind and see what was happening, and there was a Zero—right on my tail and shooting like mad.

Carpenter and his wingman managed to use their superior speed to escape without significant damage, having learned the hard way to heed the warnings.

Poor weather precluded all flying the next day. To pass the time, a punching bag and a Ping-Pong table were erected near the ready tent. At about the same time, initial drawings of the new squadron insignia were shown, and the pilots welcomed a bold theme from Harry Hollmeyer. The Horse had linked the idea of Corsairs and swashbucklers from pirate days of old to create a skull-and-crossbones design, using the bent wings of a banking Corsair to form the cross. A skull replaced the F4U's cowling to "scare the hell out of Jap pilots." A longtime aviation buff, Hollmeyer knew that Royal Air Force squadrons favored Latin mottos, and the Marines had *Semper Fidelis*. He made his squadron's motto *Semper Vincere:* always to conquer. Thus in the waning days of July, the Marines of VMF-214 proudly tried on their new name—the Swashbucklers.

After Vince Carpenter's encounter on July 26, there was no more shooting for the rest of the month. The only other opportunity developed on the thirtieth, when seven Zeros followed Pace's and Burnett's divisions from Kahili to

Rendova after a B-24 strike, but the Japanese stayed out of range. This time the Marines refused the bait.

Sometime during the last days of July—the exact date is guesswork—Pete Folger's injured leg forced him back into the field hospital. The wound had never healed properly, and after weeks of festering in the tropical climate the infection had gone clear to the bone. Pete was in and out of sick bay throughout the early days of August, but eventually the situation turned life-threatening and he was evacuated to Lion One, the big naval hospital on Espiritu Santo. A major operation to scrape the infected bone and weeks of recuperation finally put Folger back on his feet, but the coffee man's service with the Swashbucklers was finished.

To compensate for Folger's loss, the squadron welcomed a familiar face back into the fold on the last day of the month. Charlie Lanphier rejoined his squadron mates, having completed a temporary ground assignment that had carried him as far as Rendova. He enthralled his friends with tales of neurosis and self-inflicted wounds among the ground troops, who had encountered vicious fighting on Munda under gruesome conditions. In turn, he learned that VMF-214's participation in the New Georgia campaign had been relatively benign thus far.

As July gave way to August the situation changed. On the first of the month, Dave Rankin and Vince Carpenter took their divisions back to Kahili to cover a dozen SBDs and the same number of TBFs. The bombers struck with precision, hitting four out of five Japanese ships anchored off the end of the airfield in the face of intense AA fire. During their egress several Zeros again shadowed the formation, trying to lure away the fighters, but the Marines stayed close to the bombers. Just past the Shortland Islands, however, an emboldened Japanese pilot suddenly dived from above and opened fire before flitting away. Rankin's plane took a 20mm explosive round in the engine that knocked out the blower section, but he was able to reach Banika safely.

That the enemy pilot singled out Rankin was probably not coincidental, for Rankin was flying Pace's ship that day with a large number one painted on each side of the fuselage. Though it was not particularly troubling for Rankin, that single hit created a chain of events that would one day prove far more devastating.

Meanwhile another pilot encountered trouble on the way back from Kahili. Jim Taylor, leading the second section behind Vince Carpenter, was already low on gas when his engine began acting up. For a pilot with mechanical trouble over water, discretion meant finding the nearest suitable field, and he opted for Segi even though it had a notoriously short runway. "Being more than a little bit nervous, I landed much too hot," he recalled, "and I just ran out of runway." The Corsair went over on its back at the end of the strip, but Taylor was able to scramble out, helped by several infantrymen. After catching a ride to the Russells, he returned to duty the next day, unhurt and a little wiser.

Three days later the squadron got into its first large-scale scrap since early April. It was a confusing battle involving cases of mistaken identity between Japanese *Ki*-61 Tonys and New Zealand P-40s. The set-to began on Wednesday morning, August 4, after sixteen Corsairs from VMF-124 first strafed the Shortland-Faisi area with eight Swashbucklers providing top cover as they hightailed for home. Smiley Burnett and Chief Synar had their divisions aloft to do the job, making the rendezvous over Rendova, when four of VMF-124's Corsairs began to lag behind—one with engine trouble. The Chief's division shifted with them toward the island of Kolombangara. They were at six thousand feet when a ground radar controller, call sign Saturn, spotted bogeys on the screen and gave the Swashbucklers a vector. Served well by his acute vision, Synar saw the incoming planes first and initiated a climbing turn to intercept them over Munda.

Without warning, an enemy plane came out of a cloud on Synar's right. Unlike some of the earlier encounters, this Japanese pilot was aggressive. He dived at Chief and then reversed to come up from underneath and splatter the Corsair with bullets. At least one round entered the cockpit and struck the wing fold handle, sending fragments into Synar's thigh and buttocks. A second plane swooped in behind.

Synar's wingman was Bob Hanson, on his first-ever combat mission. The young wrestler was quick to react when he saw the two enemy fighters jump Synar; crossing over he drew a bead on the first one. Much to Synar's relief, Hanson "shot his ass off." Chief was forced to break off from the fight, bleeding and uncertain about the severity of his wound, to land at Segi for treatment. Hanson did not escape unscathed. A couple of Japanese fighters got behind him and shot his Corsair in the right wing as he turned to climb above Blanche Channel. One 20mm round exploded between the guns, another knocked a sizable chunk from the outer flap, and a third, along with several 7.7mm bullets, holed the right stabilizer.

Synar's second section got involved at about the same time as Bennie O'Dell and Chalky Cavanagh climbed to fourteen thousand feet after Saturn advised them of a dogfight over Rendova. The two Marines thought they saw a flight of P-40s, then realized it was nine or ten Zeros making a run on P-40s below. O'Dell nosed over and opened fire first, satisfied to see pieces flying off a Zero as it went down. Cavanagh stayed on his wing as both Corsairs pulled up and fired at another Zero. He saw his rounds connecting with the Zero—it turned away belching smoke—but it could be counted only as a probable.

After becoming separated from O'Dell, Cavanagh joined several P-40s circling Rendova for a few quiet minutes, then decided to head northeast to look for Corsairs instead. He located what he thought were two Kittyhawks and made a nearly fatal mistake by giving them the join-up signal, dipping his nose down, then up. The two fighters, actually *Ki*-61s, were only too happy to oblige. Cavanagh saw tracers flashing past his canopy as the fighters maneuvered behind him and opened fire. "Hell, this is stupid," he said to himself, and he shoved the stick forward to dive away.

Smiley Burnett's division had also become separated near Kolombangara. Charlie Lanphier, with Al Jensen on his wing, circled back over the Kula Gulf when the first bogey report came over the radio, then headed toward Munda at 27,000 feet. When they sighted nearly a dozen Zeros below them, the Marines rolled over and pounced on the last vee. Lanphier drilled one just behind the wing root and it promptly went down. Jensen hit another but could not witness its demise, thus getting credit for a probable. Both Marines, low on gas, landed at Segi to refuel before continuing to the Russells.

The last two players were Smiley Burnett and his wingman, Vic Scarborough. They climbed extremely high—34,000 feet—and circled over the Kula Gulf looking for bogeys that were expected to come from Kolombangara. The Marines became separated and Scarborough missed the action altogether, but Burnett sighted half a dozen Zeros 9,000 feet below and gamely plunged into them. For all his faults, lack of courage was not one. Luck was not his either. When he squeezed the trigger nothing happened; his guns had frozen. He leveled off and headed for Rendova, listening to plenty of bogey calls on the radio, but remaining out of the fight.

When the pilots landed, their new ACIO, Capt. Donald Hatch, did his best to sort out the details of the engagement. The fighter that Hanson shot down was listed as a Zero in the action report, but it had passed extremely close to Synar, who "was able to see clearly the white spinner and the in-line engine with the rows of exhaust stacks on each side." The rookie had undoubtedly splashed a Tony, his first enemy plane in what would ultimately become an unbeatable record. The Japanese fighters, with an inverted V-12 in-line engine, closely resembled the New Zealand P-40s, especially when flashing past on opposite headings at combined speeds exceeding seven hundred knots. The 68th and 78th Sentais of the Japanese Army Air Force (JAAF) did operate Tonys in the region until August 1943, but until now the Swashbucklers had never encountered them.

Doubts about aircraft identification raised the specter of friendly fire. One observation in the war diary strongly supports the notion that the Swashbucklers encountered both Japanese and Kiwi look-alikes, perhaps even shooting at the wrong ones: "The Nips have painted their 0's [*sic*] with the P-40 markings—white spinner, lines on wings, stabilizer and rudder. We'll still shoot 'em down!" Ironically RNZAF Kittyhawk markings were developed expressly to prevent confusion between their P-40s and the Japanese *Ki*-61s. Propeller cones and vertical stabilizers were white, with bold diagonal white stripes on the wings and fuselage. Fortunately (for the Kiwis), no P-40s were shot down this day.

In any case, the Swashbucklers were not particularly concerned with mistaken identity. They had met the enemy again, caused him harm, and could revel in the fact that the fight ended favorably. At the cost of a few bullet holes, they claimed a Tony and two Zeros, with two more Zeros counted as probables. Chief Synar's injuries proved relatively minor, and after a quick patching at Segi's field hospital he returned to the Russells in a J2F. At Banika, three Japanese flags were added to the prop blades jammed into the coral near the squadron's ready tent. Including the night skirmish over the beleaguered *Chincoteague,* the squadron's score now stood at sixteen confirmed planes. The pilots themselves had barely been scratched, and not even the sight of the sleek *Ki*-61s could dampen their confidence.

A few days was all it took for their fortune to begin shifting. Munda fell on August 5, but the Japanese did not readily concede the skies overhead, and the aerial contest became hotter than anything the squadron had previously experienced. There had been only one scrap during the entire first tour, but now scrambles and dogfights occurred on almost a daily basis. The lopsided victories could not last.

On the sixth, Smiley Burnett and Vince Carpenter launched their divisions to escort a P-38 photo plane (F-5A) while it overflew the Shortlands accompanied by eight Fighting Falcons from VMF-221. The strike hugged the waves no more than fifty to two hundred feet above the surface, then over the Treasuries the F-5A made a half circle before racing at high speed for its run over the Shortlands. It was all Burnett and the others could do to keep up, and the Marines began to string behind as they cut flat out across Morgusaisai Island and Kulitanai Bay.

Suddenly they ran into a sky full of opposition. From a base along the shoreline, several floatplanes were in the process of taking off while others were already in the air, waiting. Some were Rufes—floatplane versions of the A6M and surprisingly nimble despite their seagoing appendages; others were two-seater Jakes. At least a dozen Zeros, likely from nearly Ballale, were circling several thousand feet above with tremendous tactical advantage.

Formation integrity unraveled as the marines separated to fend for themselves. A Jake came at the Corsairs from the right, and Al Jensen swung out to fire a burst from five hundred yards. Smiley Burnett, slightly above, also turned and fired a long burst from head-on. The Jake exploded and plunged into the water, leaving a column of black smoke to mark its impact just offshore from the jungle.

Vic Scarborough, flying on Burnett's left wing, spied a floatplane ahead that had just lifted from the water. It was barely above the trees when the North Carolinian caught it with a steady stream of bullets. He watched it "crack into the trees at the edge of the shore and burn." He was so close to the wreckage that he could see the rear gunner struggling to get out. Then Scarborough swung around to the south with Burnett as intense antiaircraft fire from the nearby base burst all around them. Zeros were still above and it was getting plenty hot. Because the F-5A was already heading for home, the two Marines followed.

Leading Burnett's second section, Al Jensen had his hands full. He got in a nondeflection burst at a Jake that had just taken off and was boldly turning into the streaking Corsairs. His heavy slugs hammered the engine and cockpit, and the Jake dropped back toward the trees, where it crashed and burned. Next he opened fire briefly from long range on another floatplane that was already being chased by other Corsairs, then flipped around in a split–S. Pouring on the coal to catch Burnett, he saw a Zero coming down on the tail of an F4U, and he reefed his machine around in a sharp, climbing turn. Triggering his guns with thirty degrees of deflection, Jensen watched the enemy fighter hit the water.

Suddenly a Zero came down on his tail, and he dived back toward the water to shake the enemy plane. Two more Zeros turned in when he started to climb again, so he took a snap shot at one and kept going. Coming around Morgusaisai and turning south toward home, he spied two or three Zeros hassling with Corsairs. He pulled up into them and raked a Zero from the wing root to the tail at full deflection until several of his guns jammed. This plane also fell flaming into the sea, his third kill of the day for the ex–enlisted pilot. With two knocked down on April 7, Jensen had just made the exclusive list of Marine Corps aces, making him the first to achieve that status while flying with VMF-214.

In all, three Swashbucklers in the first division had accounted for five planes without receiving so much as a bullet hole in return, but in Vince Carpenter's division the situation was far less favorable. Big John Fidler and Bill Blakeslee were trailing on the outside of the formation as it swept over the Shortlands, then turned sharply to the south. Momentum carried them like a cracked whip toward the waiting Japanese.

As several Zeros pounced from above, Fidler heard the

terrible noise of bullets striking his Corsair and flying turned into self-preservation.

> I went right down to the deck and flew as close to the ocean as I could get. I was flying as fast as I could go, but didn't know how to get away from them. They were just sitting up there, taking potshots at us.

Fidler's plane had already been holed several times when he hit on a novel idea. Kicking full rudder but holding the stick level, he sent his Corsair into a sideways skid. The Japanese, trying to aim in front, missed because his plane was crabbing in a different direction. Their rounds splashed harmlessly off to the side, and as they drew away from their own base they finally gave up.

When Fidler was convinced it was safe, he climbed to get his bearings. Bill Blakeslee was nowhere to be seen, nor was anyone else for that matter, friendly or otherwise. Worse, one or more bullets had come through the right side of Fidler's cockpit into the electrical panel, knocking out his compass and fuel gauge. It was high noon and the sun was straight overhead, yielding no clue as to which direction was east or west. Fidler reasoned that he was somewhere south of the Treasuries, but without a compass he could not tell which way was southeast toward home.

He had still more innovative ideas up his sleeve, however, and loosened his harness to reach behind his back and open the jungle pack attached to his parachute. Worming around blindly with one hand, he located the survival kit and dug out the waterproof match case with its little magnetic compass in the cap. As he banked the Corsair in a circle, the tiny needle turned in its case and held steady on magnetic north; the ten-cent device worked. Fidler could now point himself southeast, and before long the New Georgia islands hove into view. From there getting home was a piece of cake.

Bill Blakeslee never did come back. No one had seen or

heard from the newly commissioned lieutenant, who as tail-end Charlie would have been easy pickings for the swarming Zeros. Big John was the last one back, his relief at escaping tempered by the bitterness of losing a wingman. He knew he had been extremely fortunate to get back with nothing worse than some holes in his plane. "I went to the Doc and he gave me a big belt of brandy. I unwound after a while, but that was really a bad, bad experience."

Because no one had seen Blakeslee go down, he was listed as missing in action. Unlike the defensive air war over Guadalcanal, where a downed aviator could be rescued and return to fight again (as was the case with Smiley Burnett on April 7), the fights were now taking place over enemy territory or the waters in between. Not knowing whether Blakeslee had been killed outright, had bailed out and was adrift in his raft, or had possibly been captured, the squadron remained hopeful. "It is assumed that he made a forced landing . . . and will show up shortly," one wrote.

August 6 was also a costly day operationally. Tony Eisele was asked to test-fly one of two F4Us that had received a new engine. It had been overheating at thirty thousand feet and the mechanics could find nothing wrong, so the civilian technical representative from Pratt & Whitney wanted it flown again, to an even higher altitude, while the pilot jotted down various instrument readings on his knee board.

Eisele took off that afternoon and climbed to thirty thousand feet, where the cylinder head temperature soon redlined. Following instructions he continued to climb, but smoke suddenly billowed out of the engine and the plane began to shake violently. The Pratt & Whitney was done for, and Eisele slid back the hood to get out. The blast of frigid air reminded him of an article he had read about the dangers of bailing out above thirty thousand feet. A pilot swinging in his parachute could die before reaching oxygen-rich air, and if he delayed opening his chute he might pass out before reaching a safe altitude and never pull the D ring.

Eisele sat back down and kept his oxygen mask on while descending to twenty thousand feet, where the engine, propeller, and smoke stopped abruptly. With the engine frozen and the propeller not windmilling, his rate of descent increased, but he thought he could glide to the field and save the airplane. As he descended through five thousand feet he lowered the flaps and landing gear and turned into the wind toward Banika, but realized that the headwind was too strong.

Now a water landing was inevitable. He doubted there was enough hydraulic pressure to raise the wheels, but he placed the gear handle in the up position anyway and chose a likely landing spot just offshore. Then a new concern cropped up. The first Marine to make a water landing in an F4U was Ken Walsh, Eisele's former tent mate at Espiritu Santo, who had experienced great difficulty getting out of his sinking plane. The hood had slammed shut when the plane struck the water, and Walsh barely escaped by using a large knife to chop through the Plexiglas as the Corsair sank. Eisele knew of two less fortunate pilots who had drowned, and he did not intend to become the third. Just before hitting the water, he grabbed the corners of the windscreen with both hands and jammed his elbows against the sliding hood. The canopy indeed released, but his trick worked and he suffered only bruises above both elbows. Before the plane came to a halt, he released the safety harness so that when the long nose dug in he was thrown clear of the cockpit.

Swimming back to the Corsair, Eisele made a decision that might have been ill advised but showed his dedication.

> I grabbed the tail of the plane and worked my way to the cockpit as the plane went under. I wanted to recover my knee pad as I had kept notes of all the instrument readings on the way up and down. Although I was near shore, it began to get dark and I felt the pressure building,

so I swam back up and got in my life raft. I later learned that the water was over 100' deep there.

A crash boat was soon on the scene to take Eisele back to the fighter strip, where Bill Pace met him with a towel and a dry flight suit. He wanted to hear the details, for his own plane would be ready to test the following day. Although Eisele's knee pad had gone down with the plane, he remembered most of the engine readings and passed them along to Henry Miller and the engineering section.

The next day, Pace's Corsair number one was ready for a test of its new engine, replaced after a 20mm shell had knocked out the blower section five days earlier. The skipper took it up at 1030 and conducted a normal test procedure for approximately an hour before the engine failed. He was observed descending rapidly from high altitude, perhaps attempting a dead-stick landing at Banika, just as Eisele had tried less than eighteen hours before. But Pace wasn't going to make the field either; a Douglas R4D occupied the strip.

Some thought Pace saw the transport and deliberately tried to avoid it; others guessed that he misjudged his rate of descent. In any case, he was coming in short of the strip as his silent Corsair descended toward the water just offshore. At the last moment, he apparently changed his mind about ditching, released his harness, and stood up in the cockpit. Whether he jumped first or pulled the ripcord in an attempt to let the parachute pull him out of the plane is uncertain, but he left the Corsair at only a hundred feet above the water. It was simply too low for his chute to open. The F4U careened into three feet of water with a huge shower of spray and coral at about the same time that Pace struck the surface of the channel. Two men manning an antiaircraft gun swam out and supported him until the crash boat arrived, but there was nothing to be done. At his speed and trajectory, the water might as well have been concrete, and he had died instantly.

Fortune had smiled upon VMF-214 for months, but in a span of barely twenty-four hours the skipper was dead, another pilot was missing in action, and three valuable planes were lost. Pace's body was held for burial the next day while pieces of his F4U, some of which had wound up on the beach just a hundred feet short of the strip, were collected for engineers to analyze. Henry Miller suspected that the engine failed for the same reason as Eisele's—breakdown of the number thirteen cylinder due to overheating. His hunch was confirmed when Pace's engine was found to have a broken master rod and some broken articulator rods.

At 1400 on the afternoon of August 8, the remains of Maj. William H. Pace were buried with full military honors in Banika cemetery number one; a bent propeller blade salvaged from the wreck served as his marker. The funeral was "simple, sincere, and nicely carried out."

Forty minutes later, four Swashbucklers took off to escort B-25s on a search for enemy shipping around Rendova and Kolombangara. Henry Miller, Ledge Hazelwood, OK Williams, and Ovis Hunter joined forces with twelve Fighting Falcons of VMF-221. When the search turned up nothing of interest, Miller led his and one other division on an impromptu strafing run to Rekata Bay. Pumping eighteen hundred bullets from his own plane, Miller and the others thoroughly shot up a fuel and ammo dump, reported later by a coastwatcher as "burning like hell."

Miller flew again the next morning, leading twelve Swashbucklers as high cover for a B-24 strike intended for Kahili. They hit Vila instead when the primary target was obscured by weather, but in a repeat of the July 26 debacle only a handful of Corsairs completed the mission. Again it was engine trouble that forced five of the lieutenants to return early. One optimistically advised that the "engine offers many complex difficulties," but the Pratt & Whitney people and Marine mechanics scratched their heads in frustration.

Following Pace's death, Miller quietly became the new executive officer of the squadron. Unlikely as it seemed,

Smiley Burnett was appointed commanding officer, an advance that did not sit well with some. The smallish Burnett was not outwardly disliked—his personality and behavior on the ground were acceptable enough, and with two enemy planes to his credit his gunnery skills and bravery were not in dispute—but he had never gained his fellow pilots' confidence. So low was their regard that one pilot suggested (to Henry Miller) that Burnett should no longer lead his own division. "Part of the afternoon I spent trying to straighten out Carl Dunbar on his idea about Smiley flying wing on Carpenter," Miller wrote. No doubt others felt the same way, but Miller knew the value of squadron integrity, which would cease to exist unless Burnett were a leader in the air as well as on the ground.

The rumblings represented the beginning of a difficult spell that permanently affected the Swashbucklers' morale. Their enthusiasm and bonhomie of old had been irrevocably altered by misfortune, mechanical troubles, and unwanted personnel changes. In a broader scope, it looked as though the air war would remain grim for some time, now that much of the aerial fighting was taking place over enemy territory. The Japanese seemed to have an inexhaustible supply of planes.

Munda's fall on August 5 meant the Allies had another airfield available, and Seabees moved in to make improvements even before the far end of the strip was secured. Marine aviators put it to good use after Brig. Gen. Francis P. Mulcahy, ComAirNewGeorgia, set up camp. VMF-123 and -124 were operating from the improved strip by August 14. Just one day later, three divisions of Swashbucklers led by their new commanding officer took off from Banika and landed at Munda, gassed their planes, and took off again for a two-hour patrol.*

*A Presidential Unit Citation later awarded to VMF-214 erroneously credited them with being the first to operate from Munda.

They found conditions on the ground appalling. In some ways, the push through the New Georgia jungle had been even more vicious than that on Guadalcanal. The Japanese had defended it fiercely from reinforced coconut-log pillboxes "dug in like so many chiggers," and the surrounding vegetation had been blasted by many tons of bombs and artillery. Unlike the Russells' picturesque scenes, Munda offered only ugly devastation—ground-up earth, denuded trees, unburied enemy bodies. And the island was not secure. Although a perimeter of ground Marines defended the airfield, Japanese troops still occupied the high ground and kept the strip under sporadic artillery fire. Dubbed "Pistol Pete" and "Millimeter Mike," the guns lobbed shells onto the strip and camp area during the day. Washing Machine Charlie took over by night.

August 15 was also the day of amphibious landings on Vella Lavella, the next hop up the island chain. (Bull Halsey had decided to bypass Kolombangara with its ten thousand Japanese troops; cut off, they would be left to rot on the vine.) The Swashbucklers were tasked with guarding Munda while the other two squadrons covered the landings. VMF-123 and -124 had a big day over the Barakoma beachhead on Vella Lavella, where the Japanese sent raid after raid from Kahili, only ninety miles away. In sharp contrast it was quiet above Munda, just half that distance from Vella Lavella.

After the patrol, Smiley Burnett and two others flew their planes back to the Russells. Four lieutenants rode back on a SCAT transport, having left their planes behind as spares. Lieutenants Carpenter, Scarborough, Lanphier, Jensen, and Paul A. Knipping spent the next few days on Munda, where the living conditions were the worst the squadron had yet encountered. Only the crudest improvements had been completed since the field was activated, making for a couple of miserable nights.

Back on the Russells it was a better day for eight other Swashbucklers. Henry Miller was supposed to have the day off, but in the morning George Britt, now the ops officer of MAG-21, sent him to Guadalcanal to represent the air group's fighter pilots in a planning conference. After the meeting, several high-ranking officers asked Miller's opinion about a strafing attack on Kahili using Corsairs, then sent the former attorney back to Banika with the go-ahead to make it happen. As soon as he landed, Miller got together with Pete Folger (who was just back from the hospital) and Don Hatch to work out the details. At 1500 they called the rest of Miller's division and Dave Rankin's pilots into the ready tent to brief the spontaneous mission—a dusk strafing of the vaunted Japanese field. To ensure complete surprise, the pilots were ordered to hold their fire until there was no recourse. After that, Miller told them, "go ahead and shoot your heart out."

Borrowing a page from John Condon's planning of the Yamamoto intercept back in April, Miller designed a circuitous route to avoid detection. Ten Corsairs roared down Banika's strip at 1636 and set a course across the Slot toward the big island of Choiseul. Two F4Us were spares; when Harry Hollmeyer dropped out with a failing fuel pump, Scrappy Deetz slid into his place. After a hundred miles with no further aborts, Joe Curran reversed course and flew back to Banika.

The remaining eight strike Corsairs continued at just a hundred feet, flying northwest until they reached a prescribed turning point more than 230 miles from Banika, then turned left and flew southeast toward Bougainville—a direction entirely unexpected by the Japanese. With the setting sun behind their right shoulders, the Marines purged wing tanks and accelerated to 210 knots as they raced toward Kahili, dropping to wave-top height and forming into a line abreast when they neared the coast. Jim Taylor noticed that his altimeter was reading many feet below sea level, due no doubt to a change in barometric pressure, but knowing that the instrument reading was false did not help his adrenaline-charged nerves.

The Marines blasted across the beach so low they had to pull up to clear the palms, then alternately dipped and bobbed as they hugged the contours of the hills en route to Kahili. Cresting the last rise, they spied the field to their left and made a slight correction, then found an unexpected bonus. Above the strip more than twenty Vals and Zeros circled in the landing pattern, ripe and defenseless after their return from a strike against the Barakoma beachhead.

Henry Miller noted the time, incredibly just a minute and a half off his estimated time of arrival, as the Corsairs bore down on unsuspecting targets. Following his edict, the Marines held their fire until Ledge Hazelwood reportedly squeezed first. Within an instant, forty-eight heavy machine guns began cutting a half-mile-wide swath through enemy planes and the airfield below.

Dave Rankin lined up on two aircraft being refueled on the ground, each connected to a gas truck and surrounded by personnel. He "caught them all square," then looked up to find himself on a collision course with the control tower. Jinking to avoid it, he was close enough to glimpse a big black and white clock as he roared past. "No," he reported, "I couldn't tell what time it was."

Lieutenant Edwin J. Hernan, Jr., was nearly involved in a collision, too, so close to hitting two Zeros that he later said, "If I ever see those two pilots I'll recognize them." He didn't get any shots into them, but he did destroy another fighter on the ground.

Tommy Tomlinson caught a Zero in his line of fire and sent it curving off into the trees, smoking. It was recorded first as a probable, then later upgraded to a victory. Jim Taylor and Ovis Hunter each found a slow, fixed-gear Val in their gunsights and made short work of both. Hunter's Val had only enough altitude to roll over and plunge to earth on its back. Taylor held in the trigger and destroyed another plane on the ground.

Henry Miller, for all his planning, did not find such rewarding targets in his sights. Cutting diagonally across the end of the strip, he sprayed an area where a fuel dump was thought to exist but was disappointed when it didn't explode. Continuing flat out, he spotted a beached cargo vessel showing signs of life and gave it a good burst.

The Japanese had been caught so entirely flat-footed that none of the Marines saw a single tracer round of return fire. Throttles to the stops, all eight Corsairs crossed back over the beach and dropped to the wave tops as they raced away to the southwest. Twenty miles farther they slowed and regrouped, then turned east for the flight home. Miller's immaculate planning was reaffirmed when they landed at Banika—three minutes behind his ETA.

In their rapid pass over Kahili, the Marines had fired their guns for only about ten seconds each (a check of the ammo canisters revealed that an average of 800 rounds had been expended). Miller used another 400 shooting at the beached vessel, meaning that a total of 6,500 slugs had torn through personnel, equipment, and airplanes. Intelligence officer Don Hatch described VMF-214's strafing of Kahili as "the first attempt at such a mission," but twenty-one F4Us preceding a B-24 bombing strike on July 26 had earlier sprayed the field with more than a hundred guns. However, the Swashbucklers' raid was likely the first time Corsairs hit Kahili in a dedicated strafing, planned as an independent mission from start to finish. It had gone without a hitch, remarkable considering the brevity with which the whole affair was conducted. From speculation to planning to execution, the mission had been accomplished in just a few hours. Even better, the victory props in front of the ready tent now boasted three new Japanese flags.

Over the next seven days the squadron had no further encounters with Japanese aircraft, but it was a busy week all the same. For starters, the ground echelon pulled out of the Russells and retired to Espiritu Santo, an evolution that took five days beginning on August 16. The enlisted troops, having serviced fighters in the forward area for five months, more than deserved a rest. Within a few days

VMF-214's aviators became acquainted with the replacement ground crew supplied by VMF-215, but the changeover hardly merited their attention. The pilots were plenty busy themselves, conducting patrols and escorts from Banika and the hellhole called Munda.

An unusual administrative event occurred on August 19 when VMF-214's control was transferred from MAG-21 on Banika to MAG-11, hundreds of miles away on Espiritu Santo. The Swashbucklers had completed only four weeks of the anticipated six-week combat tour, making their exchange to MAG-11 premature. The veteran pilots in particular felt that they were losing an old friend, having been in Col. Ray Hopper's air group since Ewa. Hopper likewise had a soft spot for VMF-214. He was a regular fixture at their evening parties, especially when the quartet performed.

Down on Buttons, a relatively unknown lieutenant colonel named Joe A. Smoak commanded MAG-11. A dive-bomber pilot who had been George Britt's division leader in an SBD squadron a few years earlier, Smoak was described as "a capable pilot, about six feet tall and a little portly." He was a no-nonsense graduate of the Naval Academy known for maintaining a meticulous appearance, particular to a fault. Leading strictly by the book, he expected the same of others and demanded that his officers should exhibit appropriate behavior. He did not suffer fools, a trait that would clash with another Marine's opposite polarity in a few weeks.

Meanwhile, a few divisions at a time, more Swashbucklers rotated through Munda for temporary duty. Miller landed with three divisions on the morning of August 17, followed by Chief Synar's division the next day. They flew several patrols of no consequence during their brief stay and had time to explore the war-ravaged area, feel the tension of incoming artillery. The Japanese gunners were more than pesky. Pistol Pete dropped a round that missed Tommy Tomlinson and the revetment he was standing in by just a few yards; shrapnel splattered the revetment walls and grazed two blades of his Corsair's propeller. During the previous evening, some soldiers waiting to eat were not so lucky. "Nips were lobbing shells in from Arundel [Island]. Everyone left camp as a few were killed while standing in chow line," wrote Dave Rankin, who spent a sleepless night.

In some ways, Munda's utter lack of organization was more troubling than the Japanese. The visiting pilots had to scrounge for everything, including a place to sleep. Some huddled under the ready tent near the strip. Decaying bodies of Japanese soldiers lay unburied, scattered among the debris.

Fortunately the Swashbucklers' stay proved a short one. By late afternoon on August 18, all had boarded SCATs or flew F4Us to Banika, some bearing souvenirs collected from the battlefield. Fed up with Munda's dismal conditions, those who thought they were escaping soon learned otherwise: within two days Dave Rankin, Jim Taylor, and Ed Hernan were sick with dysentery.

One notable mission was launched from the Russells on August 20. Two divisions were tasked with strafing Rekata Bay, where they sprayed several wrecked planes on the beach and some freshly painted aircraft farther inland, but as one Marine reported, "Those lousy Nips had rigged up about 16 dummy floatplanes." The risky low-level attack was all for naught.

Early the next day, ten Swashbucklers headed back to Munda. As soon as they arrived and refueled, Miller's and Eisele's divisions hurried aloft to join a division led by Maj. Robert G. Owens of VMF-215, the Fighting Corsairs. Operations were still snafued at Munda and no one gave them the radio frequency for Barakoma's fighter director, so the Marines missed a potential contact when the Japanese sent a raid over Vella Lavella that morning. Miller's division accompanied Owens on another patrol, launching at 1345. Once again the radio frequencies were fouled up although

Miller could receive the fighter director on a ship below them, who in turn relayed information between Barakoma and the fighters.

Thirty minutes after departure they received word of bogeys approaching the Barakoma beachhead. The early warning radar, handicapped by large blind spots from the surrounding hills, was unable to relay the enemy's altitude. Despite several glimpses of incoming aircraft, the Marines could not make the intercept before the Japanese struck. Several near misses chewed the shallow water around four LSTs drawn up on the beach while Bob Owens led the Corsairs in hot pursuit of the withdrawing attackers. He had chased them approximately twenty miles beyond Vella Lavella when an unfavorable setup developed—a pack of Zeros was descending from above—and Owens turned for home. The Swashbucklers, suddenly the quarry, also wheeled around. Before turning, David Moak managed to get a long burst into a Zeke, with no observed results. Another Zeke sneaked up behind Tommy Tomlinson.* Joe Curran turned toward the Japanese fighter, feigning attack to drive it off Tomlinson's tail. The Swashbucklers returned to Munda without further contact and pancaked to receive good news. A coastwatcher reported an enemy plane down in flames west of Munda; Moak was the only one known to have pulled the trigger, he was given credit. The 201 Kokutai did lose one pilot on August 21.

When bad weather prevailed for the next two days, promotions and health matters dominated the brief entries in the squadron diary. On August 22, just a few months after receiving his field commission, former enlisted pilot James Taylor was advanced to first lieutenant, followed by Smiley Burnett's promotion to major the next day. Pete Folger

*This was the first time that VMF-214's war diary reflected the Allied identification for the A6M. An incorrect reference to a Zeke was made in the action report of August 4, 1943, in describing the squadron's first encounter with a *Ki*-61 Tony.

was evacuated again to the hospital on Espiritu, hoping to get his leg healed in time for another visit to Sydney. Three pilots were grounded with dysentery, Munda's unsanitary conditions likely the culprit, and Ledge Hazelwood came down with malaria, which got everyone taking their Atabrine. But the mosquitoes had already had their feast, and Tommy Tomlinson soon joined the ranks of the feverish.

Bugs or no bugs, the whole squadron was ordered back to Munda in an effort to relieve pressure on the fighters already stationed there. Frequent contact with the Japanese had whittled away fighter cover, and VMF-214 could plug the gaps. While Hazelwood and Tomlinson remained in sick bay, twenty-seven pilots plus Don Hatch and Doc Bookman were scheduled to depart the Russells on August 24. Twelve pilots were to fly F4Us and the others to ride a transport, but at the last minute the Corsairs were assigned as escorts for a B-24 strike to Kahili. Confusion reigned. In the end, only three Swashbucklers completed the escort mission; the rest landed early at Munda with a host of engine and oxygen system troubles.

Of the three who finished the strike, one had a close encounter on the way home. The B-24s ran into heavy weather east of Bougainville and turned to bomb their secondary target, Vila, whereupon Jack Petit became separated from the others over the Shortlands. Heading home at thirty thousand feet, he spied Zeros below and immediately nosed over. Attacking the tail-end Charlie, he shot off its right elevator. The brown Zeke wobbled, then dived toward the surface, which earned Petit a probable. Rather than mixing it up with the rest, he continued diving until he was safely out of their way before continuing to Munda.

The next day was busy with an early scramble (no contacts), a sizable strike to Kolombangara later in the morning, and an evening patrol that ended in confusion. One pilot raced in and pancaked first, getting things out of normal sequence, then Charlie Lanphier braked his Corsair too hard and it nosed up, hanging precariously for a moment before falling back onto its tail wheel with a stalled engine. Behind him came Bob Hanson, who didn't hear the warnings and didn't see Charlie until it was almost too late. Hanson braked even harder, and his F4U went all the way over on its back. Neither pilot was hurt, but it was a hell of a way to lose an airplane.

Between the efforts of Pistol Pete and Washing Machine Charlie, the Swashbucklers were under Condition Red almost constantly on Munda. Ignoring the disruptions, the squadron had one of the most active days in its brief history on August 26 with thirty-four sorties beginning just after dawn. A mission was added in midafternoon when ComAirNewGeorgia learned of two barges in a cove on Kolombangara. (In their effort to resupply the thousands of troops cut off by Halsey's bypassing operation, the Japanese resorted to the risk of daylight detection.) Two divisions led by Dick Sigel and Dave Rankin found both barges and left them burning.

Miller's and Synar's divisions took off at 1520 for a roving patrol, after which Miller's flight was directed to cover B-24s returning from a strike on Kahili. As Miller climbed through seventeen thousand feet, he detected fighters "swinging Jap-like above the bombers" and initially thought that a Japanese strike was inbound. Then he saw two drifting clouds of black smoke and realized that the bombers had just flamed two attacking Zeros, but by the time he approached there was no sign of the enemy.

Such was not the case for Bob Hanson, whose supercharger had been giving him trouble. With his engine stuck in neutral blower he fell behind the division, which was now in position above the Liberators and hanging just beneath a layer of clouds. The mechanical trouble worked to his advantage, however, for a lone Zeke suddenly dropped out of the cloud layer, shot at Ed Hernan, and rolled away. Just as the pilot brought his Zeke back to wings level, Hanson gave it a short burst. Seeing no result, he closed in, sighted carefully, and squeezed again. This time the Zeke gushed flame from the left wing root, zoomed briefly, and fell away, leaving a trail of greasy smoke.

Other Swashbucklers had their hands full with a different B-24 raid. Vic Scarborough's division took off at 1520 and headed east to pick up a formation of Liberators in conjunction with several P-40s, but Charlie Lanphier turned back early because of a fuel problem and Paul Knipping accompanied him for protection. Scarborough and Al Jensen remained with the bombers, weaving overhead at thirty thousand feet. Just as the Liberators began their bomb run, four Japanese fighters appeared and the two Marines dived toward them. Scarborough exploded one on his first pass, then pulled up to see two *Ki*-61 Tonys coming straight for him, one on a collision course. The North Carolinian never wavered, holding in the trigger as the Tony approached head-on. The fighter burst into flames as it passed beneath his Corsair.

Al Jensen dived with Scarborough on the first pass but found himself in the same situation that Mac McCall had encountered the previous month—only one gun was working. The remaining enemy fighters retreated into a cloud, but the unflappable Jensen followed and went on instruments as he closed to within seventy-five yards of a Zeke from below and flamed it with one gun.

Scarborough used a cloud for defense when two more Tonys got on his tail. They went around the cloud, and Scarborough popped out to find them right alongside. Catching one in a full-deflection shot, he downed his third aircraft of the afternoon, watching as it flipped onto its back for the final plunge. The Tarheel, the second in the squadron to score three in a day, joined the Swashbucklers' short list of aces.

Two days later Al Jensen was back in the spotlight, conducting what Marine Corps aviation historian Robert Sherrod called "one of the great single-handed feats of the Pacific war." A dozen Swashbucklers rolled out of their cots at 0345 on August 28 for a dawn strafing attack on Kahili, but right from the start things were snafued. Late orders resulted in a mix-up in the allocation of Corsairs, and pilots had difficulty finding their assigned planes in the dark. Putting an exclamation point on the confusion, a Washing Machine Charlie arrived over the strip just as the pilots were warming up their engines. They could only sit in their cockpits, unnerved, as he laid five bombs in the water alongside the strip.

The original plan called for VMF-215's Bob Owens to lead one of his divisions and three Swashbuckler divisions to Kahili, where eight planes would do the shooting while eight remained overhead as cover. But the mix-ups and Condition Red resulted in only one other Fighting Corsair pilot getting aloft on time. Al Jensen, Vic Scarborough, and Charlie Lanphier managed to join up just as Owens was directed to proceed with the attack. He led the small group on a high-speed cruise to the northwest until they neared Fauro Island, where a small weather front appeared. Its size was deceiving. As Owens held his course, the Marines entered a squall that turned out to be extremely turbulent. Encountering violent thermals that bounced their planes upward as much as four thousand feet, they were forced to split up. Al Jensen briefly saw one other fighter, but it disappeared from view inside the storm and he popped out alone.

His spontaneous action that followed was later described by Sherrod.

> Jensen came out of it upside down, smack over the Japanese field. He flipped his plane over at the north end and started strafing the aircraft lined up along the runway.

This was a curious and unnecessary dramatization. Jensen's debriefing resulted in a wealth of information that eventually filled two typed pages in Don Hatch's official intelligence report, including specifics such as altitudes, locations, times, radio calls, even power settings. Jensen did not come out of the storm over Kahili upside down. He emerged upright north of Fauro Island, some twenty miles east of Kahili, at an altitude of twelve hundred feet. Thinking that he heard Bob Owens calling "Let's go!" on the radio, he realized that the tactical advantage of attacking Kahili before daylight would soon be lost. At that point Jensen decided to attack from his current position and shoved the throttle to full military power. The big Pratt & Whitney responded, pulling forty-two inches of manifold pressure at more than 2,500 rpm as Jensen dropped down to the wave tops and cut a wide arc across the Bougainville Strait. After reaching the beach he hugged the terrain, pulling up to clear the hills north of Tonolei Harbor, where an eight-hundred-foot peak to the north served as a landmark and convenient backdrop. Sighting Kahili to his left, he stood the Corsair on its left wing and reefed it around, then leveled off to aim for the northwest corner of the facility. He could see the tower "looming up in the increasing morning light," then sighted about a dozen medium bombers parked tightly together on the ramp at the north end.

Boring in at less than a hundred feet, Jensen triggered his guns at the clustered bombers from six hundred yards. The sky brightened with the reflection of a brilliant flash as he flew past. Crossing the strip diagonally to the east, he held in the trigger and sprayed what appeared to be three or four dive-bombers parked on the east side. Then he let go of the trigger as he rolled right and recrossed the runway halfway down the strip.

At this point he became aware of small-caliber tracer floating past his right wing. Looking ahead he saw eight or nine Zeros parked side by side at the far end of the strip, near the water's edge. Lining up, he squeezed again, able to see a pilot sitting in the cockpit of the first fighter as he zoomed over. Skimming the water now, he turned left to stay as far as possible from the heavily defended island of Ballale. He stole a look back to see "two good fires blazing," then made a beeline for Munda. Checking his plane after landing, he determined that he had expended eight hundred to a thousand rounds—slightly more than a third of his ammunition.

During his debriefing, Jensen estimated the number of planes in each of the three clusters he fired upon, thereby determining that twenty-three to twenty-five enemy aircraft had been parked along Kahili's strip. He did not claim to have destroyed them all; VMF-214's handwritten war diary praised him for "ruining about 3 Bettys, 2 Vals and 10 Zeros with pilots warming up engines." Jensen's estimate of the total planes on the ground proved remarkably accurate. (A reconnaissance photograph taken the next day showed that twenty-four Japanese aircraft had been destroyed). Upon that basis Jensen was later awarded a Navy Cross.

But there were conflicting statements, enough to suggest that Jensen might not have acted alone. Vic Scarborough was a distant witness, having emerged from the storm above the south end of Fauro Island at five thousand feet. He climbed to fifteen thousand feet in the direction of the Shortlands and found a clear area from which he could observe Kahili and render assistance if needed. From this vantage point he saw "fires blossom at both ends of the runway," where the medium bombers and fighters were seen parked close together. He believed that three or four planes had done the strafing. Neither Scarborough nor Jensen reported fires in the middle of the complex where the dive-bombers were parked, meaning that someone else added to the destruction before the next day's photo run. Sadly the only other Swashbuckler who could account for such damage did not return from the mission.

Charlie Lanphier was the final pilot to enter the squall over Fauro Island, and that was the last the squadron saw of him. Throughout the rest of the day, several flights including a division from VMF-215 poked among the island beaches and channels. Charlie had gone down once before on an enemy-held island and returned none the worse for the wear, but this time he was not found. He was listed as missing with this hopeful afterthought in the handwritten diary: "Our fingers are crossed, Charlie."

Unknown to the Swashbucklers, Lanphier was still alive. Perhaps the storm knocked him down, but the more plausible explanation was Japanese AA fire. The final tally of destroyed Japanese planes at Kahili was likely Lanphier's parting achievement, though a lack of American eyewitnesses makes his participation speculative. What is known is that Charlie was captured on Bougainville by the Japanese and transported to the Kempei Tai (military police) prison at Rabaul. There he met and befriended Lt. James A. McMurria, a B-24 pilot from the 90th Bomb Group, based on New Guinea.

Theirs was a partisanship born of indescribable suffering. They were kept on a starvation diet of two small balls of rice per day with a ration of water. Allied bombings destroyed the vegetable gardens, and at one point the prisoners went without rice for six weeks. Diseased, starved, covered with festering sores, they resorted to any measure for scraps of food. When a man began to bloat and "bite the air," his fellow captives knew his death was imminent. Eventually they contrived to tell the guards of a special mourning ritual. It was customary, they said, to place a bowl of rice at the dead man's head and a pineapple at his feet while the living gathered around to smoke cigarettes and say good things about him. Respectful of the dead, the Japanese provided the items. "As soon as the natives took the body out, we'd go for the food," reported McMurria. "We tried to be decent, but we were starving to death." As it turned out, the Japanese hastened the demise of many prisoners, executing four times as many as died slowly from malnutrition.

These horrors became known only after McMurria

emerged at the war's end with 8 gaunt companions out of 126 known military prisoners.* Charlie Lanphier was not among them. After months of deprivation and suffering from beriberi and other scourges, he began to fade. One day he crawled to McMurria and told him, "Jim, I'm not going to make it. If I had a milkshake I could make it. But I don't. And I can't." Three days later—McMurria thought it was May 15, 1944—Charlie died.

The Swashbucklers soldiered on through the last days of August, participants in a giant aerial slugfest between two weary heavyweights. With New Georgia as center ring, Japan and the Allies stood toe to toe, trading blows. The Allied hammers fell during daylight as they relentlessly pounded Bougainville's airfields with bomber strikes. The Japanese came after dark, hitting Munda, the Russells, and Guadalcanal almost nightly with sleep-depriving raids. The enemy bombers did not have to come all the way to the Allied bases or release their munitions to cause disruption; it was enough to tickle the radar warning systems and set off air-raid sirens. Many a night the Swashbucklers were rousted from their cots and into sweltering dugouts only to learn after an hour or so that the alarm had been false. There was no way to tell for certain if the alarms were real until the bombs fell, which was often enough to make the men heed every warning.

Sorely did they miss the sleep. The schedule had them flying from before dawn until after dark, and between flights they passed the time among the rot, filth, and stench

*An American survivor, Jose L. Holquin, compiled a list of 126 military captives imprisoned at Rabaul, not including plantation owners, missionaries, and many others held as civilians. Of the military captives, 64 were executed, 18 died of starvation or disease, 1 was shot during an escape attempt, and 18 were transported to Japan. Another 16 captives were transferred to Heitei prisons (Navy custody) or listed as "fate unknown"; American researcher Henry Sakaida stated that none of the naval prisoners survived.

of Munda's devastated landscape. It was Guadalcanal all over again, only worse. In addition to horrid living conditions and sleepless nights, combat tension ran high. There was a good chance they would encounter tenacious enemy pilots on practically every flight, and now there were more strafing missions, each fraught with particular risks. The F4U had already earned a reputation as an ideal daylight weapon for interdicting Japanese barge traffic, making its use as a gun platform increasingly popular.

The day following Charlie Lanphier's disappearance, coastwatchers reported two barges hidden in a cove on Kolombangara. ComAirNewGeorgia ordered a division of Swashbucklers aloft to find and destroy them, and Vince Carpenter took three others aloft just before lunch. They could not locate the reported barges, but they did find and strafe several suspected Japanese huts along the beach, perhaps unaware that similar attacks had been causing casualties among friendly natives. In the process they located a different barge in another cove and burned it, which was later confirmed by a coastwatcher.

When more small vessels were reported that afternoon, Chief Synar guided his division at low level toward the sightings in Tombulu Bay. Along the way they stumbled across a coastal vessel with a single stack, apparently stuck on a reef. The Swashbucklers' heavy slugs shattered the lightly constructed steamer, starting fires after only two passes. Continuing, they found the reported barges and set upon them. In what could only have been pure mayhem for the Japanese, individual Corsairs made eighteen withering runs and left the two craft in flames.

August 30 proved quieter, but only for the Swashbucklers. One division launched early to cover B-24s returning from a Kahili strike, and two others patrolled over a task force unit as it landed on Vella Lavella. A few scrambles this day and the next missed contacts by a hair's breadth. Pilots in other units had as much action as they could handle, however, including Ken Walsh, Tony Eisele's former tent mate and the high scorer in VMF-124 with sixteen planes. On this day he tangled single-handedly with a huge pack of fighters, adding four more Zekes to his record before others knocked his Corsair out of action. He splashed into the warm water off Vella Lavella and was picked up, but he had scored his last victory. Walsh became the first Corsair pilot to receive a Medal of Honor and was sent home, a celebrity.

At 0900 the next morning, Henry Miller scrambled with Jensen, Bernard, Hunter, and Hernan to meet an attack over Vella Lavella, but they were too late to find the Japanese. It proved to be a milestone anyway; it was the Swashbucklers' last combat flight. Six pilots had returned to the Russells the day before, having received notice that their relief squadron was in place. Now another dozen departed via SCAT transport. All were grateful to leave New Georgia's unhealthy conditions behind. Dave Rankin, still sick with dysentery, had tried an hour's flight on August 27, but the All-American football player was so weakened that he returned to Banika the following day. Scrappy Deetz and Joe Curran had also fallen ill and were unable to fly.

By the evening of August 31, only a handful of Swashbucklers were left to spend a final night at Munda. Among the last to leave the next morning was the seemingly indefatigable Henry Miller, who had logged more flight hours than anyone else in the squadron. During the week on Munda he had flown twelve sorties for more than twenty-four combined hours, exceeding the next highest man by at least four hours. In striking contrast, the interim commanding officer, Burnett, had accumulated barely nine hours. Dave Rankin, sick for the entire period, was the only pilot to log fewer hours than Burnett.

After the last group returned to Banika, on September 1, the entire squadron gathered for a photograph that afternoon (except Bob Hanson, who missed it), followed by a party that lasted well into the evening. The next day the Swashbucklers bid farewell to the lovely Russell Islands and boarded transports for the thirty-minute flight to Guadalcanal. There they spent the night in the Hotel de Gink, the transient officers' quarters. They arose at 0400 on the third for the long flight to Espiritu Santo, most riding SCAT transports while six pilots ferried war-weary Corsairs ("and old beat-up crates they were") to the service squadron on Buttons.

Thus ended VMF-214's second tour of combat in the Solomons, just a few days shy of six weeks in length. According to their officially recognized claims, fourteen Swashbucklers had participated in the aerial destruction of twenty Japanese aircraft, with three others probably destroyed and a few damaged. Almost thirty planes had been destroyed on the ground, with Al Jensen (and probably Charlie Lanphier) accounting for most. But claims were one thing; their own losses had been heavy, too. As if confirming the pilots' early concerns about the Corsair, operational accidents had destroyed no less than six airplanes and killed Bill Pace. The enemy caused grief as well, bringing down two of the Swashbucklers. Charlie Lanphier's squadron mates would not learn until much later that he was currently a prisoner of the Japanese, and Bill Blakeslee's name was placed on the Prisoner of War and Missing Persons Detachment list on September 6. He never came back, and of course neither did Charlie.

The Swashbucklers arrived at Turtle Bay on September 3 to find conditions far more crowded than during their previous stay almost six weeks earlier. Swarms of replacement pilots occupied new encampment areas, swelling the old coconut groves into sizable plywood cities. The arrangements were orderly, however, and the Swashbucklers managed to locate their assigned Dallas huts without much confusion.

No sooner had the Swashbucklers dumped their gear, however, than disturbing rumors shattered their pleasant return to Turtle Bay. The scuttlebutt was that another squadron was going to take their number; the Swashbucklers would be broken up. The news was one more blow to their morale, already "plenty low despite Sydney's proximity." Henry Miller detected a note of truth in the rumor and mailed a letter of protest to George Britt, hoping he might be able to intervene. Then Miller went to MAG-11 headquarters with Smiley Burnett and Doc Bookman to see what else could be done. Rumors and future plans were discussed over lunch. By the time they departed, Miller believed that they "had accomplished something."

Apparently the group staff had given them a false sense of security, intentionally or otherwise. The squadron number was indeed spoken for (or soon would be), and big changes were on the horizon. Still the Swashbucklers were not broken up forthwith. Indeed thirty pilots from VMF-124 and a ground officer from the headquarters squadron were *added* to the roster on September 7. At first glance the inclusion of these new arrivals appeared to be a simple matter of administrative control, and the Swashbucklers were scarcely aware of the roster change, according to their various diaries. The two groups were quartered independently, and any interaction that took place between them was purely coincidental.

The Swashbucklers' attention was on Sydney. Several dive-bomber squadrons were ahead of them in the rotation, leaving almost two weeks to kill, so they passed the time on Espiritu by swimming, playing games, and drinking their daily ration of beer. As revealed by various diary entries, the effect of six weeks of combat and the conditions on Munda had been sobering. "Tenseness wearing off" was a repeated phrase.

The Marines found several ways to ease stress. Despite the maturing effects of war they were still youngsters, given to prankishness and exuberance when conditions allowed. One day, as if to prove they had not been permanently aged beyond their years, several of them endeavored to record the flatulent effects induced by drinking warm beer—a farting contest. The winning time, an astronomical 17-and-a-half seconds, was "witnessed and suffered by four other squadron members," then duly recorded in the handwritten war diary on September 8.

The squadron's return to Espiritu enabled the aviators to reunite with their original ground echelon, which they commemorated on September 9 with an all-hands party featuring forty-three cases of stockpiled beer. Two days later Pete Folger was released from the hospital, confident that he would get to accompany his old squadron mates to Sydney, and joined them for a few days of swimming, sunbathing, volleyball, and evening libations. Doc Bookman passed the time creatively by building a small sailboat from scrounged materials and christening it *Noskie Boskie*. He launched it with a bottle of beer on September 17, though it would not be completely fitted out until the squadron returned from Sydney. It was a heartwarming sight for those who watched as the seaworthy craft sailed across the lagoon. But Pete Folger was bitterly disappointed when complications from his persistent leg infection landed him back in the hospital. He would miss the long-anticipated trip Down Under.

The next morning at 0230, having divided into two groups for transportation arrangements, the first echelon of Swashbucklers departed for Australia. The second group made it only part of the way to Tontouta on September 19 before weather closed in and forced their return to Buttons. But within two days both groups were "madly engaged in the Pursuit of Happiness."

They enjoyed a week of leave much like the one they had experienced almost four months before: afternoons at the Snake Pit in the Hotel Australia, meeting girls at the Tivoli Ballet, renewing old acquaintances, an even bigger squadron party at Prince's. During that particular shindig on September 25, Aussie drinking companion Arthur Paton was commissioned as an honorary major. He even had "wings" pinned on—a corkscrew. The week seemed scarcely to have begun when it was time to go, and "many sad hearts were left behind once again" as the Marines departed for Tontouta. This time, thanks to Harry Hollmeyer, they returned to the South Pacific with orange-and-black patches identifying them as Swashbucklers. Not bothering with official approval, Hollmeyer had arranged for a Sydney seamstress to create the insignia from his design.

The men were not destined to enjoy the patches for long as a unit. Both echelons of Swashbucklers were back on Espiritu by September 30, there to discover with surprise and disgust that the earlier rumors had been true after all. The group of pilots who had been added to their roster in early September was already in combat as Marine Fighting Squadron 214. Henry Miller's reaction spoke for all of the Swashbucklers when he arrived at Turtle Bay "to find the rape of 214 well under way, with our number gone . . ."

The second incarnation of VMF-214 had actually begun three weeks earlier on September 7, but that particular day was unremarkable as far as the Swashbucklers were concerned. Judging by their handwritten diary, they were interested in little besides planning a party. Ignorance was bliss. They were unaware of being laterally transferred to the squadron's ground echelon while the new group of pilots became the flight echelon. The two units were independent to the point of submitting separate war diaries at the end of the month, and as such they shared the squadron number only briefly. Because no official Marine Corps documents exist to explain the dissolution of the Swashbucklers, it is something of an enigma. "Daily routine" was the single entry in the MAG-11 war diary for September 7; the squadron diaries and enlarged roster reveal only that personnel changes occurred.

Heretofore, Marine fighter squadrons served a total of three six-week combat tours in the forward area, retiring to a rear base for a few weeks between each tour to rest and replace the pilots lost in battle or fallen ill. After completing three tours, the squadron's number and its original pilots (there were sometimes few remaining) sailed back to "Uncle Sugar," the United States. Pilots brought in as replacements between tours were obligated to remain overseas and were transferred to other squadrons to complete the balance individually. It was a simple pattern, and it worked; seven of the first eight Corsair-equipped squadrons to fight in the Solomons adhered to it. VMF-214 was the lone exception.

It was no secret that the Swashbucklers, disillusioned with their interim commanding officer, were suffering from low morale by the end of their second tour. Their lack of confidence in Smiley Burnett had festered for months, stripping all vestiges of respect, and their complaints—sometimes veiled, sometimes openly derisive—revealed exasperation. Considering the amount of time that Ray Hopper and George Britt spent among the pilots, the MAG-21 staff surely overheard the griping, making it reasonable to assume that higher echelons also knew of the trouble.

Despite their low morale the Swashbucklers were still twenty-six pilots strong, a healthy figure compared to many other fighter squadrons. Twenty-one had flown together for two tours and knew their trade well. Tony Eisele and Chief Synar were headed home, their obligations fulfilled, but the rest were available for at least one more tour. Replacing the commanding officer with a capable major to lead this seasoned group would seem, on the surface, a simple solution. Indeed an experienced fighter pilot of the correct rank had been campaigning, loudly, for several weeks to get just this kind of assignment.

He would get his wish, but not with the Swashbucklers.

10

"HE COULD FLY BETTER DRUNK . . ."

He was born in western Idaho on the fourth day of the twelfth December in the new century and grew up thinking his name was Gregory Hallenbeck. He had his first flight in the autumn of 1919, when a Jenny biplane swooped low over his St. Marie's schoolyard and landed in a nearby hayfield. With his friend John Theriault in tow, Greg ran on chubby legs to find the Jenny, and when the two boys reached it they met barnstormer Clyde Pangborn. He promised the boys a fifteen-minute flight over their little town, for a fee, so they ran all the way to the lumber store where Greg's dad worked. Ellsworth Hallenbeck gave them the money and they trotted back to the hayfield for their rides. Sitting side by side in the front seat, they tossed the barnstormer's leaflets out of the cockpit. After they landed, little Hallenbeck told Pangborn that he, too, would be a pilot when he grew up.

Hallenbeck held steadfastly to his dream while growing up in Washington. He graduated from Lincoln High School in Tacoma, then majored in aeronautical engineering at the University of Washington. There he swam and wrestled on the varsity teams, once holding the 160-pound Pacific Northwest Intercollegiate Middleweight title. As a senior he had a steady girlfriend, Helene Clark, a senior at Roosevelt High School. In the spring of 1934 he graduated into the Depression's dismal job market but was fortunate to land a job as a draftsman for Boeing Aircraft. He and Helene were married on July 29.

Within a year he was restless, mired in dull routine. Then came eye-catching Navy advertisements seeking qualified men to enter the service as aviation cadets. It was a path by which he could realize his childhood dream. Upon investigating the idea at Naval Reserve Air Base, Seattle (popularly known as Sand Point), Hallenbeck learned there was a catch—cadets had to be single. He took the physical exams anyway, then was informed that he needed a birth certificate. The seemingly minor requirement became complicated.

When he sent to Idaho for a copy of his birth certificate (he was born in Coeur d'Alene), an official responded that no record of a Gregory Hallenbeck for the given date could be found. The explanation soon came from his mother, Grace, who disclosed that Ellsworth Hallenbeck was not his biological father, nor was Greg's last name legally Hallenbeck. His real father was a small-town dentist, Dr. Charles B. Boyington, whom Grace had divorced a year after Greg was born. Greg was three when she remarried, but he was never formally adopted.

The revelation was a blessing of sorts. Armed with an Idaho birth certificate showing his name to be Gregory (no middle name) Boyington, he could begin his military career as "an unmarried man." He reported to the elimination base at Sand Point on May 15, 1935; his first child was born nine days later.

Boyington soloed handily and qualified for cadet training, but he did not receive further orders for several months. In order to feed his family he went back to Boeing, "hating every minute of it." Finally he was called up. He accepted his appointment as an aviation cadet on February 18, 1936, with orders to report to Pensacola for flight training. There, in the Florida Panhandle town known as the Cradle of Naval Aviation, his drinking career began as well. After tasting hard liquor for the first time during a cadet party, he said to his fellows: "I don't know why I stayed away from this stuff for so long, because this was made for me." Soon the weekend parties turned into serious binges, and he later admitted to being "a blackout artist from the start."

Excesses aside, he was a natural flyer, and the aeronautical engineering background allowed him to breeze through exams. His wrestler's strength and sense of balance gave him flying skills that ranked him high among his classmates. He earned his wings of gold in March 1937, then accepted a rare commission into the regular Marine Corps less than four months later. Such commissions were coveted. Only a hundred were offered annually during those lean years and were considered probationary for two years. During that time, recipients could not be married (the Corps lacked funding to support dependents), and commissions could be forfeited at any time for cause. At the end of the two years, professional exams were administered and the scores were combined with the men's fitness reports. The net score determined an officer's lineal ranking upon permanent commissioning.

The lengthy probation was a financial burden for Boyington. Second lieutenants earned little during the Depression, and besides his own needs he had to secretly house Helene and his new son, Gregory, Jr., first in Quantico, then Philadelphia (where he attended the Basic School for officers), and finally San Diego. He had been obligated to purchase, on credit, expensive uniforms for different seasons and occasions. Then there were bar tabs at officers' clubs, which he could not seem to avoid.

In 1940 he returned to Pensacola, this time as a flight instructor. By now his weakness for alcohol was taking its toll on his reputation, and he was in deep financial trouble, the cost of maintaining a separate residence to keep his family hidden having finally caught up. And a sizable family it was. On the heels of his son's birth had come two girls, Janet Sue in 1938 and Gloria in 1940.

Within a year of returning to Pensacola his marriage was a shambles. A trail of unpaid bills from across the country and letters from "nasty people" at his former duty stations went all the way to headquarters, where they landed on the desk of the commandant, Maj. Gen. Thomas Holcomb. He put Boyington on a strict repayment program that required him to account for the bills in writing every month, an embarrassing situation and potentially ruinous for his career.

One summer night in 1941, Boyington stepped from Palafox Street into the air-conditioned bar of the San Carlos Hotel, Pensacola's grandest establishment. As he related the story years later, he was there not to celebrate but to commiserate. He was near rock bottom, and drinking had become an escape. Payday was still a few days away and he was flat broke. "I wasn't one of those methodical chaps that kept his check stubs straight," he later admitted. "I knew darn well that it was gone, but I wrote out a check for twenty bucks and they cashed it."

Then someone at the bar told him it was his lucky day. A man in an upstairs suite was recruiting pilots to fly with the Chinese Nationalists against the Japanese. Boyington went to investigate and met a man wearing Army wings on his civilian suit who claimed membership in the *Lafayette Escadrille,* a famed World War I volunteer outfit. This was Richard Aldworth, employed by the Central Aircraft Manufacturing Company (CAMCO) of China (so the guise went) as a recruiter. His job was to lure American pilots into so-called advanced instruction and training units, but it was all a front. The CAMCO units were actually fighter squadrons within the American Volunteer Group.

Aldworth was not all that he portrayed. He was never on the *Escadrille* roster, and there were far-fetched elements to his recruiting pitch. (The Japanese all wore thick lenses, they were mechanically inept, and nine out of ten Japanese planes would be unarmed transports.) Boyington was skeptical until the mention of bonus money grabbed his attention. The Chinese would pay five hundred dollars for every airplane confirmed destroyed, on the ground or in the air, in addition to a salary that was double his current Marine pay.

But he would have to resign his hard-won commission and go overseas as a civilian with a doctored passport, although Aldworth promised that he could later be reinstated.

For Boyington this was an unexpected bonus: He could leave the country in virtual secrecy and escape his debts. On August 26, 1941, he resigned his first lieutenant's commission and was employed the next day by CAMCO. Next came a long journey to the Far East with the third (and last) contingent of AVG pilots to sail overseas.

If the twenty-eight-year-old former Marine thought the clouds would suddenly lift upon reaching Burma, he was wrong. His reputation had preceded him, as Olga Greenlaw, the supposed "wife" of the AVG's executive officer and one of three females on the roster, explained.

> Among the AVG fliers who had already arrived in Burma by the end of August 1941, he was the subject of considerable speculation. A batch of new pilots was about to arrive, and among them was a Marine captain—fellow named Boyington who, it was rumored, was a rough, tough, cantankerous leatherneck who could fly like a falcon and had never been beaten in a dogfight. Why, the youngsters wanted to know, was this old duffer, who must be approaching the venerable age of thirty, coming out to this rathole? Marine Corps captain's bars were hard to get and meant something, so why would any sensible fellow give them up? There was a catch to it somewhere. Had the Marines kicked him out? Was it money trouble? Was he running away from something? . . . The boys placed two strikes against him before they ever saw him.

Greenlaw had inadvertently elevated Boyington's former rank. The AVG's charismatic commander, Claire Lee Chennault, had already organized the group into three squadrons with leaders in place, so when Boyington arrived in Toungoo he was offered a secondary position as flight leader (and paid fifty dollars per month more than regular pilots), equivalent in rank to an Army Air Corps captain. He was posted to the 1st Pursuit Squadron, the Adam & Eves.

First impressions did not improve when Boyington's initial flight in a P-40 ended unfavorably. Before a gallery of curious pilots wanting to judge his skill for themselves, Boyington ground-looped and damaged a wing.

"What's the matter, captain?" asked one of the pilots playfully when Boyington climbed down. "Lil' old shark get away from you?"

Boyington remembered it differently in his autobiography, explaining that he began to swerve off the strip and jammed the throttle forward to bring the Curtiss fighter around for another attempt. He claimed the only damage was a broken manifold pressure gauge, which burst when he cobbed on the power.

Whichever account was closest to the truth, his relationship with the AVG began poorly and deteriorated from there. He did not remember kindly Olga's choice of mates—balding, beak-nosed civilian Harvey Greenlaw—and he used strong-arm tactics with at least one other aviator, according to his own testimony.

> They had every reason in the world to beat me up at any time, but one night somebody did it, and I didn't remember or didn't know who. The next morning I woke up quite early and I asked who did it.
>
> It was Jack [Newkirk] who was found asleep in his cot. Well, my philosophy was to have people fear [me] and then they won't bother [me] at those inopportune times when I am unable to fight—not that I disliked it—I loved it, and so I kicked this fellow off the cot. Of course, he never did get to his feet, and I'm sorry to say I walked on his face rather severely, and a few other places. Anyhow, people let me alone when I was walking around blacked out.

Although Boyington did not get along with several pilots, in the Russian-Mexican temptress Olga Greenlaw he found a confidante and more. She was alluring, well proportioned, was as tall as most men, and she had vivid green eyes and long lashes. Boyington was a frequent visitor, she admitted. Lonely and uneasy, he gradually divulged his past, including concern about his children and the situation on the home front.

Judging from Olga's breathless description that followed her first meeting with Boyington, she found him equally irresistible.

> Not too tall, dressed in rain-soaked khaki shorts and unbuttoned shirt which exposed a barrel chest and bull neck supporting a square-cut face with powerful jaws, thick lips, flattish nose, broad forehead and protruding, heavy-lidded eyes. His waist and hips seemed much too slender for his massive torso and shoulders and his curly hair was wet.

If Greenlaw assuaged Boyington's melancholy, she was unable to help that he was plagued with hard luck. He missed several opportunities for action, then was passed over for a squadron leader slot when the Adam & Eves' commander was killed.* Increasingly bored and frustrated, he often complained, "I came out here to fight, and all I do is sit around and wait."

His bad luck continued. First he suffered dual knee injuries during an operational accident, then exacerbated them by stumbling, drunk, over a thirty-foot embankment during a night air raid. After that, most of his flying was relegated to engine checks on rebuilt P-40s. He eventually saw limited action and was paid by the Chinese for a few

*This was Greenlaw's version. In an exhaustively researched history of the Flying Tigers, Daniel Ford wrote that Boyington declined an offer to lead the squadron.

destroyed aircraft, but much of his time with the group was characterized by drinking and hell-raising.

In the meantime his wife had returned to Seattle with the three children. Citing alleged abuse, she filed for divorce barely a month after Boyington's departure; a judge granted the divorce decree, giving her custody of the children, on November 7, 1941.

By April, Boyington was thoroughly disillusioned with the Flying Tigers and limped up to Olga at Kunming, China, to tell her he was quitting. She begged him not to, reminding him of Chennault's ruling that every resignation after Pearl Harbor would be considered a dishonorable discharge. "T' hell with it," he said. "I'm getting out of this comic-opera outfit." True to his word, he caught a Chinese National Airways Company transport across the Hump to Calcutta, then hopped on a British airliner to Karachi.

Leaving that port city proved more challenging, however. Authorization was required to board military transportation back to the States, but Chennault would not give it. Instead he got the last word by declaring Boyington dishonorably discharged. Chennault's disdain was further evidenced by his suggestion that the 10th Air Force, newly arrived in India, draft the ex-Marine as a second lieutenant. Olga Greenlaw reported a slightly more sympathetic version in which Boyington went to Delhi and applied for induction (such was his desire to wear an American uniform), but the 10th Air Force "apparently shared the general opinion that he was no damned good and never would be" and rejected the stunned ex-Tiger.

Regardless of the exact circumstances, Boyington shipped out on the SS *Brazil* for New York. During the lengthy transit he literally stumbled onto a new woman and dallied with her for the rest of the trip. Mrs. Lucy Malcolmson was a former New York showgirl who had married a wealthy, older executive in Bombay years before. With America now in the war, Stewart Malcolmson thought that sending his wife home was the safe thing to do. Instead she became involved with Boyington, and sometime during the voyage they drew up an agreement that made her trustee of his estate. He obviously anticipated reinstatement in the Marine Corps, for he arranged for her to draw from his future allotments and authorized the money to be used for the care of his children.

When the ship docked in July, he made his way to Washington, D.C., and applied for reinstatment, then traveled to his mother's home in the state of Washington to wait. Lucy was aboard the same train west of Chicago; she met his mother in Okanogan and visited there briefly before traveling to San Francisco.

In August, Boyington filed for custody of his children, claiming that his ex-wife was an unfit parent. Ironically the same judge that granted Helene's decree nine months earlier now issued another, giving the children to Boyington. No word arrived from the Marine Corps, and with three extra mouths to feed Boyington was eventually forced to seek work. He finally had to settle for his former collegiate job, parking cars for a Seattle garage. After two months passed at this menial position he became deeply frustrated. The two older children went to live with his mother while little Gloria was placed in the custody of his ex-wife's sister.

In desperation, Boyington decided to unstick the wheels of bureaucracy. After consuming a bottle of bourbon one night, he wrote a letter to an "assistant Secretary of the Navy," then dictated it over the telephone as a three-page Western Union telegram. Within its rambling contents, he claimed to be an ace in the AVG with six aerial victories. The cable may have ended up in the hands of Secretary of the Navy Frank Knox, publisher of the *Chicago Daily News* before President Roosevelt added him to his cabinet as a Republican counterbalance. How else to explain such fast results, for Boyington was back in the Corps within days. He also had a significant head start toward the future, because someone powerful in Washington, either Knox himself or an official at headquarters, had given him recognition for six victories.

Boyington's new status apparently happened without so much as an interview (he reported straight to the West Coast) and without confirmation from anyone in the AVG. Had someone at headquarters attempted confirmation, Boyington's official score would almost certainly have been lower. According to AVG records, he was paid for only three and a half victories: two fighters in aerial combat over Rangoon on February 6, 1942, and another plane-and-a-half destroyed on the ground during a strafing attack in Thailand on March 24. Noted authors, historians, and former members of the AVG have agreed upon that figure for several decades.

Further evidence was uncovered during an exhaustive study of aerial victory credits during the 1980s conducted by Dr. Frank J. Olynyk, who discovered a loose and untraceable sheet (not by itself a strong document) listing "Confirmed Air Victories—AVGs," at the Albert F. Simpson Historical Research Center in Montgomery, Alabama. The entry opposite "Boyington, G." was 3½, partially clouding the issue because of the words "Air Victories" in the title of the document.

But the overall number is consistent with other accounts. Robert B. Hotz listed 3½ for Boyington in his 1943 book, *With General Chennault: The Story of the Flying Tigers,* and the same figure appears in AVG records maintained separately by the San Diego Aerospace Museum. Another definitive analysis was conducted by historian Robert L. Sherrod for the 1987 reissue of his landmark *History of Marine Corps Aviation in World War II*. In its preface, Sherrod fretted for two pages over the controversy surrounding Boyington's claims. He quoted one compelling statement from Medal of Honor winner Brig. Gen. James H. Howard, USAF (Ret.), who in no uncertain terms told Sherrod, "I was president of the AVG confirmation board in 1942, and I know he should be credited with only 3½ planes and that's what he was paid for."

Boyington described six victories in the autobiography he penned sixteen years after departing the AVG, but was vague about dates. His description of the first engagement, during which two Japanese fighters went down in flames, matches exactly a documented fight that did occur on January 29, 1942. He was not, however, among the nine AVG pilots credited with victories that day. Next he mentioned a day "in the middle of February" when squadron leader Robert Sandell died attempting a slow roll (this actually occurred on February 7), which set the stage for a single victory the following day. The Japanese fighter reportedly crashed into the bay seventy miles from Rangoon. The last three victories were described as a triple shoot-down on one flight, also "around the middle of February."

American Volunteer Group chronicler Daniel Ford performed a detailed comparison of Japanese and AVG records and found that the Flying Tigers' claims far exceeded Japanese losses. This was no great surprise (although it rankled surviving Tigers) and showed that the Chinese could not have located enough wrecks to confirm every claim. Ford did allude to an additional document, indicating that "Boyington and Hill each had one more victory than was credited to their bonus accounts."

The critical issue is that the Chinese paid for confirmed aircraft whether their destruction occurred on the ground or in the air, but the U.S. naval services recognized (for individual records) only aircraft destroyed in the air. Erring on the side of generosity, Boyington would have been credited with no more than three *aerial* victories if the Marine Corps had investigated his claim. He was officially awarded six, however, apparently on the basis of his Western Union telegram.

Now that he was at last reinstated, Boyington donned a uniform bearing the temporary rank of major in the Marine

Corps Reserves, bid farewell to his mother and children, and headed for Southern California. He invited Lucy Malcolmson to San Diego for a visit, then boarded the liner *Lurline* on January 7, 1943, for the long journey overseas.

Major John Condon was also en route to the South Pacific aboard *Lurline,* a fast transport converted from a luxury liner, and recalled that during this early stage of the war she still offered amenities served by her original civilian crew.

> They had to practice to keep their proficiency up. The food was in cold storage, and we ate pretty well. It made me nervous, like they were filling me up to go to the slaughter. But I thought it was a pretty fancy way to go out to Noumea.

Boyington then made his way by plane to Espiritu Santo, where his first duty was an unglamorous assignment as Turtle Bay's operations officer. Eventually he worked his way into a combat tour as the executive officer of VMF-122, but after several weeks on Guadalcanal with no enemy encounters the squadron withdrew for a rest period and a wild week of leave in Sydney.

When the squadron returned to Espiritu to regroup, Boyington assumed command. He continued to play hard and drink harder until one night his boisterous behavior brought his coveted assignment to a screeching halt. His downfall was that the more he drank, the more belligerent he became, and his love of wrestling got him in trouble.

During a drinking spree in the Dallas huts on June 7, he made the regretful decision to brawl with Timothy Moynihan, a much-decorated Marine with a battlefield commission who was formerly an All-American center at Notre Dame. His weight was in the neighborhood of two hundred pounds—very large by contemporary standards. Depending on the account, Moynihan either threw Boyington bodily out of the hut or put a twisting leg lock on him, but the end result was the same—a broken left ankle. Boyington was officially placed in hospital status at Lion One as of June 9, then was evacuated to Auckland's MOB-4. He crossed paths with Tony Eisele, who observed that Boyington's drinking never ceased. In fact, alcohol was more accessible in town, if Boyington was willing to stump down the road on crutches to reach it. He was. The brawling resumed, too, despite the fact that his leg was still in a cast.

Dealing with injuries from a drunken brawl proved far easier than passing the flight physical to return to combat status. Still limping when he was released from the hospital, Boyington struggled to get a flight surgeon's approval. Without revealing his exact method, he later wrote, "I was finally able to con the poor doc into letting me by in spite of his better judgment."

Boyington jumped into a Corsair that was ready to be ferried to Espiritu, but was not welcomed back with open arms. In a sort of fighter pilot exile, he was assigned to various units in administrative capacities that denied him a sense of attachment. During one stint he commanded VMF-112 for seventeen days as a caretaker while the flight echelon enjoyed R and R prior to shipping back to the States. Shortly before the squadron sailed in mid-August, he was transferred to VMF-124, merely a lateral shift of his name from one roster to another.

Such was the setting in midsummer 1943 when Boyington began a verbal campaign to land some kind of flying job. He was "bored to distraction," frustrated enough to fly anything—even dive-bombers if it came to that. Finally, as had happened in the past when he needed out of a situation, circumstances and fortuitous timing came to his rescue.

Among the eight original Corsair-equipped squadrons in the Solomons, half were scheduled to depart for the States between July and September.* Two fresh squadrons arrived

*VMF-122 in July, VMF-112 in August, and VMF-121 and -124 in September.

in August but the remaining outfits were spread thin, leaving serious gaps in fighter strength. Bull Halsey, smack in the middle of a major campaign, needed another fighter outfit immediately.

Herein lies the best explanation for the dissolution of the Swashbucklers. Boyington was available to lead them on a third tour, but they were not ready to be led. They had earned a rest, and it would be weeks before they returned from Sydney and were capable of heading back into the fray. Halsey could not afford to wait. From the very top came a sense of urgency to get another squadron ready for combat. The quick solution was to cobble together a new outfit from replacement pilots and give them the Swashbucklers' number.

Boyington wrote that he fostered the idea independently, then presented it to Col. Lawson H. M. "Sandy" Sanderson, a former commanding officer of MAG-11. (Boyington referred to him as the "group commander," but Sanderson had been transferred to the staff of the 1st Marine Air Wing months earlier.) An even stronger sympathetic ear belonged to the 1st MAW's assistant commanding general, Brig. Gen. James T. Moore. Widely rumored to be one of Boyington's drinking associates, Moore had a soft spot for the brash fighter pilot and the authority to endorse the squadron idea up the chain of command.

The pilots whom Boyington would need were readily available, legacies of sorts from an alphabet soup of famed fighter squadrons. Some were fresh replacements currently assigned to VMF-112, the Wolfpack squadron that had fought from Henderson Field during the crucial battle in late 1942. Switching to Corsairs in May, VMF-112 split into forward and rear echelons with the latter based at Turtle Bay as a catchall for replacements. The rear echelon had filled with unassigned lieutenants, who had arrived overseas in greater numbers than there were squadron slots. Boyington had served as the echelon's commanding officer from July 26 to August 11, and several experienced pilots obligated to one or two more combat tours were also available. Soon after the foreward echelon sailed for the States in mid-August, Boyington received back-channel approval to commence gathering pilots from this "replacement pool" for the purpose of forming a new squadron.

For the opportunistic Boyington, absent from combat for more than a year and with precious little flying since leaving the AVG, yet another opportunity to reverse an unsatisfactory situation presented itself. He had been woefully underemployed as an administrator, "going mentally crazier by the day," and now the fates were offering him another chance.

In his attempt to get back into combat, he set a legend in motion.

11

"POOR LITTLE LAMBS"

When the original Wolfpack aviators of VMF-112 sailed for the States on August 14, taking their number with them, Greg Boyington and some thirty rear echelon pilots were laterally transferred to VMF-124.* Well acquainted with several of the pilots who were veterans from his first Corsair outfit, Boyington later portrayed most of them as novices between nineteen and twenty-two years old and remarked twice in his autobiography that only three had prior combat experience. "The rest," he wrote, "had never been in an active squadron, let alone seen a Japanese aircraft."

Actually three times that number were veterans with plenty of combat experience. Fully one-third of the squadron had completed at least one combat tour. Six had claimed Japanese planes or been bloodied themselves, but they received no credit from Boyington. Even among the nonveterans, four pilots had acquired invaluable flight experience as instructors, and three others initially trained with the Royal Canadian Air Force before switching to naval aviation.

Among the three veterans Boyington acknowledged was a major who would be the new executive officer. Stanley R. Bailey, twenty-six, had been an instructor with Boyington during their prewar days in Pensacola and considered

*VMF-124's forward echelon was still at Munda in the middle of its third and last combat tour, and the ground echelon at Espiritu took over as the "replacement pool." In the end, twenty-seven of this group remained with Boyington; a few others were later transferred to the "sick list."

him a friend, although the two had little in common. It was probably Bailey's Yankee roots (he was born in Quebec and raised in Vermont) that made his personality so diametrically different from that of Boyington. Bailey epitomized Marine Corps starch by adhering strictly to old-school conventions and codes of honor. A swagger stick suited his description of etiquette (a riding crop in his case), justly earned as a skilled equestrian on military jumping teams. His most distinguishing feature was his broad head, anchored by a prominent chin and capped with a heavy brow. Like his commanding officer, Bailey was a plane killer, having downed two Mitsubishi G4M Bettys during previous tours with VMF-122. First Lieutenants John F. Begert and Henry M. Bourgeois were the only other veterans whom Boyington named. Begert grew up in the midwestern prairies, as did a surprising number of young men drawn to naval aviation. In two tours with VMF-122 he had downed one Zero. Hank Bourgeois, a twenty-two-year-old New Orleans native, began his combat career in Wildcats with the same outfit, then moved to Corsairs in VMF-112 for his second tour. There he shot down a Sally and a Zero.

June 30, the day that Bourgeois got the Sally, began a remarkable series of events. Bourgeois had just been scrambled into lousy weather and was heading toward Munda when his wingman developed that old Corsair nemesis—engine trouble—and turned back. Bourgeois followed in an attempt to shepherd him home but lost sight of him while descending through the heavy clouds. His wingman vanished. Bourgeois climbed again, en route to Munda, when he stumbled upon the Sally and opened fire. It went down trailing smoke but not before shooting out Bourgeois's radio. Alone among the towering storm clouds, Bourgeois began to experience the creeping, helpless sensation of being lost.

Turning to a general heading that he hoped would lead back to Guadalcanal, he descended slowly through the clouds until he broke through the undercast. There, just a few hundred feet above the wave tops, were nine SBDs. "Hell, they know where they're going," he figured aloud and promptly latched onto the rear of the formation. But they were just as confused and soon split into two groups. Forced to choose, Bourgeois remained with the formation leader's group as five other SBDs veered off in a different direction.

Soon Bourgeois realized that he had not made the right choice.

> The five guys were smart and knew where the beam was that got them to Guadalcanal, but I followed the leader. We ended up on Rennell Island, which is about a hundred nautical miles south of Guadalcanal. It wasn't even on the strip maps. I had enough fuel and could have flown back to base if I had known where I was. The SBDs just peeled off and made water landings one by one in the lagoon. I flew around for a while because I didn't know what to do, and thought I might as well land, too.

Bourgeois tightened his harness, jettisoned the hood, and lowered the flaps, then set his Corsair down a hundred yards off the beach. The huge nose dug in and pulled the rest of the plane down so quickly that he had no time to retrieve his rubber boat. As his heavy boots and jungle pack dragged him down, Bourgeois tugged the inflation toggles on his Mae West. One failed and the other leaked. Panic set in as he struggled to stay afloat. Just as he began to founder, an outrigger canoe shot out from the shoreline, and several husky natives hauled him in.

It was late afternoon as the natives led him to a lean-to shelter through heavy jungle made gloomier by storm clouds and misting rain. No one spoke English, not even a pidgin variety. Bourgeois suffered their silence with growing concern. Some of the fierce-looking men carried clubs, and their own blood trickled from slashed eyebrows. But he was given a bowl of warm rice, and when exhaustion overcame anxiety he managed to sleep through the night.

In the morning he was paddled to the main village, where the "Super Chief" lived, and his outlook improved.

> I was the first to get there. The other eight Marines—four pilots and four gunners—were paddled there later. When I arrived I was treated royally, and they kept talking about Marines and Japs. They could speak pretty good pidgin English and wanted to know if I was number one. I kept saying, "I'm number one, I'm number one," so they thought I was in charge of everything. Later the rest of the Marines arrived, and the natives did some cooking for us and fed us pretty well. Since I had said that I was number one, I got to sleep in the Chief's hut with one of his daughters.

At dawn on the second day, several large natives gestured for Bourgeois to accompany them. They paddled to a small island, then led him through the jungle to a lean-to where a young woman lay on a grass bed in great discomfort, obviously in labor. The natives expected Bourgeois to perform, so he knelt beside her, placed his hand upon her forehead, then gave an attendant several aspirin tablets from his first-aid kit. His doctoring finished, he was escorted back to the main village.

Later that afternoon a Catalina landed in the lagoon and taxied to the beach. Bourgeois remembered to tell the Dumbo's corpsman about the pregnant woman.

> He went out and took a look at her, came back and said she needed help and was obviously overdue. The next day, after they took us back to Guadalcanal, they sent a doctor down with a team, and the baby was born. When the doctor came back he told me that the chief was so happy they named the boy "Boo-gawa." The chief

sent me some carved wooden scepters, which I still have. Then I discovered that the reason all the elders had their brows bleeding was that the chief of their village had died. They had cut their brows, like a crown of thorns, in mourning.

The youngster from New Orleans earned credit for the Sally and a new nickname as well: "Doctor Boo."

One pilot whom Boyington did not mention but should have remembered from earlier days was Capt. Robert T. Ewing, a twenty-three-year-old from Indiana whose ski-jump nose had earned him the handle of "Rootsnoot." He had sailed with Boyington on the *Lurline* from San Diego. His record—three victories and a probable—bettered the credit that the AVG would have officially given Boyington.

Another veteran member had even more victories, but his name never appeared in Boyington's account. Originally trained as a dive-bomber pilot, Henry A. McCartney, Jr., was a wet-behind-the-ears second lieutenant when he reached Noumea in November 1942. He joined VMSB-142 on Espiritu Santo but had completed only a few flights with the outfit when an announcement crackled over the loudspeakers. Pilots interested in joining a new fighter squadron were wanted immediately at the mess hall. "You never saw a guy travel so fast," he remembered. VMO-251, formerly an observation unit, was being re-formed into a fighter outfit, and McCartney signed on. He flew F4Fs for one tour on Guadalcanal and downed a Betty, then was reassigned to Corsairs in VMF-121, where he shot down three Zekes.*

Reaching that score was anything but easy. On July 2, his shorthanded flight of seven Corsairs was escorting B-24s to Kahili when they were jumped from above by fifty Zeros. In what McCartney laconically described as "a really

*His first Zeke, recorded as a "smoker"on June 30, 1943, was later upgraded to a confirmed victory.

good rhubarb," the outnumbered Marines used evasive tactics and some nearby clouds to draw the Zeros away from the bombers, then managed to claw down six of the enemy while losing one of their own. McCartney was credited with one of the Zekes, but his own day was ended when a Japanese pilot put seventy-five bullets into his Corsair.

Hunkered down in front of the armor plate, McCartney finally evaded the Zeke, although one of the arrows gave him a scare.

> The armor plate protects your back, but [the Zeke] was at such an angle that an armor-piercing round came through the fuselage just past the armor plate, and the next thing I knew, my foot was jammed up against the instrument panel. I got it back down and continued to fly, and after I got back to base found that a 7.7mm had nicked the heel of my Marine Corps boot and had thrown my foot up into the instrument panel.

It was a close scrape for the twenty-five-year-old Long Islander, and his Corsair was a flying wreck. Its left aileron was sawed off, there were holes in both wing tanks, and the horizontal stabilizer was chewed in half, hanging at a crazy angle. McCartney struggled to keep the damaged fighter aloft. It wanted to fly in the direction of the good aileron, forcing him to cross his legs and brace them against the stick in order to muscle the Corsair back to Munda. Mechanics later found the spent bullet that struck his foot, and he kept it as a souvenir. The Corsair became a source of salvaged parts.

Another young man who had experienced the wrong end of a Zero was 2d Lt. Virgil G. Ray. Twenty-two and slender, he had enlisted in the Corps in 1940 after a year and a half of aeronautical engineering at North Carolina State. Following boot camp at Parris Island, he took competitive exams and was one of a handful of applicants selected from dozens of hopefuls for aviation training. Winged as an

NAP, he was a master technical sergeant for part of a tour with VMF-122, then received a field commission in April. The future looked good for the former flying sergeant, until a harrowing experience changed his perspective. On July 18 his plane was badly damaged over Kahili; miraculously he was able to nurse the Corsair back to Segi's short strip for a crash landing. His aircraft had absorbed five 20mm cannon shells and thirty machine-gun bullets and poured smoke all the way. Blinded by the streaming plume, his hydraulics gone and the engine frozen, Ray somehow managed to drop it dead-stick onto the strip. He emerged from the wreckage in a state of shock.

Paul A. Mullen was the seventh of Boyington's pilots to encounter the Japanese. He was born and raised in Pittsburgh, graduated in 1940 from Notre Dame with a degree in English, then worked for a newspaper and dabbled in theater. During one tour with VMF-122, he shot down a Zero and shared a half-credit for another. Like Virgil Ray he took a turn on the receiving end. The day before Ray's encounter, a Zero laced Mullen's Corsair with twenty-seven machine-gun bullets and one cannon round. The single explosive shell entered the cockpit and wounded Mullen in the leg.

Another Pennsylvanian with combat savvy was Sanders S. Sims. The twenty-two-year-old first lieutenant had completed three years at the University of Pennsylvania, where he played football and hockey, before joining the ranks of aviation cadets. When he left San Diego in April he had the great fortune to ship out on the *Japara,* a Dutch freighter chartered by the Navy. It had been one of the last ships out of Batavia, the site of a Heineken brewery, and its hold still contained thousands of cases of beer, "a lovely convenience for traveling."

The war was not always so accommodating for Sims. During a huge melee on June 30 while the task force made the initial landings on New Georgia, he was flying wing on VMF-122's executive officer when the latter's engine suddenly failed. As Maj. Joseph H. "Hunter" Reinburg began dropping from twenty thousand feet, Sims dutifully stayed with him for protection, but they were jumped by a swarm of Zeros—too many for Sims to handle. Hunter Reinburg was eventually shot down, although he was picked up unharmed. Diving out of trouble, Sims pulled up to find another Corsair alongside and a Betty straight ahead. The Japanese bomber was making for the fleet, so Sims gave chase with his partner, ignoring the fact that their path took them into friendly fire from several destroyers below. One ship's gunnery was almost too good. As Sims later acknowledged, "I got a lot of shots in my airplane at various times, but I never got hit so often as by this American destroyer." He escaped with shrapnel holes in the bottom of his Corsair, then caught up with the enemy bomber and flamed it. When the other pilot claimed to have missed, Sims received full credit.

The ninth combat veteran to join Boyington's new outfit was 1st Lt. William N. Case. Twenty-two years old, with a new bride named Ellen back in Vancouver, Washington, Case was a member of the first cadre of students to train at mainside, Corpus Christi. His early training days were marked by misadventures. During one formal ceremony, he stood in the hot Texas sun wearing lunch under his cap. "I'm probably the only Naval Aviation Cadet who went through his commissioning with an egg salad sandwich on his head."

Advanced fighter training at North Island was more exciting. Case had a midair collision while flying SNJs, then crashed into a concrete revetment after an engine failed during takeoff in an F4F. Fortunately he was blamed for neither, and he completed the syllabus in time to sail on the *Lurline* with Boyington for the South Pacific. After an uneventful combat tour with VMF-122, Case was transferred to VMF-112 for his second tour, where he witnessed plenty of action and scored one Zero over Kahili.

Fascinated by combat and positive that he would not be

hit or killed, Case became a keen, detached observer. Zeros greatly impressed him with "how maneuverable, mobile and pretty they actually were."

An encounter with a Tony reinforced Case's sense of invincibility, although the head-on pass left him shaking with adrenaline.

> This guy was shooting at me from way out and coming straight at me, and I was coming straight at him. I started to fire and he was firing all the time. His tracers looked like little orange balls and the big cannon rounds looked like orange tennis balls. They came in a stream but seemed to lose velocity and fall below the incoming direction of my Corsair. I tried to put the pipper right on the spinner of his prop but he didn't flame or go down. At the very last minute he flipped up on a wing and yanked off to the side, and missed me. A strong impression I had was of the large size of the Japanese insignia when the pilot turned away. It was the first time that I had seen an aircraft marking that positively identified him as a Nipponese. I went steaming on ahead, and suddenly realized that I'd not had even the faintest notion of taking evasive action against a collision. Right then, I knew that I should've been smarter than I was. And the fact that I didn't kill the pilot or burn the bird saved my life, because he was able to take the evasion and pull off. He didn't come back around on me. Gratefully, that was one target that I missed.

In addition to the nine veterans on Boyington's roster, most of the eighteen new replacements culled from VMF-112's rear echelon were surprisingly senior, including one captain and fifteen first lieutenants.

Twenty-four-year-old George M. Ashmun, sporting captain's bars, had reached his advanced rank as a result of time in service while training and teaching in the States. He had been plowed back into the training command as an instructor, then spent six additional months of operational training on the West Coast.

Three of the first lieutenants were former instructors at Jacksonville's Lee Field, where they accumulated considerable flight time. John F. Bolt's logbook was already fat when he arrived on Espiritu in June, and by the end of August he had logged forty-nine more hours in F4Us, bringing his total to nearly seven hundred hours. Likewise Edwin L. Olander and Rolland N. Rinabarger carried logbooks thick with valuable instructor time. Bill Case, by comparison, had less than five hundred total hours after two combat tours. Although nothing could substitute for the lessons born of combat, those accumulated instructor hours equated to high levels of skill and discipline. Consequently Boyington assigned all four of the former instructors as section leaders.

Three others had begun with the Royal Canadian Air Force. First Lieutenants William D. Heier, Christopher L. Magee, and Donald J. Moore arrived on Espiritu with less flight time than the instructors, but they had gained the benefit of Canadian instruction that included superior instrument training. Heier's selection into fighters had not been obstacle free. Short in the torso, he worried about passing the standards for fighter pilots to the point of hanging from doorways to try to stretch his frame. A compassionate flight surgeon let him sleep on a cot in the dispensary the night before his physical, then measured him the instant he arose, reasoning that the relaxed spine would be fractionally longer before it had a chance to compress. Heier made the cut, but due to his small frame (and the fact that he looked impossibly young), he was soon nicknamed "Junior."

Chris Magee, raised on Chicago's South Side, had the heart of an adventurer. When war came to Europe in 1939, he and a friend headed to New Orleans and walked the docks for a month as they tried to book passage on any ship sailing toward the conflict. Stumped by neutrality laws, they reluctantly went home to Chicago, but Magee soon headed for Canada with hopes of flying in the RCAF. (His second cousin, John Gillespie Magee, Jr., had been successful in joining as an American pilot; he wrote the immortal poem *High Flight* not long before a collision over the English Channel took his life.) Chris was almost finished with training on Prince Edward Island when Navy recruiters arrived from the States and offered him a deal as a fighter pilot. Chris's logbook showed almost four hundred flight hours, including fifty-six in Corsairs since his arrival on Espiritu.

The remaining nine first lieutenants represented a significant improvement in training over the raw replacements who had been thrust into battle the previous year. Robert A. Alexander, Robert M. Bragdon, Warren T. Emrich, Don H. Fisher, Denmark Groover, Jr., Edwin A. Harper, Walter R. Harris, James J. Hill, and Burney L. Tucker were more proficient as the result of an expanded syllabus. They were carrier qualified, for one thing, graduates of intense procedural training with roughly a hundred hours more than their nonqualified predecessors.

Among the new squadron mates were faces familiar to the former flight instructors. Don Fisher, for instance, had been a year ahead of John Bolt at the University of Florida, but Bolt finished flight training first and was an instructor at Jacksonville's Lee Field when Fisher arrived as his first student.

Fisher was already a good pilot. Having a dentist father who owned a collection of sport planes during the 1930s helped Fisher progress rapidly through cadet training. He reached the South Pacific with such confidence that he offered a bold challenge.

> I didn't know this guy Boyington, but he was a major—an elderly fellow—and we were scheduled to fly on a gunnery hop. I said, "I'll tell you what, Major, I'll shoot you for a case of beer."
>
> "You're covered, son."

At that time, a case of beer may not have sounded like a lot, but we were rationed two beers a day, so a case was a pretty heavy debt. I always thought that I was a pretty good gunner. So we took off, and I radioed him, "What are we going to do—high sides, abeams, low sides, or overheads?" He said, "Well, we'll just do a little bit of everything. You follow me."

We got up there, and that's the first time I'd ever done a tail chase over and around the sleeve. Our training had been more formal: you'd do a high-side, come back up, do a high-side from the other side. But we just did a tail chase around that sleeve. He was shooting red and I was shooting blue, and I must have had ten or fifteen hits, which was pretty good shooting. But hell, that sleeve was red. I never saw so many holes in a sleeve in my whole life.

Fisher, who was as good at requisitioning as he was at flying, paid his debt, although his ability to gather luxuries resulted in a new nickname and some good-natured teasing from his squadron mates. He later explained why they called him "Mo."

It was an ethnic joke. I was from Miami Beach and had a knack for acquiring things that were difficult to get. On a couple of occasions I acquired a case of boned chicken—had it right under my bunk in my tent. A case of beer wasn't a real problem for me.

A few other newcomers were tagged with similarly lighthearted monikers. Bob Bragdon, a 1939 Princeton graduate with a degree in psychology, was "Meathead." Denmark Groover's short, spikey hair yielded "Quill Skull" or plain "Quill." Ed Harper naturally became "Harpo." A few were known by more conventional nicknames derived from their initials or distinguishing features, such as "J. J." Hill and "Red" Harris. Chris Magee was occasionally called "Maggie," though few dared; he had hauled a set of weights all the way to the South Pacific and could be found toning his well-defined muscles with them on a regular basis. At such times he wore only nylon swim trunks and a bandana, keeping the latter tied around his neck when it was not serving as a sweat cap. Neither article left his body except when he showered. Magee's esoteric interests belied his tough, piratelike appearance. He was into metaphysics, a beatnik long before the next decade's free-spirited generation was even defined, and his intellectual ability sometimes left his fellow pilots shaking their heads.

More conventional were the "Yamheads," the collective nickname given to several pilots from the Deep South. Burney Tucker, who had been raised in a small town near Nashville, attended Tennessee State, where he played quarterback in football and center in basketball and competed in multiple field events on the track team. Denny Groover, barely past his twenty-first birthday, hailed from a tiny Georgia town just a few miles above the Florida line. He had finished two years of prelaw at the University of Georgia and endeared himself to the other Marines with his silky accent as he gently drew out vowels with the refinement of an old Georgia gentleman. The most gentlemanly Southerner of all, the "King of the Yamheads," was Navy lieutenant James M. Reames, the new flight surgeon. Born and raised in Arkansas, the twenty-six-year-old had interned at the Philadelphia Naval Hospital, then completed the aviation medicine course in Pensacola. He first served in the South Pacific as an attending physician aboard evacuation transports (R4Ds converted into hospital planes) as they ferried wounded from Guadalcanal.

Not to be overlooked, the two second lieutenants on the roster were relatively experienced despite their boyish looks. Bruce J. Matheson was indeed youthful at twenty-one, but he had just as many flight hours as the "first louies," about four hundred by the time the first combat tour began. Robert W. McClurg had arrived in the Pacific with only twenty-one hours of fighter time in his logbook, then flew briefly with the original Swashbucklers.

McClurg was not a converted SBD pilot, as Boyington claimed, but he did struggle early. He had wrestled with the Corsair, especially during landings, and was replaced by Chief Synar prior to the combat tour. By now he had accumulated more flight time in F4Us, though Greg Boyington remained skeptical of his ability. "You're never gonna get home, kid," he told McClurg, but he decided to take him anyway. The Pennsylvanian acknowledged that his new commanding officer was his ticket for survival and vowed to stick close.

Boyington wrote of another former SBD pilot, identifying him only as "Shorty," who was less fortunate than McClurg. Attempting to correct a bounce induced by a poor landing, the pilot jammed full throttle to go around but failed to counter the sudden torque. As Boyington explained it:

> The propeller was doing a good job of corkscrewing the plane and Shorty in an inverted attitude through the coconut trees. We were able to raise the heavy plane up enough to free our little SBD friend from the overturned position he ended up in. Shorty was conscious, but one of Chief Sitting Bull's Indians couldn't have done a more thorough job of scalping.

Only one such accident occurred at Turtle Bay during this period. The pilot was a member of VMF-222, recently arrived after service on Midway. The scenario of the crash compares so closely with Boyington's story that there is little doubt they are one and the same. Second Lieutenant Richard L. Hobbs was taking off on the morning of August 25 when his Corsair veered sharply to the left and struck an earth berm between the strip and a taxiway on the north side of the field. The F4U bounced into the air, then rolled inverted and landed upside down in the taxiway. Its engine tumbled another seventy-five feet. The spinning prop tore away, cartwheeled along the flight line, struck a bystander and three parked Corsairs, and came to rest in a ditch. Hobbs escaped with only minor injuries, but the bystander suffered a fractured skull and a broken left arm. Another crewman, jumping from a parked Corsair to escape, broke his foot.

Training flights commenced during the last half of August and continued for the first six days of September, then stopped abruptly. On September 7, in an event unnoticed by the Swashbucklers resting at Turtle Bay, the rear echelon of VMF-124 was reassigned as VMF-214's flight echelon. Greg Boyington and his group of pilots now made up an independent squadron with its own number. The change was accompanied by a week's hiatus from flying, however, because VMF-214 was an "inactive squadron" currently without aircraft.

On the day of their transfer, Greg Boyington and his twenty-seven pilots gathered with the flight surgeon for a group photograph. They were milling about near a parked Corsair when the last new officer arrived. First Lieutenant Frank E. Walton Jr. had been sent from the headquarters squadron of the 1st MAW to serve as the intelligence officer. Looking for a pilot named Major Boyington, Walton spotted oak leaves on Stan Bailey's collar and saluted him as he reported for duty. It was an honest mistake. Boyington, who was dressed in rumpled, nondescript utility clothing and was standing off to one side, was practically invisible among the other pilots.

Walton soon established himself as one of the most influential members of the squadron as far as life on the ground was concerned. At thirty-four—older than most of the pilots by ten to twelve years—he was willing to oblige them as a paternal figure. His interest in looking after them was not a case of patronization but stemmed from leadership and organizational skills. They came naturally to the muscular

Californian, a once-famed swimmer who had established a world record in 1930 for the 150-yard backstroke. More recently he had been a Los Angeles police sergeant who ran war traffic control for the entire city. The big redhead was also a writer. In 1936 E. P. Dutton published his book, *The Sea Is My Workshop,* about lifeguarding in Southern California, although it did not sell many copies. Nonetheless Walton's police background and gift for writing could not have been better paired for the job of ACIO. He penned his first war diary entry on September 7. Because there was nothing of interest to write about, he economically repeated the same sentence for each of the next four days: "Operations and training, Espiritu Santos [*sic*]."

Walton did not indicate what the training was, but it all took place on the ground while the men waited to acquire Corsairs and move into combat. In the meantime, several photographs of Boyington and his pilots were staged for publicity. In one sequence, they gathered around a Dallas hut (still marked as VMF-124's ready room) for a mock briefing while Boyington squatted obligingly, pretending to scratch diagrams in the dirt. Next they simulated a scramble by running to nearby Corsairs. Another performance took place at the fighter strip, where movie and still cameras whirred while Rollie Rinabarger climbed in and out of a parked Corsair. Most of the pilots, Boyington included, donned swim trunks to cavort on the beach, and several swam out to a large floating raft, then jumped and splashed like boys at summer camp.

The photographs were processed on September 11, the same day that Maj. Gen. Ralph J. Mitchell, commanding general of the 1st MAW, gave Greg Boyington verbal orders to reposition his new outfit to Guadalcanal. This was the news he had waited weeks to hear. They would take twenty Corsairs, meaning that eight pilots and both ground officers would have to ride up to the 'Canal via SCAT transport. Boyington wisely named all but one of the combat veterans to ride the transport, allowing the least experienced pilots to log several more hours in Corsairs during the 550-plus-mile trip to Cactus.

Among the twenty Corsairs with their variegated hues of blue camouflage were a few of the newly introduced F4U-1A models, which represented several significant improvements. The most notable feature was a new bulged hood, or "bubbletop," with a raised pilot's seat for better visibility. The tail wheel assembly had been lengthened for the same reason. A small spoiler that had been added to the right wing greatly reduced the tendency suffered by the birdcage version to stall in the landing configuration. Touching down in the big bird was also more forgiving, thanks to softer oleos in the main gear struts.

Early on the morning of September 12, Frank Walton, Doc Reames, and eight pilots climbed aboard a truck for a ride across Espiritu to the bomber strip. Their R4D departed at 0730 and landed several hours later at Henderson Field, where another truck took them to Fighter One to meet Boyington and the Corsair drivers.

They had made the flight without incident save for this episode witnessed by Don Fisher.

> Bragdon had to relieve himself. The Corsair's stick had a unique bend, and the relief tube was in front of it. If you didn't know it was there, you couldn't see it. Bragdon was looking all over and couldn't find the relief tube, so he got his canteen cup out and took a leak in his canteen. Okay, that's fine . . . now what's he gonna do with it? I knew what was going on and was just dying. Bragdon was cranking the canopy open and was going to pour it out, but the slipstream blew it out of the canteen all over him.

After lunch and a briefing by Fighter Intelligence, all twenty Corsairs roared back into the sky for the short hop to the Russell Islands, this time with most of the combat veterans strapped into the fighters. Walton, Reames, and the remaining pilots spent the night on Guadalcanal, then arrived on Banika the next morning before 0800. In the meantime, Boyington and the others had already attended a briefing for an escort mission, though their only assignment was to spend the day on scramble alert.

Later that night, according to Walton, the squadron decided collectively to create a new name. Few were aware that their predecessors were already known as the Swashbucklers, nor would they have cared; theirs was an entirely new outfit needing to make its own statement. Feeling somewhat like unwanted orphans from the replacement pool, they were enthusiastic about an early suggestion for "Boyington's Bastards" (or "Boyington's Black Bastards," depending on the account). Walton mentioned it the following day to Capt. John L. DeChant, MAG-21's public relations officer, who deemed "bastard" too strong for the chaste newspaper readers back home.

The pilots' first idea had lasted one day. By Walton's chronology it was Tuesday, September 14, when the pilots went back to the drawing board and invented the subtle perfection of Black Sheep. Boyington took credit for the idea in his book; Walton named Bill Case as the creator of the original design.

Another recollection came from Pen Johnson, a battle-tested war correspondent and artist.

> [Boyington] suddenly blew into my tent announcing that he had heard that I was an artist and he wanted me to help him design a squadron insignia . . . It had to include as its motif a black sheep, as his squadron was to be named after this docile farmyard animal. To get what artists call "scrap," [we] spent all day . . . trying to find out whether sheep had long tails with big or little ears. A PFC Marine farm boy finally put us straight.

Johnson remembered the location as Espiritu, not the Russells, perhaps placing the date of the occasion a few days earlier than Walton's estimate, but in either case the finished artwork bears his signature. The design cleverly made reference to bastard ancestry the old-fashioned way, depicting a coat of arms branded with a black diagonal slash called a bar sinister. The cowl and gull wings of a Corsair formed the shield's crest, and a forlorn black sheep occupied center stage. In a matter of days the squadron had created a whole new identity, one perfectly suited to its unorthodox reactivation as a unit and equally appropriate to its commanding officer as an individual.

12

THE BULLETS FLY

Even though the Black Sheep were now officially on a combat tour, there was little for Frank Walton to write about at the end of their first full day in the Russells, September 13. After being briefed on an escort mission, the pilots passed the rest of Sunday sitting in the ready tent waiting for something to happen. Nothing did.

The major who briefed them was none other than George Britt, whose tenure as VMF-214's commander had ended only three months earlier. One of Britt's regular duties as MAG-21's operations officer was to fly a fast, stripped-down Corsair to Guadalcanal every day, collect the next day's operations plan from Fighter Command, and hasten back to conduct the appropriate briefings.* Though it was not the fighter squadron assignment he would have preferred, the job was rewarding, and the Russell Islands offered the most idyllic living in the eastern Solomons. There were other perks as well. Britt shared an electrified Dallas hut with the MAG-21 supply officer, who had procured one of the rarest luxuries in the entire area, a refrigerator, stocked with cold beer.

As Britt recalled, it did not take long for Boyington to find out.

* Lacking guns and armor plate, this Corsair was rebuilt from so many salvaged parts that it did not have a Bureau of Aeronautics registration number. It was affectionately known as NoBuNo.

> Somehow, when Boyington arrived he smelled that beer, and he became a constant visitor. He had a nose for wherever the alcohol was. When I had been in Sydney I bought a bottle of Australian brandy, and later discovered that it was so awful I just threw the bottle in my trunk and forgot about it. One evening when Boyington was visiting the hut, I broke out that bottle of brandy and said, "Do you want this?" He took a swig and said, "Boy, that's good!" So I was able to get rid of the brandy.

Two days after reaching the Russells, the Black Sheep participated in their first combat assignment. It was not the mission described years later by Boyington, who had them arriving in the Russells on September 15 and shooting down Japanese in a huge fight early the next morning. The drama of a big dogfight on the squadron's first mission might have been irresistible, but it did not happen.

Instead the inaugural mission began on September 14 at 0835, when the first F4Us began rolling down Banika's strip for a bomber escort assignment. Although Boyington had never been on an escort mission, he gave a brief lecture about staying with the bombers, as later described by Stan Bailey.

> He gave us his aggressive combat theories the day we got down to business: "Fighter aircraft are designed and fighter pilots trained to fight. If we don't contact the enemy when he's around, something's wrong. There's only one exception and that's bomber escort. If we attack . . . it means we've been lured away from our job."

The first mission had the potential to be a tough one—shepherding twelve B-24s to Kahili. The ground crew at Banika had worked their magic, making ready all twenty of the Corsairs flown up earlier from Espiritu, and four more fighters were borrowed from VMF-123. Shortly after takeoff one pilot aborted when his wing tanks failed to feed, but the remaining twenty-three Black Sheep began weaving above the bombers in three stacked layers. The formation headed northwest, following the Slot between Fauro Island and Choiseul, before turning to initiate their bombing run from northwest of Kahili. Boyington assigned eight of his veterans throughout the group as division or section leaders. The rest were neophytes who caught their first glimpse of battle as they approached the enemy airfield.

A thick column of black smoke stretched a mile and a half into the sky, testimony to a previous strike. Dust trails appeared on Kahili's strip below as a half-dozen enemy planes scrambled. As the Liberators began dropping their loads in a straggling column of vees, about fifty bursts of heavy-caliber antiaircraft fire smeared the blue sky around them, mostly behind the formation.

Not surprisingly, many of the Army's bombs geysered into the sea off the strip, although a few landed in a dispersal area near the strip. The B-24s showed poor discipline on the return leg, and eventually the formation unraveled so that the bombers were stretched along five miles of airspace. The Marines kept their eyes peeled, but whatever had been streaking down Kahili's strip never materialized and there were no contacts with Japanese fighters. All Corsairs returned safely, though several made brief stopovers at Munda to correct minor problems. From the fighter pilots' viewpoint, it had been a well-executed introductory mission, albeit quiet.

So was Tuesday's event, an escort mission to the north of Choiseul where four B-24s made a photoreconnaissance run, though the squadron's early success with its Corsairs began to ebb. Of the twenty-four that launched (five were borrowed), four returned early with various mechanical troubles and two wingmen accompanied their leaders home. One of the latter was Lt. Burney L. Tucker, tail-end Charlie in Stan Bailey's division. When John Bolt's F4U developed engine trouble, Tucker followed him to Segi for repairs. Tucker was the last man to land at the end of the day but the first Black Sheep to wreck an airplane when brake failure turned it into a salvage job.

It was not until Wednesday afternoon, on the squadron's third mission, that the big fight Boyington wrote of finally occurred. It was indeed one for the record books. The Black Sheep were assigned to escort a mixed force of TBF Avengers and SBD Dauntlesses to Ballale, the heavily defended island base just off the tip of Bougainville. Like many of their missions, this was an interservice affair, with the Dauntlesses and Avengers at thirteen thousand feet, P-40s providing low cover, a flight of Navy F6F Hellcats at seventeen thousand feet, and the Black Sheep perched four thousand feet higher. In all, it was one of the largest Allied formations yet assembled in the Solomons.

Takeoff commenced at 1300 as divisions led by Majors Boyington and Bailey, Captain Ewing, and Lieutenants Beggert, Case, and McCartney led two dozen Black Sheep from the Banika strip in seven minutes. More than a hundred aircraft, most having departed earlier from Guadalcanal, circled between Kolombangara and Vella Lavella, then headed west up the Slot. At the Shortlands the assembled force circled again to the right. The bombers had just commenced their run toward the target from the far side of Ballale at approximately 1450 when an estimated thirty to forty Zeros "spilled out of the clouds."

The defenders, mostly Zekes, were flown by the 204 Kokutai, and in this instance their records matched the Marines' estimates closely. The 204 sortied twenty-six Zeros against "100+ fighters/bombers," and elements of the 201 Kokutai were probably engaged as well. The opposing groups clashed over Ballale in an enormous free-for-all that lasted half an hour.

It was a twisting, rolling, free-falling, gut-squeezing fight. Ribbons of tracers lanced through the sky from sea level to four miles high. Vapor trails streamed from the wingtips of g-loaded fighters that hurtled past in screaming power dives. Others were seen in mortal plunges, blurred shapes moving too fast to be identified. With so many planes in three-dimensional motion, it was dangerous to fixate on any one and fatal to fly straight and level. A swarm of enemies was surely boring in from behind.

The melee became a rite of passage for sixteen Black Sheep, their first big test. In the blink of an eye they had to absorb what they were seeing, remember the most vital points of their training, and try to react, all while their hearts pounded in their ears, perspiration burst from every pore, their tongues turned to cotton, and they forgot to breathe.

Chris Magee later described it.

> All I could do was keep spinning my neck and looking . . . everything was happening so fast. I was looking out one side, and all of a sudden I saw a plane—a Japanese plane that was kind of a brownish color—right at about the same level or a slightly lower altitude. And suddenly I saw the wings just go up both sides of the canopy, and between the front and the back it looked like a flower just blossoming out of this thing. There was a big ball of fire, and out of the middle of the fire comes a guy. He pulled his chute and opened it right there at twelve thousand feet.

Magee noted the enemy fighter's brownish paint scheme, whereas other pilots described mottled shades of green or even hues approaching black depending on the angle of the sun. The Zeros' prominent cowlings, which were painted black, perhaps dominated what the mind recorded, but there was no mistaking the Marines' first glimpse of those huge red disks, the Japanese icon of the sun, that emblazoned the enemy fighters' wings and fuselages.

The Black Sheep initiated the first engagement with the advantage of altitude. Virtually every division made an overhead pass beginning with Stan Bailey, who dived on a "circling hive" of Zekes with Bob Alexander, John Bolt, and Burney Tucker in tow. The exec singled out a Zeke and made a pass from its rear quarter, but the Japanese pilot saw him and flipped away. Bailey followed, but only Alexander was able to stay with him. Bolt's section was left behind, now on its own.

After chasing his target down to ten thousand feet, Bailey opened fire. The Zeke fled, smoking, into a cloud. The relentless New Englander followed it into the vapor, where he promptly lost sight of Alexander, then popped back into clear sky. Another Zeke spotted Bailey, opened fire, and chased him back into the cloud for a few moments. When Bailey poked the nose of his Corsair out again, there was the Zeke, waiting to pounce. Four times Bailey tried to sneak out, and four times his adversary cut him off. Finally Bailey went on instruments and, staying within the layer, turned southeast toward friendly territory.

When Bailey next emerged into clear air, the Zeke was gone, but another was down below, making runs at a helpless pilot dangling in a parachute. Bailey dived, but the nimble fighter yanked into a loop and came down on his own tail, whereupon Bailey had to dive again to evade, using his Corsair's superior weight and speed. Circling back, he spotted yet another enemy fighter and was turning in to it when the puckering sound of bullets striking metal grabbed his attention. There were three Zekes behind him. After diving away yet again, Bailey finally decided he'd had enough. The fight had degraded to his disadvantage ever since that first overhead run, and with his plane riddled it was past time to head home.

Some of the rookies had better luck. Bailey's wingman, twenty-two-year-old Bob Alexander, had remained with the exec during the first pass but pulled off when he descended through ten thousand feet. Intent on chasing his target, Bailey had not seen three Zekes about to dive on them, but Alexander yanked hard into the trio and scattered them. Then he "went hunting." Soon he spotted a pair of Zekes a thousand feet below and nosed over toward the wingman in a trailing position on the right. Closing rapidly from astern, he squeezed the trigger at two hundred yards and could see his heavy slugs sawing into the Zeke's fuselage and cockpit. Pieces flew as smoke began to stream from the Zeke's right side. As Alexander passed within fifty feet, he looked into the cockpit, now seething with fire. Cutting across the path of this flaming torch, he drew a bead on the leader, but the agile Zeke rolled to the right and pulled into a split-S.

Maintaining his altitude and keeping his head on a swivel, Alexander spotted four more Zekes just as the leader of this group peeled off to make a run on him. Alexander pushed his Corsair over in a diving right turn to elude them, then made certain the threat was gone before pulling back up into what looked like a swirling fracas. He soon discovered an unusual Japanese fighter discipline that would become a common sight: a dozen or more Zekes turning and slow-rolling in a giant circle. The Japanese were performing their version of the Lufbery Circle, a defensive posture not unlike circling the wagons.* The premise was that any pilot trying to get behind a Zero in the circle put himself at great risk—several other enemy planes would be on him in an instant—but the circle was rendered ineffective if left alone. Alexander knew better than to tangle with this pack by himself and dived out, his fighting finished for the day.

Another Marine in his first shooting engagement was Don Fisher. Greg Boyington, who had once humbled Fisher out of a case of beer during a gunnery hop, nonetheless placed the big Floridian on his own wing. It was a wise decision. When the fight commenced, Boyington reefed his Corsair around in a hard left turn. Fisher tried to follow but

*Named for Gervais Raoul Lufbery, 1885–1918, a key member of the American-manned *Lafayette Escadrille* in World War I.

was sucked back, leaving about two hundred yards of separation. A Zeke promptly sailed through this gap from the left, then reversed course to initiate a right-quarter pass at Boyington's F4U. It was a beautiful setup for Fisher; as he triggered his guns the Zeke began a slow roll to the left. It was on its back when Fisher sent another burst directly into the cockpit. "I was right behind him, and he blew," Fisher remembered. "The wings went each way. They couldn't take the beating of those six fifties—once you were on them, they were done."

Fisher's gunnery had turned out to be as good as he hoped, and his day was not yet done. Looking around for Boyington, he spotted another Corsair heading toward him with a Zeke on its tail. Fisher snapped off a burst and missed, but the Zeke pulled up and initiated the same maneuver that Fisher had just witnessed—a slow roll to the left. This Zeke was also on its back when Fisher fired a long burst. The Zeke began smoking, then spun off into a tight spiral for a thousand feet until flames streaked back. Separated from his division now, Fisher climbed up and eventually found the bombers, then followed them home.

Boyington, meanwhile, apparently never saw the Zeke that Fisher shot off his rear quarter until it began to burn. Years later he described a sense of bewilderment as the fight began, until a stream of tracers flashing past his right wing snapped him back to reality. He didn't see anything of his second section either (Virgil Ray leading, backed up by Red Harris) after Don Fisher pulled up to flame the Zeke. Several single-handed engagements followed, details of which appeared in the official action report compiled that day by Frank Walton as well as in the story Boyington wrote fifteen years later. The two accounts were roughly in agreement, but the former—written within hours of the event—is considered more reliable.

According to the war diary, the first Japanese fighter Boyington saw was a clipped-wing A6M3 Hamp whose pilot was apparently as confused as Boyington had been. The

Japanese pilot pulled alongside Boyington's Corsair, waggled his wings in the standard join-up signal, then accelerated ahead and passed within a hundred feet. A surprised Boyington, who had not even remembered to arm his guns, flipped the switches and opened fire from 150 feet. With its cockpit aflame, the Hamp rolled left, plunged straight down, and hit the water about ten miles east of Ballale.

Boyington circled left and spotted two unidentified Corsairs, then took the lead and turned them toward Kahili. Staying just under a cloud layer, he headed toward a large formation of circling Zeros—possibly the same group sighted by Bob Alexander. The other two Corsairs departed, so Boyington pulled up into the clouds and climbed in a spiral to 24,000 feet. Toward Vella Lavella he sighted more Zeros, nearly two miles below, making high stern runs at friendly bombers without pressing their attacks. Boyington nosed over and picked out another Hamp. He accelerated rapidly as his Corsair dropped like an elevator, then opened fire from 300 yards astern. With his plane traveling at approximately 500 feet per second, he readily closed the gap. He was only a few yards behind the Hamp when it disintegrated completely, causing him to instinctively raise one arm across his face to protect it from flying debris. Fortunate to miss the tumbling engine, he emerged from the shower of exploded pieces with dents in the cowling and leading edges of his Corsair.

As Boyington turned to the right and climbed back into the sun, he spotted a pair of Navy F6Fs flying close formation on the right flank of the retreating bombers just as another Hamp commenced a firing run on the Hellcats. Boyington could see tracers streaking past the F6Fs, which had parked too close to the bombers to maneuver. But the Japanese pilot overran them and pulled up sharply into a loop, which gave Boyington an opportunity. Nimble though the Japanese fighter was, its airspeed decayed as it neared the top of the loop, and Boyington caught it flush. Spewing flames and flat on its back, the Hamp drifted through the loop and plummeted as Boyington passed through its blazing arc.

As he climbed again to eighteen thousand feet, Boyington estimated that he was a third of the way back to Vella Lavella, about twenty miles east of Ballale. By now the Zeros were turning away from the retreating bombers and heading home, but Boyington thought he saw a loner moving west at six thousand feet. This time, instead of diving with excessive speed, he pulled power to idle and glided down. When the Japanese pilot started a gentle left turn, Boyington became suspicious. Searching to his right he spotted a bouncer waiting to spring the trap. He immediately turned in toward the would-be ambusher, approached it head-on, opened fire at three hundred yards, and held in the trigger. He saw pieces of cowling fly off as the Japanese yanked up and passed overhead. Boyington chandelled up and left, then quickly reversed course to chase down the Hamp, which was now streaming heavy smoke. Climbing toward Ballale, Boyington watched the stricken fighter motor along for ten miles in a flat glide until it finally hit the water.

The bait Zero was no longer in sight, so Boyington climbed back into the sun to ten thousand feet, having decided that "a fair day's work" had been accomplished. But soon another section of Zeros turned toward him, directly abeam and half a mile below. Boyington kicked the rudder and charged at the lead Hamp, which broke to the right and climbed. He shifted his aim to the second Zero, then opened fire at a reported six hundred yards—a third of a mile. This one smoked, but rather than pursue it Boyington pointed his Corsair southeast and returned to ten thousand feet, because he was running low on both fuel and ammunition.*

Boyington mistook for a Zero a single plane he sighted

*Beyond the account in the action report, there is no record that this was scored a probable.

heading toward Vella Lavella at three thousand feet. But when two more planes appeared from the opposite direction and circled back to make a pass at the single, Boyington realized it was a damaged Corsair under attack. As he nosed over to drive off the two aircraft by opening fire at extreme range, one of the antagonists yanked straight up. Boyington pulled with it, firing all the way as it commenced a slow roll and burst into flames. But now his own fighter was in a precarious situation. The heavy Corsair ran out of airspeed, stalled, then pitched over in an inverted spin. After struggling to recover the aircraft, Boyington could not find the other Corsair. Critically low on fuel, he headed south once more.

At the Banika airstrip, the off-duty pilots waited with Frank Walton and Doc Reames for the Black Sheep to return. By 1630 all but two of the airplanes had straggled back to the Russells. For the next hour the flight surgeon tended to sweat-soaked pilots, some paradoxically shivering from the adrenaline rush of combat (they would almost crumple once the hormone wore off). Other pilots gathered around the intelligence officer while he recorded their statements and sorted out events.

Those who made it back claimed six Zeros shot down and eight others probably destroyed, all Zekes. In addition to Bob Alexander's single and Don Fisher's two slow-rolling flamers, John Begert had burned two more. One had been witnessed by Chris Magee, who saw the pilot emerge from the flames and pull his parachute at twelve thousand feet.

Boyish-looking Bob McClurg, who had struggled earlier with the Swashbucklers before gaining Boyington's grudging acceptance, proved himself by defeating a Zeke in a bold head-on encounter. McClurg had just watched the Zeke shoot a Navy Hellcat down in flames, but his reactions were slow. When the enemy plane turned toward him, he thought it was flashing its lights at him. With a jolt he realized those were muzzle blasts from its cannon and machine guns. He fired by instinct and saw pieces fly off the Zeke's cowling. Another burst caused more chunks of its engine to fly apart. Then the planes rolled past each other canopy to canopy. McClurg could see the pilot struggling inside as flames filled the cockpit. "I was scared to death," he recalled. "My tongue was swollen up the size of a pear."

Of the eight probables, two were credited to Hank McCartney and singles went to Stan Bailey, Bill Case, Virgil Ray, Chris Magee, Ed Olander, and Bruce Matheson. In all, six neophyte Marines had scored victories or probables in their first shooting engagement. Other Marines, including John Bolt, missed opportunities. "The first time I saw a meatball it was a full deflection, and he just *zipped* by," Bolt recalled. "It was a great big meatball, with the sun over my shoulder. I was in a state of shock." Later in the same fight he encountered another Zero head-on and never fired his guns.

But at least Bolt made it back. By late afternoon Greg Boyington and Bob Ewing were unaccounted for, and it soon became obvious that they could not still be airborne on their original fuel supply. When last seen, Ewing was leading his division in a scissors above the bombers at 23,000 feet, then commenced a diving right turn at full throttle toward a gaggle of sixteen Zeros. He had begun crowding toward Moon Mullen and Tom Emrich, who were lined up on his left in the second section. His wingman, McClurg, crossed under in an attempt to stay with Ewing but fell behind and was separated from the rest. Ewing kept crowding against Mullen, apparently intent on getting into firing position behind a target. Mullen continued to give way until he spotted a Zero diving steeply on a Corsair below. Then he cut under Ewing and managed a short burst at the Zero before pulling back around to rejoin his division leader. By then, Ewing was nowhere in sight. The Black Sheep continued to wait by the ready tent, checking their watches and speculating what could have happened to the missing pilots—especially the skipper—on their first mission. "We timed for his fuel to run out," Denmark Groover remembered, "and we thought he had gone gosling."

More than an hour passed before they finally heard the familiar sound of a single Pratt & Whitney. It was Boyington, who pancaked at 1755 and taxied over to a revetment, his soot-stained Corsair pocked with dents. After climbing down, he explained to his exuberant squadron mates that he had managed to shoot down five planes but had barely enough fuel to make it to Munda. The ground crew there had counted just thirty rounds of ammunition and ten gallons of gas before they serviced his plane.

The pilots' jubilation began to subside with they realized that Bob Ewing was not coming back. Boyington surmised that the damaged F4U he saw under attack was Ewing's: "That slowed-down, oil-smeared, and shell-riddled Corsair couldn't have gone much further." If that was the case, the slender Purdue man did not go down early in the fight. Perhaps he managed to survive another thirty minutes, but he was a statistic in any case—the first Black Sheep to go down in battle. John Begert and Moon Mullen, having been with Ewing since their days together in VMF-122, were given the unhappy job of itemizing his possessions. They produced two lists, one of government property, the other of personal effects. The articles in the first were redistributed; those in the second were bundled up for eventual return to Ewing's next of kin. Even the little items were documented and signed for, everything from a model airplane to safety razors to thirteen books and pictures of loved ones.

On the positive side, the Black Sheep and their fast-starting commander earned credit for eleven victories and eight probables in their first fight. Frank Walton cross-examined participants to determine the accuracy of their individual claims, then made his conclusions based on their recollections after a heart-pounding melee.

But as happened in practically every recorded engagement, the total claims were mathematically impossible when compared with the recorded Japanese losses, especially considering that other squadrons claimed kills that day. Two Navy F6F outfits in action over Ballale received credit for five Zekes and a Tony shot down, plus another Zeke probably destroyed. American claims for the day totaled seventeen Japanese planes destroyed and nine probables—coincidentally the same number of planes sortied by the 204 Kokutai. That air group lost five pilots, the 201 Kokutai only one. Obviously the Hellcats and Corsairs had double- and triple-teamed against the victims.

As Bruce Matheson recalled, the details of the action were often impossible to validate.

> [Walton] would tend to sort this out. He'd say, "Now, wait a minute, you said this," and somebody else would say, "Yeah, but I was over here and I'm sure I shot it." Frank would say, "Is there a possibility you two guys were shooting at the same airplane?" Hell, yes; there may have been three or four of us shooting at this poor sucker before he finally blew up.

On this particular day the Japanese exaggerated even more wildly. The 204 claimed four F4Us downed and two others "uncertain," though Bob Ewing was the only Corsair pilot lost in the entire area. With so much confusion in the air, contention over specific claims was inevitable. In the case of the Black Sheep's first combat, an argument arose when a Navy pilot landed his F6F at Banika and complained that Greg Boyington had taken credit for some of his victories.

George Britt became involved as the mediator.

> [The Navy pilot] was mad as hell that Boyington claimed the same planes, but Boyington was very adamant that he was the one to get credit, and he got it.

His story sounded more plausible. "Sour grapes," said Boyington, after the lieutenant commander stormed out of the operations hut.

The Black Sheep's stay in the idyllic Russells was a short one. Early Friday morning, September 17, an R4D carrying Frank Walton, Doc Reames, and three fighter pilots departed for Munda; the rest launched in Corsairs to act as escort for a photoreconnaissance of Choiseul. After searching nearly thirty minutes in vain for the photo planes—apparently the rendezvous point was incorrect—Boyington and the others gave up looking and pancaked at Munda.

Five hours later, divisions led by Stan Bailey and Hank Bourgeois took off to conduct a two-and-a-half-hour sweep for pilots downed during earlier dogfights, especially Bob Ewing. Crisscrossing the waters from Vella Lavella to Ballale and the Shortlands, then retracing their path, they encountered surface glare that thwarted their efforts. There was no sign of Ewing. Boyington later wrote that a sun-blackened corpse found floating in a raft several days later might have been the missing pilot, but the PBY sent to investigate did not risk a water landing for a dead man.

The Black Sheep soon discovered just how comfortable the camps on Espiritu and the Russells had actually been. Gone were the relative luxuries of plywood Dallas huts and electric lights; now they moved into sagging, dirty canvas tents infested with rats, lizards, giant crabs, and bugs. Foxholes cut into the wooden floors collected water, which turned rancid, then condensed and added to the perpetual humidity. Tent walls, bedding, and clothing were never truly dry. Mealtimes offered little respite (other than a chance to congregate in the chow line) because of the monotonous diet of Spam, beans, SOS, and bland dehydrated packaged food, all washed down with bitter coffee or warm water. "Flies were having a field day," wrote Walton. Like his predecessors on Guadalcanal, he learned what it was like to fight the insects for the food.

On a quiet night their crude living arrangements would have taken getting used to, but their first night at Munda was far from peaceful. The first air-raid alert awakened them at 0100. Hardly had they settled back onto their sweaty cots when the sirens went off again, this time accompanied by the whistle and crunch of bombs, then again an hour later, and once more at 0445. Moon Mullen stood an eight-hour scramble alert, but for some reason he remained on the ground during the recurring raids.

No one slept through that hot, sticky night. Several Black Sheep were already up and dressed when the last raid came, minutes before the first division was scheduled to take off on a task force escort mission. When the all clear sounded, those scheduled for flights piled onto a vehicle—often a sagging, overloaded jeep, perhaps a larger weapons carrier—for a ride down to the flight line.

The pilots did not have preassigned Corsairs. No one, including Boyington, had a personal airplane. Instead the jeep rolled down the line past the revetments, where an enlisted plane captain waiting by each Corsair signaled either "thumbs up" or "thumbs down." In the dark he used a hooded flashlight. If the signal was affirmative, a pilot jumped from the jeep and climbed in; if the plane was grounded, the jeep simply rolled to the next plane in line.

Bruce Matheson later remarked on the informalities.

> Off you'd go with no idea what the tail numbers were, whose squadron [the aircraft] belonged to, nothing. They were just airplanes, there to be flown. Looking back on it, the absence of record-keeping was unbelievable. We kept our own logbooks. There were no Yellow Sheets. There was no such thing as writing down anything, when you came back from a hop, which had to do with maintenance. When you came back, some young

kid naked to the waist would bring you in, put chocks under it and say, "What about it?" You'd say, "It's okay," or "fix the radio," and walk away from it.

After finding four ready Corsairs, Hank Bourgeois led his division airborne at 0525 Saturday morning to provide convoy patrol above a naval force on its way to a landing on Vella Lavella. During the rest of the day, the Black Sheep flew thirty-one sorties to maintain this protective umbrella. The convoy, filled with troops and cargo, was too big to go unnoticed by the Japanese network of coast-watchers among the islands. Soon the enemy launched a sizable raid from Bougainville.

When the Barakoma radar controller called the bogey inbound shortly past noon, two divisions of Black Sheep were already on station. Bill Case's flight climbed to 23,000 feet, but scattered layers of cumulus clouds made it difficult to see into the distance. Case was easing down when radar called the bogey at twenty-five miles. Lanky Rollie Rinabarger spotted them first—an estimated forty to fifty Vals guarded by thirty Zeros, just below a cloud layer at 18,000 feet. His estimate was good: The 204 Kokutai had sortied a mix of thirty-two Zekes and Hamps. The Vals probably came from the 582 Kokutai, though the records were later destroyed at Rabaul.

Once again the Japanese fighter pilots pulled into a huge circle some two miles across to repeat the phenomenon of two days before. Case dived, then glimpsed a flight of four Hamps with a thousand-foot advantage just waiting for him to commit. He yanked up into the bouncers. The rest of the Corsairs continued toward the giant Lufbery Circle, which proved dicey to penetrate. Rollie Rinabarger, Bob Bragdon, and Denmark Groover were able to get short bursts at selected Zeros, but the little fighters simply chandelled or split-Sed away before the Marines could get close. When Bragdon tried to get behind one, it pulled into a short, skidding chandelle, then half stalled. He overran it, and it rolled onto his tail. After diving out and crossing under Denny Groover, he lost both of them.

Case, meanwhile, pulled back up to 23,000 feet and was now alone, flying in and out of clouds and sunshine. Soon he saw three Corsairs a mile below and dived to join up. Zeros were still flying in a circle below these Marines, probably from VMF-213, who rolled over to initiate a firing run. Case lagged behind, looking for a bouncer. Sure enough a Zeke came curving in from the right and made a beam run on the third Corsair. Case rolled into an overhead pass and settled behind the unsuspecting pilot, who never stood a chance.

> I got onto this one Zero and he didn't take any evasive action. He didn't see me, or maybe he thought he was the sacrificial goat. He finally made one long, gentle turn around a cloud, and then went into a cloud. I was so close behind him that I could see him inside the cloud—this was fifty feet or less. I was at idle rpm, slowing down so I didn't overrun him. He just came out of the cloud straight and level, and I fired away at him. [But] the prop on a Corsair was about thirteen feet six inches, and the guns were set outboard of that, so I was missing him. Too much spread. I spent about 2,000 rounds figuring that out. I finally put the pipper up above his tail and about six or eight feet to the side and shot that way, and hit him with three guns at a time.

Case followed the smoking Zero down to eleven thousand feet when it finally began to burn from the left wing, followed by two puffs from the fuselage. Soon it was engulfed in flames and nosing over for the terminal plunge. Case had his first victory as a Black Sheep (he had claimed a probable two days before) and his second overall.

John Begert and two of his division's pilots had departed Munda at 1130, but Chris Magee was delayed because of mechanical trouble. By the time Magee changed Corsairs,

Begert and the others were nowhere in sight, so he leveled off and patrolled alone before joining three other F4Us. Soon they spotted thirty Vals below. The enemy dive-bombers had split into two groups. The nearest segment, which appeared to have pickled its bombs without attacking the convoy, was now headed back toward Bougainville.

Magee initiated a run from thirteen thousand feet, then followed the other three Corsairs as they dropped onto the Vals from behind. When one of the dive-bombers broke loose to evade, he turned with it and squeezed three medium bursts. The Val erupted and dropped toward the sea.

Turning, Magee spotted more Vals—fifteen in this group—boring toward the ships at Barakoma Beach. Ignoring friendly AA, he followed.

> The Japanese were going into a straight dive, so I headed into the dive with them. Of course, by then the antiaircraft was all around us, but you don't even think of that. It's not a case of choosing . . . there's no choice involved. I got in there with them, and could see the bursts going off, but nobody was getting hit apparently. The [Vals] kept going down, and I kept in there, firing.

Magee trapped several Vals down on the water. Then he began making beam runs back and forth across the rear of the fleeing formation, like a big cat worrying wildebeests, until he cut one from the pack. Magee pounced, raking the Val with a long burst that "blew it to pieces," then picked out another straggler. He was starting a beam run on this one when it turned toward him, and the two planes closed fast. As he hosed off a long burst, Magee was satisfied to see the Val fly through his bullets before it passed beneath him.

Away from his own ships and intent on chasing the Vals, Magee did not see a pack of Zeros until they had him dead to rights. He was saved only by his armor plate and his speed. He heard the sound of bullets striking metal "like a hail storm on a tin roof" and saw holes appearing in his wings. His reaction was to kick the rudder hard right, then left, to send his big fighter into a skid as he dived with what little altitude remained, then he turned back toward friendly ships. He glanced behind him and saw the Zeros, which chose not to pursue him into the convoy's guns.

Having shaken them, Magee could have turned for home but instead climbed back on station over the fleet, where he resumed patrolling for another fifteen minutes. Only when a division of P-40s appeared did he depart the area. He landed at Munda with a tire shot out and thirty bullet holes in his Corsair. When Frank Walton finished Magee's debriefing, he told the Chicagoan that he was recommending him for a Navy Cross. "Hell," Magee reportedly scoffed. "I don't want any medals. Just killing the yellow bastards is enough fun for me!" The Navy's highest award for valor was eventually pinned on his blouse, although the citation included several yet-unfought actions.

Magee's was the only Black Sheep fighter to receive battle damage, but September 18 was a costly day for their sister squadron. VMF-213 lost three Corsairs with only one pilot rescued. Likewise two of the 204 Kokutai's fighter pilots failed to return. No comparable records for the Val air group have been located to validate Magee's claims. His two kills and one probable were significant nonetheless. Throughout the rest of the war, all but the very last Japanese plane the Black Sheep dueled with were fighters.

On Sunday morning, two divisions conducted a search of the Vella Lavella area to locate Maj. W. H. Clarke, one of the Hellhawks missing from the previous day's action. The results were negative and almost costly: Bob Alexander's engine quit on the way back to Munda and he barely made the field for a dead-stick landing. Hank Bourgeois and Bill Case led their divisions as medium and high cover for an afternoon strike by SBDs, TBFs, and B-25s on Vila where the fighter pilots had a ringside seat for observing the bomber's pinpoint accuracy once the moderate AA fire had been suppressed.

That night, hoping to give Munda's bleary-eyed ground troops and airmen some peace, Greg Boyington decided to take off alone and defend the field against Washing Machine Charlies. He departed an hour past midnight on Monday, September 20, and stayed aloft for four hours, dropping down occasionally to conserve his oxygen supply. Several times he saw what appeared to be a signal light flashing from a location on the east side of Kolombangara and suspected an enemy coastwatcher at work. The behavior of the Japanese bombers seemed to bear out his theory. Whenever he dropped down to go off oxygen, any of several bogies milling about would close toward Munda until Boyington climbed back on station, then they would retreat and keep their distance.

Just after he pancaked at 0500, and before the dawn patrol could reach altitude, a Betty raced in and dropped a stick of bombs on the field. John Begert, scrambling to reach a Corsair during the raid, was knocked flat by a bomb blast and sustained minor injuries. The Betty did not strike with impunity, however; two Hellhawk F4Us chased it seventy miles toward Bougainville and shot it into the water.

Twenty-five minutes after he'd been bowled over, Begert and his division (J. J. Hill, George Ashmun, and Chris Magee) took off to provide aerial coverage for the admiral who was responsible for the squadron's impromptu inception. Bull Halsey departed Rendova Harbor aboard a PT boat for a two-hour transit to Barokorua Island. He received protection from rotating divisions of Black Sheep all the way in addition to the return trip later in the day. That he knew the Corsairs overhead were manned by his stopgap band of fighter pilots is doubtful, but later he did take time to personally meet several of his better-known protégés during a brief visit to the Black Sheep's strip alert tent at Munda.

Later on Monday, seven Black Sheep led by Stan Bailey

and Moon Mullen launched to escort a strike of SBDs and TBFs to Kolombangara. Six made the rendezvous point (Tom Emrich's engine failed a few minutes after takeoff and he returned intact) fifteen minutes early, where they found the bombers already in their dives. In the face of intense, heavy-caliber AA fire, the bombers thoroughly covered the target, Parapatu Point, losing one TBF that came down in the Kula Gulf. While the Black Sheep guarded the skies, its crew climbed into a rubber boat and were soon picked up by a PT boat.

The following day was dedicated to two strafing missions, with dramatic results. The first mission was launched at 0835 as Boyington and Begert led their divisions toward Choiseul, where a Japanese cargo vessel and several barges had been sighted. Two of the Black Sheep returned early with mechanical trouble, but the rest managed to locate the reported vessel, a seventy-foot Chinese junk that appeared occupied.

Chris Magee's action over the target soon elevated him to legendary status among his squadron mates, for he happened to have brought along a piece of unauthorized ordnance.

> There was some kind of boat or yacht over across the channel. We flew over there and started strafing the thing, and I had this grenade I'd taken along with me. I pushed the canopy back on one of the runs we were making, got all set up and then pulled the ring, and couldn't get it out! It really takes two hands to do that. The first time, I tried to pull it with my teeth—I saw that in the old movies. Well, it didn't work like it works in the movies: I almost pulled my teeth out, instead. So when we circled around and came back for another run, I used both hands and held it until we got to the right spot, then threw it over the side. Of course when I threw it, the slipstream hit my arm and threw it back. But the thing went down all right, and it was really one of those lucky shots.

It went off just above the deck. Boyington yelled, "They're firing at us!" With that close a shot, it looked like AA or something. So I told them, "Forget it, that was a grenade."

The Black Sheep left the vessel burning and flew to where the barges had been reported, found one with ten men working on it, and put it to the torch. On the return trip to Munda, Chris Magee discovered that the excitement was not yet over: His engine quit near the field and forced a dead-stick landing. Circling in a figure eight to lose altitude, he lowered his landing gear and flaps, then discovered that he was about to undershoot Munda's coral strip. He tried raising the gear with what little hydraulic pressure remained, hoping to reduce drag and milk his heavy glider closer to the strip. The boys down at the ready tent saw him disappear below the palm trees. "Oh God," someone said, "there goes a plane. That's the end of that aircraft."

To their amazement the windmilling F4U appeared again just above the trees, then dropped to the field. Once clear of the trees, Magee used the emergency CO_2 bottle beside his seat to blow down the gear, and his wheels locked into place just thirty feet above the deck. His grenade-throwing days were over, but that episode and his nonchalant handling of the subsequent emergency resulted in a new name: "Wild Man." His teammates never looked at him the same way again. In later years Magee was popularized as a renegade pilot who habitually flew with a sack of grenades in his lap and tossed them at targets of opportunity; it was pure myth but rooted in an actual event.

Five hours later Magee was back in the air to join Boyington and ten others on the second strafing mission of the day. Their task was to strafe Kahili at dusk, though only one division (Bourgeois's) would do the shooting while the rest formed a protective escort. In addition to eight guardian Corsairs, four flights of P-40s and P-39s acted as medium and high cover, respectively. As with previous strafing missions, the formation took a northwest course along the coast of Choiseul, but this time the attackers turned to make their run across the south end of Kahili heading roughly southwest—a direction that would preclude an immediate egress over the water.

The four shooters (Bourgeois, Bill Heier, Sandy Sims, and D. J. Moore) spread out and dropped to just fifty feet, then opened fire at a thousand yards and held down triggers as they crossed the facility. Their twenty-four machine guns totally surprised a bivouac of encamped Japanese, then lanced through a cluster of Zeros parked on the south end of the strip, hit an AA position just beyond it, and finally chewed through a group of boats and personnel two miles to the west at the mouth of a river.

The strafing run was going like clockwork until a big chunk of something suddenly flew up directly in front of Junior Heier—a hazard of working so low. Instinctively he turned and flew smack into a palm tree with a shuddering bang that amputated the Corsair's left wingtip and peeled the skin from underneath. The prop and the oil cooler were damaged, too, though not enough to prevent Heier from holding the fighter steady in the sky, at least initially. With the engine vibrating badly, Heier slowed down and began receiving ground fire. A bullet penetrated the cockpit from below, passed through his flight suit, and nicked him on the shin.

Steering for Treasury Island, some thirty miles away, Heier thought about bailing out there and taking his chances with the coastwatchers. Arriving over a likely spot, he pulled back the throttle in readiness to jump but discovered that the plane was uncontrollable at reduced airspeed. He regained a semblance of stability at full power, but as he watched oil bleed from the damaged cooler he realized that the engine would shake itself apart. He decided to try for Vella Lavella, but as he approached the newly acquired island the Pratt & Whitney finally gave out. Because he had been expecting this for several minutes, he was all set to exit and rolled the Corsair inverted before releasing his seat harness.

Nothing happened. Just as with Harry Hollmeyer's bailout three months earlier, Heier's Corsair was settling and g force held him against his seat. He grabbed the stick, kicked it forward, and literally shot out of the cockpit upside down. Instead of the conventional delay, he counted only "One . . . two . . . ten!" before pulling the D ring on his parachute.

Heier was still inverted, an unhappy position when his chute opened because the opening shock snapped him upright. After that he was worried about fathering children.

> By this time, I was only about three feet tall. The airplane spiraled down and hit the water, and it was gone: no pieces. I got into my rubber boat, and here came a Japanese landing barge. I took out my .45 and got in the water by my boat. I was going to kill as many of them as I could, then let them do me. Then I heard some guy say, "The sonovabitch is around here someplace, there's his parachute!" It was the Seabees, and they were using [the barge] as a garbage scow. So I yelled, "It's me, fellas!"

Somewhere during the process of jumping and swimming, Heier lost one of his prized wool-lined Australian flying boots. When he discovered this, he heaved its companion into the sea in disgust. Later he discovered the first missing boot in shallow water, but by then the second one had disappeared. The cost of Heier's Corsair (and his boots) was deemed affordable after photos brought back by a reconnaissance flight showed more than a dozen Japanese planes burned on the ground.*

*In his book, Boyington erroneously claimed to be one of the four shooters on this mission. He also described Heier as shearing off both wingtips, then making a safe landing at Vella Lavella.

Following a day of relative quiet, the squadron's primary assignment on September 23 was to escort twenty-four SBDs and TBFs striking Jakohima, a hill-based strong AA position west of Kahili. Japanese fighters had not challenged that piece of sky for several days, but soft-spoken Denny Groover had a premonition, what he called in his demure manner "just some sort of feeling that something might happen."

He was right. Aspects of the mission began to turn sour even before it began. For one thing, the old mechanical headaches were back. Of the twenty Black Sheep scheduled to depart at 0800, five either never left the ground or aborted soon after takeoff.

The issue prompted Frank Walton to highlight some of the problems in his war diary.

> Rinabarger in particular reported the following things wrong with his plane: Temperature down, motor rough, no radio receiver, generator cut out, and according to fuel gauge had used 110 gals. of gas in 15 min. at low power. Tucker had fumes in the cockpit so bad that he had to land on oxygen . . .

Greg Boyington led the remaining fifteen Sheep to their rendezvous with the dive-bombers over Munda, where another fifteen Army P-39s and some New Zealand P-40s joined to provide low and medium cover. After circling Treasury Island, the formation was proceeding toward the target when they met a friendly bomber formation coming in the opposite direction. B-24s and their covering fighters were supposed to have hit their respective targets simultaneously, but they had already completed a strike on Kahili and were headed home.

On the heels of the bombers came another surprise. An unfriendly group of thirty to forty Zeros had followed the bombers and were about to meet Boyington's high cover

Corsairs head to head. With so many unforeseen problems—mechanical difficulties that plagued the launch, B-24s on target early, and now a swarm of angry hornets—tactical integrity was beginning to unravel among the Black Sheep. Several (including Boyington) failed to make contact with the enemy.

To make matters more confusing, Bob Alexander radioed Stan Bailey that he couldn't keep up. He had started the flight with a bad cylinder but decided to press ahead after seeing five Black Sheep already drop out. Now his Corsair was faltering. Bailey ordered him to return to base. Alexander was about to comply when several Zeros initiated a run on Bailey's tail. Alexander turned to drive them away, a bold maneuver that served only to put him in harm's way, for he soon saw "tracers whistling by his ears" as three Zeros jumped him. Using the standard escape maneuver, Alexander shoved the stick forward to dive. This proved too much for the ailing Pratt & Whitney, which stopped cold.

Fortunately Alexander's aggressors did not press home their attack, allowing him time to restart the engine, although it never regained normal power. Gradually settling lower, he twice radioed Vella Lavella that he was approaching for a straight-in emergency landing, but no one received his transmissions. Just after topping a small ridge on the north end of the island by mere feet, he found the strip still under construction and covered with heavy equipment.

With no choice but to put down his crippled bird, Alexander sideslipped to the safest-looking portion of the strip and touched down on marshy earth. He bounced and swerved, missing some vehicles but hitting a ditch and careening out of control. He unstrapped his shoulder harness and seat belt, then dived low into the roomy cockpit and hung on as the Corsair flipped. The unconventional decision literally saved his neck, for the canopy was crushed flat. Construction workers ran to the wreckage and dug him out. The first man to greet him as he emerged into the sunlight was a hometown friend from Davenport, now an ensign in the Seabees.

Over Bougainville, Alexander's division leader had not fared much better. When Alexander withdrew from Stan Bailey's wing to return to base, John Bolt slid into the vacated position, then saw the same Zeros that Alexander had seen attacking Bailey. "Dive out!" Bolt hollered on the radio, but Bailey didn't hear him over the cacophony of other calls.

Bailey eventually did jink on his own, losing the Zeros as well as the rest of his division in the process. He climbed again to rejoin some other Corsairs, but everywhere he turned, packs of Zeros made passes and occasionally holed his plane with cannon fire and bullets. Just as in the previous fight, Bailey had been singled out and was feeling the pressure, but he managed to locate the returning bombers and climbed back above them. Although he found some safety in numbers there, the tenacious Japanese stayed after the formation. Bailey occasionally turned back to keep them at bay, only to take more hits in return.

The Corsairs were two-thirds of the way back to Vella Lavella, with the Japanese still in pursuit, when Bailey saw several Zeros strafing a parachute on the water. He dived and momentarily scattered them, and again the attackers jumped onto his tail. Eventually he drew away, but his main tank was running dry and he could no longer assist the downed pilot. Bailey made it back to Munda with only fifteen gallons of gas remaining, and punctures in his Corsair from four cannon shells and thirty bullets.

Somehow the integrity of Boyington's division had dissolved, for neither he nor his section leader, Bill Case, were involved in reportable action. Instead their wingmen joined forces, and Denny Groover backed up Moon Mullen as he opened fire on a Zero at three hundred yards. Sensing that this target was bait, Mullen pulled into a climbing right turn that led them, unintentionally, into a pack of ten to twenty Zeros.

Suddenly there were targets aplenty, but as Groover discovered it did not take long for the Japanese to turn the tables.

> I was settled in on two Zeros. I had one of them smoking and was trying to make him catch on fire. We were in a turn, and while I was settled in on the left one and had him smoking, the one on the right pulled up sharply. I kept trying to get this other one on fire. I had read a story about the atrocities the Japanese had committed on nurses, and like a damn fool I let my feelings take over, saying, "You sonuvabitch, you'll never mess with another American woman." About that time I wondered where that other Zero went, and made a sharp turn. As I made that turn, BAM! My right arm and leg went dead, and my left wing was on fire.

The second Zero, which had looped over and hit Groover hard from the right rear quarter, soon was joined by several of its pals in raking his Corsair. One 20mm round punched through the cockpit's right side and exploded, shredding his flight suit with shrapnel, breaking his right arm, slicing his right leg and ankle, and smashing instruments. There was a flash of fire inside and another in the left wing from the impact of more cannon shells. Groover beat out the cockpit fire with his good hand; the other fires eventually went out when he pushed over to dive away from his attackers.

Moon Mullen also caught hell. Outnumbered by at least ten to one, he swerved into "the swarm of Zeros attempting to finish off Groover," only to receive a hail of bullets from overhead. Several entered the cockpit and one punched through the birdcage canopy, lacerating his left shoulder. Mullen pulled into the Zero and it dived out, but another bored in from the left. Mullen reversed hard and opened fire, and this Zero flew through his burst and began to smoke. As Mullen held his turn and watched, fire flickered from the Zero's cockpit and wing roots and then blossomed as the aircraft fell. Mullen dived out, located some bombers, and scissored above them for mutual protection as they headed home down the Slot.

Although Bailey, Mullen, and Groover absorbed heavy punishment, other Black Sheep fared better. John Bolt made up for not firing his guns in his first combat by knocking down two in flames this day. When Bailey had dived out earlier, Bolt headed for a cloud bank, then climbed into the sun and saw a half-dozen Zeros in a turn over Bougainville. He dived unnoticed onto the formation's tail, then opened fire when the nearest plane was at two hundred yards. The Zero suddenly leveled off and started burning. When another Zero came across his nose, Bolt simply circled behind it, gave it a short burst, and watched it burn. Climbing into the sun again, he located a third target, but when he squeezed the trigger only two guns fired. Another incentive to leave came from a 20mm cannon shell that struck his left wing. Bolt dived out and steered for home.

Hank McCartney and his well-disciplined flight were the next to witness the strange sight of Zeros in a Lufbery Circle. Fifteen fighters were chasing one another's tails and slow-rolling among themselves as he led his division on a sweeping gunnery pass through the circle, then zoomed for altitude. As McCartney turned back into the enemy, he caught a Zero in a flat turn and gave it two good bursts, closing so rapidly that he had to roll up on one wing to miss it. Then he rolled again into a split-S as two other Zeros dropped in from behind. Pulling through, he saw a Zeke flaming down and was given credit for it. The victory made him the second Black Sheep ace, although it would not become official until one of his earlier claims with VMF-121 was recognized many months later.

Ed Olander, leading McCartney's second section, pulled several hard turns with another Zeke and drew smoke; it was later scored a probable, completing the squadron's claims for the day.

The injured Denny Groover, meanwhile, was still struggling toward home and had his hands full—especially because only the left one was functioning. He kept a clear head and began an inventory, knowing that he had to control the airplane, patch himself up, then find a place to land. What appeared to be "a heck of a lot of blood" streamed from his wounds, but before he could reach a first-aid kit the engine sputtered and died. He fumbled one-handed with the fuel controls to get it started again, then returned to doctoring.

To keep the plane steady, Groover grabbed his injured right arm with his left hand and placed it holding the stick, then jammed his elbow against the side of the cockpit as a brace. This kept everything reasonably level. After pouring sulfa powder into the rips in his flight suit—the limit of his self-treatment—he turned his attention back to the airplane. Having no airspeed indicator (indeed, half the instruments were ruined), he had to land using guesswork. The radio was out, the left aileron was gone, and the rudder cables were shot away. He would find later that seven 20mm cannon shells and more than a hundred bullets had virtually wrecked the Corsair, although the Pratt & Whitney had been spared and was holding everything aloft. Groover considered Vella Lavella for an emergency landing, unaware of Alexander's misfortune there, then decided to try for Munda, which was better equipped to handle his wounds.

Quelling concerns about his approach speed and uncertainty about how to control rollout with no rudder, he brought the bullet-riddled Corsair straight in.

> I lined it up, and mostly by the seat of my pants began to feel my airspeed. Just a short distance out, I turned loose the stick right quickly with my hand and grabbed the handle on the gear and threw them down. I didn't

want to try the CO_2 bottle because I was afraid I couldn't pull it. The wheels came down, and it was the best landing I ever made in my life. I landed on the main wheels, unlike the three-point landings we normally liked to come in with. Fortunately it went just straight as an arrow to the end of the runway, then it started circling. I couldn't brake to stop it.

Too weak to move, Groover was lifted out of the cockpit and laid on a stretcher, then hauled by jeep to the squadron's ready tent. His Corsair, so badly damaged that it would not fly again, was hauled to the boneyard. Jim Reames took one look at the bleeding youngster and realized that he required more attention than the field hospital could provide. After downing a few medicinal brandies, Groover was "as high as three tall pines" when he was lifted aboard a transport for the flight to Guadalcanal's hospital. His combat tour with the Black Sheep was over.

The Japanese probably counted his plane among the five Corsairs they claimed that day (along with two probables) although only two F4Us were actually shot down, both from VMF-213. The 204 Kokutai sortied twenty-seven fighters, comparable to the American estimates, and lost one pilot.

Moon Mullen, whose wounds proved superficial, participated in another mission later that day. At 1230 he took off as a section leader for a specialized assignment. Greg Boyington led the flight, which also included Stan Bailey and Bill Case, to determine if a particular small island in the Treasury group was a suitable site for PT boats to collect downed pilots. After locating a satisfactory landing beach, they disguised the mission by swinging around to the Shortlands and strafing the Japanese seaplane base at Faisi. Their one sweep, at maximum speed and treetop height, cut up a seventy-foot steam launch under way in the channel. Judging from the cloud of steam that boiled up, the boat's hull and boiler were thoroughly sieved. There were no seaplanes evident, so the Black Sheep left their smoking handiwork behind and raced back to Munda.

Still later, seven Black Sheep departed to search for the two Hellhawks shot down during the morning rhubarb. Several Black Sheep had witnessed one of them parachuting into the water and boarding his rubber boat, and now they were out to relocate their sister squadron's missing man. Luck was on their side—barely. Several objects were spotted during the box-shaped search, including "a floating body, apparently a long time dead," but no sign of life. Four Black Sheep turned for home, but Tom Emrich, Sandy Sims, and Bob McClurg chose to search a bit longer. They, too, were about to give up but agreed to make one more circle. On the final turn they spotted yellow dye marker staining the water, found the drifting pilot, and reported his location. Although a PBY made the pickup, September was still a bad month for the Hellhawks, who lost twelve Corsairs and six pilots dead or missing.

In the most noteworthy event of the following day, September 24, Greg Boyington and Mo Fisher took off at 1015 and landed at Vella Lavella thirty minutes later for what the war diary described as the first "official" landing at the Barakoma airstrip. But VMF-221 was already operating there. Furthermore, during Bob Alexander's landing at Vella three days earlier, he turned his Corsair upside down—obviously not deemed an official landing. He was still there, as was Junior Heier, brought ashore in the garbage scow that hauled him out of the water that same day. Both planeless pilots finally boarded a Grumman J2F and were delivered to Munda around noon. Mo Fisher departed Vella in his Corsair at about the same time for the return trip, but Boyington was stuck there for five hours: VMF-221 "borrowed" his plane for a mission.

The Black Sheep had been on Munda for all of one week, but the crude living conditions were already beginning to take their toll. Some pilots seemingly had cast-iron stomachs, whereas others suffered brutally from the bacteria from unsanitary food preparation.

As if the misery of constant diarrhea was not enough, the degradation of squatting in the open caused plenty more discomfort. Bob McClurg remembered:

> When you have the G. I.s, you sit on a box—an orange crate—and everybody's lined up in front of you while you're doing your job right on the edge of the strip. "Hurry up! Hurry up!" They should have been lined up behind you. I can remember sitting there, feeling just terrible.

Physical ailments were not limited to the internal variety. In such a hot, tropical climate, the pilots had no choice but to live in sweat-drenched, unwashed clothing, their only hygiene consisting of an occasional gravity-fed shower. It was inevitable that they would suffer from fungal growth. The "creeping crud" prevailed in dark, moist areas of the body: crotches, underarms, feet. Although it was treatable, some men, Frank Walton among them, almost preferred the ailment to the cure.

> You could get it around your rectum. The doctor would have us line up, bend over and spread our cheeks, and he'd paint our rectums with this stuff like muriatic acid. I mean, goddamn, that stuff really hurt! "Oh boy," he'd say, "no bug can live in that!"

But their ills were quickly forgotten when Zeros were aloft. The squadron's next encounter came on Sunday, September 26, during a dive-bomber strike. It might have been dubbed "the Irish flight." The three Black Sheep divisions involved were led by Stan Bailey, Moon Mullen, and Hank McCartney and were joined by a division of Hellhawks under 1st Lt. Leonard W. McCleary. Again it was an interservice mission, which included sixteen Army P-39s and twenty Navy F6Fs providing close and medium cover while the F4Us flew high cover for two dozen SBDs and a dozen TBFs striking Kangu Hill, near Kahili. Using a plan similar to that of three days previously, three squadrons of Liberators covered by P-38s were to simultaneously hit Kahili.

Their timing was off again. The dive-bombers and Corsairs were motoring northwest toward the target when they met the Liberators coming fast from Kahili with an estimated thirty Zeros on their heels. The Marines were level at 17,000 feet when they sighted the bogeys, and Stan Bailey immediately led them up to 21,000 feet. The Zeros were still almost a mile higher. Fending them off seemed the best tactic, and in this they succeeded by scissoring over the Avengers. But a group of Hellcat pilots covering Dauntlesses made it difficult, as the Marines later explained with scathing criticism. Frank Walton wrote, "These pilots kept up a continual chatter of unnecessary conversation over their radios, making it almost impossible to send and receive necessary messages."

The poor radio discipline nearly cost the Black Sheep one of their own. A group of Zekes made several feints above Moon Mullen's division (Rollie Rinabarger, Meathead Bragdon, and Tom Emrich) before one pair split off and attacked. Mullen turned the division toward them, then more Zekes swooped down until sixteen to twenty were hassling with the Marines. When one got too close to Bragdon, Mullen pulled around hard to the left and hosed it from nose to tail. Flames burst from the cockpit as it went tumbling down.

At this inopportune moment, Rinabarger's engine began to overheat and detonate. His Corsair limped through the turn as he followed Mullen. He tried using the radio but was unable to break through the babbling F6F pilots. A Zeke caught him lagging, and his Corsair shuddered under a long, combined burst of machine-gun and cannon rounds. One

20mm exploded in the right horizontal stabilizer, another in the port wing tank, while a hail of 7.7mm "beat a steady tattoo" from the empennage all the way up the fuselage. Either a cannon burst or an incendiary bullet sent shrapnel through the left side of the cockpit at an angle. A chunk nicked the back edge of Rinabarger's knife, squirted into his left hip, and burned flesh as it traveled eight inches down his thigh just under the skin. Stunned by the pain, he radioed again for help and again failed to be heard through the garbage. He tried to keep up with the division, but the aggressive Zeke—and probably others—slammed the door.

A third 20mm burst in the left wing of Rinabarger's Corsair and another struck the engine cowl. It knocked apart a cylinder and broke an oil line, which instantly turned the windscreen opaque with a black sheen. A fifth 20mm exploding just behind the cockpit destroyed his radio and started a persistent fire. Yet another impacted the left wing, this time bursting the tire nestled inside and severing the flap control. Between each bass drum thump of an exploding shell came the staccato rattle of bullets.

Finally Moon Mullen reefed his Corsair around and scattered the Zeros. Rinabarger's plane trailed a long plume of smoke as he dived away. That his F4U still held together after being hit by six cannon shells and untold bullets was a tribute to its beefy construction. The heavy armor plate aft of his seat had done its job, saving him from a stunning explosion inches behind his back: "I knew I'd got a hell of a blow on the head," he later remembered, "but didn't know what had caused it."

While the Oregonian desperately dived away in his shattered airplane, Mullen, Bragdon, and Emrich scissored overhead to keep the Zeros from finishing him off. Enemy fighters "snapped at their heels" all the way back to Vella Lavella, where the Marines finally lost them in a huge weather front that had been building all afternoon. Unable to transmit a request for an emergency landing at the

Barakoma strip on Vella Lavella, Rinabarger opted to limp home to Munda. He dived from cloud to cloud as he nursed his Corsair across the last few miles of open water.

He had few options available for his landing approach. The engine was smoking and detonating, the shot-out left flap control necessitated a no-flap landing (uneven flaps were aerodynamically impossible to control), the left tire was blown, there was no airspeed indicator and no radio, visibility was obscured by oil on the windshield, and Rinabarger fought against the haze of shock from a painful wound. He wrestled the streaked, blackened Corsair to the approach end of the strip, whistled by at almost fifty knots too fast, then drifted far down the field before settling. He put it down nicely, but without directional control he was unable to avoid a grader parked along the right side of the strip. With a rending crash the right wing struck the heavy machine. The plane that had carried him home finally tore into several pieces that bounced and rolled down the strip in a cloud of coral dust.

A jeep raced out to the wreckage. Miraculously Rollie stood up in the intact fuselage, although he could get no farther. Just as the crash crew reached the plane he collapsed into their outstretched arms. An ambulance carried him up the hill to the hospital tent, where medics cut away burned flesh and probed some of the dozen or more pieces of shrapnel out of his left hip. He wanly greeted squadron mates as they came to congratulate and tease him about his narrow escape. But the afternoon ended with everyone scrambling for the nearest dugout. A Japanese raid caught the whole area napping, with the whine of falling bombs reaching them even before the sirens blew. Rinabarger soon discovered that Navy corpsmen could be as dangerous as the enemy.

> Bombs started coming down and two guys picked me up on the stretcher that I was lying on and headed for a dugout not very far away. About the time the bombs

started to hit, the guy in the front of the stretcher put it down and ran into the dugout. Hell, the guy on the rear . . . he deserved a medal. He ran back to the tent and got a mattress and threw it over me and threw himself on top of the mattress.

Rinabarger was still feeling bad the next day when a transport finally evacuated him to Guadalcanal. There he spent several weeks healing, but the environment ultimately got the best of him. Blood poisoning and other complications nearly finished what the Japanese had not been able to do. Although he would later try to come back, illness ultimately knocked him out of the war. He never flew another combat mission.

In the meantime the other pilots debriefed the day's fight. Moon Mullen was given credit for the Zeke he had flamed and Hank McCartney shared a probable with Bruce Matheson. The Marines' estimate of the number of Zeros lent some credence to the Japanese records. The 204 Kokutai sortied twenty-five fighters and claimed two F4Us shot down. One Corsair belonging to VMF-213 was indeed lost during the Kangu Hill mission, though its pilot was rescued, and no doubt the Japanese thought that Rinabarger's smoking Corsair had fallen into the sea. The Kokutais reported no losses of their own.

The bullets flew again on Monday as the clashes with Japanese defenders over and around the south end of Bougainville intensified. Two Black Sheep divisions had completed the dawn patrol when word arrived from Strike Command that twelve Corsairs were needed to cover a squadron of B-24s, but they had only fifteen minutes to find ready Corsairs before takeoff in order to rendezvous on time.

Hank Bourgeois and John Begert took their divisions aloft first; Greg Boyington got airborne late, accompanied by Mo Fisher, Bill Case, and Red Harris. Bourgeois's instruments froze up and he turned back to Munda with Junior Heier, leaving only six Corsairs to cover twenty-seven

Liberators. Boyington's division was instructed to fly directly to Kahili for an impromptu fighter sweep—possibly the impetus for a tactic he later employed with regularity.

After climbing up the Slot at full military power, Boyington reached Kahili shortly past noon, about twenty-five minutes before the scheduled drop. As the Corsairs passed over the airfield, Boyington glanced up and saw a twin-tail aircraft heading north with two intermittent streams of smoke trailing behind it. Thinking this was a signal for the defending fighters to take off, Boyington led his flight down to intercept them. But he saw only two fighters on the field—both apparently mocked-up dummies.

The Marines climbed for altitude again, then caught sight of twenty Zeros approaching from the southeast. Still climbing, Boyington circled to gain height advantage, then dived but lost Fisher in the plunge. He selected a Zero and squeezed the trigger, but nothing happened. In the official report, Walton generously allowed that Boyington's guns had jammed, although he had not flown to a freezing altitude, and electrical failure of all six guns was rare. Bill Case discovered later what really happened.

Flying in Boyington's second section, Case made several descending turns while chasing the same Zero. He held his fire whenever Boyington's plane drifted near his gunsight. Case later described it as "going straight down the funnel while these guys were doing a corkscrew right underneath me." After the flight, Boyington asked who had been on his wing. Case spoke up, and Boyington gave him credit for shooting down the fighter. "You were on his ass," said a surprised Case. "I was just coming along for the ride!"

"I forgot to put my master gun switch on," Boyington confessed, "and I couldn't get a round in him."

After realizing his mistake, Boyington had armed his guns and dived on another column of Zekes below. This time, opening fire at a selected target from six hundred feet, he was rewarded by the sight of pieces tearing away from the Zeke's tail. The plane angled downward at thirty degrees and crashed into the water near Kahili's strip. Defying one of his own edicts, Boyington followed it down through the clouds and nearly hit the water himself—his second error of the day. After recovering, he made an atypical, halfhearted attempt to locate other enemy planes before returning to Munda.

Mo Fisher, in the meantime, had already holed one Zeke that subsequently split-Sed away. He rolled into a high stern run on another and shot a long burst from about two hundred feet, drawing smoke before the Zeke made the sanctuary of a cloud. Fisher followed it in, and when they popped into the clear he was still on the Zeke's tail. There was no need to shoot again: This one slanted into the water near the Shortlands. After patrolling for a while, during which he saw several aircraft falling in flames, Fisher radioed Boyington and was instructed to return to base.

John Begert and his group of six Corsairs, which had managed to join the bombers just minutes before they reached the target, were promptly set upon by fifteen to twenty Zekes. After chasing them away, the Corsairs climbed again for altitude, then entered a storm cloud, which kept them busy for several minutes. By the time they cleared the turbulence, Sandy Sims and D. J. Moore had become separated. When a dozen or more Zekes jumped them almost immediately, Moore slid wide and blasted one that had curved behind Sims. As Moore rejoined his section leader, he looked back and watched the falling Zeke burn. Sims found himself low on fuel, throttled back to conserve what was left, and turned for Vella Lavella, but Moore saw Japanese fighters harassing the bombers and reversed course to assist them.

Bill Case saw the same thing. He had just popped out of the storm near Treasury Island and radioed his wingman, "Harris, we've got to go back." The pair climbed toward the bomber formation, scissoring all the way, while as many as forty Zeros descended upon them and made repeated feints before heading for the rear of the Liberators.

Case and Harris pulled around into an overhead run and briefly scattered the enemy fighters, but the numbers were overwhelming. One made a run on Harris's tail. Case had just turned in toward it when a 20mm exploded in his right wing, followed by a stream of tracers that flashed by as he dived under Harris.

Leveling off again, Case looked around but could not find his wingman. Suddenly another hail of bullets spattered his plane. He dived out once more, evaded the latest attack, and looked for Harris. This time he could see four planes headed for the water, well in the distance; he thought it might be Harris with three Zeros on his tail. Later he saw a splash as a plane struck the surface about twenty-five miles southeast of Treasury Island.

By now the rest of the Zeros were gone. Case's plane seemed okay and the windscreen looked clear, so he climbed back above the bombers and scissored overhead as they crawled home. But the damage had already been done. "Corsair, you're losing gas and oil, get the hell home," radioed one of the Liberators. When Case, who was flying one of the early birdcage Corsairs with a belly window, glanced between the foot rails, he saw a steady stream of oil flowing past the Plexiglas. Increasing the revolutions per minute did not increase the rate of flow, so he wound up the engine and raced for Vella Lavella at top speed. The minutes he saved were crucial. Just as he cleared the strip's approach, his oil pressure dropped and the engine quit. The strip was still under improvement, but Case had enough speed to hop over a bulldozer, swerve around a grader, and coast to a stop at the far end.

As Case climbed down, several Seabees came up to him. "What is it with you?" one demanded. After Case explained the reason for his emergency landing, they turned helpful. Case was impressed with their ingenuity.

> They unsnapped the cowl and looked into there, and wiped off a whole bunch of oil. I'd had a round go right

through the oil reservoir, a twenty-five-gallon tank which fed that monster, and the hole was in the bottom so I got the chance to use it all up. One of them said, "Well, a fella tried to come in here yesterday, and he didn't make it. His Corsair's over there. It nosed up and we didn't know what to do with it. Why don't I go over there and look?"

He brought back the reservoir from this other bird, and pulled the one out from my poor old, sloppy airplane. Then they rolled a couple of drums of aviation fuel and a drum of oil down. I was only three hours on the ground there. These were just backyard mechanics who knew how to take things apart and put them back together again. It was a wonderful experience to have that kind of support. Anyway, I cranked it up, and didn't even pull the oil strainers to see if there were any chips in there. I ran it up and it sounded good, got full takeoff power and didn't have any heavy equipment in front of me that time, so I roared on up. I made a low pass over the field for them for a "Thank you," and headed off for Munda.

When Case got back to base—three hours late—he discovered that many of his personal belongings had already been claimed, including the bottle of booze he'd been saving since his last visit to Sydney. He didn't raise a stink but went to chow instead. When he returned to his tent, most of the belongings had been returned. Admitting that it was embarrassing for everyone involved, he said, "Nobody told me that they'd had any part in it, and I never asked."

But Red Harris's belongings could not be returned to their owner. Later in the day three divisions of Black Sheep launched to search for him and another pilot down, escorting a J2F that could effect the pickup if results were positive. But even after talking with Case to get Harris's estimated position, the pilot of the "Duck" flew around the Vella Gulf some fifty miles out of position. Naturally there was no rescue. Harris's name was placed in the Prisoner of

War and Missing Persons Detachment; his wife, Maurine, continued to teach in a school near San Diego, waiting for good news that would never come.

Once again the Japanese were surprisingly accurate. They claimed one F4U shot down and one "undetermined," equating to Harris and Case, while losing one of their own.

Frank Walton recorded the Black Sheep's four victories, then seized an opportunity to get the pilots "some of the recognition they deserved." To a correspondent from the *Chicago Daily News* waiting outside the ready tent, he mentioned that J. J. Hill, Chris Magee, and Bruce Matheson were Windy City boys. Walton opened his green war diary and showed their short biographies to George Weller, then invited the newspaperman to talk to the pilots in person. Weller later produced a half-dozen articles on the squadron that were widely syndicated.

Walton, the former champion swimmer in the Hollywood Athletic Club, found it easy to shake hands with reporters. No stranger to publicity, he knew how to work it to advantage as he involved pressmen such as Jack DeChant and Pen Johnson in the Black Sheep's early history. They were soon joined by Weller and others who sought the story of the independent Boyington and his hotshot pilots.

Even without Walton's inside scoop, Boyington was a magnet for the press on his own merits. In a *Daily News* article, Weller described the September 16 battle in which Boyington became the first Corsair ace in a day. Such impressive victories made good copy by themselves, but Boyington's powerful physique, impetuous behavior, and frank, witty statements added spice to his achievements.

The essence of his personality could be summed up in one word—charisma—and he had it in spades. The press loved to describe him as "swashbuckling," ironic considering VMF-214's previous identity. If he swaggered, it was justified because of his association with the legendary Flying Tigers; that name *meant* something. And if he lacked recruiting-poster looks, he countered by appearing dangerous whenever his smile vanished or his eyes narrowed to calculating slits.

Boyington's own pilots were thoroughly charmed by his behavior, as Ed Olander recalled.

> We loved him. And we felt great that we had a leader who had been in combat, was pugnacious in nature and wily by instinct. I don't know about grace, but he was well protected. He took us many places that we might not have gone otherwise because he was so aggressive.

Boyington's aggressiveness was sometimes displayed as belligerence, though few considered the trait a flaw. After all, he was in the business of fighting. His drinking binges were not generally looked upon with disdain, either, not since Ulysses S. Grant had proved eighty years earlier that a commander's addiction was acceptable as long as he was winning. (Besides, any hell-bent-for-leather cowboy was more fun to cheer for than a teetotaler.) Boyington had an ally in the person of General Moore, who seemed to watch over him as a vicarious parent.

Nonetheless some were not admirers of Boyington's behavior and looked askance at his reputation as a Marine Corps officer. He exhibited a cavalier attitude toward military protocol, maintained a careless appearance, and allowed his pilots to address him with offhand names. But because the style obviously worked within his own squadron, there was little to criticize in his overall success.

Regarding the nicknames, Boyington was commonly addressed as "Skipper" or "Greg," with an occasional use of "Gramps" in deference to his age. The first was acceptable enough, but for subordinates to call a commanding officer by the other two choices would have normally been a serious breach among old-school regulars. In the hugely expanded war machine, however, there had not been time to imbue the spirit of etiquette into thousands of reservists.

The rules were relaxed, which suited Boyington just fine. Surprisingly, for all its later renown, the nickname the pilots did not use in person was "Pappy." It made a sole appearance in their Yale-adapted drinking song, but it would not find its way into printed use until early 1944.

Regardless of what the pilots called Greg Boyington, they were devoted to him and trusted the homespun wisdom he was willing to share from eight years of flying. When he spoke they hung on every word, especially when it sounded like this:

> I'm supposed to be boss, so you're supposed to do what I tell you to. But that doesn't mean you have to "sir" me or lick my boots to get anything. We're just a flying football team and I'm the captain.

Aside from the Black Sheep's aerial achievements in two weeks of combat, another month remained of their six-week tour and exhaustion was already beginning to wear them down. Living conditions in the flimsy tents were abysmal, the food was even worse, and sleep—the minimum revitalization a combat pilot needed to function properly—was frequently denied. The Washing Machine Charlies' almost-nightly forays were nerve-racking at best, and people on the ground were occasionally killed. There is no record of any Black Sheep being physically hurt after John Begert's close call on September 20, but the psychological effects were real enough.

There were other hazards, too, as Walton remembered after a night when unwelcome visitors shared their foxhole.

> Boyington, Reames and I were in a tent, and we had a foxhole right outside that was always full of water. When the raid siren sounded, Reames put his leg down in there, and it was full of rats swimming around. He said, "Boy, I'm never gonna get down in there," but

when the bombs started dropping we all jumped in, rats and all. The hell with those.

Steeling themselves against the lack of sleep, the pilots flew above unfriendly territory against overwhelming numbers of enemy fighters. Those numbers seemed to be increasing, despite the Marines' best efforts. "Gee, Frank, when is this all gonna end?" one asked Walton in private. "You get up there, and there's more of them there today than there were yesterday. And there are gonna be more of 'em tomorrow."

Walton gave the only encouragement he could, telling them, "It's like a string of freight cars: if you keep cutting off the front ones you're eventually going to get to the back, because they cannot keep supplying them in the rear. The other elements . . . are cutting off their supplies back there."

It was a relief, therefore, when Tuesday, September 28, was filled with relatively benign assignments—local sector patrols and combat air patrol (CAP) for Allied ship movements. Hank McCartney's division was off before dawn to shepherd a force of five destroyers, then flew a local patrol early that afternoon. When two other divisions relieved him, Mac took his wingman on a hunting expedition. Searching the east coast of Kolombangara, he and Bruce Matheson sighted twelve to fifteen troops in a rowboat and a raft at the mouth of Kape Harbor. The Marines rolled in and strafed them repeatedly, killing most of the Japanese and beaching the boat, then they flew off and patrolled to the north for a few minutes before returning to the scene. This time they were met with small-arms fire from the jungle, which they promptly silenced by hosing the brush.

Payback came later that evening as the Black Sheep endured no less than five air raids. The bombs fell until well after midnight.

Another search-and-destroy mission to prosecute barge traffic was ordered for late Wednesday afternoon. As of the previous July, the legendary high-speed runs of the Tokyo Express had been reduced to a trickle after several fierce naval actions forced the Japanese to increasingly risk daylight detection to evacuate their starving garrison on Kolombangara. At night, however, as many as a hundred Daihatsu barges and a few destroyers crisscrossed the channel from Choiseul, which kept radar-equipped American destroyers and PT boats busy. In this fashion, more than 3,800 Japanese escaped from Kolombangara on Tuesday night.

Three divisions of Black Sheep were scheduled for Wednesday afternoon's search. Stan Bailey, Hank Bourgeois, and Mac McCartney led twelve Corsairs aloft at 1645 and strafed two barges along the west coast of Choiseul with no observed fires. At about the same time, John Begert's three-plane division completed a task force assignment and went hunting; they burned two forty-footers off Kolombangara. That night the Black Sheep received the welcome news that their two-week stint on Munda would end the next day, and they could retire to the relative luxury of the Russell Islands in the afternoon. An encouraged Stan Bailey planned one more strafing performance for his division, to be conducted after their dawn patrol on Thursday morning, the last day of September.

While the Black Sheep slept (fitfully, due to air raids), four PT boats rumbled slowly out of New Georgia's Lever Harbor and into the Kula Gulf for another long night of barge interdiction. Led by Lt. Craig C. Smith, the commander of Motor Torpedo Boat Squadron 6, the boats separated into two sections to search for traffic with their mast-mounted radars. His PT-126 and Lt. (jg) Leighton C. Wood's PT-124 took one sector while PT-116 and -189 searched another. Each eighty-foot Elco craft was more of a gunboat than a torpedo boat, their early four-torpedo loads having been reduced in favor of additional automatic weapons. Their topsides fairly bristled with heavy machine guns, light weapons, a rapid-firing Oerlikon 20mm cannon, and even a modified 37mm cannon taken from the nose of a P-39.

It took nearly two hours to reach their assigned stations close offshore Kolombangara. In the blackness they soon observed the eerie glow of flares and the flash and rumble of gunfire to the northeast, which continued sporadically throughout the night as the destroyers found plenty of targets. Shortly past 0500 the two sections rendezvoused to return to Lever Harbor as planned. Half a mile from Kolombangara a lookout spotted a barge's wake, and the boats reversed course to investigate. The target was lost in the darkness, but Lieutenant Smith decided to check the island's northeast coast in case damaged barges had been beached after the destroyer action. An hour later, two were located along Kolombangara's shore, and the PTs closed to a quarter mile before raking them with machine-gun and cannon fire. Two more were found within the next forty-five minutes, the last near a promontory called Ropa Point. Smith brought his 126 boat in close to engage it with the heavy gun.

To avoid mistaken identity, the PT boats were supposed to withdraw from Kolombangara's shoreline by daybreak, permitting aircraft to take over and sweep the surrounding waterways and beaches. So intent were they on hunting down and strafing targets that nobody among the four boats seemed to notice that they had extended beyond their assigned patrol area, or that the sun was already climbing high in the east. The realization hit them like ice water at 0740 when a column of three dark fighters curved gracefully around Kolombangara's jungle-covered slope. The gull wings of Corsairs were unmistakable. The trio rolled out, sun flashing through canopies as they bored in at just three hundred feet.

Two hours earlier, Stan Bailey's division had departed Munda for its scheduled dawn patrol. Section leader John Bolt's oxygen system failed and he returned early, leaving Burney Tucker to slide behind Bob Alexander and complete the assignment. As they came around Kolombangara to look for barges, Bailey signaled for them to form a column, and Alexander dropped back to the third position. Rounding the conical shore from the Kula Gulf, Bailey spotted four objects on the water that appeared to be barges, the nearest only seventy-five yards off the beach. It was a good hour past dawn, and no American vessels were to be so close to shore.

"Don't fire until I give the word," Bailey cautioned, wanting to be sure of his target. Radio communications had been excellent throughout the flight, which gave him every reason to expect the other two pilots to heed his warning. The Corsairs rolled level and spread out. From the boats, Alexander's plane appeared to be in the middle of the formation, trailing Stan Bailey and Burney Tucker. The latter, who had just recognized the boats as friendly and turned off his guns, heard Bailey at the same instant call, "Hold fire, they are our own PT boats." Tucker and Bailey waggled their wings as they roared over PT-126 ahead of Alexander.

From his station in the tiny, open bridge of PT-124, Leighton Wood had been watching Craig Smith's boat strafe the last Japanese barge. Now one of his gunners spotted the approaching planes and alerted the twenty-three-year-old skipper, for whom the next few seconds unfolded in slow motion.

> The Corsairs were right on the water, wing to wing, and we promptly started to track them in—at least my 20mm and stern dual fifties did. As they approached, we held up our American flag and shot up the current recognition flare. We noticed that the two [outboard] flyers recognized us and waggled their wings, but the middle plane dropped his nose and put a cone of .50-caliber fire in the water probably fifty yards from the 126. Then he just walked it up the water and across the stern. About five people standing around the 20mm on the stern all

fell. My people, and I'm sure other boats, immediately opened fire.

No one could say for certain why Bob Alexander riddled the 126's stern. Nobody ordered the gunners to return fire, but they did—probably out of pure reflex. Craig Smith later reported that PT-126's starboard twin-.50 mount scored with one short burst, and Alexander's Corsair never pulled up. It curved toward Kolombangara, swept through the canopy of trees, mushed into the jungle about five hundred feet inland, then exploded in a greasy ball of fire. Most of the spilled fuel burned quickly. By the time Stan Bailey circled back over the spot, he was unable to see anything except "a black, burned swath under the trees directly on the beach, and scattered pieces of debris still burning."

The carnage on Craig Smith's boat was even worse. Ensign John F. Daley, a member of the torpedo boat squadron for all of one week, had been standing near the Oerlikon when Alexander opened fire; now he lay sprawled among the splinters with red froth bubbling from two large holes in his chest. Gunner's Mate First Class Thomas M. Ross, manning the weapon, had been blown off the stern and was nowhere to be seen. Down in the engine room, MoMM2 Bertis I. Paul died instantly when Alexander's slugs tore through the thin deck.

Leighton Wood brought the 124 alongside to assist. One of 126's engines had been knocked out, so Craig Smith ordered the faster boat to rush John Daley back to Lever Harbor. Wood's executive officer drove the 124 hard while he administered first aid to the gravely wounded ensign, trying to keep his lungs from collapsing, but Daly was beyond help. At the scene, PT-116 idled in a search for the missing gunner's mate but found only his watch cap.

The informal board that was convened published its findings within a few days. Roughly equal blame was shared between Bob Alexander and Craig Smith, the latter having submitted a statement along with Stan Bailey and Burney Tucker. No one mentioned a recognition flare. According to Smith's testimony, as soon as the Corsairs were identified he gave immediate orders for full speed ahead and full right rudder—the curving wake being a standard recognition signal in addition to showing the American flag. Bailey and Tucker were probably directly overhead and thus would not have seen the 124 boat's flare. Perhaps Alexander did see it from the corner of his eye and assumed the boats were shooting first, though why he failed to heed Bailey's radio warning is a mystery, considering that communications had been excellent prior to the incident. Several of Alexander's squadron mates suggested later that he had aggressive tendencies and took risks. As one put it, "He had an attitude that he was going to win that war, and it got him in trouble." L. C. Wood's mention of a recognition flare raises the interesting possibility that Alexander responded to what he perceived as aggression, but the mistake cost four American lives.*

September had turned downright bloody for the Black Sheep. Alexander was declared missing but had undoubtedly been killed. Ewing and Harris were still missing, Groover and Rinabarger were out of action for the duration of the tour, and seven Corsairs had been destroyed. The month might have ended with more losses, because the Black Sheep were scrambled to intercept a large bogey later that same morning. Hank Bourgeois led seven F4Us to 21,000 feet, where they observed a force of forty to fifty Zekes climbing through 15,000 feet. He then led his Corsairs up to 24,000 feet, but incredibly the Zekes got there at the same time, having climbed 9,000 feet in the time it took Bourgeois to climb 3,000 feet. Outnumbered at least six to one, the Marines were content to keep their distance while

*Craig Smith personally shouldered the blame and was inconsolable. "His nerves were shot," L. C. Wood wrote. Relieved of command, Smith was hospitalized for treatment and did not return to combat duty.

Always charismatic, frequently unorthodox, Gregory Boyington commanded VMF-214 for only four months, yet he gave the Black Sheep enduring fame.

John Fidler prepares to board an F4F Wildcat at Ewa, December 1942. The blue-gray over light gray color scheme and circular national insignia were standard until mid-1943. (McCall collection)

VMF-214 was seven months old when the officers and men gathered at Ewa for this stylized formation in mid-February 1943, one week before deploying overseas. (National Archives)

Doc Kraft poses on Vic Scarborough's crash-landed F4F-4 after the air battle of April 7, 1943. A Japanese 20mm explosive round punched a large hole in the fuselage. (Britt collection)

Ledge Hazelwood works out during the second tour on the Russell Islands. VMF-214's ready tent and MAG-21's operations hut are in the background. (McCall collection)

The Swashbucklers (27 pilots, 2 ground officers) at Banika, Russell Islands, September 1, 1943. (Williams collection)

Vic Scarborough, Bob Hanson, and Al Jensen apply victory flags to a propeller blade at Munda after downing five Japanese planes on August 26, 1943. (Williams collection)

During an overnight stop at Efate in late September 1943, Bob Hanson beckons to a squadron mate while Drury McCall, Ed Hernan, and O. K. Williams look on. (Williams collection)

Case, Rinabarger, Fisher, Bourgeois, Begert, Ewing, Groover, and Tucker stand as Boyington kneels with Bailey, Ray, and Alexander at Turtle Bay, early September 1943. (Walton collection)

Bill Case (note Australian boots), Rollie Rinabarger, John Begert, and Henry Bourgeois mock a scramble from the parachute riggers' tent at Turtle Bay. (Walton collection)

Trim pilots gathered at the Turtle Bay lagoon, where swimming was a favorite pastime. Greg Boyington (far right, profile) later wrote, "[Walton] swam our asses off." (National Archives)

Impressive row of birdcage Corsairs on Turtle Bay's crushed coral. Engines have been started, pilots are strapped in, and linemen wait to guide the planes out. (Walton collection)

Rinabarger (division leader), Emrich, Harris, and Groover over Espiritu Santo. Note taped cowl seams, indicating chronic fuel leaks; second section retains old national insignia. (Walton collection)

Boyington prepares to heave himself into an F4U-1. The heavy parachute harness and its bulky ’chute, raft, and jungle packs are described in chapters 5 and 20. (Walton collection)

Boyington in a birdcage F4U with the seat lowered, making the cockpit seem even more expansive. Release cables, rearview mirror blister are evident in the sliding canopy. (USMC)

Big flaps splayed like feathers, a VMF-214 birdcage F4U is seconds away from a classic main wheel (vice 3-point) landing at Turtle Bay. (National Archives via Sullivan)

Crushed coral taxi way, probably at the Russells or Vella Lavella, is crowded with Black Sheep F4Us rolling toward the duty runway for a mission. (Walton collection)

Boyington finds humor in fighting a losing battle against the filth and debris at Munda. (Walton collection)

Few smiles are evident among the Black Sheep during a breather at the Russells in early October 1943. One pilot was dead, four others were MIA or hospitalized with wounds. (Walton collection)

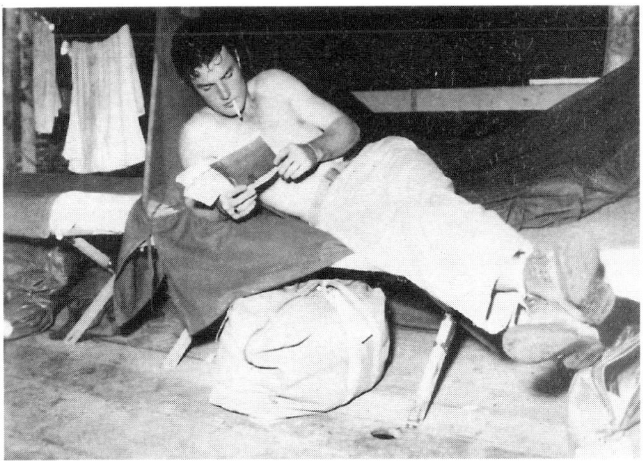

His hair matted with sweat, Bruce Matheson enjoys a quiet moment. The limit of a pilot's personal space in the combat zone: an army cot and a few standard-issue bags. (Olander collection)

Interiors of hard-shell Dallas huts—many boasting electricity and mattresses—were relatively spacious. Note the Black Sheep patch on Tom Emrich's leather flight jacket. (Walton collection)

The Chicago contingent: Bruce Matheson, J. J. Hill, and Chris Magee, who wears the ever-present bandana knotted around his neck. (Losch collection)

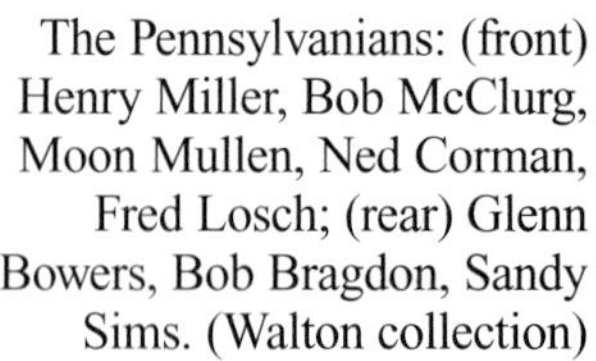

The Pennsylvanians: (front) Henry Miller, Bob McClurg, Moon Mullen, Ned Corman, Fred Losch; (rear) Glenn Bowers, Bob Bragdon, Sandy Sims. (Walton collection)

Stripped to shorts and boondockers in the tropical heat, Tom Emrich, Don Fisher, Bob Bragdon, and Ed Olander engage in an intense game of bridge at Turtle Bay. (Olander collection)

The irrepressible John Bolt enjoys a cigar. Throat microphone kept hands free for other tasks in the cockpit. (Bolt collection)

"Lucybelle" and other strictly noncombat graphics were applied briefly to this F4U-1A at Turtle Bay on November 26, 1943, between tours. "They ran a publicity game out there even during a real war," Boyington said. (Walton collection)

Sagging jeep delivers Tucker, Chatham, Avey, Harper, Bolt, Bailey (driver, A.P. correspondent), Reames, Doswell, Groover, and Fisher to the flight line on Vella Lavella. (Bolt collection)

Soaked with rain and sweat after a late mission, Tom Emrich, Bill Hobbs, Fred Avey, and Burney Tucker share a moment of mirth on Vella Lavella. (Walton collection)

Bob McClurg, J. J. Hill, Bill Heier, and Chris Magee (now with goatee) happily demonstrate how fighter pilots "talk" with their hands. (Hill collection)

An unlucky jackpot for Denny Groover, who overturned F4U-1A #17777 at Torokina on December 16, 1943, at the conclusion of a Cherry Blossom patrol. (National Archives)

Bill Crocker straddles an F4U-1A's cockpit at Torokina on December 18, 1943, backed by rows of Allied fighters (note F6Fs, P-40s). The planned mission to Rabaul was later aborted. (National Archives via Sullivan)

The Black Sheep received promotional items shipped by the St. Louis Cardinals, including one ball cap for each plane shot down. Chris Magee and Greg Boyington exchanged caps for victory flags. (Walton collection)

The first-tour veterans donned the new caps and toted bats as they crowded onto the sturdy wings of 17740 in a Vella Lavella revetment. (Walton collection)

Later, aces Bob McClurg, Moon Mullen, and Ed Olander hammed for a publicity shot on the same Corsair with newly acquired caps and bats. (McClurg collection)

Christmas Eve, 1943, Vella Lavella. Frank Walton sits beside Boyington, who wears a prized derby passed around by a neighboring squadron's pilot. Vought rep Lou Markey faces the camera. (Walton collection)

VMF-214's third incarnation was at full strength (43 pilots in flight jackets) at MCAS Santa Barbara in December 1944, just prior to dividing into carrier and rear echelons. (Free collection)

This FG-1 came to grief in the "bean patch" at Oxnard on August 15, 1944, when the wheels folded during field carrier landing practice. Stan "Red" Free was uninjured. (Free collection)

Radial aircraft engines were inherently oily and dirty, as this mech's hands testify. Free (center) called this "a bunch of pilots acting like we knew what we were doing." (Free collection)

Midnite II with Al Sibbernsen, the Nebraskan who acquired the ram as a replacement for the original Midnite after it was killed accidentally in August 1944. (Free collection)

Ralph Husted's arrested landing on *Franklin* began normally on February 28, 1945, but as the Corsair slowed, its full belly tank detached and hit the prop, spraying fuel. (National Archives)

The observer at left has covered his face in sympathetic reaction as Husted is burned alive. The wind-fed blaze took an hour to extinguish. (National Archives)

Jubilant Black Sheep carry Boyington from the ramp at NAS Alameda on September 12, 1945, the night he returned to the West Coast after twenty months as a POW. (Walton collection)

Boyington's first stop on the War Bond tour was a three-day visit to Seattle beginning September 17, 1945. A crowd estimated at 5,000 gathered for this downtown rally. (Walton collection)

Boyington receives the Medal of Honor from Harry Truman on the morning of October 5, 1945, eighteen months after the medal had been awarded "posthumously."

the Japanese chased them to Kolombangara; neither side forced contact and the Black Sheep pancaked at 1230.

Later that afternoon, most of the pilots boarded a transport and flew to the Russells, with eight others following in Corsairs. The combat tour was far from over, but at least they could look forward to a spell of decent food, electricity, and Dallas huts in the friendlier setting of Banika.

In their first two weeks of combat, the Black Sheep had flown nearly six hundred sorties, most from a poorly equipped advance base, and established a blistering record. They had encountered the enemy in numbers that the Swashbucklers could not have imagined, claiming twenty-three aerial victories and eleven probables while sustaining five casualties, a seven-to-one ratio.

By strange coincidence, the Swashbucklers were even now riding inside other transports, still officially members of VMF-214 as they winged their way back from a week's leave in Sydney. How amazing the changes a day would bring.

13

"COME ON UP AND FIGHT!"

Among the different echelons of Marine Fighting Squadron 214 scattered throughout the New Hebrides and Solomon Islands, the importance of October 1 varied greatly.

On Espiritu Santo, the Swashbucklers had returned from Sydney only the day before to learn the fate of their group. "Shooting us in as replacements and all because of one man," someone wrote in a last diary entry, no doubt referring to Greg Boyington. "God bless us! We'll need it!"

By the end of the day, seventeen pilots had already been transferred to other squadrons, and the rest eventually joined them. Henry Miller was the lone Swashbuckler to stay on Espiritu. He spent the next several weeks instructing new replacement pilots assigned to MAG-11's headquarters squadron.

In the first three weeks of October, mechanical failures and crashes resulted in the loss of five Corsairs and three pilots; six more planes were damaged. The final chapter in the story of one dead trainee did not unfold for more than fifty years. Miller recalled the details.

> Wayland Bennett—a very nice fellow from Texarkana—was seen to go straight down into the jungle. The pilot flying with him thought he saw a wing fold. I never believed that, because I don't think that a Corsair wing could fold; it was probably the strongest part of the whole plane. But that's what they said. As

you can imagine, the jungle from the air is like water. Once something goes into it, the jungle closes over. It's gone. We searched very carefully that day and for a couple days afterward, but found no trace of it, no trace of him. I wrote a letter to his family.

The almost incredible part of it is that in 1988, somebody called from Texas who knew the family, and he said they wanted to go out and find Wayland's body. They wanted to know exactly where it went in. I didn't know where it went in at the time, and I certainly didn't know all these years later. I didn't discourage them; I said, "Well, I wish you luck, but you're going to have a tough job."

And then, believe it or not, in the summer of 1994, somebody from the family called up again. They went out there and did find the airplane and found his body, still in the cockpit. I would have assumed that over all those years the soft jungle would have absorbed anything that hit it that hard. But they identified him by his class ring and numbers on the airplane. They brought what was left of the body home and had a big military ceremony in Texarkana.*

By the end of October, all of the other Swashbucklers departed for combat tours with other squadrons. Vince Carpenter, John Fidler, Howard Cavanagh, Carol Bernard, and Jim Taylor joined VMF-211; Al Jensen, Vic Scarborough, Dave Rankin, and Dick Sigel went to VMF-212. The remainder joined VMF-215, the Fighting Corsairs, and returned to the fray for their second tour. Later over Rabaul they would be engaged in some of the most intense aerial fighting of the Pacific war.

*An expedition member attempted to link Bennett with VMF-214 by calling him "The Lost Black Sheep," but Bennett was never a member of the squadron. At the time of his death, he was still weeks away from assignment to an operational unit.

Ledge Hazelwood did not make it that far. Barely two weeks into his third and final tour, he made a strafing attack against a boat on Bougainville that was already out of commission. The vessel was beached but still had teeth, as Joe Curran remembered. "A gunner had some sort of weapon there, and he got pretty proficient. Hazelwood was going to strafe this ol' boat, and the guy got him."

Several saw the handsome Princeton man's Corsair go straight in, so there was no point in listing him as missing.

Two other former Swashbucklers became aces in the squadron. Ed Hernan had been practically anonymous as a replacement pilot in VMF-214, but during his second tour with the Fighting Corsairs he downed eight planes over Rabaul.

No F4U driver could match the incredible scoring run achieved by Bob Hanson with the Fighting Corsairs. He had already claimed two victories as a Swashbuckler, then dropped three more during his first tour with VMF-215. But it was during his second tour with them that he became a holy terror. He was credited with five fighters on January 14, 1944, then rang up a startling fifteen more victories by the end of the month, for a total of twenty planes in a seventeen-day span. His rise, unfortunately, was too meteoric to last. On February 3, the day before his twenty-fourth birthday, he fell victim to ground fire on Cape St. George. Like Ledge Hazelwood, he descended to strafe an essentially worthless ground target, and AA fire brought him down. Hanson was the last of three F4U pilots to receive the Medal of Honor, which in this case was presented to his mother.*

While the Swashbucklers were learning of their fate on October 1, the Black Sheep were more than five hundred

*In addition to spending time in India, Bob Hanson and Greg Boyington shared other commonalities. Both were collegiate wrestlers, members of VMF-214 (not concurrently), the only Corsair aces-in-a-day in the Solomons, and recipients of the last two Medals of Honor awarded Corsair pilots.

miles to the north, feeling civilized again at Banika after completing two weeks at Munda. Several weeks still remained of their combat tour, but the Russell Islands were "a million miles away in comfort." Few missions were planned, so they had time to recuperate. A photographic mission scheduled for Saturday, October 2, was scratched because of weather; so was a Kahili strike on Sunday. Some divisions were chalked on the blackboard for scramble alerts, but no one took off. Finally Greg Boyington and John Begert took their divisions on a strike escort on Monday morning.

For this mission, an SBD attack against AA positions on Malabeta Hill, near Kahili, the Black Sheep used eight Corsairs brought back from Munda for overhaul. The aircraft had supposedly accumulated too many hours for continued combat operations, yet they were now being pressed into service from a strip 135 miles farther from the target than where they had earlier been based. Two of Boyington's fighters didn't last an hour, and the rest wheezed up to the rendezvous point only to learn that the dive-bombers were on their way home. As with numerous other attacks, this strike had been coordinated with a B-24 mission over Kahili, so Boyington climbed and continued northward.

Fifty miles from the enemy base, the Black Sheep spotted dust clouds as fighters rose from the strip to challenge them. Their estimate of thirty Zekes in separate groups of eight and four was remarkably accurate. Lieutenant (jg) Fukuda, of the 204 Kokutai, led a scramble of twenty-eight Zeros that day to defend against B-24s, P-38s, and F4Us.

As the little Japanese fighters streaked up to meet them, Boyington dropped onto the first division in a high stern run. The speed differential was almost more than he could overcome. He opened up on the nearest Zeke from three hundred yards as it climbed in a right turn, then cut the throttle and sent his Corsair skidding sideways to prevent an overrun. After getting it under control, he "settled back on the Zero's tail, opened fire again and chopped the Jap's tail to pieces." He then wheeled around to the left side of the group and attacked the next Zeke in line from its seven o'clock high. He had fired only a few rounds when the pilot jumped from the cockpit and his parachute spilled out, the color of raw silk. The Japanese pilot's decision not to die for the emperor nearly backfired: The chute streamered for a mile before it finally popped open.

Almost immediately Boyington chased down a third Zeke and opened fire from directly astern, squeezing all the way as he closed the gap. The Zeke's right wing root flared and it went down burning. All three Zekes had fallen in less than a minute. Now tracers flashed by Boyington's canopy, and he dived to ten thousand feet before shaking off the aggressor.

While Boyington sashayed with the Zekes, John Begert's section leader, George Ashmun, became the first Black Sheep to observe an unusual Japanese defensive weapon. When the quiet twenty-four-year-old from Far Hills, New Jersey, became separated from the others, he climbed to 25,000 feet over Ballale and saw a huge aerial explosion west of Kahili. The enemy had resorted to dropping phosphorus bombs against the Liberator formations. They were ineffective as weapons (Ashmun saw no aircraft near the detonation), but their fireworks were spectacular. Enormous white tentacles curling slowly out of the center of the burst were bright against the backdrop of blue sky.

Ashmun found his own people more dangerous. Seeing P-38 Lightnings flying top cover for Liberators as they circled Fauro Island, Ashmun turned toward them to assist. As he approached, a pair of the twin-boomed fighters broke toward him, and he rolled to flash his white-painted belly and national insignia. The Corsair's white central wing box and blue outer wing panels should have been a sure recognition signal, but tracers from one of the Lightnings flickered past his canopy. "P-38, that's an F4U you're shooting at," shouted a bomber crewman. Ashmun kicked and twisted his plane to show every angle of his Corsair, then tucked alongside a Liberator's flank. Tracers whizzed by once more, so this time he prudently dived for home.

Back on the ground, Frank Walton queried the P-38 pilot and recorded his excuse in the action report: "Well, I didn't know there were going to be any Corsairs around." Another pilot offered that some of their boys were "kinda trigger happy." Apparently it was unnecessary to add that they were also poor shots.

Frank Walton's creativity in writing action reports was soon to be squelched by a new directive issued to intelligence officers requiring them to use official forms for the reports. As Walton completed this first action report for October, he realized that the formatted outline left no room for the likes of his earlier creative writing (the September 16 report, entitled "Zeros Spilled Out of the Clouds," was a thirteen-page masterpiece), although he did supply some vivid details in the narrative section.

No one flew on Tuesday, October 5, and only one division was airborne the next day. On Thursday, three divisions departed the Russells at 0610 and landed at Munda, flew two task force cover missions, then returned to the Russells. The next day the cycle was repeated but substituted local patrols for task unit coverage. This type of rotating assignment gave most of the pilots several days off, just the tonic they needed to shed the lingering tensions from their stay at Munda.

Like the Swashbucklers, the Black Sheep had their own choral group, anchored by the voices of George Ashmun, Moon Mullen, Bruce Matheson, Sandy Sims, and Ed Olander. "Whenever any three or more of them got together in the evening," wrote Walton, "it naturally turned into a songfest with the whole squadron joining in." Moon Mullen, a handy poet, made significant contributions to their repertoire.

During off-duty hours, the squadron often dispersed into distinctly different groups. Some veteran pilots and newcomers were drawn to the company of Stan Bailey, whom

Hank McCartney described as "a real fine fellow and not much of a hell-raiser." Others gravitated to the charismatic Boyington, an acknowleged master at finding something to drink even when supplies seemed low. As John Bolt put it, "He would mooch it, borrow it or browbeat it out of members of the squadron who he thought had booze."

This was corroborated in an unpublished manuscript by Frank Walton, who described a night at Munda.

> A group of us sat with Boyington under the olive drab canvas of the pyramidal tent we lived in. The tropical rain drummed on the taut canvas and ran down the open sides in sheets. We wore only underwear shorts and field shoes. The hot, humid air made the sweat run down our sides and between our shoulder blades. The flickering light from a lantern barely beat back the jungle dark.
>
> Boyington was about half drunk. He fixed one after another of us with a half-sly, half-baleful eye and demanded: "Who's holding out? One of you guys has a bottle of whiskey stashed somewhere. Come on, don't be a heel. Get it out."

Later that night, after one of the junior pilots caved in, Walton and Doc Reames were wakened by the sound of wild thrashing outside their tent. They found Boyington rolling in the mud and completely covered in black jungle slime. They stood him in the downpour to rinse him off "as we would a child in the shower."

Boyington was off the flight schedule for much of early October, even after the squadron returned to Munda on the tenth, their breather over. They landed on New Georgia at 0905 that morning, and within half an hour twenty Black Sheep, minus Boyington, jumped into Corsairs to escort a strike. Boyington had not flown, in fact, for almost a week, which made the following statement in his autobiography seem all the more incongruous: "In the month of October we were flown to a frazzle. There was no such thing as rest, or a day off, a situation I had never experienced before."

For the Sunday-morning mission—another coordinated strike with B-24s over Kahili while dive-bombers hit the Malabeta Hill AA site—McCartney's and Begert's flights were assigned high cover for the Liberators. Army P-38s were also assigned, but they disappeared near Kolombangara soon after the rendezvous. This was not the first time the Lightnings had seemingly vanished, which lent further credence to the Marines' scornful nickname for them, "high-altitude foxholes." On the other hand, two Corsairs aborted for mechanical reasons, which left only six to cover the Liberators.

Adding to the Army's woes, the bombing was none too accurate. About half the loads fell into the water off the end of the strip, "killing many small fish," whereas the heavy-caliber AA fire from Ballale and Kahili was on target. Two of the big bombers were hit as the formation made its clearing turn, and they lagged behind pouring smoke. Soon they were jumped by twelve to fifteen Zekes, and one Liberator went down in flames. Only four of the crew parachuted out of the plunging ship; they were strafed in their parachutes by a Zeke. The six remaining Black Sheep raced to the aid of the second cripple. Ed Olander caught one enemy fighter and flamed it, for his first confirmed victory; he also scored a probable and reported that a Liberator's gunner flamed another. Olander was the only Marine to record claims that day. The Japanese indeed lost two pilots from the 201 Kokutai, which was back in action for the first time since late September.

Over at Malabeta Hill, the other three Black Sheep divisions covered the dive-bombers as they tipped toward the earth. One bomb scored a direct hit on a large gun position; others thoroughly pummeled the entire site as the fighter pilots watched from ringside seats.

After comparing the methods and results between

Navy/Marine dive-bombers and the Army's level bombers, the fighter pilots continued to regard the latter with contempt, as Bruce Matheson remembered.

> We had a pretty poor opinion of them for a number of reasons, all factual. Their bombing accuracy was deplorable, and there was nothing worse than to escort these people to and fro, particularly if you get involved in dogfights, and then see them lay a beautiful stream of bombs off the end of the runway out in the water. Or even worse, on more than one occasion they broke formation before they even got to the target, and of course we didn't know where we were because they were doing the navigation.

Greg Boyington finally flew again on Monday, October 11, when he led three divisions over Kahili as cover for a mixed bag of Liberators and dive-bombers. The B-24s released from 22,500 feet and dropped most of their bombs into the water. Soon a handful of Zeros climbed from below. Bill Case, who was leading Boyington's second section, almost unintentionally caused the demise of one approaching bandit.

> We dropped down below the B-24s, and this fellow was still a mile away. I thought maybe I'd better warm up my guns to make sure they were functioning if he did come into us. So I got my gun switches on and checked them out. He was still climbing up and was almost directly in front of us by this time but about half a mile away. I fired my guns to check the spread of the tracer bullets and everything was fine. I used all the mil lead down to the engine cowl as the Zero was still at extreme range. All of a sudden, he flipped over and went straight down. He was still a half mile in front of us. They said that the Zero had burned and crashed, but I hadn't seen its destruction. I was the only person in the formation

who had fired my guns, so obviously it was a lucky, wild-assed shot.

Case's surprising victory was almost certainly one of four casualties suffered that day by the 201 Kokutai. Uncharacteristically Greg Boyington had nothing to report from that mission or the next. On Tuesday afternoon he led three divisions from Munda at 1400 for a planned fighter sweep of Kahili with P-40s as the low flight—bait, in other words. But an hour later he landed with his wingman, Mo Fisher. Both had suffered engine trouble, as did Bob McClurg. The nine remaining Black Sheep flew a bit farther, then turned back when they found much of Bougainville socked in by weather.

If the lull was unproductive for Greg Boyington, who had flown two inconsequential missions following an unexplained week-long hiatus, an ongoing problem with another pilot was far more serious. Virgil Ray's name had virtually been wiped from the chalkboard at his own request. He had approached Walton—the group's acknowledged confidant—one day, saying, "I can't cut it anymore." Evidently the trauma of being shot down on his previous tour had knocked the fight out of him, and his conspicuous absence from the flight log reveals as much. He flew two strike escorts in mid-September (claiming a probable) but finished the month with only three "miscellaneous" flights. In all he accumulated barely eleven hours for the entire month, compared with the squadron average of twenty-one flights and approximately forty-six hours during the same period.

Greg Boyington had compassion; he kept Ray in the lineup but scheduled him for noncombat hops such as mail runs to Guadalcanal. The other pilots accepted the situation. "He wasn't an extrovert to begin with," remembered Jim Hill, "and pretty much kept to himself. Nobody treated him badly. We all kind of sympathized with him and hoped he'd come out of it, but he was satisfied with the assignment."

Ray did not fly at all during the first twelve days of

October—mail runs had not been necessary during their hiatus in the Russells—but soon after the pilots returned to Munda he was sent out. He took off at 1100 on Wednesday morning, October 13, and landed at the Russells, then proceeded to Guadalcanal. After returning to the Russells he began the final leg to Munda at 1630. He never showed up.

The only plausible reason for Ray's mysterious disappearance was a storm, a big one, that had developed between the Russells and New Georgia. The next morning, Stan Bailey's division scoured the entire perimeter of the eastern New Georgia group, but the results were negative.

Just past noon on Thursday, October 14, Bill Case led a division consisting of Mo Fisher, Tom Emrich, and Bob McClurg on a shipping patrol. Half the flight aborted with engine trouble, then Casey and Long Tom were vectored hither and yon by ground radar before taking a heading toward Kahili. Twenty miles beyond Vella Lavella, radar called a snooper inbound.

Injecting some of his typical dry humor, Case later recounted the dynamics of a two-versus-two encounter.

> Finally we spotted them—a pair of Zeros doing their patrol out of Kahili. We had about a 4,000-foot advantage in altitude. We turned in toward them and they finally saw us. They turned in toward me and started to climb rapidly to try to make contact. They dropped their little external fuel tanks, and I tried to pull in around behind them. That seemed to be going fine, but then they did something that I didn't recognize as being part of their air discipline. They could climb straight up for a long way before they fell off on a wing—they had a zoom characteristic because it was such a light airplane. So although they were in front of us, and therefore in a critical position, I'm quite sure what they were trying to do was pull us up into a stall, and they were going to flip over and be on our tails. It didn't happen, though, because we had all this extra speed from [descending] to get at them. So they went up, and we

went up. We fired, and I could see the tracers going up toward the bird I had on the left. My wingman had a free shot at the one on his right. We went up and up, and up, and up. I kept wondering, "Are the guns going to jam because there are zero g's on the ammo belts?" But they kept firing and we kept closing on them. Then the Zeros flipped off in opposite directions. I stayed with the one I was on, and chased him and chased him and chased him. Finally he just dived away from me, and I never got a bit of fire or even smoke out of that bird.

I had been in a whole series of little waltzes with that guy, and I thought, "My gracious, here I am, passing through 4,000 feet going straight down, and it's about time your ol' Dad has to pull up and miss those big waves." So I pulled out, and found that I was at *fourteen* thousand feet instead of four thousand. I had completely lost ten thousand feet in my concentration. That was a dumb thing. I looked around to see where this character was that I'd been chasing, since I'd found out that I was 10,000 feet higher than I thought I'd been, and I saw a splash. It would either be the splash from a 100-gallon drop tank they had jettisoned, or it was an airplane. But I was now back at 16,000 feet—no way it was that little tank. So I reported this, and they said, "Well, you got yourself a bird."

If Casey's claim seemed less than airtight, Japanese records would agree. Neither the 201 nor 204 Kokutai reported casualties on October 14, though the possibility exists that the pilot ditched and was rescued. Case was given credit—he thought confirmation might have been issued by the radar controller—which made him the second Black Sheep ace. Tom Emrich, meanwhile, knocked pieces off the other Zeke's tail, but it turned on him and gave chase before finally breaking off to hightail home.

Friday morning's mission brought even better results. Two divisions (Bourgeois and Olander) were to escort B-24s to the Kangu Hill supply dump near Kahili. Greg Boyington's division was scheduled to take off late to sweep the area for fighters after the bombers departed the target. It did not work out that way. The various elements took off and made their rendezvous on schedule, but the bomber formation zigzagged before proceeding to the target. Consequently Boyington's division—Burney Tucker on his wing, Case and Emrich in the second section—arrived ahead of the bombers and watched dust trails as Zeros scrambled to intercept.

Circling while the Liberators completed their drop, Boyington had a tremendous advantage as he lowered his four Corsairs to engage a dozen Zekes long before they could get to the bombers. In quick work, Case and Emrich downed two apiece and Tucker claimed his first. Boyington put away another (his tenth as a Black Sheep) and also claimed three probables. The Japanese did indeed lose big on October 15, with seven pilots killed among the 201, 204, and 253 air groups. The totals match for once, but some of the Japanese fighter losses were incurred while they escorted Vals from the 582 Kokutai during an attack against Allied ships.

What was supposed to have been a tail-end fighter sweep had unintentionally become a successful preemptive ambush for Boyington, who felt that an identical strike should be planned for that purpose. Walton greased the skids in his conclusion of the day's action report: "It is recommended that such a fighter sweep be sent up early on every strike to engage the enemy fighters." The logic was inarguable, but the next day's mission had already been scheduled with another tail-end sweep.

The dawn patrol pancaked at 0650 on October 16 and reported a heavy front building up. At about 0800 three divisions (Bailey, Begert, and Bourgeois) took off to provide medium cover for an SBD strike at Kara airfield, followed an hour later by two more divisions (Boyington and Olander) to act as the fighter sweep for Liberators returning from a Kahili strike.

Stan Bailey's three divisions joined up with the SBDs on schedule, but as they approached the target they were thwarted by zero visibility and ceiling. Following alternate instructions that had been given earlier to strafe barge traffic around the Shortlands, Bourgeois led his division down to the surface. Tail-end Charlie in the flight was Don "D. J." Moore, a Texan whose infectious grin had established him as one of the most likeable pilots in the outfit. It was all he could do to hold formation as the division weaved around storm clouds and bounced in the turbulence. When the flight broke into clear air a mile southeast of Vella Lavella, Moore spotted a small bargelike craft with several people in it. Thinking that the division was still near the Shortlands, he opened fire. His target turned out to be a Higgins landing craft. Fortunately he observed no results from his 3-second burst, and no complaints were heard from the boat's occupants.

Greg Boyington's two divisions also struggled with the weather. "The clouds were way the hell up there, towering over the bombers' altitude," recalled John Bolt, leading Olander's second section. "The bombers went into some clouds and we lost them; we didn't know where the hell we were." The fighters, who had been busy weaving over the bombers, were all too happy to let the Army handle the navigation.

Separated from the bombers, Boyington needed to get a visual fix on their position in order to lead them back to Munda. The only way to do that was to find a hole in the undercast and drop through it, so the eight Corsairs closed up as he led them down through an opening in the clouds. Suddenly Boyington discovered that they had already overflown part of Bougainville; they were well past Kahili now, somewhere in the vicinity of Empress Augusta Bay. It was ticklish to be so deep into enemy territory while trying to avoid detection and staying beneath the overcast.

Soon they approached Kahili, which seemed all the bigger. "Stick in close, stick in close," Boyington radioed as they inched around Kahili's northern perimeter and out over Tonolei Harbor. Passing low over the wave tops, the Black Sheep were surprised to see tremendous barge activity in progress. The harbor was full of tempting targets as the Japanese took advantage of the overcast.

But Boyington ordered them to stay quiet. "Nobody shoot," he radioed, and they continued across the harbor without incident. As they reached the open sea, Boyington took an easterly heading instead of turning southeast toward Munda. Eventually he located Choiseul, then turned south for Vella Lavella. By this time his erratic route had taken its toll on their fuel supply, especially for tail-ender Tom Emrich, who had jockeyed his throttle more than the rest.

A few miles short of Vella Lavella, Emrich's engine ran dry. He later described the sensation when he was forced to ditch.

> As soon as I hit I couldn't see anything, and as the airplane was going down I was visualizing that I was dead. All I could see was this spray of water. The next thing I knew the airplane decelerated and the water was right up to the base of the windshield. The tail was about thirty degrees up, and when the spray stopped I could see out. Then I tried to get up. Of course, I still had the seat belts and everything tied on, so I had to undo those. I got out with all my gear and jumped on a wing, and about five seconds later the airplane went down and disappeared.

Emrich climbed into his rubber raft and waited for the crash boat while several Corsairs circled overhead. Boyington and McClurg, who had enough fuel to reach Munda, steered for home base. Case landed at Vella Lavella to refuel, as did all of Olander's division after waiting to make certain that Emrich had been safely picked up.

Instead of preparing for the short flight to Munda, however, one member of the group at Vella Lavella ardently campaigned to return to Bougainville, where all the big game was ripe for strafing. "Come on, guys! Let's go back up there and shoot up those barges," urged John Bolt. "This is perfect! If we get jumped by Zeros, all we have to do is pull up on instruments, get in the cloud cover, and we're safe."

"Oh, Jesus," someone replied. "The Skipper'll be pissed off about that!"

Bolt pressed them. "If we try to get an okay to go back, it's never coming through," he argued. "The damned command structure is so ponderous, it will never be able to approve a flight like this." But no one volunteered to go with him.

Bolt had a mechanical dilemma as well; his gunsight had burned out when a plug-in electrical connection shorted. Bill Case solved the problem by unplugging the connector from his own Corsair and giving it to Bolt, who roared off, without orders, once his plane was serviced. He climbed to fifteen thousand feet to get a fix off the western tip of Choiseul before turning toward Bougainville. Then he dropped back to the water and raced into the mouth of Tonolei Harbor, which he found just as before—full of boats of all descriptions. The Japanese in them were surely stunned to hear the piercing shriek of air through the Corsair's oil coolers—"Whistling Death," they had come to call it. When Bolt saw two dozen troops sitting in a forty-foot barge, he aimed the bright image in his repaired gunsight at them. In an instant they were dead or dying and their vessel was on fire.

Next Bolt saw an empty barge in his path, which did not burn, then a tug resembling a Chinese junk with no sails, which did. He found a small cargo vessel towing a smaller boat, noting that the first had a purple numeral four on its wheelhouse. He thoroughly sieved it with a withering stream of incendiaries and armor-piercing rounds.

When he reached the end of the harbor, he pulled up into a wingover, then dropped back down to the water and raced for home. The hills behind him hid his silhouette. "I was only taken under fire from one gun," he later reported as he described orange balls of tracers from a 20mm weapon. "They just floated by."

When Bolt pancaked at Munda at 1330, Boyington was indeed furious, but Bolt defended his action.

> When [Boyington] was chewing me out, I told him I didn't understand why we didn't strafe them on the way out. In fact, in my mind, the thing to have done would've been to rev up those engines and strafe Kahili. We were already in a terrible pickle, and I didn't think that shooting them up a little bit was going to increase the danger that much.

It was difficult to argue with success. Boyington had to swallow any lingering criticism the next day with the arrival of a telegram from the Old Man himself.

> THAT ONE MAN WAR . . . CONDUCTED BY LIEUT BOLT AGAINST JAP STUFF IN TONOLEI, WARM HEART (STOP) HALSEY

But Halsey's cryptic note could not undo all of the damage. "Boyington never cottoned to me much after that," Bolt admitted. His statement was later justified by Boyington's treatment of the situation. In his autobiography he claimed that he recommended Bolt for the nation's second-highest medal: "This boy was awarded the Navy Cross." But Boyington had done no such thing; instead he effectively buried the Tonolei Harbor strike in a citation for a Distinguished Flying Cross, which was awarded routinely when Bolt subsequently claimed his third aircraft on another mission.

It was apparently Boyington's last word on the matter,

however, for he put personal opinions aside to include Bolt on the next day's preemptive fighter sweep. The boat killer was in Olander's division, which joined three others (led by Boyington, Begert, and Bourgeois) for the singular purpose of drawing Japanese fighters into the air.

The Corsairs hurtled down Munda's crushed coral strip at 0815 on October 17, accompanied by seven Fighting Falcons from VMF-221. Division leaders Begert and Bourgeois soon turned back—the latter because of an intensely painful sinus attack resulting from a tropical cold—which left twenty-one F4Us en route to Kahili. With the seven Fighting Falcons at six thousand feet to act as bait, the Corsairs reached the enemy base an hour after takeoff and made a lazy circle in the sky overhead. Dust arose as an estimated forty Zeros took off in pairs and threes, then converged into two groups, one circling northeast toward Choiseul, the other southeast near the Shortlands. Boyington could not have envisioned a sweeter setup. With the immeasurable tactical advantage of altitude, his Corsairs descended in sweeping turns onto the nearly defenseless Zeros. Puffs of smoke appeared as AA gunners began firing from the ground.

Boyington took his division down to 10,000 feet and engaged fifteen to twenty Zekes. Other Black Sheep still circling above met fifteen more at 18,000 feet, and yet another fifteen to twenty Zekes and Hamps approached from the west at 22,000 feet. Their estimate of up to fifty-five enemy planes was extremely accurate: The 204Ku sortied thirty-two Zeros and the 253Ku sent twenty-four. In a melee that swirled across hundreds of square miles, from the Shortlands to Fauro Island to Bougainville, seventy-six combatants yanked their planes around the sky. Soon the blue was streaked with vapor trails, streams of gun smoke, and the ugly black whorls of exploding gas tanks.

The Black Sheep scored again and again, although in Frank Walton's report the drama of earlier episodes was unfortunately replaced with efficient data.

Type Enemy a/c: Zeke
Pilot or Gunner: Lt. E. L. Olander
Where Hit, Angle: High, 12 o'clock
Damage Claimed: Destroyed

And so it went: one for Matheson from seven o'clock level; one for Bolt from dead astern; two for Magee and the same for Tucker; three more for Boyington; two for Heier.

Years later Walton claimed, "The 21 Marines had, without a single loss, shot down 20 Zeros for sure and God only knew how many probables—the battle was too violent to worry about probables." His report shows twelve destroyed and two probables for the Black Sheep, with no mention of VMF-221, although one Fighting Falcon claimed two Zekes destroyed and one probable.

The Japanese did suffer heavily, losing three pilots apiece from the 204Ku and 253Ku and one from the 201Ku who was killed over Fauro Island. The Black Sheep also reported that two pilots bailed out of their Zekes, which brought total Japanese losses to probably nine aircraft. For once, they had actually lost greater than 60 percent of what the Marines claimed.

On the receiving end, Bruce Matheson and Ed Harper, both wingmen with no one to guard their own backs, earned Purple Hearts. Harper in particular had a difficult time with a large pack of Zeros and was fortunate to make it back alive.

> I picked myself a Zero out of a group . . . got on top of him, and he was split-Sing under me and I was doing wingovers on top of him. We almost got down to the water right in the middle of Kahili harbor when I found myself in trouble. Before I could get a decent shot at him I looked around, and six or eight Zeros were clustered around me; I was pretty well pinned down on the water. My target must have been screaming for help on

his radio. I actually thought, What a lousy place to get shot down. I never once thought I was going to get killed, but I was almost sure I was going to get shot down. I started jinking and carrying on, and headed toward a small cloud about a mile or so away. I finally popped into that cloud, but by that time I had taken quite a few holes. They were literally using me for target practice. The game changed from me chasing a Zero to just trying to survive. Tracer was flying over me and under me. I'd go down and they'd fire over me; I'd pull up and they'd fire under me.

The significant thing is that when I got into this cloud—just a puffy little thing—I could turn in the cloud and pop out the other side. It was just like squat tag—I felt completely safe. I noticed my flight suit was wet. I had been sweating but was so busy I didn't recognize it until after.

"Harpo," wounded in the neck, finally managed to dive out the bottom of the cloud and race to Munda, where he made a belly landing due to a ruined hydraulic system. Peppered with bullet holes, his Corsair was written off.

Matheson, hit in the legs, nursed a Corsair tattered with more than a hundred bullet holes and two 20mm hits through a storm cell before reaching Munda; his plane would take a week to repair. D. J. Moore's Corsair had likewise absorbed bullets and cannon rounds but could be fixed in a day. Those were the only debits on the squadron's balance sheet. Jim Reames patched Harpo's neck wound and Matheson's leg lacerations and anesthetized them with Le Jon brandy; they were back in the air the following day.

Ed Olander's postmission euphoria was tempered by a mild scolding from the skipper. "Boyington always did a lot of shooting," he began. This day, Olander saw him chasing down a fourth Zeke after expending his ammunition on the first three.

> I came out of the sun all by myself and saw a Zero headed back to Ballale with a Corsair right on his tail. They were going 90 degrees to me, so I couldn't shoot at the Zero without chancing that I'd hit the Corsair, which was practically chewing the tail off the Zero. When I got back and described it, Boyington said, "For Christ's sake, I was the guy there! Why didn't you shoot him?"

It was the only time Boyington chewed him out, and it served to reinforce Olander's dedication to his leadership. It was hard to fault a man who would risk having his own men hit him in order to kill a Zero.

The following afternoon Boyington, Begert, and Olander took their divisions on a repeat of the Sunday fighter sweep—*after* flying medium cover for an SBD strike over dreaded Ballale in the morning. During the back-to-back combat missions, they sweated through five total hours of flying toward the enemy, fighting him, then flying home.

The Ballale strike was a large, cooperative mission with Army B-24s, P-38s, and P-39s, Marine SBDs and TBFs, and New Zealand P-40s commencing at 0900 on Monday morning. Two separate groups of Zeros—including fifteen Zekes level at the Black Sheep's altitude—seemed content to keep their distance.

The Marines, staying close above the bombers, were rewarded by the results of the strike, which were recorded in the war diary.

> The bombing was the best the VMF-214 pilots ever saw. The AA positions around the perimeter of Ballale were well hit. TBF bombs crossed the runway, and the bombs from the B-24s walked right down the runway.

Right above enemy territory, Bob McClurg began experiencing engine trouble, an ignition problem known as "mag flash." The unpressurized magnetos would occasionally arc at high altitude, which momentarily cut the ignition. McClurg's started flashing over Ballale before the ignition quit altogether. He nosed over and got the engine started again at fifteen thousand feet, where the air was dense, but the Pratt & Whitney performed so poorly that he turned toward Choiseul and prepared for an emergency landing. Looking down as he crossed Fauro Island, he spotted two slate-colored Zekes climbing beneath him and heading in the same direction. "You buggers!" he muttered and eased down behind them. They never knew he was there.

Like a hunter with buck fever, McClurg opened fire on the trailing Zeke from 800 yards—extreme range—and watched as his tracers lost velocity and fell short. But he held down the trigger, closed the distance, and raised the nose until his rounds tore through the Zeke's fuselage. The aircraft curled to the right and plunged into the water without burning. McClurg throttled back, slid to the left, and fired on the lead Zeke from 250 yards, again pulling until his shots entered the cockpit. Like the first, this Zeke nosed over and splashed.

The engine continued to miss as McClurg babied the Corsair back to Munda and reported his claims. "That's gonna have to be verified," Walton told him and left McClurg to wait. Soon came good news: An Army pilot flying low cover in a P-39 had seen the whole thing, and the Pennsylvanian had his confirmation.

For the afternoon mission, Burney Tucker replaced McClurg on Boyington's wing in the fighter sweep, which was made up of twelve Black Sheep and eight Corsairs from VMF-221. One of the Fighting Falcons was Jim Swett, now a captain after earning a Medal of Honor over Guadalcanal when the two squadrons fought together on April 7. With Boyington leading, the twenty Corsairs took off at 1530 and flew directly to Kara airfield. As they circled it once at fifteen thousand feet, they received medium-intensity AA fire that was initially below them but soon began bursting accurately at their level. Boyington then moved his Corsairs over to Kahili and circled it twice while the AA fire continued to intensify. The Marines counted sixty planes on the enemy airfield, but none rose up to fight. Boyington used the radio to berate them, shouting, "Come on up and fight, you yellow bastards!"

According to Black Sheep lore, several such taunting incidents between Boyington and English-speaking Japanese controllers took place, and some have been documented. The first was a well-known query—"Major Boyington, what is your position?"—that probably occurred on October 17. This time, in response to Boyington's direct challenge, the controller allegedly radioed in formal English, "Why don't you come down, Major Boyington?"

Neither of these exchanges was mentioned in the otherwise highly detailed mission reports compiled by Frank Walton, a notable omission. Information that the enemy was not only listening to tactical frequencies but actually broadcasting to an individual by name should have been significant news from an intelligence officer's point of view. Walton did write in his book, however, that Boyington not only called the Japanese but answered their challenge by instructing his pilots to remain at altitude while he dived on the enemy base single-handed, strafed the field in the face of AA fire, then rejoined his flight and resumed the taunting. "The flight of Marines audaciously circling and mocking them was too much for the Nip commander. Japanese pilots raced out to their planes, and one after the other they took off until there were 40 Sons of Heaven."

The statement is difficult to reconcile with Walton's own war diary, which reported only half as many enemy fighters and did not mention Boyington's strafing run. Normally Walton was meticulous in his record keeping, especially because the newly distributed ACA-1 forms required thorough documentation of enemy contacts—even to a calculation of average fuel consumption and rounds of ammunition expended. When Burney Tucker reported a strafing run on the Shortlands after that same mission, Walton described it in detail.

Another shadow of doubt is cast by the element of time. From Boyington's orbit at fifteen thousand feet, it would have taken him long minutes to descend, strafe Kahili, and climb back up—all while his outfit circled vulnerably in the midst of accurate AA fire. This was unorthodox, even for someone as compulsive as Boyington.

Bruce Matheson, a wingman on this flight, later observed:

> [Boyington] was leading this fighter sweep, and when you lead a formation of fighters, they go where you go. Had he said to somebody, "You keep making lazy circles in the sky while I go down 10,000 feet, then I'll be back up to join you," I would have remembered that. It would have been most significant.

Ed Olander agreed with Matheson's thoughts regarding the alleged strafing, but he remembered hearing Boyington call down to the Japanese. "He did taunt them, and they did eventually come up."

Climbing in a circle from Kahili were twelve to fifteen Zekes, a few Hamps, and a Tony. "Well, they're going to make it easy for us," radioed Boyington. "Let's go get 'em. Pick out your target." He led them down to eleven thousand feet. Suddenly the Corsairs scattered "like the spring on a broken clock" as they dived onto the Japanese. They hit the enemy a mile above the earth halfway between Kahili and Ballale, and in a matter of minutes they claimed eight Zekes destroyed and two probables.

George Ashmun had been leading John Begert's second section but diverted with engine trouble, leaving wingman Chris Magee with an opportunity to fly unfettered. He was credited with a triple, which made him the third Black Sheep ace. Greg Boyington misspelled his name but gave due credit: "McGhee didn't seem to be wasting much extra lead this day, as I saw him flame three on first bursts."

Jim Hill, the lanky Chicagoan who was flying on Begert's wing, claimed his first; other singles were scored by Mullen, Case, Olander, and Boyington. Ed Harper and Sandy Sims earned the probables. The Fighting Falcons were given credit for six fighters destroyed and four probables, meaning that the Marines' combined claims equaled twenty destroyed or given little probability of returning to base—the same number of aircraft the Japanese were estimated to have sortied in the first place. They admitted to losing a total of six pilots for the whole day—certainly a serious debit—but Bob McClurg had already received credit for two that morning.

Although the Marines' claims were wildly high, the Japanese actually did lose at least fifteen fighters and thirteen valuable pilots—the equivalent of half a squadron—in two days. In exchange only one Marine pilot, VMF-221's 1st Lt. Milton E. Schneider, was reported missing in action. The Black Sheep were justifiably exuberant, having completely dominated their foe while receiving only a handful of bullet holes in two planes. One of those bullets was a close call, however, and could easily have doubled the Marine casualty list.

Bill Case had already been told that this would be his last combat mission. He had made it through three six-week tours and had a bride waiting back home. As a matter of habit, he had *always* flown with his seat raised as high as it would go because of his short torso, but this particular day he made an exception.

> On this flight, I ran it to the top, and looked at the gunsight—turned it on to make sure it was working—and ran the seat down a notch. I looked at the gunsight again, and still had about sixty mils of lead before the image touched the cowl. I thought, That looks pretty good for today, so I left my seat down. That was the only time in

the South Pacific that I didn't fly with my seat all the way up.

That afternoon, having already downed his eighth and last enemy plane, Case was flying comfortably at twenty thousand feet when a single 7.7mm bullet came angling through his birdcage canopy from directly behind. Instead of drilling him in the back of the head—as it certainly would have if he had not lowered the seat—the bullet clipped the top of his helmet, cut his scalp, and pushed his head forward. The slug struck the bulletproof glass inside the front windscreen, then ricocheted down into the tube of optical lenses in the gunsight, which exploded in a shower of glass particles. Case had not been wearing his protective goggles, but because his head was shoved down, the glass peppered his forehead instead of blinding him. Lowering the seat—a seemingly insignificant decision—had saved him not once but twice, sparing Ellen Case a widow's telegram.

In a trailblazing month, from September 16 to October 18, the squadron was credited with fifty-seven aerial victories and nineteen probables, which attracted a great deal of attention. It was likely at this juncture that the man most responsible for the impromptu creation was on New Georgia, where he took the time to shake hands with Greg Boyington.

What began as a casual visit left a big impression on several Black Sheep, including Bruce Matheson.

A few of us were on fighter strip alert. They got us all together and we kind of stood at a half-assed mode of attention, and this . . . man came up with an open khaki shirt. He wore an old cap, and I looked at it and saw there were a lot of stars there. I realized later that this was Admiral Halsey. He was a little old man, but he had a lot of stars and he had come out personally to visit Boyington.

The squadron had now been in the forward area for five weeks, and its combat tour was winding down. With the exception of flying a thirty-minute hop to Vella Lavella a few days hence, Bill Case was removed from the flight schedule as Boyington promised, but there was still a bit of flying left for others—some of it unexpected.

On Monday evening, October 18, Frank Walton announced that the relief squadron had arrived and the Black Sheep would be flying to the Russells the next morning. It was all the incentive the men needed for a celebration. The whole outfit vacated their smelly tents, moved into a new plywood hut equipped with enough folding cots to accommodate all of them, and started cadging liquor from wherever they could get it. After personal contributions had been rounded up, the men descended upon Doc Reames and his footlocker stocked with medicinal brandy. He consented, and the party went on until well past 0200 on Tuesday morning.

It was not yet 0400 when Frank Walton was rudely awakened by an operations officer with orders to strafe Kahili. A few men stirred in the darkened hut. "These men have been in combat for forty-two days, they need rest," Doc Reames groaned, but his protest fell on deaf ears. Boyington, still drunk, could barely focus his eyes as he stood swaying beside his cot. "Never mind, Doc. They want Kahili strafed, we'll strafe it. Who wants to go with me?"

George Ashmun—as likely as any of them to be sober—volunteered, along with Chris Magee and Bob McClurg. Boyington, no stranger to flying after a night of heavy drinking, explained years later how he managed to make himself function.

> I crawled out on my hands and knees most of the time; sometimes I had my skivvie shorts on, most of the time nothing. I would get out there beside my tent like a dog on all fours and I would look up about a block to where the mess hall light was, but I didn't see one light, I saw

> three, four, five or six sometimes. I knew that I would kill myself taking off in the dark if I could see more than one light there, when I knew there was only one.
>
> A nice little tub . . . was parked under the eves [*sic*] of my tent, and in the early morning I wanted to feel awfully cool in the rainwater. When I saw these lights I crawled over and dunked my head and shoulders up to here and said, "Boooo, booooo, booooo, booooo."
>
> I went on like that, and I would bring the lights down a few, and then I would repeat this process until I would get it down to one light.

After pulling on some clothes, Boyington shuffled across the crushed coral of the flight line when the beam from Doc Reames's flashlight played on his feet. "Hell, Greg," he exclaimed, "you don't have any shoes on."

"I don't need shoes to fly an airplane."

"You'll certainly need them if you go down," argued Reames. He untied his own and insisted that Boyington put them on before climbing into a Corsair. The pilot complied.

Boyington's hastily organized plan was to split the division into two sections. Ashmun and Magee would strafe Kara and he and McClurg would take on Kahili. Soon after the Black Sheep lifted into the inky blackness at 0450, they encountered a turbulent weather system. Ashmun lost sight of the others and steered alone to Choiseul, where he circled on instruments for a few minutes to prevent outpacing the others. Turning toward Kara, he saw Fauro Island in the moonlight and decided instead to make a single pass at Ballale. At forty feet off the ground he raced the length of the strip and held down the trigger for about ten seconds while he sprayed the revetment area. Except for sighting an empty raft amid several oil slicks, he had an uneventful return flight to Munda and pancaked only an hour and forty minutes after takeoff.

In the meantime, Greg Boyington had turned on his

running lights to make it easier for Magee and McClurg to stay with him in the heavy weather. Over Choiseul he inexplicably turned them off, then nosed over and was lost from sight.

Magee continued toward Kara with McClurg, searching in the darkness, and later remembered:

> Normally you'd be able to see a coral strip with enough moonlight, but there was all this ground fog. So we flew around looking, and by luck I finally saw the strip . . . then dived right straight in. We went down below the treetops, because there were trees on both sides of that strip. We went right down the center. I didn't think at the moment where McClurg might be, flying my wing.
>
> All of a sudden, when we were halfway down the strip and firing, I saw a flash off to the side and above the trees, as if someone had struck a match. Just then I thought, My God, that's the tower!

That flash of light was McClurg's lucky charm; he was so close to the tower that he had to roll to avoid it. After straightening out, he and Chris Magee expended seven hundred rounds apiece on five aircraft parked at the far end of the strip. Twisting in their seats for a look back, they saw that the planes were in flames.

Greg Boyington, who flew alone to Kahili, could barely find it in the darkness. After dropping low and running the length of the strip, unable to see anything to shoot, he made the bold decision to attempt another pass. Leveling off at just forty feet, he sprayed three bombers parked at the northwest end, which drew ground fire, then he headed toward the water. He flashed across Tonolei Harbor and opened fire on an anchored warship, reportedly a destroyer, before concluding his morning with some barge hunting along the northern tip of Choiseul. He strafed one barge at the mouth of the Mulamabuli River. In his book he wrote that he could see George Ashmun strafing Kahili at the same time and wondered how they missed each other in the dark. Perhaps he was still seeing double: Ashmun had strafed Ballale and gone home.

Instead of returning to Munda as did the others, Boyington pancaked at Vella Lavella. No official explanation was given for the diversion, though a fuel or mechanical problem would likely have been noted by Frank Walton. Chris Magee volunteered the reason years later. "[Boyington] had heard someone up the line had a quart of booze at Vella Lavella."

Whether or not Boyington actively searched for another drink before 0700 (or found somebody willing to give him one), it was to his credit that he had completed the daring attack on Kahili while still under the influence of what was supposed to be the squadron's farewell party. Alcohol might have emboldened him to volunteer for the mission in the first place, but his pilots loved the example he set by personally accepting tough assignments. That he was sometimes hung over, or put tobacco under his eyelids to stay awake, did not concern them. Bruce Matheson later said:

> [Boyington] was an alcoholic in the days when we didn't know what an alcoholic was. But I've always maintained that he could fly better drunk than most people could sober. If there was a natural born pilot, he was one: extremely aggressive, and to me, absolutely fearless.

Later that morning, twelve Corsairs participated in a coordinated multiservice strike on Kara. A few Japanese planes were seen taking off, but they never challenged the formation. More rewarding, only fifteen to twenty enemy aircraft were observed at the northeast end of the Kahili strip, apparently all that remained of the once-formidable enemy base. On Wednesday, one Black Sheep division flew an uneventful dawn patrol. Two others that escorted a relatively small SBD strike to Bougainville late in the afternoon received no opposition over their target whatsoever. The balance of aerial superiority over Bougainville had shifted dramatically in favor of the Allies.

Early on the morning of October 21, Greg Boyington and fifteen other Black Sheep ferried Corsairs to Vella Lavella for use by squadrons now operating from the new advance base, then boarded an R4D bound for the Russells. The Black Sheep still at Munda hopped on another transport for the same destination, and soon both arrived at Banika with a collective sigh of relief. Now that the combat tour was over, the miseries of Munda became just a memory for the squadron. Munda had served its purpose as the forward base on New Georgia, having permitted the Black Sheep and Swashbucklers alike to strike at the Japanese strongholds on Bougainville and surrounding islands, and VMF-214 would never again operate as a unit from that ruined place.

The Black Sheep were not destined to return to combat with the same esprit de corps enjoyed by the current group. Not that their camaraderie would diminish, but a new policy dictated that the size of the squadron would soon swell from seven fighter divisions to ten. Of the twenty-eight pilots in the original Black Sheep, six did not accompany the squadron back to the Russells (four were dead or missing and two others had been evacuated with wounds). Another four carried scars from lesser wounds. Had any of the Black Sheep been fatalistic enough to consider their casualty rate over Bougainville—almost 40 percent—they might have paled at the knowledge of just how long and bloody the road to Rabaul was going to be.

14

A LITTLE TROUBLE IN PARADISE

That the Black Sheep were going to fight over Rabaul was inevitable, they knew, but those days were too far into the future to trouble them now. Much more immediate was their desire to unwind from the rigors of the recent combat tour. There were beaches to enjoy, decent meals to replenish tired bodies, drinks to soothe worn nerves. For Frank Walton it was a luxury to write "no flying" in the war diary.

The squadron was temporarily housed in a long Dallas hut with a row of cots lining the walls. With beer in good supply and the Choral Society in full voice, evenings passed quickly.

One night the entertainment went beyond the ordinary. As the men lounged on cots, Boyington and a man identified only as "a visiting pilot from another squadron" argued the merits of boxing versus wrestling. The Black Sheep skipper was confident that the wrestler would win; the boxer was equally self-assured. As the beer flowed, their discussion became more heated, with neither pilot willing to budge. Inevitably they talked themselves into proving their respective points.

Frank Walton was elected as referee, and cots and furniture were pushed out of the way. Boyington crouched in a wrestler's stance; the stocky challenger danced lightly in the classic pose, one hand cocked near his chin, the other poised to jab. The two men circled in silence for a few moments until the boxer came in with two quick flicks, then backed out of reach as blood trickled from Boyington's nose. The wrestler tried to get close enough to grapple, but the other pilot fended him off and continued—as Walton later wrote—"to jab, jab, jab until Boyington's face was a bloody mess."

Despite the blows, Boyington gradually cut off the boxer's circle. With a sudden rush Boyington got his arms about the other's waist and threw him to the floor, then he pounced, grabbed his opponent by the throat, and pounded his head against the floorboards. After a moment, Walton stepped in and tapped Boyington on the shoulder. "Okay, Greg, you've proved your point. Let him go."

Boyington turned his puffy eyes to Walton, said "That's okay," and continued to bounce the blue-faced boxer's head off the floor. A few more spectators waded in and separated the fighters, who then retreated to cots and resumed sipping beer.

"That was a lucky hold you got," said the boxer.

"No, it will always end the same way," Boyington insisted. "The wrestler will always win."

But the boxer was not satisfied, and Boyington was obliged to prove his point again a few minutes later. Much more wary this time, the boxer landed several solid blows while trying to avoid Boyington's grasp, but the result was the same: Once the Black Sheep skipper got a tackling grip, it was all over. At the age of thirty, Boyington was still in his prime, though he had obviously forgotten any lessons learned from the broken leg sustained in the same type of brawling.

On Sunday, October 24, Denny Groover returned to the Black Sheep with a green light to resume flying, just in time to join the whole outfit as they flew the next morning to Guadalcanal. After changing planes they rode down to Buttons, then settled into another set of Dallas huts. Their routine changed little, save for the availability of fancier clubs stocked with real liquor. Days were spent beachcombing, playing cards, and catching up on mail; darkness brought movies, drinks, and songfests. The veterans' tales of Sydney whetted the appetites of those anticipating their first trip. One prerequisite for getting there came on Wednesday, when Doc Reames administered Schneider tests—checking the men's pulse and blood pressure—and malaria smears.

The last day of the month was celebrated by welcoming Rollie Rinabarger back after he'd recuperated from wounds received on September 26, but he still did not look good. Weeks of weight loss and bouts of blood poisoning had taken their toll. Nonetheless the Black Sheep were back to twenty-six in the fold, counting Doc Reames and Frank Walton. On November 3 the first half (divided alphabetically) departed for Tontouta and Down Under; the next group of thirteen followed a day later.

To the veterans of previous visits, Sydney was unchanged. A week's leave with fine food, late parties, lovely ladies, and sights for touring provided the same rich experience as before. After having adjusted to the rigors of island life, the men found the city something of a shock to the system.

Frank Walton did not spare the time to write while he was on leave but soon thereafter sent a full description of Sydney's gastronomic and cultural offerings to his wife, who built B-17s on the Vega Aircraft assembly line.

> Nov. 13, 1943
>
> My darling little rigger,
>
> Here we are, back at home base after a long, hard but thoroughly enjoyable trip to Sydney, Australia. Yes, we got orders for the whole squadron for a rest and recreation trip . . .
>
> Sydney is a town of about 1½ million or more and it was a welcome sight to see streets, buildings, automobiles, and civilians again. We had a real vacation. I started off by eating a cool baker's dozen eggs for breakfast, drank 11 milkshakes the first day, ate a T-bone steak for lunch and a filet mignon for dinner the first day.

After that I settled down to a breakfast of 6 eggs, 4 milk-shakes and only 1 steak daily.

I went to the Australia Hotel and really lolled in the lap of luxury, getting a steam bath, sweat, and a rub, a shave, haircut, massage (facial) and even a manicure. It was wonderful to be back in civilization again. I looked eagerly about for excitement but found myself strangely disquieted and realized that I was still many, many thousands of miles away from my baby, and as long as you weren't there I couldn't really enjoy myself. I went to the horse races, to the zoo and the aquarium—saw the Koala bears and the duckbilled platypus—you've probably had that last strange animal in your crossword puzzles . . .

Went to the movies, all very old but well displayed, orchestras with them and the people here crowd them so that you have to get reserved seats to all of them.

The money system is not hard for an old mathematician like me to grasp—a pound is worth [$]3.27 and has 20 shillings in it. 2 sixpence pieces make a shilling and 2 threepence pieces make a sixpence, of course . . .

Streetcars are trams and drugstores are chemists.

Butter, tea and sugar, but not coffee, are rationed—however, there is a ceiling price on everything so that the grocery stores hide out the better stuff, like the big, nice tomatoes, etc. for their customers who pay double or triple—a lot like the U.S., eh? You can buy anything in the black market, which flourishes openly—almost—provided you can pay the outrageous prices.

The civilians get 3 gallons of gas a month (I mean petrol) so most of them have installed huge, unwieldy contraptions on the front or rear bumpers . . . They are about 5 feet square, weigh about 300 pounds and burn coke. Others have huge gas bags on top of their car. The bags are about 12–15 feet long, 6 feet wide and 5 feet deep, and are filled with natural gas. One filling will run the car about 15 miles. Seems hardly worth the bother. Streetcar service is excellent and the fare only a penny.

Very few civilians have telephones and you have to have a radio license to keep a radio in your home—they call them "wirelesses." The programs are all government produced . . . are really lousy, and most go off at 11 pm—no swing shift programs here.

The people are quite fond of Americans generally and the Marines in particular, because they know the Marine landing on Guadalcanal saved Australia . . .

While the Black Sheep enjoyed the charming city, orders were being processed to transfer a handful of the three-tour veterans into VMF-213, which was currently preparing to depart for the States. Stan Bailey, John Begert, Hank Bourgeois, Bill Case, and Hank McCartney enjoyed their vacation in Sydney, but when their visit ended and they returned to Espiritu Santo it was time to say farewell to the Black Sheep and the South Pacific. Despite the squadron's exhaustion from a week of playing in Sydney, it joined with the Hellhawks of VMF-213 to throw a party. Among the tired Marines heading home, only Stan Bailey would find a future place with the Black Sheep.

The remaining nineteen pilots appeared haggard after so much overindulgence. Doc Reames gave them another Schneider test and exclaimed, "Your readings are worse than before you went. You're more run down now!"

They had two weeks to recover. More important, in that same period they had to integrate nineteen replacements who had checked in during their absence, along with two more who arrived within a few days of their return to Espiritu. The newcomers brought the squadron's total strength to forty pilots, as required by a recent directive.

One of the new arrivals was a career Marine who would take over Stan Bailey's role as executive officer. Major Pierre M. Carnagey, in the Corps for three years and recently advanced to the rank, was one of the few experienced pilots who did not enter combat during the early part of the conflict. He finally came west in February 1943 and joined VMF-222; he worked out of Midway all summer before arriving in the Solomons for one combat tour, most of it at Munda. A legitimate veteran, Carnagey had been shot down once over the Vella Gulf, and his own guns scored two probable Zeros. Prior to shipping overseas, the blond, photogenic twenty-seven-year-old graduate of the University of Southern California had settled in Corpus Christi with his wife, Mary Jeanette. She was a nurse's aide whom he called the "prettiest damned wife a man could have."

Another experienced pilot was Capt. Marion J. March, better known as "Rusty." At twenty-eight he was one of the older pilots in the squadron, having graduated from Stanford five years earlier. Like Carnagey, he entered the Marines before the war started only to spin his wheels as an instructor at Corpus Christi for two years. "That did me no good as far as combat was concerned," he later said. "I got scared as much by student pilots as I would have in combat."

Greg Boyington sometimes boasted that he was the oldest active fighter pilot in the Marine Corps (and wrote that all of his pilots were between the ages of nineteen and twenty-two), but he was not even the oldest in his own squadron. A former Hellhawk from VMF-213 named Fred V. Avey turned thirty-one a week ahead of Boyington. Avey was still a first lieutenant when he checked in, and his promotion to captain followed soon after. In the process of logging nearly seventy combat hours in Corsairs, Avey had downed a Zero on September 18, then received half credit for a Washing Machine Charlie in a dramatic night action. He was section leader in a division led by Capt. James N. Cupp that took off from Munda in the wee hours of September 21 and chased a Betty in the moonlight. When the Japanese bomber shot Cupp down in flames, he bailed out over Vella Lavella with third-degree burns "from his shorts to his shoetops." Avey stitched the bomber across both wings and watched it belly into the water, then strafed it when a crew member emerged from a hatch. In the end he shared credit for downing it with another pilot who claimed hits, though no one had seen him nearby. "Tiger Fred" was also married; his wife, Mae, was at home in Portland, Oregon.

J. Cameron Dustin, a veteran of two previous tours, was a youthful captain. Only twenty-two, the Nebraskan had been in the South Pacific a long time, having arrived on the *Lurline* with Boyington. His combat service began on Guadalcanal in VMF-123, then a Wildcat squadron (which VMF-214 replaced when it arrived on the 'Canal in mid-March). Later that summer he scored a Zero probable during his first Corsair tour. Walton described him this way: "Rusty [*sic*] is one of those quiet boys who somehow managed to have two trips to Sydney and a 5-week tour in Aukland under his belt before he headed north for his third trip. He musta learned how in the books he had his nose thrust into most of the day."

Another newcomer wearing captain's bars was Gelon H. Doswell, a teammate of Dustin's for two tours in VMF-123. Born and raised in New Orleans, the twenty-three-year-old had a wife and a newborn daughter in the Crescent City; little Ann was already seven months old, but "Dos" had never seen her.

First Lieutenant James E. Brubaker likewise had family concerns. The twenty-one-year-old veteran of a single tour with VMF-213 had departed the States on June 22. He later learned that his brother, a B-17 bombardier, had been shot down over Germany that very day. Neither theater would be kind to the Brubaker clan in this war.

Another of the new pilots arrived from a situation similar to that of former Swashbuckler Tony Eisele. First Lieutenant Bruce J. Ffoulkes was an original member of VMF-214 returning to the squadron after a long hiatus. He had first joined the squadron in 1942 with the likes of Vince Carpenter and Charlie Lanphier but was then detached to Palmyra for seven months of boredom before coming west to join VMF-213. Ffoulkes's tour as a Hellhawk had been largely uneventful. The twenty-five-year-old Southern Californian was engaged to Harriet Banfield, who waited out the war in Portland, Oregon, near Fred Avey's wife.

Last of the experienced arrivals was the indomitable Henry Miller, who was rejoining the squadron for an unprecedented third tour. Assigned as the operations officer and promoted to major upon arrival, he brought along thirteen second lieutenants from the MAG-11 headquarters squadron.* Miller and two other instructors had personally trained them for the past several weeks to familiarize them with the Corsair.

Of the whole bunch, only skinny Pennsylvanian Fred S. Losch had arrived with previous flight time in the airplane—a surprising 108 hours. It was an unusual luxury considering his upbringing and early military training—both studies in primitive living. He grew up in the hills of central Pennsylvania near the tiny town of Larryville, worked a family farm that lacked indoor plumbing and electricity, and finished eight grades in a one-room schoolhouse before going to high school in neighboring Jersey Shore. He roomed with his older brother in order to attend Geneva College, near Pittsburgh, then joined the Navy the day after Pearl Harbor. As a member of the first class to train at a brand-new elimination base near Kokomo, Indiana, still without permanent buildings or even a strip, he learned to fly from a cow pasture. The parachute loft was an old chicken coop.

*Harry R. Bartl, Glenn L. Bowers, John S. Brown, Rufus M. Chatham, J. Ned Corman, William L. Crocker, Jr., William H. Hobbs, Jr., Herbert Holden, Jr., Alfred L. Johnson, Harry C. Johnson, Perry T. Lane, Jr., Fred S. Losch, and Alan D. Marker.

Losch's fortunes changed after he selected the Marines and earned his wings at Pensacola. Sent to Jacksonville for advanced fighter training, he was one of five lucky students selected to train exclusively with Maj. John F. Dobbin, a veteran ace from the bitter fighting on Guadalcanal. "He couldn't hear, and looked about twenty years older than he really was," recalled Losch, "but he was a hell of a good pilot." Dobbin had a handful of F4Us at his disposal—the first in the training command—and gave his fortunate students unparalleled fighter training.

One-fifth of the revamped squadron hailed from a single state. In addition to Henry Miller and Fred Losch, two other arrivals from Pennsylvania were Glenn L. Bowers and J. Ned Corman, who shared uncommonly parallel careers. Both were students at Penn State, where they learned to fly together in the civilian pilot training (CPT) program, then remained in the same training and operational squadrons throughout the war. Four other veteran Black Sheep—Bob Bragdon, Bob McClurg, Moon Mullen, and Sandy Sims—were also natives of the Keystone State. Illinois boasted the most-represented single community, with four pilots from Chicago: J. J. Hill, Chris Magee, Bruce Matheson, and new arrival Alan D. Marker.

Among Henry Miller's other students, two had come to the South Pacific with an hour or so in Corsairs, but the rest had no experience whatsoever. In four weeks Miller had managed to sign off about thirty hours into each of their logbooks, although not without difficulty. Harry C. Johnson, another married youngster, lost a hydraulic line in mid-October and was forced to make a belly landing. Twenty-three-year-old Herbert Holden, Jr., disappeared from his division four days later during a morning hop when his engine failed. The New Jersey lad hit the silk, then spent the rest of the day in the water. Badly sunburned, he swam ashore and returned to the squadron the next day. Three days after Holden's accident, Al Marker lost his vision when his goggles slipped during takeoff; he went off the side of the strip and knocked two feet of wing off his birdcage Corsair.

At first glance it would seem that inclusion of more than a dozen inexperienced replacements was a significant liability. By comparison, however, VMF-214 had entered its first tour in March with no combat-experienced pilots, and about one-third of Greg Boyington's original Black Sheep had been veterans. Now the balance of experience had tilted toward two-thirds of the total group.

In addition to receiving new pilots, the flight echelon was temporarily reunited with the squadron's enlisted men. Park Avenue bachelor Arthur Little was still assigned as the commanding officer of the ground echelon, having been with the unit now for an entire year. Administrative duties, including the tedious job of chief censor, consumed most of his time, so that now Little's melodramatic prose was largely limited to squadron memos. Still it was a big organization to manage. Along with 5 subordinate ground officers were 269 enlisted men—cooks, clerks, plane captains, drivers, custodians, laundry workers, and especially mechanics. As before, the reunion between flight and ground echelons would be brief.

Flying resumed on November 17. Boyington had once postulated that a pilot needed fifty hours to become truly familiar with an airplane, which meant that most of his newcomers were about twenty hours short. Training flights included bomber escort, high-altitude dummy gunnery runs, and division tactics. During the latter, division leaders tinkered with assignments to find the best possible blend of experience and ability among the members. Finally they flew plenty of "interception" hops: Two divisions of Corsairs charged at each other head-on from a considerable distance, and as soon as one had the other in sight the battle was on.

One day, as the whole squadron gathered to brief the day's training exercises in the ready room, the newcomers gained an unexpected appreciation for what the veterans recently had endured at Munda. Glenn Bowers, for one, got a laugh out of their combat jitters.

> Somebody detonated some dynamite nearby. I don't know what they were building, but there was a big blast and all of the veteran pilots immediately dived flat on the floor. Us new boys were sitting there in our chairs. [The veterans] were reacting, having been up there where the bombs were dropping, and flattened themselves out real quick.

While the new members settled in, one veteran tinkered between flights with an idea that would benefit all of them. John Bolt had already proved his fortitude by taking his Corsair up to Bougainville for a single-handed strafing run, which more than made up for his first melee when he had handled his Corsair "in a state of shock." The young Floridian had since become a determined student of aerial fighting, with three Zekes to show for it. As his experience grew, he became analytical not only of tactics but of equipment; he soon began to question the effectiveness of the standard machine-gun belting. Bullets were automatically fed from canisters in the Corsair's gun bays by means of metal belts, with incendiary, tracer, and armor-piercing (AP) rounds linked one after the other in repeated sequence.

Bolt did not believe this was the best use of the ammunition. Not one to palaver about it, he borrowed a long-barreled .50-caliber Browning M2 from the ordnancemen, hauled it over to the "boneyard," and began firing belt loads of different bullets into wrecked F4Fs to measure their effect. It was not merely for fun; he analyzed the results carefully.

> I shot into the planes' pilot armor. All the rounds, i.e., tracer, incendiary, and AP, would penetrate the armor if their hit on it was direct. The incendiary had a low-order

explosion on impact, so that if it hit farther back on the fuselage it would impact the armor over a few square inches of area and not penetrate. However, there appeared to be enough punch in the incendiary to knock off a cylinder or certainly a pilot.

Because Bolt's tests were limited to wrecked Wildcats in the junk pile, he temporarily suspended them with the idea of trying new experiments later. Meanwhile he proved resourceful as well as innovative, particularly with regard to food. The diet on Espiritu was a vast improvement over the fare in the combat area, but the quality and flavor of the food had a military sameness to it. Bolt enlisted the help of others to improve the menu from time to time. Meathead Bragdon was an avid hunter, and they occasionally ventured into the jungle after game birds and animals.

Freshly caught fish were also a treat, although catching them by fishing or spearing did not always satisfy Bolt. He and Bragdon decided to use a more efficient method.

There was some type of tuna that would run up at night and feed in the fresh water in the spring. There was a French stone bridge over it, about eight feet wide and not more than four or five feet off the water. I could get a fish fry for the squadron by mining the stream, which was sufficiently wide that it would take three to five charges. My pal, Bob Bragdon, would lay wires down next to a battery, and we'd have the charges numbered. I'd get up on the bridge and see the fish leave the fresh water and start downstream. I'd say, "Get ready on number one—shoot it!"

KABOOM! The school of fish would turn back and try to make another run through. I'd say, "Get ready, get ready! Here they come—by three! Get ready on three!" KABOOM!

Then we'd go out and pick up these nice, white-meat fish. Once I shot a school of mullet and had 240 fish.

They were not big mullet, but they were good frying size.

Another opportunity for fine dining was provided through an acquaintance of Bolt's who lived in another camp that was having trouble with wild hogs at its garbage dump. The camp commanding officer refused to let anyone shoot them and erected a fence instead. Bolt came up with a plan that would eliminate the hogs and provide a feast at the same time. He took Bragdon again as an accomplice.

> We sat around and drank with those guys for an hour or two after dark. We opened the gate and all the pigs in the neighborhood went in there, then we sneaked over and slapped the gate closed. God, we had pigs! We had the multitude all penned up.
>
> But old Papa Pig was a formidable character. We were not supposed to shoot because of the CO's edict, so instead we got these steel stakes and were going to club 'em. Papa Pig had long tusks that were razor sharp, and he probably weighed about 400 pounds. He would charge at this fence, and it was like the whole fence was coming down. So we decided that nobody wanted to deal with him, opened the gate and let Papa out. Three or four of his wives ran out and a couple of small ones, but we went in and [clubbed] six pigs.

Courtesy of a little practical ingenuity, the Black Sheep enjoyed a huge pig roast and beer party. There was enough to go around, even to the ground echelon. Newcomers and veterans alike shared enormous slabs of roasted pork and clutched bottles of beer with arms about one another's shoulders in joyous camaraderie. The squadron had blended quickly.

Greg Boyington appeared in an uncharacteristically neat uniform complete with a regulation garrison cap on his head. The reason behind the sudden change in appearance was a portly lieutenant colonel named Joe A. Smoak, the commander of MAG-11 since mid-July. Boyington had already gone behind Smoak once—by engaging the support of senior allies in the 1st Marine Air Wing to organize the Black Sheep in August—and Smoak apparently harbored vindictive intentions. When Boyington returned from combat, Smoak came down hard and cited an untidy camp. Boyington vowed to keep the squadron squared away for the rest of its stay.

Despite this compliance, their mutual disdain for each other rapidly intensified. For starters, Boyington's cavalier behavior and periods of drunkenness galled Smoak, a meticulous Naval Academy product who ruled strictly by the book. There is little doubt that professional jealousy festered beneath Smoak's skin, because his nemesis consistently made headlines as a fighter ace in spite of his unsavory conduct. For his part, Boyington considered Smoak a fat, arrogant authoritarian looking for any excuse to hang him. Even worse, he was a dive-bomber pilot. The man Boyington referred to as "Colonel Lard" in his book almost succeeded in undermining his career.

About a week after the Black Sheep returned from leave in Australia, Smoak dropped what amounted to a bomb on Boyington by arranging to have him transferred as the operations officer for the newly opened Vella Lavella strip. Boyington spilled the bad news to Frank Walton, who promptly urged him to learn whether James Moore, Boyington's old drinking general, was aware of the orders. Boyington drove off in a jeep in the middle of the afternoon on Friday, November 19, and was gone for the entire evening.

Suddenly realizing that he had underestimated Boyington's intensity, Smoak tried hourly to locate him but didn't dare call on General Moore. Boyington finally returned, drunk and happy: Moore had gone ballistic and canceled Smoak's orders. Smoak took a weak stab at retribution again by ordering Boyington to report to his hut the first thing Saturday morning.

Boyington returned from the meeting carrying paperwork not often issued to Marine Corps majors—an order for his own arrest. Smoak had unearthed an obscure general order prohibiting officers from making trips to the 1st MAW "for personal or departmental benefits without specific permission of the Group Commander." The order had been written ten months earlier—long before Boyington sailed to the South Pacific or Smoak came to the Wing—and Smoak used it to punish Boyington for going over his head.

Smoak's contrivance, dated November 20, placed Boyington under arrest for a ten-day period "for disobedience of orders." He was to remain within the perimeter of the immediate airfield, a limitation that Smoak knew would keep him out of the officers' clubs.

Although he was not confined to quarters, Boyington spent most of his nonflying time in his Dallas hut. He was "in hack," in military jargon, and Joe Smoak went to great lengths, even posting a man near Boyington's hut, to make sure that his orders were being followed. Despite the watchdog, nothing could daunt Boyington's own pilots from helping out. As Glenn Bowers recalled, "He needed some booze. We got some whiskey in a Coke bottle and rapped on the shutter, passed it in there and walked away nonchalantly."

General Moore's hands were tied regarding Boyington's arrest—Smoak had kept within strictly legal rights and could place detrimental information in Boyington's service record—but the wily general had other ways of bringing pressure to bear. Ralph Mitchell, commanding general of the 1st MAW, had earlier received a glowing commendation from AirSols Fighter Command on Boyington's performance. It said that his first tour had been characterized by "a brilliant combat record, readiness to undertake the most hazardous types of missions, and a superior type of leadership." The November 15 letter further praised Boyington as "one of the five outstanding fighter combat pilots that have operated in this theater since the beginning of operations." That last put him in mighty tall cotton alongside the likes of Guadalcanal heroes Joe Foss, Bob Galer, Joe Bauer, and Jimmy Swett, each a Medal of Honor recipient. As assistant commanding general of the wing, Moore saw to it that the commendation was officially forwarded to Joe Smoak, who received it a few days after arresting Boyington.

Time, or lack of it, was also on Boyington's side. Moore had already overruled Smoak on the matter of Boyington's continuing assignment with the squadron, which was scheduled to return to combat duty on November 27. Not even Smoak could prevent that from happening. Thus at 0430 on a Saturday morning, only a week into his ten-day arrest period, Boyington and twelve others took off from Espiritu via SCAT transport and pancaked at Guadalcanal four hours later. After an hour to refuel they left again, this time landing at Vella Lavella in time for lunch.

Having departed so early in the morning, Boyington probably did not have orders in hand releasing him from arrest. Jumping the gun was just one more way of thumbing his nose at Smoak. Frank Walton carried the original signed copy of the release when he departed Espiritu the following day with the rest of the Black Sheep, and he kept the yellowing sheet for the next fifty years. Smoak signed below the following words, which he must have hated to state: "You are hereby released from arrest this date and restored to duty, as your services cannot be spared."

General Moore later extracted additional retribution for MAG-11's meddling. According to Walton's account, Smoak himself was demoted to the Vella Lavella operations job the next day. It probably did not occur quite that rapidly, but Smoak was indeed replaced as MAG-11 commander within two weeks.

As had happened so often in the past, Greg Boyington managed to dodge another unfavorable situation. Not all of his pilots did, however. As they waited near their R4D during refueling on Guadalcanal, Rollie Rinabarger started to collapse. Ed Olander tried to prop him up, but he blacked out and crumpled to the dirt. "Doc grabbed me and threw me back in the hospital," Rinabarger later recalled. Already thin, he was so run down that it took him months to recover. He was eventually transported back to the States on the hospital ship *Hope,* then recuperated in Oakland until the following June. The Black Sheep, having lost a man before the tour even began, went into combat with thirty-nine pilots.

On Espiritu, meanwhile, adjutant Arthur Little published one of his patented hyperbolic memorandums to the ground echelon, hardly bothering to be subtle about the fact that Boyington had been in hack for a week.

> 1. Major Boyington, your "Skipper," together with your pilots left us last night for another hitch in their well-worn belt of combat duty. They are already winging their way northward to meet the enemy. And, judging by past performances, by the time you read this may have knocked down a few more Jap planes to add to the impressive record of your Squadron, of which we are all so proud.
>
> 2. Major Boyington is still your Commanding Officer—make no mistake about that . . . Last night, busy as he was in getting away, he turned to me and said almost apologetically, "You know, I only wish I had had more time with the men . . ."

The enlisted men might have shared a wink or two about the notion that Boyington got away, but few could have swallowed that final quote. Having been confined to the airfield for a week, he had plenty of time to spend with them if he wished. Boyington lived to fly; otherwise he worried little about the welfare of his squadron. He was tenacious in the air, but his presence on the ground was another matter. As one of the pilots put it, "Boyington was a horror as a CO. Frank was . . . the glue that kept us together."

Boyington would probably have agreed as long as he had an enemy airplane in his sights. A few slow weeks would pass before he got his next chance.

15

ISLANDS IN THE SUN

When the Black Sheep returned from Sydney in mid-November, they learned the details of Bull Halsey's latest Allied advance in the Solomons. Back on November 1, just as they were preparing to begin their leave, the 3d Marine Division commenced amphibious landings at Empress Augusta Bay on Bougainville. After consulting with Gen. Douglas MacArthur and his own advisers, Halsey had decided the best place to assault the biggest island in the Solomons was its lightly defended middle, even though the Japanese still had five airfields and a seaplane base within a sixty-five-mile radius.

Once Halsey secured a perimeter beachhead, it would have to be tenaciously defended against Japanese air and ground attack from multiple directions. To prepare for the invasion, repeated bombings and fighter sweeps by AirSols had reached their crescendo the previous month and finally rendered the enemy bases on Bougainville useless. However, once the assault force reached Empress Augusta Bay, four operational Japanese fields at Rabaul were barely two hundred miles distant.

On November 1, the Japanese sent several large air raids to turn back the landings. They were met by some of the AirSols fighters that maintained a constant patrol overhead, Bob Hanson among them. The former Swashbuckler scored three victories to became an ace that day, but he got wet when his plane was shot out from under him (he was picked up unhurt later in the afternoon).

Before the Black Sheep left Espiritu for Vella Lavella, Frank Walton tried to be circumspect in a letter to his wife, Carol, by hinting that the squadron might set foot on Bougainville when it resumed its combat tour. He was only partially correct. The squadron would eventually operate from a new coral airstrip along Bougainville's shoreline at Cape Torokina, but it would be only a staging point, and Walton would remain on Vella Lavella for the entire tour.

A month after the assault on Bougainville, the ground battle was still in progress as the Black Sheep positioned themselves to contribute to the campaign. Their first mission on Sunday, November 28, was a local patrol over the big island, which was roughly an hour's flight to the northwest of Vella Lavella. While half the squadron was still en route from Guadalcanal, three divisions (Boyington, Carnagey, and Miller) took off at 0855 in pre-positioned Corsairs (Glenn Bowers was left behind due to a flat tire). Boyington led an uneventful patrol before taking them down for a couple of strafing forays.

Unfortunately the Black Sheep were unable to complete even one mission of their new tour without an operational loss. John Brown, a twenty-five-year-old former Purdue halfback, ran out of fuel during the return leg and was forced to ditch his Corsair near the northwest tip of Vella Lavella. A Higgins boat picked him up promptly; he arrived back at the outfit on Monday morning just as the last fourteen Black Sheep off-loaded their gear from a transport.

Frank Walton was pleased to describe their new home as "a lovely little island." As the northwest anchor of the New Georgia group, Vella Lavella was the first island Halsey took after bypassing Kolombangara. The handful of Japanese garrisoned on the island were quickly mopped up, an action that saved the jungles and coconut groves from the violence that had defaced Munda. A new airstrip scraped out of the southeast corner adjacent to the Barakoma beachhead had already seen its share of Black Sheep who were either making emergency stops or defending the skies overhead.

Now they had come to stay on the island for the next six weeks. It was hot and steamy—and they would live in yet another tent city—but the unspoiled condition of the picturesque island was a vast improvement over the wretched environment they had endured during their last tour on Munda.

On Monday morning the squadron blazed a minor historical trail. J. C. Dustin took off with Glenn Bowers, Rufus Chatham, and Ed Olander for a Cherry Blossom patrol (the code name for Bougainville), although Olander had to land a few minutes after their departure when his wheels failed to retract. The others reported on station just in time to receive a unique request for close air support. Japanese mortar positions were giving the ground Marines a tough time as they attempted to widen the bubble of American-controlled territory, and the Corsairs were needed to strafe the positions.

Rudimentary attempts, particularly by dive-bombing squadrons, had been tried in August on New Georgia, but there had been no formal training or procedures established for coordinated close support. The only navigational aids the Black Sheep carried were simple strip maps, which were useless for plotting coordinates. The embattled troops overcame this by creating an ingenious signaling device. Piecing together several muslin panels on the ground, they formed an enormous white arrow, then radioed the fighters overhead and told them to spray the jungle five hundred yards beyond the tip of the arrow. Making a total of eight runs in echelon formation, Dustin, Bowers, and Mack Chatham smothered the terrain, observing plenty of smoke as they effectively silenced the mortars. Frank Walton later wrote that they put 25,000 rounds into enemy positions, but their Corsairs carried only 7,200 rounds among them. Even so, it was an effective demonstration of the versatile fighter's capability.

November concluded quietly with a few task force escorts and Cherry Blossom patrols, the latter often ending with a Charlie search for targets of opportunity. (Able and

Baker were other areas designated for freelance hunting.) Greg Boyington took three of his old-timers on such a run on Tuesday, November 30. Gunning alongside Bob McClurg, Chris Magee, and D. J. Moore, the four veterans set fire to a sizable stucco building in a small harbor. Otherwise there was little for Frank Walton to describe in his war diary. Japanese aircraft were nowhere to be seen, so there was no need for air combat action reports.

The situation did not change throughout the first half of December. The Japanese appeared to have quit flying altogether, due in large part to another aborted attempt by Adm. Mineichi Koga to thwart Halsey's island-hopping momentum. In late October, Koga had ordered 173 aircraft off their Third Air Fleet carriers and sent them to the airfields surrounding Rabaul where they joined approximately 200 aircraft from the Eleventh Air Fleet—all that survived after fifteen months of fighting in the eastern and central Solomons.

During the first weeks of November, Koga's ships and aerial forces attempted several strikes, including four relatively minor surface engagements and six "great air operations." Koga boasted that fifty Allied ships were sunk, but the United States actually lost only one old four-stacker destroyer during the predawn hours of November 17. By then, Koga had already withdrawn the tattered remnants of his Third Air Fleet to Truk. Of the 173 carrier planes he had thrown into the meat grinder, only 52 survived less than two weeks later, which left the battle-weary Eleventh Air Fleet gasping. It was no wonder they refused to challenge the Marines over Bougainville.

A graphic illustration came on December 1, when Pierre Carnagey led eight Black Sheep as high cover for a strike on Chabai, along the north coast of Bougainville. The forty-eight SBDs and twenty-four TBFs found the primary target socked in, so the formation did an about-face and steered for its secondary objective, the once-formidable Ballale. Just a few weeks previously they would have encountered fierce resistance anytime they were in the vicinity; now the Zeros were nonexistent. Antiaircraft fire remained accurate (one dive-bomber was seen to go in, with only one chute opening), but it was all the Japanese could muster.

Days passed with similar results. Cherry Blossom patrols over Bougainville and Empress Augusta Bay were mixed with an occasional strike escort and impromptu strafing runs, but the Japanese never took to the sky. On Saturday, December 4, Boyington led four divisions on a large strike that included sixteen other Corsairs escorting eighteen B-25s to Chabai. Here the flak was light, so while the Mitchells turned south after their drops, Pierre Carnagey's flight loitered for half an hour, then howled down from eight thousand feet to strafe buildings and a supply dump. Flying just twenty feet above the ground at three hundred knots, they bored past thoroughly surprised gunners. That afternoon, having completed routine Cherry Blossom patrols, several divisions scattered to strafe targets of opportunity. Boyington's division worked its way around to the Shortlands and strafed an AA position at Faisi in which several gunners on the ground were killed.

Only four Cherry Blossom patrols were scheduled for Sunday, which allowed a handful of Black Sheep to embark on a solemn mission. For the past week they had looked across the Vella Gulf at Kolombangara's conical peak, contemplated Bob Alexander's fiery crash there in September, and wondered if they might still be able to find him. Frank Walton talked a PT boat crew into taking them on the thirty-five-mile journey to investigate. Although the Japanese had already evacuated the volcanic island, Walton joined Greg Boyington, Doc Reames, D. J. Moore, Moon Mullen, Bob McClurg, and Burney Tucker—the only remaining member who saw where Alexander crashed—in arming himself before going ashore.

The next day Walton described their effort in a letter to his wife.

6 December 1943

Darling Carol,

Yesterday morning I strapped on a .45, climbed on one of those things John Williams works on, [and] went to a nearby island to look for one of our men who crashed there last September. We landed, looked around and found the plane in a million pieces, and found the boy, too, his bones huddled up in a pitifully small pile.

We scooped out a shallow grave, laid his remains in there, painted his name on one blade of his propeller, set it up as a headstone, carried some clean white rocks from the beach and put [them] around it, stood and saluted and wished him well. What a hell of a place to die—7000 miles from home on a godforsaken, Jap-infested island. We didn't see any Japs although we fully expected to, and we were ashore for some 3 hours.

Somehow, we hope, his bones will rest more peacefully after having had a friendly hand lay them away.

At least his father will know, too, that he's definitely gone and not live for years in a false hope that he'll turn up some day . . .

Things are still quiet in this area—looks as though my boys have the Jap fliers scared to death. We hear they're refusing to fly in the daytime because our boys have been giving them so much hell. We're all hoping things will pick up before long . . .

But things did not pick up, not for the better part of two weeks, and the Black Sheep continued to chafe at the lack of aerial opposition. Another measure of just how quiet things had become was illustrated by Strike Command on December 6 when Greg Boyington and J. C. Dustin led two divisions as high cover for an attack on the Kieta Harbor supply area. Along with eight P-40s assigned as medium cover, the Black Sheep provided the sum total of fighter protection. Six weeks earlier it would have been ludicrous to send only sixteen fighters to protect no less than seventy-two TBFs and

SBDs, yet Strike Command's assessment proved accurate. Not a single Japanese aircraft challenged the formation.

There was one advantage to the lull. Free from the punishing stress of constant aerial combat, the replacements and veterans had a relatively peaceful opportunity to develop into a cohesive unit. The second lieutenants already knew one another well, having spent weeks together in training before joining the Black Sheep, and soon made their own contributions to the entire group.

Herb Holden added his singing voice and vocal arrangements to the Choral Society, and Fred Losch found humor to be an ally.

> I weighed 128 pounds and was very dark. We were horsing around and I was going to wrestle Walton or somebody. Matheson said, "Oh, for Christ's sake, sit down. You look like an Indian rope trick artist." From then on, all through the service, nobody ever knew my real name. My name was Rope [Trick], and still is today.

Twenty-two-year-old Perry T. Lane was a native of Vermont, but unlike Stan Bailey, his stoic predecessor from that Yankee state, he was always near the parties. "My mother warned me to avoid drinking and gambling," Lane said to Frank Walton, "but I can't see where her advice has done me much good." Having been raised in the mountains, he hated the tropical heat. In Pensacola he filled out a request form listing the South Pacific as his last choice for assignment, but that had not done him much good either.

There were two Bill Juniors: William L. Crocker, Jr., and William H. Hobbs, Jr. The first, a Yankee from Worcester, Massachusetts, was a skilled midnight requisitioner. "Whatever you wanted," Walton said of the twenty-three-year-old, "Crock could get it for you—and at wholesale."

Hobbs, one of several married newcomers, spent a lot of time writing to his bride, Ann, who was living in Missouri. When he smiled, which was often, his wide grin and button nose made him look like a teenager; he was twenty-two but looked almost too young to be wed.

Two other new arrivals soon became the Mutt and Jeff of the Black Sheep. Tall, skinny Harry C. Johnson, twenty-two years old and a native of Birmingham, Alabama, soon earned a spot among the Yamheads because of his oratorial skills with a "southern lingo thick enough to cut with a dull knife." He was the perfect foil for Alfred L. Johnson, twenty-three, an undersized New Yorker known for his rapier wit.

Some of the newcomers were high-spirited, such as freckle-faced Harry R. Bartl, from Sacramento, California. He was a big-band aficionado and loved to dance, so much so that Walton wrote: "Those that know him insist that more than one cute little California chick bears a broken heart because Red, choosing between her and the Palladium, picked the latter."

As could be expected, however, the biggest boost to the squadron's esprit de corps came from the veterans. They won over the newcomers by example, as Glenn Bowers recalled.

> It was just like one big family. Nobody had the feeling that they were better than another guy. That's the way it was, and that's what made it so good. Even Boyington. He'd never ask anybody to do anything that he wouldn't do himself. In the Black Sheep squadron, there were no specially assigned airplanes. Boyington came out to the flight line and he just took one like everybody else. He didn't have his own plane. The operations officer didn't have his own plane, like other squadrons where they'd only fly their plane. That made for better camaraderie than anything.

As the doldrums continued, John Bolt took advantage of the situation by resuming his earlier experiments with the belting methods used in the machine guns. After witnessing the various effects of ammunition on wrecked aircraft in the Espiritu boneyard, he was particularly interested in further testing the capability of incendiary bullets. The general consensus was that tracer rounds were responsible for igniting fuel in Japanese fighters—in addition to helping pilots adjust the placement of their bullets—but Bolt suspected otherwise.

He conducted tests on Vella Lavella by placing fifty-five-gallon drums partially filled with gasoline at the end of an old dock, where fires could be easily extinguished. He strapped down another machine gun and compared the effects of tracer and incendiary rounds. This experiment removed any doubts.

> These tests illustrated rather clearly that the incendiary was the killer on the Zero. I got Boyington to come up to the dock a few hundred yards from the airfield. He was sold as soon as he saw the demonstration. We immediately went to belting something like ten tracers on the lead of the belt into the gun for a boresight test. After the lead-in we used about six incendiaries [for each] AP and tracer for the remainder of the 400 rounds.

It would be some time before Bolt's new belting method could be tried out on enemy aircraft, for the Japanese were still nowhere in sight. The Marines' own airplanes, on the other hand, were giving them fits. Rarely was a mission completed without one or more Black Sheep turning back with mechanical difficulties. Although the majority of Corsairs on hand were improved F4U-1A models, primitive maintenance conditions combined with the harsh environment and operational tempo continued to take their toll. During one division's Cherry Blossom patrol on December 5, for example, Bob Bragdon pancaked early for an oil leak, and Denny Groover landed at Ondonga due to temporary closure of the Barakoma strip. The brakes on Groover's Corsair failed and it went over onto its back; he was unhurt but the aircraft was a washout.

Only one mission was scheduled for each of the next two uneventful days, and the Black Sheep logged all of sixteen sorties. A bright spot came on December 8, however, when J. C. Dustin's division took off for a Cherry Blossom patrol. Four hours later, low on fuel, they pancaked at the new airstrip on Cape Torokina. Their stopover was of some historic importance, for another squadron was later given credit for making the first landing—fully two days later.* Indeed the field had not been completed when the three Marines (Bruce Matheson had returned to Vella leaking fuel) appeared overhead; they had to orbit while Seabees moved grading equipment, then they had to touch down on soft loam. When Ed Olander got back, he cautioned Boyington and the others about the condition of the surface: "The place was a quagmire."

Boyington flew up alone two days later to see for himself. He examined the strip and the facilities for several hours before returning in the afternoon, after swinging around the Shortlands on the way home to strafe two villages. "You must be crazy," he said to Olander when he landed. "It was dry as a desert. It looked like it hadn't rained in a long time." Apparently the Seabees had finished packing the strip, then let the sun bake it; later they covered it with Marston matting.

At 0450 on December 11, Boyington took off with two divisions for a grinding 4.6-hour Cherry Blossom patrol, then landed at the new Torokina strip to refuel. The pilots snooped around the Bougainville encampment for most of the day before manning their planes for the hour's hop

*According to Robert Sherrod: "Ground crews of VMF-212 and VMF-215 arrived at Torokina on December 9, the day before the 71st Seabees finished the airstrip; on December 10, 17 F4Us of VMF-216 were the first to land, followed by 6 SBDs and 4 SCAT transports."

back to Vella Lavella. Late that afternoon, Sandy Sims began a new precedent in the squadron's association with Torokina by flying there to spend the night, then arising early for the dawn patrol Sunday morning.

Boyington took off alone on Sunday morning, this time landing at Munda where he shared some ideas with General Moore, and returned to Vella Lavella shortly after lunch. The Black Sheep skipper was tired of the inactivity and hoped General Moore could find a way to unstick the logjam. If Japanese airpower was finished on Bougainville, perhaps they could hit them at Rabaul.

The exact reach of Moore's influence is unknown, but it helped that another Marine general was now ComAirSols. Ralph Mitchell had assumed command of all aircraft in the Solomons in November and was handed the exclusive job of concluding the air war against Rabaul. The Army's Fifth Air Force, operating out of New Guinea, had targeted the stronghold during October and early November but halted its strikes, claiming that Rabaul was "no longer a satisfactory base for any kind of operations."

AirSols knew better. His pilots would likewise discover that there was plenty of sting left in the Rabaul hornet's nest. The Japanese had repaired damaged runways, brought replacement aircraft from Truk, and even now counted a few hundred planes at the four operational fields ringing Rabaul. Whether Boyington's visit to General Moore was a direct catalyst or merely good timing is unclear, but on Wednesday evening the air ops officer at Barakoma published the following note in Thursday's flight plan: "All squadron commanders report to ComAirSols, Munda, 1430 for conference."

When the time came, Boyington hopped in an F4U and roared off to the New Georgia strip. He returned to Barakoma less than two and a half hours later—all smiles. Tomorrow, he reported, they would see the notorious stronghold of Rabaul for the first time. AirSols had directed him to lead a dedicated fighter sweep.

It was a great honor. Boyington's aircraft would be the first land-based, single-engine Allied fighters to appear over Rabaul, surely an ominous sign for the enemy. As such, Boyington was probably unconcerned about news that his squadron had written off two more airplanes in the past few days, the latest just hours earlier.

The first incident had occurred on December 12, when Henry Miller's division escorted three R4Ds to Torokina. The mission was routine until Al Marker, the last Black Sheep down, drifted off the Marston mat and hooked a wheel in the soft loam. He was still going seventy-five knots when the heavy fighter suddenly flipped onto its back with a tremendous bang.

> I was just in a state of shock. I wasn't even knocked out. I was bleeding profusely from the head, I remember that. My arm had gotten caught between the throttle and the fuselage someway, so it was broken. I remember this guy coming, and he said, "Is the switch off?" He was worried about the whole damn thing blowing up. So I flipped the switch off, and they cut me out of the airplane.

Marker's injuries were serious enough to land him in the hospital for the next six weeks, which effectively ended his tenure with the Black Sheep after only a few flights. Then, a few hours before Boyington's trip to Munda on December 16, George Ashmun and Bob Bragdon brought their divisions into Torokina after a three-hour Cherry Blossom patrol. Denny Groover, the last one down, got off the Marston mat, but he hit a gun emplacement and his Corsair flipped. "As it was going over, my only thought was that I was gonna get my damn neck broke when this thing hit," he recalled. Fortunately he had lowered the seat enough that the empennage and armor plate cushioned the blow, but the vertical stabilizer was crushed flat. A few Marines helped the groggy pilot scratch his way out of the cockpit, then relieved him of his .45 and wristwatch. The mere fact that he had overturned two Corsairs in eleven days might have caused a more superstitious pilot to think twice about the side number of his planes. The first accident occurred in number 888, the second in 777.

Greg Boyington, meanwhile, overlooked the cumulative loss of four Corsairs and one injured pilot in order to focus his attention on the fighter sweep. General Mitchell, perhaps trying to appease all of the squadrons clamoring to be included, had placed three different types of fighters from eight squadrons on his wing. It made his leadership of the sweep a huge responsibility. In addition to eight of his own Black Sheep, Boyington would shepherd eight apiece from VMF-222 and VMF-223 on Vella Lavella, eight Corsairs from VMF-216 based at Ondonga, eight Navy F6Fs from VF-40 at Barakoma, another sixteen Hellcats from VF-33 at Ondonga, and twenty-four P-40s from the 14th and 16th Squadrons of the Royal New Zealand Air Force (RNZAF), also at Ondonga. The sweep had become a conglomeration of eighty planes.*

At 0515 on Friday, December 17, the big event commenced as Boyington released the brakes in an old birdcage Corsair on Vella Lavella, followed in the next four minutes by Bob McClurg, Chris Magee, D. J. Moore, Sandy Sims, John Brown, Junior Heier, and Bruce Ffoulkes. When they landed at Torokina a little more than an hour later, Ffoulkes veered off the Marston mat and nosed over. His Corsair was not badly damaged, having perched on its nose instead of going all the way over, and he was able to borrow another F4U to complete the mission. Later Bob Bragdon joined as the ninth Black Sheep (having spent the previous night on Bougainville) to make up for mechanical dropouts from other units. By the

*In *Once They Were Eagles,* Frank Walton implied that he was the primary briefer for the whole strike, but only about a third of the participants were based on Vella Lavella.

time all of the participants refueled and took off for Rabaul some two hours later, at least seventy-eight fighters were involved, still a ponderous group.

The original plan called for the New Zealanders to approach the enemy at 10,000 to 15,000 feet, with the Navy Hellcats 5,000 feet above them and the Marine Corsairs on top at 26,000 feet, but it proved impossible to get so many mismatched types to join up with any semblance of order. One Kiwi P-40 remained at Torokina with a bad starter and two others turned back with various mechanical problems. Wing commander Trevor O. Freeman raced ahead with the remaining Kittyhawks without waiting for the American fighters to reach altitude. Boyington, who later claimed that Freeman was in charge of the entire sweep, directed his own pilots on a course parallel to the Bougainville coast, then turned west to dodge a large front sitting squarely in their path.

For the Marines, the ocean beneath their wings represented the largest expanse of open water that any of them had covered on a combat flight. There were no friendly islands between Bougainville and Rabaul for safe haven in the event of trouble. Anyone going down in the open ocean faced long odds for rescue, one reason why Moon Mullen's song *In a Rowboat at Rabaul* had become widely popular throughout the region.

Under radio silence, a fighter plane's cockpit could be an awfully lonely place. The pilots remained quiet as they flew in a cobalt blue sky four miles above the sea. Between them and the sparkling water were a few scattered clouds, brillantly white against their own shadows. The ascending sun warmed their shoulders as it refracted through the Plexiglas canopies and glared from the glass dials of the instrument panels, but their throats were dry from breathing pure oxygen through ill-fitting masks and from thinking of Rabaul and the waiting enemy beyond their whirling propellers.

Adrenaline and pulse rates notched higher when the first green-carpeted landmass appeared on the horizon. This was the southern tip of New Ireland, which resembled a foot at the end of a long, skinny leg, and they knew to stay well south of its concentrated AA emplacements. The narrow waters of St. George's Channel and the tip of Cape Gazelle slid into view next, then the mountains that ringed Rabaul, and finally Simpson Harbor itself. The low-lying terrain that spread before them southeast of the harbor revealed the enemy airfields at Tobera and Rapopo. The American fighters commenced climbing just as Sandy Sims's engine began to misfire, and he could not keep pace. Regretfully he turned away and John Brown went with him, prudence dictating the use of the buddy system over enemy territory.

Trevor Freeman's Kittyhawks, which now sailed over the Gazelle Peninsula well ahead of the Americans, were met by twelve Zeros of the 204 Kokutai. Soon another fifteen Zeros from the 201 and more from the 253 joined the fight. Freeman downed one, yelling, "Tojo eats Spam!" into his microphone before several other Japanese fighters pounced. Freeman was last seen circling a valley over New Ireland as his Kittyhawk spewed smoke or glycol. The latter was liquid coolant, the lifeblood of in-line engines, and without it his V-12 Allison would last only minutes. Two squadron mates covered Freeman while he searched for a place to bail out. They had been briefed, in case of trouble, to make their way to a village near the Weilan River and contact a native named Boski. But before Freeman could jump, more Zeros piled on and drove away the covering Kittyhawks. The wing commander was never seen again.

Flight Officer John O. McFarlane, of the 16th Squadron, also went down after a midair collision with a Zero over the channel. He evidently parachuted and was captured, for his name appeared on the list of 126 military captives to pass through the Kempei Tai prison at Rabaul, but he did not survive the war. Petty Officer Masajiro Kawato, who collided with the unlucky Kiwi, was rescued despite a lack of formal search-and-rescue units at Rabaul.*

Meanwhile Greg Boyington steered his fighter force toward Lakunai, where intelligence had estimated a hundred planes, including sixty-five fighters. The field was located near the water, just inside the northeastern ring of mountains surrounding Rabaul and Simpson Harbor like the letter *C*. Arriving overhead at 26,000 feet, the Marines counted an estimated thirty to forty fighters lined up at the strip, but they were not taking off.

"Come on up and fight!" Boyington yelled on the radio. An answer came, likely from thirty-two-year-old Edward Chikaki Honda, a former Japanese baseball star raised in the Territory of Hawaii. As one of four Nisei at Rabaul headquarters, he was more familiar with Yankee vernacular than his counterparts at Kahili had been; he chided, "Come on down, sucker!"

Boyington did just that. In an action that this time was well documented in Walton's report, the major fired about nine hundred rounds in an effort to rile the Japanese pilots. Few lifted off, and there would be no more shooting for Boyington for the rest of the mission.

Bob McClurg experienced better luck, though he bent the rules severely.

> I looked down and saw this Rufe floatplane. Now, the thing you don't do is break formation, you stay with your division. I was flying a loose pattern . . . when I saw this sucker down there. So I just dropped back a little bit and

*One Japanese officer said during interrogations after the war: "Seaplanes, subs and destroyers were sometimes used to search for downed fliers. But this depended entirely on the will of the division commander." Kawato enjoyed notoriety some decades later in both Japan and the United States by claiming to have shot down Boyington on January 3, 1944. He peddled a book at air shows—often at a table adjoining Boyington's—until his story was debunked.

sneaked down there. He was sitting there just flying straight and level. Nothing to it. I got back in formation and [Boyington] looked over at me shaking his fist at me for breaking formation. He gave me this finger wag: "Don't pull that shit."

Boyington wrote of McClurg's seaplane incident and called it the only claim of the day, then described refueling his division at Bougainville before taking them to the Shortlands for an impromptu strafing mission in which they shot up a coastal steamer. But the fighter sweeps over Rabaul were exhausting missions by themselves, and the circumstances Boyington described had actually occurred some months earlier, on September 23, when he led a division from Munda to Faisi and strafed a steamer.

McClurg was not the only Black Sheep to score. D. J. Moore sighted Japanese planes as they approached Rabaul—a column of seven Zekes in this case—and waggled his wings. Boyington apparently missed the signal and continued toward Lakunai, so Moore descended behind the last Zeke and crept up unnoticed. But when he squeezed the trigger nothing happened.

Moore pulled away from his target, reefed the Corsair around, and charged his guns, then rolled wings level behind a second Zeke. Again nothing but silence from his guns. He chandelled up and away, rolled out behind another Zero, and charged his guns again. This time they blazed forth and knocked a wing off the doomed Zeke. As he circled south and headed out of the harbor's mouth in a climb, he spotted Kiwis and Zekes locked in a fight; one of the latter hit the water.

As the New Zealanders broke off the action and turned toward Bougainville, Moore saw a single Zeke pass over them on its way to Rabaul. After dropping down in a high stern run, he commenced firing at three hundred yards with a long burst, then followed his target through a slow roll and watched it crash without burning in the water opposite the Vunakanau airdrome. It turned out to be the last of three claims by the Black Sheep, including McClurg's floatplane version of the Zero.

Moore soon discovered that his jammed guns were not the end of his troubles. On his way back to Torokina he encountered heavy weather—perhaps the same front the formation had skirted on its way to Rabaul—and owing to a faulty compass he missed the west coast of Bougainville. Critically low on fuel, he spotted small islands below, an overwhelming relief to any man sweating out his fuel gauge with only clouds and dark water around him.

As luck would have it, Moore had stumbled upon the Treasuries, grabbed by the Allies in late October during a diversionary assault before the main Bougainville landings. Even better, the 87th Seabees were in the process of building an airstrip on Sterling, so Moore had an actual landing site. He zoomed the field once, circled and fired his guns harmlessly to warn the workers that he was coming in, then set the Corsair down.

The fighter was rolling to a stop when Moore's luck ran out. A boulder protruding from the unfinished strip caused the F4U to go over on its back, and none too gently. In addition to a lacerated left arm, Moore sustained a blow to the head severe enough to knock him unconscious. Workmen extricated him from the wreckage, then liberated his helmet and goggles, the Corsair's clock, and other sundry items before Moore came to. It would take three days and a Dumbo ride for the stray Sheep to return to Vella Lavella; even then, Doc Reames grounded him for another four days.

Meanwhile Boyington and McClurg pancaked without incident back at Torokina almost three and a half hours after taking off. Chris Magee had patrolled over Rabaul for thirty-five minutes with no encounters, then stretched his fuel to land at Vella Lavella. In similar fashion Junior Heier and Bruce Ffoulkes circled Rabaul for almost half an hour at thirty thousand feet before they withdrew.

Among the rest, only Bob Bragdon had something of value to report when the day was done. He had arrived over Rabaul several minutes behind the others and joined with another Corsair upon reaching the enemy stronghold. Boldly he decided to strafe Rabaul city, but the other aircraft did not accompany him. Bragdon was further chagrined to discover as he dived on the town that his guns would not fire. He climbed back up, leveled at five thousand feet, and was heading out of the harbor when tracers flickered past his wings. Twisting around, he saw six Tonys on his tail.

Bragdon later gave Walton a thorough description of the Tonys' unusual markings.

> They were a vivid California blue, shiny with white tails. They had white diagonals on the wings and white . . . longitudinal stripes on the fuselage extending from the rear of the cockpit to the tail assembly. The meat balls were indistinct; it was difficult to make them out against their blue background. Roundels were definitely on the fuselage and possibly on the upper wing surfaces.

The planes gave chase, and Bragdon dived into a cloud, checked his bearings as he jammed the throttle forward, and turned for home. He soon had the big Pratt & Whitney at full revolutions per minute and manifold pressure as he streaked away at nearly four hundred knots, but even then he managed to open the distance on his pursuers only slowly. They stayed with him for the next sixty-five miles before he finally lost them.

That Bragdon saw fighters with in-line engines and unique graphics is not in question, but they were almost certainly New Zealand P-40s, not Tonys. If a Kiwi opened fire on Bragdon by mistake, there was certainly precedent, as George Ashmun knew well after a P-38 shot at him repeatedly. Ironically the New Zealanders painted their fighters with bold markings to prevent confusion with the

Tony's similar shape; there were white slashes on the wings and vertical stabilizer, exactly as Bragdon described. His reference to indistinct roundels was an interesting choice of the word, which is commonly used to describe RAF-style markings but is rarely used in reference to the Japanese "meatball." Royal New Zealand Air Force roundels were blue, which might have attracted his attention. As for the chase, the Kiwis departed Rabaul in the same direction and probably in just as big a hurry. Their Kittyhawk III variant of the P-40 had a respectable top speed of more than 360 knots.

In addition to Bragdon, several Black Sheep (and many other American pilots) continued to sight and claim Tonys in the vicinity during the coming days and weeks. Postwar interrogations revealed that the Japanese Army Air Force (JAAF) did not operate Tonys at Rabaul after August 1943, when the 68th and 78th Sentais withdrew to Wewak, New Guinea. Even allowing that the desperate Japanese repaired a few Tonys that were left behind, it is extremely unlikely that six would have been aloft at one time.

Shortly after Bragdon streaked back to Torokina, all of the Black Sheep who had stopped for fuel took off again and landed at Vella Lavella, which concluded the first fighter sweep of Rabaul. When Boyington reported to the intelligence tent for his debriefing with Walton, he threw down his helmet in disgust, frustrated by the lack of enemy response. The Black Sheep claimed three enemy planes against no losses of their own (Moore's accident at Sterling notwithstanding), and the other Corsair squadrons had come away empty-handed. One ensign from VF-33 claimed a Zeke, and the Kiwis claimed five shot down against the loss of two pilots. Boyington's force of nearly eighty planes had claimed only nine of the enemy, but he would have been doubly incensed to learn that the Japanese actually lost only one pilot and two planes. The obvious conclusion was that the Allied sweep had been too large and unwieldy to be effectively controlled.

Walton promptly broadcast the skipper's recommendation.

> Major Boyington is of the opinion that far too many fighter planes were sent on the sweep. He thinks 24 sufficient. He is also strongly of the opinion that all planes should be the same type—thus eliminating the necessity for continually checking on other planes in the sky.

The next morning, Pierre Carnagey led three divisions to Torokina before dawn to participate in a big strike, but they were back at Vella Lavella by midmorning after the mission was scrubbed by poor weather. The strength of the nor'wester was evident in their transit times. It required almost half an hour longer to battle headwinds into Torokina than it did to scoot back. Instead of sitting idle, Carnagey and eight others refueled their Corsairs and launched to strafe targets all along the east coast of Buka.

Few sorties went out during the next three days, although a Rabaul strike scheduled for December 21 did look promising. Boyington positioned three divisions at Torokina early that morning, but again the mission was canceled. The return hop to Vella Lavella concluded the squadron's operations for the entire day and was followed by only two uneventful assignments the next day.

Suddenly the combat tour was more than half over and only two pilots, McClurg and Moore, had fired their guns at enemy planes. It was difficult to believe that the air war could have changed so dramatically in such a short time, particularly because the squadron was within spitting distance of Kahili and Ballale, once the most fearsome pair of enemy bases in the central Solomons. On a personal level, Greg Boyington's remarkable first tour had earned him fourteen confirmed victories in a thirty-three-day span. Because of his AVG claims, the Marine Corps recognized a grand total of twenty, which put him within sight of the all-time American record of twenty-six. But more than two months had passed since his last victory, and at the current rate his odds of shooting down six more enemy aircraft in less than three weeks looked poor indeed. There would be no other opportunities, he knew. He had used up the last of his charm to talk his way into this combat assignment. There wasn't a prayer of getting another.

16

BLACK SHEEP FALLING

On Wednesday afternoon, three days before Christmas and almost a week since their first low-yielding attempt, the Black Sheep learned they would have another crack at Rabaul the next day. The operations order was posted, and the pilots gathered excitedly in the operations hut to talk about the large-scale strike scheduled for Thursday morning, its objective summed up in a single sentence: "Destroy enemy aircraft by aggressive offensive action." Sixteen F4Us from VMF-214 would participate, half covering a formation of B-24s, the other half joining a fighter sweep. As with earlier missions over Kahili, the fighter sweep was planned to arrive *after* the bombers departed Rabaul; apparently recognition for the success of preemptive sweeps was slow in coming.

It would be a large raid by Pacific standards, with 120 aircraft (of which only twenty-four were bombers) flying to Rabaul in two groups. Three Marine squadrons supplying two divisions of fighters apiece (Pierre Carnagey leading the Black Sheep contingent) would join twenty-four Hellcats from VF-33 and VF-40 to protect the Liberators. One hour and fifteen minutes later, forty-eight fighters would handle the poststrike sweep. The elements included eight Black Sheep and twelve airplanes from Maj. Marion E. Carl's VMF-223 at low altitude; the Army was providing twenty-eight Lightnings to cover the medium and high airspace. Carl, the Marine Corps' first ace, would be in tactical command of the fighter sweep.

Pierre Carnagey was the first Black Sheep to depart Vella Lavella on Thursday morning, followed in quick succession by the other pilots assigned as medium cover for the B-24s. After waiting forty minutes, Greg Boyington led his eight Corsairs aloft. Henry Miller and John Bolt sped to Torokina an hour and a half after Boyington, having been added to the flight plan at the last minute. Somewhat surprisingly, more than half of the Black Sheep Corsairs, ten of eighteen, were older birdcage models. All reached Torokina without incident and refueled, and Carnagey's eight Corsairs were airborne on schedule by 1130. Getting two dozen bombers and four dozen fighters sorted out over Bougainville proved difficult; by the time the formation was en route to Rabaul, it was fifteen minutes late.

As the strike droned across the open ocean toward New Britain, Carnagey's wingman developed trouble. Rusty March, in one of the new Corsairs, discovered that his fuel pump was out. Carnagey sent him back, with Bill Hobbs as escort. Half of Carnagey's division was now gone, so he and Jimmy Brubaker—both flying birdcage models—formed their own section.

Nearing New Britain, the formation turned right to parallel the coastline until they had passed north of Rabaul, then turned west. They flew beyond the target before making a sweeping left turn to attack the city and harbor out of the northwest. Visibility was not as good as it had been during the sweep six days earlier. This day it was hampered by a cloud layer at seven thousand feet, with plenty of scattered cumulus clouds up to four miles high. There was also a headwind; because of it, the formation was now half an hour behind schedule.

After reaching their turn point northwest of Rabaul, the bombers settled into their runs and separated into two groups at 21,000 feet. Intense AA fire of medium and heavy caliber began bursting at their level, though it appeared that the wind aloft was pushing the trajectories off to the left. At the same time, however, fifteen to twenty

Zekes jumped the forward section of Liberators from above and caught several of the Navy Hellcats out of position. Of the twenty-four that were supposed to be providing cover, only four or five were present and remained there while the Zekes made overhead passes at the bombers.

The heavies shouldered through and unleashed their bomb loads at 1330 with good effect on Rabaul town and the harbor area. Several fires burned in the city. Eyewitnesses reported that among the nine ships in Karavia Bay, one sank, another was smoking badly and settling at the stern, and a third was burning fiercely. In Simpson Harbor a large transport's back was broken, its bow and stern rising from the water while it submerged amidships, wreathed in smoke.

As the bombers egressed, the forward group was now blanketed by a dozen Hellcats scissoring fifteen hundred feet above them, but the Liberators in the second group were protected by only a handful of Black Sheep. Suddenly phosphorus aerial bombs began detonating all over the sky, each one erupting into a fifty-foot cloud with long white tentacles arching away from the core. Some thirty bursts were counted, with no ill effect on the bombers.

At the rear of the group, J. C. Dustin's division guarded one side of the formation while Carnagey and Brubaker covered the opposite with their two-plane section. Beyond Rabaul the Liberators came under attack again by fifteen Zeros. The Black Sheep stayed close and scissored to fend them off. For the next twenty minutes, groups of Zekes and apparently a few refurbished Tonys attacked in a running battle that moved east of Rabaul. A Liberator was hit in one engine; the pilot feathered the prop and held his ship in formation. The enemy fighters dived well below after making their overhead runs. Several had started back toward Rabaul just as Marion Carl's forty-eight fighters swept in at 1350, as much ahead of schedule as the bombers were late.

The timing was perfect. Greg Boyington's Corsairs were eighteen thousand feet over St. George's Channel when he spotted the bombers to his right. "This is it, fellows," he called on the radio as he turned in toward the fight. He looked down and saw a lone Zeke more than a mile below him, running for Rabaul, and within moments the Black Sheep had scattered. Unlike the discipline necessary for bomber escorts, this was every man for himself. Initiating a solo run on the Zeke, Boyington curled behind it in a descending turn as he closed to within fifty feet. The Mitsubishi never deviated from its heading. Boyington triggered a short burst; the fighter ignited and its pilot immediately bailed out.

As Boyington climbed over the channel to eleven thousand feet, he detected two more Zekes a thousand feet below. One appeared damaged as it flew straight and level while its wingman scissored above. Boyington glided down behind the cripple in a level stern run, then closed this time to a hundred feet before squeezing off a short burst. The pilot jumped free when his Zeke began to burn. His wingman made the mistake of descending to three hundred feet over the spot where the parachute drifted to the water, so he had no room to maneuver. Boyington came down out of the sun and opened fire from point-blank range. Zeke number three burned, rolled on its back, and smacked into the sea upside down.

Boyington now climbed three miles high and circled Simpson Harbor. Twenty minutes passed before he encountered more enemy aircraft, a formation of nine Zekes crossing eight thousand feet below. Once again he throttled back and came out of the sun in a shallow glide, and once again the hapless pilot in the rearmost plane was completely unaware of his approach. According to Walton's reconstruction, Boyington "opened fire at 100 yards, closing fast and firing continuously till he passed under and out to the side. Pieces flew off the Zeke's cowling and then it burst into flame and went down burning." The other Zekes scattered like quail, then regrouped and chased Boyington for ten minutes before he was finally able to elude them.

Surprisingly the lightweight fighters appeared to be gaining even after Boyington put his Corsair into a dive, but he reportedly pulled away in a shallow climb at high speed.

Bob McClurg had become separated from Boyington early, then spotted a Zeke already being chased by another Corsair. When the Zeke kicked out to the right, the Corsair skidded wide and McClurg dropped down in a high-energy tail chase. His throttle was all the way back in an effort to avoid overshooting the Zeke, and he even opened the cowl flaps as extra speed brakes. Twisting and turning, he pushed the fleeing Zeke down to the water, mushing through the air as he opened fire at a hundred yards. Momentarily the Zeke leveled off, then dipped its nose and bounced twice off the water's surface before plunging in.

McClurg pushed the power back on, remembering to close the cowl flaps as he soared up into a left chandelle, then climbed to four thousand feet. As he checked around, two Zekes came over his right shoulder and were already pulling to his five o'clock. He jammed the throttle forward again, set the mixture to full rich, and revved the Pratt & Whitney to 2,750 rpm as he dashed for a cloud with the Zekes gaining. Upon reaching the cloud he reversed hard to the right and pulled for all he was worth; his vision turned gray and then almost black from the g force. When he popped back out of the fleecy mist, he saw the Zekes directly ahead. Both immediately rolled over and split-Sed so sharply down to their right that McClurg could not kick the rudder enough to lead them with his guns. But by thumbing the rudder trim tab, he regained the advantage and led the second Zeke as it bottomed out. White vapor trails streamed from wingtips as the mottled green Japanese fighter and the blue Corsair pulled hard to the right, but McClurg had the proper deflection and caught the Zeke from 150 yards with two short bursts. Its left wing folded an instant after the right as the unarmored fighter came apart in a fireball, "leaving only a big cloud of black smoke and little pieces falling."

At the beginning of the fight, Chris Magee had been leading Boyington's second section with Ed Harper as his wingman. They had just started after two Zekes when Magee caught sight of another out of the corner of his eye. Near his level, it was only three hundred yards away and closing fast on an opposite heading. With no time to set up a firing run, Magee simply dropped his nose and sprayed bullets in front of the Zeke, which flew right through them. Another Zeke crossed his nose from the left, blocking his view of the results, so he lifted the Corsair's nose and snapped off a shot at the second Zeke from four hundred yards. It promptly rolled over and pulled out of sight. A third Zeke now appeared off to his left about three hundred feet below; Magee started down behind it in a curling left turn and squeezed the trigger at three hundred yards. This one also flipped away, but the Wild Man followed.

The high-energy maneuvering began causing a malfunctioning connection in his oxygen system; the O_2 failed completely when Magee pulled hard behind the Zeke and opened fire. Once more the Zeke initiated a split-S, but Magee anticipated the move, scooped his nose to catch the Zeke just as it got over on its back, and gave it a steady burst as he flashed by. The Japanese fighter nosed over and plunged straight into the sea with a dead or wounded pilot.

As Magee climbed back to twenty thousand feet, his oxygen began flowing intermittently but quit again whenever he maneuvered. He became disoriented from hypoxia such that when Junior Heier tried later to join, Magee waved him off, unable to recognize a friend. Fortunately Magee had the presence to dive down to denser air and activate his emergency oxygen. When his head cleared, he turned for home.

Magee was in a birdcage Corsair that day, as was Sandy Sims's entire division behind Greg Boyington. Neither Sandy nor his wingman, John Brown, registered claims, but Junior Heier, who was leading the second section, hit pay dirt. Like the others, he and Bruce Ffoulkes started the fight at eighteen thousand feet. After spotting fifteen Zekes crossing St. George's Channel a thousand feet above, Heier climbed two thousand feet, located a Zeke to his left, and swung around to commence a deflection shot from its three o'clock. He opened fire at two hundred yards, pulled lead as the distance closed to half that, and was rewarded with a burst of fire out of the Zeke's engine. But it was not a fatal hit. The Japanese pilot split-Sed down and continued to roll in a complete spiral as he plunged for a mile and a half. Heier twisted around with him but leveled out at thirteen thousand feet, then watched the Zeke until it pulled level a mile below and ducked into a cloud. Maintaining his altitude advantage, Heier followed him in a slight left turn. When Heier came out of the cloud, the Zeke was four thousand feet below and a mile ahead.

Heier chopped the throttle, let his heavy Corsair slide down, and actually dipped below the Zeke before coming up for a belly shot from behind. Only one gun fired when Heier squeezed the trigger, but it was enough.

> I was having to do esses to keep from over-running him. He pulled up very slowly and started a nice, easy turn to the left and I could see these holes all over his plane. There was this nice little white smoke coming out the side that was gradually turning black. I got down and kind of alongside of him and I couldn't even see anything of the pilot. He was down in the cockpit.

The crippled fighter eased down until it hit the water in a flat glide, then bounced and skittered across the surface. It finally came to rest on the surface and remained afloat as Heier passed overhead. Bruce Ffoulkes, still on his wing as he recharged his guns and began climbing toward a cloud, called, "Where are you going?"

Heier radioed back: "Climbing out from under; we're under the fight. We have to climb out, then come back on top."

"Well, it's behind us," Ffoulkes responded. "I'm going back."

"Don't climb up under it, you'll get your ass shot off," warned Heier, but Ffoulkes insisted. "Good luck," Heier called. He never saw his wingman again.

Just then a Tony (they were still being reported around Rabaul) blocked Heier's path to a nearby cloud and turned to enter it just ahead of him. Heier closed to within fifty yards and fired as he kicked the rudder back and forth to swing his nose. He saw his bullets strike the in-line-engine fighter from its nose back to the tail before it vanished in the mist.

Heier went on instruments and climbed to eight thousand feet, then poked out in time to see four more Tonys arcing around the cloud in a column below and to his left. He rolled over and came down on the last one from its high four o'clock, firing at a hundred yards and boring in until the fighter exploded. Its left wing twirled away as the rest of the fireball tumbled into the sea.

Another Tony appeared three thousand feet higher off to his right, and Heier began climbing. Slowly he gained on the sleek fighter, then closed from its right rear quarter until he reached three hundred yards. The Tony snapped to its right when Heier fired; he could turn with it, his Corsair slowed by the climb. The Tony reversed to the left and raced for a nearby cloud, then made another left turn, which gave Heier a clear shot. Just short of the cloud the Tony rolled left again and Heier overshot, unable to avoid skidding into the whiteness. When he popped back out, the Tony was gone. Heier found a Corsair to join with, but the pilot was flying erratically and refused his attempts to close. Not knowing that this was the oxygen-starved Magee, Heier abandoned the idea and steered for Bougainville alone.

John Bolt and Henry Miller, who had attached themselves to the fighter sweep just before it left Torokina, were both able to contribute. Bolt, who had not yet employed his machine-gun belting ideas in combat, was at twenty thousand feet when the fight began, and he peeled off against a flight of Zekes a mile below. He opened fire from long range and scored hits on one fighter's wing, but his momentum carried him through the formation. Climbing back, he found a lone Zeke at eight thousand feet and set up an overhead run, but the Japanese pilot saw him coming and ran. They scissored a few times, then the Zeke flattened out and streaked away.

Bolt straightened out and had closed to within four hundred yards behind the Zeke when a tremendous explosion rocked his Corsair. A phosphorus bomb that was jettisoned by the Zeke had detonated between them. Flying through the thick white cloud, Bolt caught the Mitsubishi when it entered a right turn. He squeezed the trigger at two hundred yards and saw his bullets impacting the Zeke's engine cowl. The aircraft settled into a shallow glide, then drifted from eight thousand feet all the way to the coast of New Ireland. While Bolt circled overhead at eight thousand feet, the Zeke crashed into the jungle near the mouth of the Warangoi River.

Another Zeke appeared, this one coming from Bolt's right quarter a few thousand feet below, but when Bolt turned in toward it, the Zeke rolled up and showed one wing. With his vision momentarily hampered by glare, Bolt could not see a meatball and pulled off, thinking that a friendly was showing him a recognition signal. But when the other plane rolled level, the red disk was evident. Bolt gave chase, first opening the throttle to 2,600 rpm and forty-five inches of manifold pressure, then crowding on another 100 rpm as the Zeke fled. Trying in vain to outrace him, the Zeke took no evasive maneuvers. Bolt closed to two hundred yards before squeezing the trigger. His bullets had just reached out when the Zeke tried to enter a split-S at high speed. It was only partly over on its back when it flared, then came apart in a flaming mess that smeared across St. George's Channel.

Finally it was Henry Miller's turn. Well into his third

combat tour he had consistently logged more combat hours in VMF214 than anyone, but had not found an airborne enemy within his gunsight's reflected image since early April, more than eight months before. When the moment came, he was more than ready. He let down in a giant spiral when the melee began, then spied a single Zeke chasing a Corsair a thousand feet below. The Zeke's pilot saw him coming and tried to pull up, but Miller closed and stitched the Zeke's belly from 250 yards. As it rolled over on its back, out popped the pilot. Notebook Henry had his one and only aerial victory.

Greg Boyington did some of the day's last shooting at an unusual target of opportunity. While flying along St. George's Channel, he came across a submarine running on the surface. He swooped down for a strafing run and got in a few bursts of undetermined consequence before the sub disappeared beneath the waves. Stretching his fuel, Boyington made it all the way to Vella Lavella; he was the last Black Sheep to land. The returning pilots had been scattered across many miles, and it took Frank Walton the better part of an hour to count them all in. He finally stopped at fifteen; eighteen had gone out.

Pierre Carnagey and Jimmy Brubaker were two of the missing. They were last seen covering one side of the Liberator formation when a swarm of Zeros attacked from the rear. Whether they collided or were overwhelmed by Zeros, hit by friendly fire from the bombers, or hit by AA fire, or simply got lost after the mission was anyone's guess. Any or a combination of those causes would explain their disappearance, but they were merely scenarios for the Black Sheep to ponder. Brubaker had celebrated his twenty-second birthday less than two weeks earlier. His family in Clearwater, Florida, would soon learn from the War Department that another son was missing in action. Pierre Carnagey's wife, Mary Jeanette, would get the chilling news in Corpus Christi. Beyond that, neither family was destined to hear anything more specific about their loved ones. They would join the long list of families waiting interminably for news that would never come.

Harriet Banfield was not officially next of kin, but she received bad news just the same: Her fiancé, Bruce Ffoulkes, was the third missing Sheep. His demise was easier to explain, for he had brashly chosen to climb into harm's way despite Bill Heier's warning to the contrary. No one saw him go down or heard a distress call, but a Japanese pilot almost certainly picked him off during his vulnerable climb.

It was the costliest day yet in the squadron's history. The Black Sheep lived by divisions in four-man tents, one of which was now minus half of its occupants. In exchange, the Black Sheep claimed twelve enemy fighters along with two probables. Bolt and McClurg joined the list of squadron aces, and Boyington had done extremely well, nearly matching his earlier ace-in-a-day score with four Zekes over Rabaul. In one mission Boyington had brought his score to within two victories of the record, his tally now at twenty-four in the eyes of the Marine Corps.

Later Boyington described the four victories with a clarity not found in other parts of his autobiography. Except for his identification of the fourth plane as a Tony instead of a Zeke, most details closely match the official report compiled by Frank Walton. Boyington made one conspicuous departure from fact, however, when he moved the calendar ahead two days so that the mission occurred on Christmas instead of December 23. Considering the accuracy of the other details, his chronological alteration seems all the more glaring.

Some suggest that the discrepancy ought to be excused as an honest mistake, perhaps caused by memory loss after long years of alcoholism, but his own statement rules out that possibility.

> On the peace-on-earth-and-good-will-to-all-men day, I went around the skies slaughtering people. Don't ask

> me why it had to be on a Christmas Day, for he who can answer such a question can also answer why there have to be wars, and who starts them, and why men in machines kill other men in machines. I had not started this war, and if it were possible to write a different sort of Christmas story I would prefer to record it, or at least to have had it occur on a different day.

Such a disclaimer makes it appear that Boyington deliberately altered the date for greater philosophical and moral impact. He could not have confused the mission with another sortie closer to Christmas, because he did not fly again for four days after the fighter sweep. Apparently he was not satisfied that four aerial victories in a single mission was by itself a standout accomplishment; he thought a Christmas fight would make it more interesting.

As for the overall claims, the Marines were credited with nineteen enemy planes destroyed and five probables. The Hellcat pilots received credit for downing four more, a composite score of twenty-eight. The Japanese recorded a total of seven Zero pilots killed. The three pilots seen bailing out might have survived, which could possibly account for as many as ten Zeros shot down. Although the JAAF Sentais were reportedly long gone from Rabaul, the Marines claimed four Tonys (including one by Marion Carl) and three probables, but it is highly unlikely that seven flyable *Ki*-61s were there.* By comparison the Japanese exaggerated more wildly, claiming seven Corsairs, eleven Hellcats, and five Liberators, the latter by aerial burst bombs. Three missing Black Sheep and an ensign from VF-33 were the only American losses.

There is no recorded explanation for why Greg Boyington missed three days of flying (others in his division flew

***On the bright side, a review of RNZAF records showed that no P-40s were lost, which rules out the possibility of friendly fire. Likewise none were lost on the other dates that Tonys were claimed.**

during that time), but a Christmas Eve party might have had something to do with it. During his absence from the flight schedule, the squadron logged more than 116 hours on December 24, including participation by two divisions in a bombing strike against Rabaul's Vunakanau airdrome. Due to cloudy conditions the Japanese failed to intercept, and the bombing results were unobserved.

In another notable flight, Henry Miller, John Bolt, and Herb Holden ferried three war-weary birdcage Corsairs to Guadalcanal, where they were surveyed (stricken from the Bureau of Aeronautics registry) after being stripped of usable parts. Ironically all three of the planes lost during the previous day's fighter sweep had been birdcage models, and two of these aircraft now being surveyed had been used on the mission. In the afternoon, the pilots returned from Guadalcanal with three brand-new F4U-1As, two of which Greg Boyington would use exclusively for the remainder of his combat missions. With the exception of one short hop in a third plane, the rest of his flights were conducted in side-number 883 or 915. He was destined to suffer trouble with both.

The Black Sheep celebrated Christmas Eve with milk punch, just as Henry Miller had made a lifetime ago on Efate. They stirred five quarts of brandy into a base of powdered eggs, powdered milk, and sugar, then sang their songs and toasted their existence, remembering three who had been with them barely thirty-six hours earlier. They also worried about their skipper. "We all want to see you break the record," said Meathead Bragdon, sitting on a footlocker across from Boyington's cot, "but we don't want you to go up there and get killed doing it."

"Don't worry about me," answered the skipper. "They can't kill me. If you guys ever see me going down with thirty Zeros on my tail, don't give me up. Hell, I'll meet you in a San Diego bar and we'll all have a drink for old times' sake."

Boyington got drunk again after making this prophetic

promise, and he missed another two days of flying in decent weather. His behavior was unpredictable at such times, and he was occasionally belligerent toward his own pilots. Fred Avey discovered this while showering under the fifty-five-gallon contraption rigged near Boyington's tent.

> I had just soaped down and Boyington came drunkenly up on the stage [of] pierced steel planking, which is very sharp on raw flesh, and he wanted to wrestle. I had one awful time getting away from him. As it was, I finally talked him into going back to his tent. That was a time I was really frightened because I knew that pierced steel planking can cut like crazy when you're wet and naked.

Christmas, on a Saturday, was just another day of combat for many Black Sheep, even busier than the day before with a total of fifty-two sorties. It began before dawn when Gelon Doswell and Moon Mullen took their divisions to Torokina, gassed up, then joined a strike on Rabaul that included sixty-four Lightnings, Corsairs, Hellcats, and Kittyhawks stacked four miles high around a formation of twenty-four Liberators. The formation took a roundabout path to approach Rabaul from the northwest, but the Japanese had plenty of early warning stations on New Ireland and were waiting for them in force: twenty-two Zeros from the 201Ku, thirty from the 204, another twenty-seven from the 253. They hit just before the bombers reached Rabaul.

It was a little past noon when the Black Sheep scattered to engage the Japanese. For Burney Tucker the fight began when he spied a Zeke at twenty thousand feet crossing from his right. He dropped down and opened fire from three hundred yards in a full-deflection shot, holding in the trigger as he pulled behind the aircraft. He saw no smoke or flame but evidently killed the pilot, for the Zeke curled off to the right in a slow, descending circle and crashed into the water just off the Rabaul Peninsula.

Flying on Tucker's wing, Ned Corman was initiated into air combat when Tucker turned toward that first Zeke.

> He kept going all the way around me, right behind me. I looked over my shoulder, and here's the first Zero I've ever seen in my life, coming right up my ass. He wasn't firing, he was just coming in on me. And Burney—turning around like that—the guy dove out. Burney followed him, and I tried to follow him too. The Jap pulled up in a loop. I got on top of the loop, did the first Immelmann in that airplane that I'd ever done, rolled out, and I was right in the middle of the Japanese air force. I never could get a lead on any of them long enough to open fire. I just pushed straight forward and dove down. This all started at about 25,000 feet and I pulled out at probably about fifteen thousand. My ears were hurting so badly that I could hardly stand it, and I was getting tossed out of the cockpit because the tail was vibrating. So I eased out of that dive, looked around, and I was by myself. That's the way it happened. You were either in the middle of it, or it's, "Where'd everybody go?"

A few minutes later, Don Fisher was sailing along at 25,000 feet when a Zero above him initiated an overhead pass. He dropped a mile and leveled off to enter a cloud, then emerged from the other side with numerous Zeros scattered about. Singling one out, he ran it down from behind and shot from 200 yards, firing continuously as the distance closed until fire blossomed from its cockpit. He climbed back up to join the bombers, which mistakenly opened fire on him, so he parked a safe distance away.

Bill Crocker shot a fighter off a P-38's twin tails at 17,000 feet and saw his tracers stitch the cockpit area as the Zeke went into a flat spin. But his attention was diverted when two other Zeros appeared on his own tail. Fred Avey came over and chased them away, then discovered a pair of Tonys blocking his own path. Avey dived nearly three miles to escape them, so he thought, and leveled off near the water. With his radio out, he decided to pull out the local strip map and plot a course for home. Before he could check it, tracers flashed over his left wing and small geysers appeared in the sea. In one motion he kicked the rudder hard right and shoved forward on the stick. A black Tony with solid red wings overran him, caught by surprise. Avey kicked left rudder and brought his guns to bear. He shattered the Tony's tail; from a thousand feet it nosed over into the water.

Ned Corman had also dived out of the flight, but he did not need a strip map to know the way home. After taking off from Bougainville, he remembered some good advice and preset the reverse course in his gyrocompass. He rolled out on that heading and eventually spotted five aircraft well ahead of him. Thinking they were friendlies returning home, he approached to join them for the rest of the trip, then saw red meatballs adorning their wings.

There were five Zekes in a lazy turn to the left—three planes in front followed by two others off to the side in echelon. Corman closed on the bigger group.

> Being greedy, I thought I'd take the group with three and eased in behind them. I opened up, so far out of range that I could see my tracers falling short. I did everything wrong. I had held the trigger down and taken long bursts when they tell you to use short bursts. But anyway, as I came in on this group, I had one gun firing. That's all that was left. Evidently, I caught this guy in the wing root, because I saw a puff of smoke, and he blew. I was so close to him, I could smell smoke and hot oil. I kicked hard rudder up to the right. He just rolled over on a wing and went right straight down into the water.

Corman, Avey, and the rest of the Black Sheep returned unscathed to Vella Lavella, where Frank Walton debriefed them and recorded four victories and two probables.*

Sunday was quiet by comparison with only twenty-six flights in all, but the missions were markedly different from those of recent days. At dawn Chris Magee took a division to Torokina to spend the day on standby, then George Ashmun and Meathead Bragdon followed with two other divisions and refueled for a strike. Unlike the high-altitude raids they were accustomed to, this strike involved seven twin-engine Mitchells in a low-level bombing and strafing attack. The target, a cluster of Japanese positions on New Ireland at Cape St. George, was thick with AA emplacements. Thirty-six Corsairs and Hellcats provided overhead coverage.

The raiding party took off, joined over Bougainville, then turned west with the B-25s at a mere thousand feet. An hour later they descended to two hundred feet and separated into pairs to start their runs. The Black Sheep could not discern much of the target area as they attempted to steal glimpses through trees and heavy foliage, but they later reported that the Mitchells started only one small fire (a third of their bombs had landed in the water).

The slight damage they inflicted came at a price. One B-25 was hit by AA fire, went down a mile offshore, and submerged momentarily before coming to rest partially afloat. It had been too low for anyone to parachute, and no survivors appeared while the Black Sheep circled for fifteen minutes. A Dumbo was summoned from Torokina, but by the time the Corsairs had to depart the bomber was underwater.

*VMF-214, VMF-223, and VF-33 claimed a total of ten fighters destroyed and two probables; the 201, 204, and 253 Kokutais lost a total of two killed and one wounded. Conversely they claimed seven F4Us, but the Marines lost only one from VMF-223.

Chris Magee's standby division received the order to escort the PBY as it winged toward the crash site. Remarkably, when they arrived off Cape St. George they spotted a rubber boat with some of the bomber's crew members aboard, now just a half mile off the beach.

The Catalina touched down on the water to pick them up just as Chris Magee saw a Japanese .51-caliber machine gun open up from a nearby hill.

> They were firing on the PBY, but they hadn't hit it yet; I could see where the shells were falling short, or off to the right or left. Cape St. George had some elevation where they could look down and shoot.
>
> So I circled around to the other side of the PBY. Then I could look across the PBY and see where the bullets were hitting the water, and it made an "arrow." All I had to do was swing in and strafe them. Well they shut up, of course; that stopped them.

The strafing enabled the Catalina to complete a successful rescue and be on its way. Magee, who knew that his brother-in-law flew one of these Black Cats somewhere in the Solomons, turned for home wondering if he was at the controls of the PBY. Chris later learned otherwise, but it did not diminish his appreciation for the Dumbo crews and their numerous unheralded rescues.

Greg Boyington was back in the air at 0615 on Monday, December 27, with three Black Sheep divisions to refuel at Torokina for a fighter sweep. Although he had flown only two missions in the past ten days, by dark he would log four sorties, the first three in side-number 883—probably his most oft-photographed Corsair.* The latest mission to

*Years later Frank Walton wrote in his book that Boyington deliberately chose Lady Carol W., a plane named for Walton's wife, but number 883 had been on the island less than three days, and the name does not appear in pictures taken on December 27. It was undoubtedly applied (briefly) for the benefit of photographs taken later.

Rabaul was a dedicated fighter sweep with no bombers to worry about, and Boyington was in tactical command. Contrary to his request for a tidier force, sixty-four Corsairs and Hellcats from six different outfits had been heaped onto the operations order.

Marion Carl, participating with three of his own divisions from VMF-223, later wrote:

> Nobody could control so many aircraft simultaneously. It was a flight leader's war, with four-plane divisions usually fighting their own battles in their particular piece of sky.

After the planes took off, the landing gear on Henry Miller's Corsair failed to retract, but the rest of the fighters gradually climbed until they were stacked five miles high. As they arrived over Simpson Harbor at 1130, they were met with an astounding sight—forty Zeros chasing one another's heels in the biggest Lufbery Circle they had ever seen. It was more than five miles in diameter and canted from fourteen to twenty thousand feet. The American fighters corralled them effectively by making overhead passes and climbing back for more. As one Black Sheep said of the Japanese tactic: "Their air discipline was excellent and their headwork was zero—just poor."

Greg Boyington hounded down a Zeke at the lower end of the traffic circle, his nineteenth claim. Don Fisher blew the canopy off a Japanese fighter and watched it fall in flames from twenty thousand feet. Then he dived to burn another Zeke, which added his name to the growing list of aces. Moon Mullen joined the list as well when he added his fourth Zero as a Black Sheep to the credit and a half he brought from VMF-122. Ed Harper got his first kill after two earlier probables, and Fred Avey scored a Zeke.

All eleven participating Black Sheep returned safely to Torokina. They straggled in just after lunch with only one plane bearing minor damage—from a 7.7mm hit in its right wing—then they refueled and hopped down to Vella Lavella. Frank Walton and many others were waiting eagerly for news of the fighter sweep. Boyington's revetment was full of pilots, reporters, and photographers, one of whom snapped a picture as Boyington's Corsair rolled across the white coral. Having already shed his helmet, Boyington grinned beneath aviator-style sunglasses and held up a finger—one victory, number twenty-five. "I got a probable, too," he told Associated Press correspondent Fred Hampson after climbing down. "The hunting was fine, but I wasn't right again. God, but I'm doing some dumb things up there! I couldn't hit a bull fiddle with a whip."

But Boyington claimed his nineteenth victory Monday morning as part of an effort that saw four Corsair squadrons and two Hellcat squadrons combine for sixteen victories and three probables. The Japanese lost five pilots killed among their Kokutais, with two other Zeros damaged. None of the Hellcats was shot down. VMF-223 lost a Corsair over Rabaul but recovered the pilot. VMF-216 did not fare so well, with one pilot missing and two others dead.

After Boyington closed to within one victory of tying the record, the Black Sheep grew accustomed to big receptions whenever he landed. Anticipation had reached feverish proportions, with news correspondents and well-wishers tramping everywhere. Big headlines appeared in the newspapers. Boyington's four victories on the twenty-third had reporters salivating at the end of every mission to see if he had tied or broken the record.

No one was more keenly aware of this than Boyington, of course. The expectations had become a burden, the number twenty-six an obsession. It showed in his uncontrollable drinking, in his unpredictable temperament, and now—superb fighter pilot that he was—in his flying.

On the night of December 26, the persistent Fred Hampson made the mistake of asking Boyington if he was deliberately seeking the record. He got an angry response.

> Sure I am. Who the hell wouldn't be? I'd like to break it good and proper. If I could just get on the ball again I might even run it up to thirty or thirty-five. Lord knows the hunting's good enough when the weather lets you in there, but I'm not right. I'm not right at all.

With Hampson just one of many correspondents nosing around, Boyington had few moments of peace. Everywhere he turned, someone was asking about the record. There were even reporters among the enlisted Marines. One wearing the chevrons of a staff sergeant was Marion D. "Dan" Bailey, a combat correspondent from the Atlanta Bureau of the Associated Press. By serving as a jeep driver, he became well acquainted with many of the pilots and wired stories to their hometown papers. It was good public relations for the Corps, and as fame trickled down from Boyington, the other Black Sheep became celebrities as well. They could not help but enjoy the publicity, such as the Sunday when John Bolt's exploits were featured in a page-wide syndicated color strip.

Thus Frank Walton tried only halfheartedly to shield Boyington from the reporters because he realized that the major was on the verge of greatness. Walton exerted his influential association with correspondents just as he had done earlier with George Weller, Jack DeChant, and others, then prepared a script in anticipation of making a radio broadcast when the big day finally arrived. The Marines made a radio truck available, and Walton wrote a descriptive dialogue to set the stage before he would bring Boyington to the microphone. He even remembered to leave a blank space so that he could fill in the yet-unknown number of planes Boyington would splash.

The Marines' losses had been coming in threes. Three Black Sheep were missing after the mission on December 23, then VMF-216 suffered an equal toll on the twenty-seventh. The trend continued on the twenty-eighth, although the Black Sheep placed responsibility for these squarely on the shoulders of the pilot in tactical command.

The Marine fighter squadrons were supposed to receive the day off. Not a single sortie appeared on Tuesday's operations order when it was posted the previous afternoon, but permission for a fighter sweep was sought in order to give Boyington another crack at the record. Immediately after the okay was granted, he took three divisions to Torokina to spend the night before rising early for Tuesday's sweep. Before departing Vella Lavella, he switched Corsairs; number 883, which had carried him for more than five hours on the twenty-seventh, needed complete servicing.

At 0600 on Tuesday morning, Boyington launched toward Rabaul, joined by eleven other Black Sheep as part of an all-Marine force of forty-six Corsairs led by Maj. Rivers J. Morrell, commanding officer of VMF-216. Their numbers were reduced when Junior Heier's Corsair lost hydraulic pressure; it slowed dramatically when the wheels came down and would not retract. Sandy Sims, who led the division, elected to return with Heier and turned the lead over to Rusty March.

Major Morrell, on his first sweep as tactical commander, approached New Britain with the rest of the F4Us stacked behind him. As Walton later wrote in his war diary, the Black Sheep were critical of the way Morrell directed the formation into Rabaul.

> Taking the formation up St. George Channel, Morrell started a huge circle at 22,000', circling [north] of Rabaul at 0730, a long way South West [*sic*] into New Britain and then out over St. George Channel again, losing altitude and making such a wide sweep that enemy planes taking off from Lakunai Airdrome had plenty of time to climb to altitude before the formation had completed its first circle.
>
> Also during this time, another formation of enemy

planes climbed up in the back of the formation into the sun. When the formation engaged the enemy planes over Rabaul, those above and behind came down on them.

An estimated fifty to sixty Japanese were waiting with the advantage when the fight began. They displayed divisional and sectional integrity heretofore unseen, perhaps by borrowing a page from their attackers, in swarming over the Marines. One explanation for the overnight change in aggressiveness could be seen on the waters below: an aircraft carrier floating among the twenty large ships in Karavia Bay. The results for the Black Sheep were disastrous.

Although Morrell was cited for placing the Sheep in a difficult position, one of their own division leaders certainly exacerbated the problem. J. C. Dustin, who was nearing the end of his third combat tour, had no enemy planes to his credit, a frustration that may have caused his desire for a victory to negate common sense. When he spotted eight to ten Zeros a thousand feet above his division, he led them straight ahead in a climb that bled their airspeed down to an indicated 160 knots. Bruce Matheson hung doggedly on Dustin's wing as Ed Olander and Red Bartl followed, but they were sitting ducks. "He flew us right up into the sun," Olander remembered, "and held us on course until bullets were tearing off parts of our planes."

Olander's only hope was to break away. As a Zeke whooshed past in an overrun, Olander rolled over, followed it down, and fired a long burst from 250 yards. The Zeke never pulled out; it hit the water going straight down. Olander managed to roll to one side as more tracers snapped by his wings, then a half-dozen Zeros were hounding him from above. He dived, twisted, reversed, and skidded to dodge a hail of bullets that crowded him ever lower. Only after collecting arrows in both wings and the right elevator did he finally manage to evade.

Matheson also dived out, with a Zero hot on his heels. It pressed him for only a thousand feet or so, but when he tried to climb again the sky above was "roofed in" with Japanese fighters. He nosed over and steered for New Ireland, hoping to fly from under the fight and climb, but the enemy planes remained overhead to block him. His next resort was a haven of cumulus clouds above New Ireland, which he safely reached.

After climbing within the cloud he came out on top, then skirted the edge while keeping an eye for enemy planes that were known to lurk near clouds in wait for strays such as himself. And there they were, just as he had heard—three Zekes curling around the cloud. With a four-thousand-foot advantage, Matheson waited until the sun was behind him before turning the tables. He dropped onto the third Zeke, an unusual light tan color, then opened fire from its high six o'clock and bored in. His tracers struck the tail and walked up the fuselage, where a brilliant flash briefly lit the cockpit—the pilot's oxygen igniting—and the Zeke slid down trailing smoke. It disintegrated against a ridge on New Ireland.

But Olander and Matheson were the only ones in the division to get away. J. C. Dustin and Red Bartl evidently died in that initial fusillade of bullets and cannon shells, or they were finished off soon after. No one saw or heard.

Boyington's division fared little better. Bob McClurg was on his wing, with Chris Magee and Don Moore in the second section. Just prior to splitting up, they noticed that Don was lagging behind, a prime target for an overhead hit-and-run. That was the last they saw of the ever-capable, highly popular young Texan. He simply vanished. The Marines had faith that their big, sturdy Corsairs would absorb terrific punishment and still bring them home, which made their disappearance hard to fathom. The odds for a cripple over Rabaul were not good. Home was a long way back across open ocean, and it took only one well-placed round to knock out a compass or silence a radio . . . or a man.

Boyington and McClurg, meanwhile, selected targets for individual passes from about eighteen thousand feet. Boyington picked out a fighter several thousand feet below and initiated his run from directly astern. The Japanese fighter appeared to be black, with a thick fuselage and large meatballs on stubby, squared-off wings. When Boyington opened fire, it yanked into the vertical and zoomed with "a terrific rate of climb." Boyington tried to pull with it, expecting his Corsair's superior weight and diving speed to enable him to close, but he was left in its wake, which was marked by a trail of dirty smoke. When Boyington later described the encounter to Walton, it was recorded as a Tojo, probably destroyed. But the Nakajima *Ki*-44s did not appear at Rabaul. All things being relative, perhaps Boyington's accumulated stress and fatigue made one of the A6M3 Hamps with its clipped wings seem even more nimble than it already was.

There is nothing to indicate that Boyington reentered the fight, and he eventually landed at Torokina claiming only the probable. Two other Black Sheep did connect. Bob McClurg downed his seventh and last enemy plane, a Hamp that hit the water off Gredner Island, then added a probable by smoking a Zeke. Wild Man Magee scored his ninth, also his last, after overhauling a Tony and blasting it from just sixty yards. Magee had closed so rapidly that he had to yank the control stick to avoid a collision.

The remnants of the fighter sweep returned even more haphazardly than the day before. John Brown flew directly to Vella Lavella and landed at 0920, followed by four more Black Sheep in the next hour. Several others stopped at Torokina for gas, then flew to Vella Lavella by early afternoon. Socked in by bad weather, Boyington remained at Torokina overnight and did not bring his Corsair to Vella Lavella until late the following afternoon, possibly to avoid the strident reporters for a day.

In the end, only nine out of twelve Black Sheep returned.

Although the three missing pilots represented the only Corsair losses over Rabaul on the twenty-eighth, the Japanese somehow contrived to claim twenty-one F4Us destroyed and eight others damaged to unknown extent. As wildly exaggerated as that seemed, the Marines were even wilder in their claim of twenty-six fighters destroyed, eight probably destroyed, and ten damaged. Compared to that collective total of forty-four planes, the Japanese were hardly touched, having lost only three pilots with two additional Zeros damaged. Also remarkable is the fact that the Marines were still claiming Tonys (five destroyed and perhaps three damaged), even though a couple of VMF-216 pilots could not say for certain whether they hit radial-engine Zekes or in-line-engine Tonys.

The only Black Sheep to leave the Barakoma strip all day, Henry Miller (who had become the executive officer after Pierre Carnagey disappeared on December 23) dodged rain showers to fly an engine test on Wednesday. The dismal weather and lack of activity made Don Moore's absence all the more difficult. Of the missing pilots, he alone had been with the Black Sheep for two tours; new faces were easier to forget. Quietly his friends packed the silver trombone he had brought back from Sydney, then sent it to his family in Amarillo, Texas. Don had used it on occasion "to murder the jumping jive"; now the camp was going to be a lot quieter.

Interest picked up in the afternoon when Greg Boyington arrived from Torokina, just in time to learn that another Rabaul sweep had been posted for Thursday, December 30. It was supposed to be Marion Carl's turn to lead, but he graciously agreed to let Boyington take his place. This exchange is widely believed to have occurred a few days later on the afternoon of January 2, which would make it more interesting from a historical perspective, but the arrangement is clearly noted on the December 30 operations plan.

Carl's name had been crossed out, and Boyington's was penciled in.*

At 0615 on Thursday morning, Boyington took off for Torokina with four divisions. They landed an hour later, but poor weather canceled the fighter sweep, so he brought two divisions back to Barakoma.

The other two divisions (led by Miller and Olander) departed Torokina at 0930 to participate in a B-24 strike on Rabaul. With visibility down to half a mile, they departed on instruments. Perry Lane hit an embankment and damaged a wing. Two other Black Sheep aircraft returned early, one with an oil leak, and the rest completed only a facsimile of the original plan. The rendezvous never materialized because of the weather, so the fighters climbed instead to 32,000 feet before they found clear sky, then tried to follow the bombers. The heavies went into Rabaul without their normal close protection.

The waiting Japanese attacked the Liberators over St. George's Channel. Ed Olander, the only Black Sheep to connect, downed his fifth Zeke, which burned, and shot much of the tail off another, which disappeared into the clouds and could not be confirmed. His were the only Marine claims for the day, accompanied by three kills and a probable claimed by VF-33.

For once the claims were not greatly exaggerated. The Japanese actually had six Zeros shot up, although five managed to return to base. No Corsairs were lost, but the unprotected Liberators received a beating. One was seen to go down smoking, two others came back over the channel with props feathered, and only nineteen of the twenty-four scheduled for the mission were counted on the return flight

*Boyington described the occasion as a day in late December, but he interchanged details with events from several different dates, including December 27, when he flew four sorties. Marion Carl described it as occurring on January 2 in his autobiography.

(although probably fewer than that had actually participated).

Greg Boyington, whose fighter sweep had been scrubbed, was not on the flight schedule for the next two days. He later wrote that he was physically worn out from what he called "daily fighter-sweep jaunts over the Rabaul area," although he had flown only four—the same rotation as the other Black Sheep—during the second half of December. In his defense, two of the sweeps occurred on consecutive days, but more likely it was stress and alcohol that were causing the detrimental effect on his condition.

On the evening of December 30, ignoring Frank Walton's warning to the contrary, correspondent Fred Hampson again pressed Boyington about the record.

> [Boyington] entered the mess hall and sat down, ignoring the food and staring into space. Emerging from this reverie he bellowed, "I don't want any more correspondents or photographers or radio guys around until I do or I don't! I don't want anybody asking me about records. They're driving me nuts!"

Poor weather interfered with another strike planned for Friday, the last day of 1943. Henry Miller's and Moon Mullen's divisions were to participate, and Marion Carl was to lead sixty-four Corsairs and Hellcats to Rabaul, but after the short trip to Torokina early in the morning they learned that the whole thing was called off.

Rather than resting while he was off the flight schedule, Boyington held council in his tent on New Year's Eve by sharing canteen cups of liquor from a jug while he sat naked on his cot. At midnight several of the pilots, including Bruce Matheson, decided to observe the New Year in some manner "more colorful than just singing and drinking." To provide the color, they fired numerous shells into the night sky with Very pistols—flare guns normally used for signaling. They were having a wild time when Henry Miller rushed out and stopped them. As Matheson recalled, "The ships in the harbor had seen our display and thought it signaled an incoming air raid—and had put out to sea. Naturally, Henry was unhappy but to his eternal credit, he never did anything about it." The year 1943 did not end with a whimper.

Although Miller was awake until the wee hours, he and Bob Bragdon managed to drag their divisions into the sky at dawn and reach Torokina more or less prepared for the New Year's first mission. After refueling, they escorted fourteen Liberators to Lakunai field near Rabaul, but because of a seven-tenths overcast that blanketed the area they completed the escort without sighting the enemy.

It was a rough day nonetheless for other elements of the formation, particularly when twenty to thirty Japanese fighters mauled the bombers again; they sent one Liberator down in flames over St. George's Channel and crippled another. The latter managed to shoot two attackers out of the sky before struggling back toward Bougainville with the number three engine smoking and the prop feathered. One Corsair from VMF-321 went down, but its pilot was saved.

The wounded B-24 was probably the one that almost killed Henry Miller. The Black Sheep had scattered, and he returned alone from Rabaul, still feeling raw from lack of sleep. Bougainville now boasted a new field big enough for heavy bombers just inland from the Torokina fighter strip, so Miller was cautious to receive not only radio clearance but a green light from the tower's Aldis lamp.

That was still no guarantee of avoiding traffic, as it turned out. Major John Condon, standing near the fighter strip, was a witness.

> A B-24 was coming in with an emergency just about the time the tower cleared Henry to land. The pilot had engines shot out, some dead aboard and one main landing

gear hanging down, so the tower brought him in from the northwest end. At the same time, Henry was taxiing up and was just about off the runway near the command post of Fighter Command. I happened to be standing outside watching this emergency come in.

The B-24 pilot came in and dragged the gear right through Henry's prop. Henry was in the three-point attitude, and I don't know if he ever saw it. It took off his windscreen but miraculously didn't hurt him. It brought him to a total stop immediately, and the B-24 crashed down at the other end of the runway. Henry climbed out of the airplane in a very leisurely way, saw me and walked over. He didn't say a damn thing about what had just happened. That certainly told me what Henry Miller was made of.

The Torokina fighter strip was too narrow for a B-24 (as several Corsair pilots who had drifted off the side could testify), and the pilot stood little chance of keeping the aircraft under control on only one main wheel, but the fact that he touched down from the wrong direction helped. Striking Henry Miller's Corsair ripped the extended landing gear from the bomber, which enabled it to make a less hazardous belly landing.

While the emergency crews tended to the bomber crash (no additional casualties were attributed), Miller looked over his Corsair. Aside from a missing prop blade and windscreen, the damage appeared slight, but appearances were deceiving. The impact from the bomber's wheel had actually popped most of the rivets on the airplane, and beneath its aluminum skin the Corsair was virtually wrecked. Soon after the carcass of the B-24 was cleared, Miller's plane was towed to the scrap pile.

Meanwhile Bob Bragdon flew back from Rabaul with Rope Trick Losch on his wing. After the excitement quieted down, Losch discovered that Boyington was not the only one with a taste for medicinal brandy. Occasionally it was wise to give Bragdon a wide berth, too, especially if he was carrying a few two-ounce bottles of Le Jon. As Losch described:

> I was just flying on his wing about two feet away, and when I saw that canopy come back I'd slide out. Here would come one of those little bottles flying back, and he'd have four or five of them before we landed.

That might explain why Greg Boyington took Bragdon's place the next day to fly an early Dumbo escort to Torokina followed by a dedicated fighter sweep. Boyington left Vella Lavella at 0715 and flew up to Torokina in an old birdcage Corsair, then requested a new plane as soon as he landed. Within minutes, Bill Crocker was airborne from Vella Lavella in a Dash-1A. He dropped it off at Torokina by 0930 and departed ten minutes later in the birdcage. Ironically Crocker completed a three-hour task force assignment in the old plane later that day, whereas its replacement proved to be mechanically unsound.

Tom Emrich, Denny Groover, and Rope Trick Losch were the only other Black Sheep involved as Boyington led a fifty-six-plane fighter sweep airborne at 1020. As the formation neared Rabaul, Boyington suddenly began to lose speed. The other divisions surged ahead and soon got into a fight with the waiting Japanese, but Boyington was unable to participate. His Corsair had developed a serious oil leak that prohibited forward vision.

As Losch watched, Boyington made a desperate but futile attempt to correct the problem.

> Boyington was throwing oil. I don't mean spitting; it was coming back on that windshield. I was there, and I saw it. I've had arguments with a few so-called experts who said, "Oh, that's impossible."

> What I mean by impossible is that we slowed way down—Gramps was leading the division in a tight formation—and as he slowed down we all slowed down to keep formation; we were almost at stall speed. He pulled his canopy back, undid his safety belt, took his handkerchief and was trying to wipe the oil off the windshield. Obviously, he could only reach part way around. He was nearing the record of twenty-six planes and had all that pressure. Every time he went up, everybody was waiting back there to ask, "Well, how did you do? How did you do?" God, it was a bad scene.

Though it sounds improbable, Boyington's display of perseverance was witnessed by no less than three other pilots and was described thoroughly in the war diary reports. At best it was an act of defiance. In disgust he returned to Vella Lavella, with Emrich covering, while the remaining section fought on and compounded his chagrin by tangling with several Zekes.

For Losch it was a day of mixed fortunes that started when he and Denny Groover dived on a pair of Zekes. Losch damaged his but nearly became a victim of friendly fire in the process.

> [Groover] opened up on one and I opened up on the other. Hell, I wasn't 75 yards behind and couldn't miss him. I was shooting at him, and all of a sudden tracers were coming down between my left wing and the engine. I did a fast sort of snap-roll, a half-assed split-S, and as I looked, it was a Corsair that was shooting at me. Whether he was shooting at my Zeke or shooting at me, I'll never know.

The Zeke went into the books as damaged, but Losch did manage to down another, and Groover claimed one probable and one damaged. Their efforts brought the Navy and Marine total to fourteen victories and four probables for the day.

After joining with a Marine from another squadron for the trip back to Bougainville, Losch had an opportunity at another Zeke, but this one was flown by an expert pilot who knew how to use his little fighter's best characteristics to full advantage.

> We hadn't gone too far when two Zekes passed below us, and we rolled in on those. He hit his and it burned, and mine dove down. Man, we were heading almost straight down, and the next thing I knew the Zeke was going right up past my nose. I pulled with everything I had, and blacked out. When I came to, I was still on him and we were going straight up. I thought I had him for sure, but he just kept right on climbing. My old Corsair just got slower and slower and stalled out. When I was dead in the air and kicking it over on a wing to come down, he flipped over and came down—firing all the way—and hit the motor. I pulled out one way, and he went out another way headed for Rabaul. I headed for home, landed at Bougainville with no oil pressure, and the engine froze while I was taxiing. It was a mess. I don't know how those things could still fly, because the mechanic said, "You've got one cylinder shot off." The plane was full of holes and I just left it sitting there, off the runway.

Losch's damaged Corsair may have been one of seven that the Japanese claimed to have shot down (only one F4U was actually lost), whereas the Kokutais recorded the deaths of three pilots and one Zero damaged. It proved to be the last combat over Rabaul for the 201Ku, which withdrew the next day to Truk and was eventually garrisoned at Saipan.

Boyington landed his oil-smeared Corsair at Vella Lavella at 1350, just a few minutes ahead of the successful second section, and began campaigning for another sweep the following day. As had happened the week before, the original schedule for January 3 was light—there were no strikes planned among the fighter squadrons—but he apparently prevailed, for another Rabaul sweep was penciled in.

No doubt glad to escape the reporters, Boyington took off again less than four hours later, flying number 915 this time. Three Black Sheep (George Ashmun, J. J. Hill, and Al Johnson) accompanied him to Torokina, where they spent the night. Ed Olander's division had flown earlier to Torokina for a Dumbo escort and would remain overnight before joining Boyington on the next day's fighter sweep.

It was irregular for George Ashmun, a captain with his own division, to go along as a wingman. Cautious by nature, he had not so much as damaged an enemy plane to date, which led Ed Olander to suggest a motive. "He looked upon that trip as an opportunity . . . and thought he just might get a kill."

Boyington's night at Bougainville was quiet. "He stayed up there just to get away from the press," began John Condon, who was then head of Fighter Command for ComAirNorSols, a subordinate unit based at Torokina. Condon continued:

> We had a little camp just off Piva Trail, which was some distance away from Torokina—perhaps a few minutes. It was comfortable and we were well set; we'd been there since the first of November. [Boyington] came over and had dinner, then shot the breeze. He did not stay up and carouse around. He went to sleep.

A well-rested Greg Boyington arose early on Monday, January 3, briefed the fighter sweep with the other Corsair and Hellcat pilots, and took off from Torokina at 0630. He was in tactical command of forty-six fighters, a more manageable force than some of his earlier forays. He began with seven other Black Sheep and eight Corsairs from VMF-224, plus twelve more from VMF-211 based at Torokina and sixteen Hellcats from VF-33 at Ondonga, but mechanical problems soon began chipping away pieces of his formation. Olander turned back when his oxygen system went down; Perry Lane aborted with hydraulic failure; J. J. Hill, who was leading Boyington's second section, encountered a multitude of electrical malfunctions.

Hill had almost made it to Rabaul when his radio went out, not an uncommon problem. But when he triggered the guns to test them and nothing happened, irritation became concern.

> I thought, "What the hell am I doing here?" I was a sitting duck and finally decided, "I'm outta here." I motioned to Al Johnson that I had a bad plane and was turning back, and turned the lead over to him to stay with the flight. On my way back, my compass wasn't working, and I got lost. I was running out of fuel. There was nothing but water—not an island in sight. I wondered if I should bail out or land on the water, and finally decided, "I guess I'm going to bail out and get in my rubber boat, but nobody knows where I'm at . . ."
>
> With this, a Corsair came up in front of me and gave me the join-up signal. Here was Al Johnson; he wasn't going to let me go down. He couldn't get me on the radio and knew it was out, and then he saw I was flying in the wrong direction. He led me home. If it weren't for Al, I would not be here.

Now only half of the Black Sheep remained, and they formed into one division. George Ashmun was flying an early birdcage Corsair (ironically the same one Boyington had rejected only the day before) and stayed glued to Boyington's wing. Bruce Matheson slid into the section leader's spot, and Mack Chatham was at the tail end. The whole group was stacked from 20,000 to 24,000 feet as they winged over Cape St. George and began a long turn to the north around Rabaul. The sky was clear below their level, but a solid layer above them cast a dark shadow across New Britain, and the air itself was hazy, which lowered visibility. Boyington's reconstituted division was parked in the middle of the formation as they made a circuit so wide that it took fifteen minutes to reverse their original heading.

The incoming Americans had already been detected. Lieutenant Yamaguchi of the 204 Kokutai led thirty-three Zeros into the sky but climbed away to a safe distance from Rabaul before turning to set up an intercept. Some minutes later, Lieutenant Nakagawa, of the 253 Kokutai, led another thirty-seven Zeros from their field at Tobera. It was probably elements of the latter group—about ten to twelve Zekes—that Boyington spotted climbing over Rapopo. The Marines split into two sections and commenced overhead runs on the Mitsubishis at 0815; they agreed to the minute with the contact logged in the 253Ku's record. The 204Ku joined the fight soon after.

While George Ashmun maintained his position, Greg Boyington dropped onto a Zeke from directly astern, sent it down in flames, then continued his dive. The flamer—Boyington's twentieth victory as a Marine—was confirmed by several Marine eyewitnesses, including pilots from VMF-223. Bruce Matheson saw it. He had attacked another Zeke head-on, saw bits of cowling and chunks of its engine fly apart before it passed underneath, then yanked up and pulled hard to the right. From that vantage point he saw it falling in flames, with Boyington's victim also in view, but of the skipper himself or George Ashmun he could see nothing. They had descended into the haze.

Mack Chatham got into firing position on a straggler, but when he triggered his guns they did not respond. When recharging did no good, he concluded that an electrical connection had failed somewhere. Like J. J. Hill, his only recourse was to pull up and away from the fight and head for home. In so doing, he saw two Zekes falling.

Around Bruce Matheson the sky was suddenly empty. He circled for twenty minutes, searching through the haze for someone to join with, but the visibility never improved and he finally turned alone for Bougainville. On the way back, a voice was overheard radioing Dane Base—Bougainville's call sign—that he was making a water landing, but nothing more was heard.

At Vella Lavella, a crowd began gathering around Boyington's revetment as the time for his expected arrival drew near. Frank Walton was surely nearby with his interview script, for Fred Hampson observed, "There was a radio recording hookup and the Marine Corps and Navy photo sections had cameramen there."

Ed Olander landed first—at the same moment the Zekes and American fighters began dueling over Rabaul—but it was too soon to report anything. Forty minutes crawled past, then Al Johnson brought J. J. Hill overhead for their break turns. They taxied in bearing little information. Another two and a half hours dragged by before Bruce Matheson reported in at Torokina and spent an hour on the ground for servicing. It was past 1130, five hours since the formation had taken off that morning, before he finally relayed his Zeke to Walton and shared the news that Boyington flamed one. The record was tied. That and the fact that Perry Lane and Mack Chatham were still at Torokina was all he knew.

Eventually the remaining elements reported their activities. They claimed low-scoring results from their individual clashes over New Britain and St. George's Channel: one probable for VMF-223, two Zekes and a probable by VMF-211, three probables (two of them Tonys) for VMF-321, and two Zekes shot down by Hellcat pilots of VF-33. Morning rolled into afternoon with no reports from other airstrips. With Boyington's and Ashmun's fuel endurance long used up, it became obvious that they had to be down somewhere. How and where were the mysteries, just as with the other missing Black Sheep. On top of what the skipper had already gone through, his disappearance in the act of tying the record seemed almost too coincidental, too scripted. As Fred Hampson pointed out, "In the movies it would be labeled pure corn. Things like that don't happen."

But it had. Slowly the reporters, cameramen, and sound operators packed up their gear and moved on, leaving Boyington's revetment empty.

Aside from scrawling the words "missing in action" next to the names of Boyington and Ashmun in his green logbook, Frank Walton and the other Black Sheep realized that little else could be done that Monday afternoon. Henry Miller, suddenly the de facto commanding officer, took off with Moon Mullen at about 1430 and landed at Bougainville, but that was as far as they got. Rather than launching to look for the missing pilots (as Walton later described), they spent the night and were airborne at first light to search the Rabaul route. They covered St. George's Channel and miles of the New Ireland coast before circling south to New Britain. Just off Rapopo they came across a barge and let loose with their guns, leaving it a smoking hulk, then followed the coastline to shoot at targets of opportunity—enemy bivouac sites, plantations, more barges. Finding no sign of their missing skipper or George Ashmun, they pancaked back at Torokina.

None of the Black Sheep who remained on Vella Lavella flew that day, but Miller and Mullen stayed busy. Three hours after completing their search, the two divisions were back in the air to take part in another fighter sweep of Rabaul, this one employing between fifty and sixty Corsairs and Hellcats. Two of the Black Sheep dropped out early, including Burney Tucker in the same Corsair that had thrown oil for Boyington two days previously. The rest encountered a large force of defending Zeros over Rabaul, where three Black Sheep were able to carve a handful of fighters out of the sky.

John Bolt claimed number six, a Zeke that had been on the tail end of a vee until Bolt ducked under from behind and picked it off. Denny Groover got one smoking over

Simpson Harbor, then singled out another one, drove it down to only a thousand feet, and closed as he fired at point-blank range. Flames boiled from the left wing root, and the Zeke plunged into St. George's Channel.

As Moon Mullen pursued a Zeke from high above its left rear quarter, he saw his slugs tear away chunks of tail and fuselage but did not witness its demise. Continuing down from that encounter, he leveled off at eight thousand feet and spied another Zeke below. He dropped down in a sweeping turn that commenced from its right rear quarter, then held down the trigger as he crossed to the other side. This Zeke hit the water near Cape Gazelle and made Moon the last of the Black Sheep aces.

Judging from the records of both sides, the Americans had been significantly outnumbered. They started the mission with some sixty fighters, but apparently only half that number actually engaged fifty-six Zeros over Rabaul. The 204Ku sortied twenty-seven Zeros and the 253Ku added twenty-nine, but they counted between them only twenty-two to thirty American fighters.

This estimate was corroborated with surprising accuracy by the following remark, which appeared the same day in the VMF-214 war diary. The scathing commentary rings strongly of Henry Miller's dutiful hand.

> About 50 percent of the formation returned to base because of various mechanical difficulties, fancied or real. It seems to be becoming increasingly difficult to get fighter planes to fight. It's a matter that would bear some examination. It's one thing to insist on your plane being in proper fighting condition to fight—but quite another when fighter pilots dream up a series of fancied motor troubles and return to base before the strike gets started. Others don't even dream up a mechanical difficulty—just start calling "Let's go home" as soon as the formation enters the St. Geo. Channel. VMF-214 pilots are

anxious for the opportunity to go on these strikes. They even cut cards to see who gets to go. It seems that some of the other squadrons could use a little more aggressive approach.

Perhaps the disappearance of the seemingly invincible Gregory Boyington the day before had a widespread effect on the confidence of ComAirNorSols fighter pilots, but it was not apparent in his own squadron. In their final two days of combat flying, the Black Sheep completed eighty-five sorties, with only one pilot returning early for mechanical difficulty.

Besides routine Cherry Blossom patrols and a Dumbo escort on Wednesday, January 5, the main event was an SBD strike on shipping in the Rabaul area. John Bolt, Chris Magee, and the indefatigable Henry Miller flew their divisions to Torokina early in the morning, then launched at 0930 after refueling for the strike. But the weather was unsettled, with thick layers of clouds and occasional dark squalls full of heavy rain, and after several course changes the ragged formation turned for home. Bolt, the one pilot who was forced to return early, gave the lead to Burney Tucker, who in turn dropped the division down to one hundred feet for an impromptu search along New Britain. They saw no sign of Boyington or Ashmun but used the opportunity to strafe a lighthouse on Cape Gazelle.

Chris Magee also hugged the water to get below the ceiling, intending to strafe the Rapopo airfield, but his division could not find it in the dismal weather. They thought of strafing Lakunai but the results were the same, so they followed the coastline looking for smaller targets. They found plenty, the first being a pier stocked with twenty to thirty torpedoes. The outcome of their strafing was not reported, but the explosion of so many warheads might have knocked one or more of the Black Sheep out of the sky. Next they came across two barges, each filled with about fifty troops, and strafed them repeatedly until all of the occupants were dead. They left one barge smoking, the other afire.

The squadron's last fighter sweep over Rabaul came on Thursday, January 6, and the Black Sheep were out in force. In addition to the sixteen scheduled to participate, Harry Johnson tagged along at the last minute. He had remained overnight at Torokina after leading a PBY to examine a parachute he had sighted in the water on Wednesday, and as the scheduled planes began taking off he begged the air operations officer to let him join. The major refused, but Johnson pleaded that this was his last hope to get a Japanese plane. "Okay, go. And you're a damn fool."

Skinny Johnson was too late to catch his sixteen squadron mates, who had already joined with fifty-six other Corsairs and Hellcats en route to Cape St. George. The weather interfered with everyone's plans, however, and the formation lowered steadily to stay beneath the ceiling. When they finally had to drop all the way to twelve thousand feet, it was deemed too risky to continue with so many fighters in such shallow airspace. The sweep was called off and most participants turned back, but three divisions of Black Sheep decided to dawdle in the area where Boyington and Ashmun had disappeared; they would shoot wherever they found targets. John Bolt's flight strafed and burned a Betty in its revetment on the island of Boropop, then raked a structure and an AA position nearby. Meathead Bragdon's group ran the length of New Ireland's eastern shore and strafed anything that resembled a camp or bivouac.

Harry Johnson alone found enemy fighters aloft; he sighted twenty to thirty Zeros in echelon over Cape Gazelle. "Of course, this was always the daydream—to be able to catch them in echelon and get three or four like some of the other boys had done," he later said. Maneuvering around and through the clouds to get into position, he came across several Hellcats unexpectedly. Just then another plane approached from below on the opposite heading. Thinking it was another F6F, Johnson was surprised when a Zero streaked past. The Japanese pilot looked at him with equal astonishment.

Johnson started to reverse, then saw another Zero above and put his Corsair into a climb. Giving the enemy fighter plenty of deflection, he opened fire and watched the Zero fly through his stream of bullets. The aircraft exploded and spiraled down to the water trailing smoke.

> Well buddy, that was the start of really feeling good. I had never had any thrill like that, not anywhere near. In fact, I got so thrilled . . . the plane stalled out. That was one of those things Boyington said: "Don't wait until you hear the rain on the roof before you do something about it."

Several Zeros were now overhead, so Johnson ducked away and went home. For a while after he departed, six feathery chains of gun smoke—little puffs from each detonation of a machine-gun shell—drifted in the air, blending, fading, until the last wisp finally dissipated. It took even longer for the few hundred empty brass cartridges to flutter quietly down to the dark water and disappear into the waves. They were the last reminder of the Black Sheep in battle over the South Pacific. Another fourteen months would pass before the squadron's guns were used again in anger, and never again would they be solely responsible for bringing down a Japanese plane.

17

BLACK SHEEP SCATTERED

Harry Johnson's backhanded tribute to Greg Boyington's wisdom was an indication of the tremendous attention still directed toward the missing major. The oft-scoring ace's fame had been steadily rising, but it went meteoric with his disappearance three days earlier during the record-tying flight. Rumors, questions, and speculation forced the Black Sheep to cope with a circuslike atmosphere among the press. Conversely, because no one except for the Black Sheep and George Ashmun's next of kin knew much about George, the impact of the quiet man's absence was all the more intense for his closest friends.

Ed Olander seemed to have a hunch that Ashmun was never coming back.

> George's death bothered me more than any. We instructed together in Jacksonville, we qualified aboard a carrier together, we went on the Santa Fe *Chief* across the country together, we bunked together out there. When we got through with that second tour and returned to Espiritu Santo, I'd be heading over for chow at the mess hall and be halfway across that coconut grove when I'd remember something I'd wanted to tell George, and I'd literally start back before the realization hit me that George wasn't there.

Greg Boyington seemed almost larger than life, and his innumerable phrases of wisdom and advice echoed from everyone's lips. Disbelief that someone could best him in combat was matched only by the faith that he would show up after the war, just as he had promised.

Those intuitions were well founded. Ashmun was indeed dead; Boyington was a prisoner of the Japanese in their Kempei Tai facility at Rabaul. In fact, three days of interrogation had already passed since he was delivered to the port city by submarine. It was only the beginning of twenty months of captivity, which he ultimately survived. The Japanese never acknowledged his capture, however, and his squadron mates would not learn of his fate until the end of the war when he returned to fulfill his pledge.

In the meantime, the January 6 fighter sweep over Rabaul and Harry Johnson's final victory closed the book on the Black Sheep's second combat tour. Their recent heavy losses—eight pilots missing in a span of less than two weeks—cast a shadow over the record they had achieved. Since their initiation into combat the previous September, Boyington and his pilots had been credited with ninety-four planes destroyed and thirty probably destroyed, nearly all during hazardous round-trip missions into enemy territory.

Both combat tours would eventually be recognized as part of a forthcoming Presidential Unit Citation, but the Black Sheep had their minds elsewhere while they packed belongings and cleaned up their Barakoma camp. They departed Vella Lavella for the last time on the morning of January 8 aboard Douglas transports, stopped for fuel at Guadalcanal, and landed at Espiritu in the early afternoon. Trucks delivered them to Turtle Bay, where they moved into several Dallas huts for two weeks of relaxing, swimming, visiting the clubs, and watching evening movies.

Four out of the five members who had completed their obligatory combat tours wasted no time leaving for the States. Gelon Doswell spent his thirty-day home leave with his wife and baby daughter in New Orleans, then reported to Defense Air Base Group Two at Naval Air Station,

North Island. Moon Mullen and Sandy Sims eventually joined him there, and all three continued flying Corsairs. Most were brand-new FG-1A models ferried directly from the Goodyear factory, where they were built under license to supplement naval aviation's demand for the capable fighter. The Marines put the new ones through their paces in acceptance tests. Later Sims logged more than twenty hours in a Mitsubishi A6M2 Zero that had been captured intact on Attu in the Aleutians. He discovered the aircraft's strengths and weaknesses during a cross-country flight.

The fourth Black Sheep to depart Espiritu was Doc Reames, who was reunited with his wife, Rosalita, in Southern California and saw his son, James III, for the first time. After home leave he reported to the Marine Corps Air Station in Mojave, California ("the hottest place this side of Hell"), and was assigned to newly commissioned VMF-452. The squadron right next door, VMF-451, was commanded by VMF-214's former executive officer, Hank Ellis.

The last Black Sheep eligible to return home was Henry Miller, who had now been overseas for almost eleven months. He alone bridged the gap between VMF-214's first tours of combat and its reincarnation as the Black Sheep, and he wished to maintain that continuity. But when the Sheep arrived on Espiritu on the afternoon of January 8, they learned that the ground echelon had already returned to the States and officially taken the squadron number with them.

Subsequently the pilots were assigned to the headquarters squadron of MAG-11, but their ultimate disposition was far from certain. Miller realized that the enlisted troops had been in the South Pacific for as long as he was with nary a break and had earned their trip home, but for his part he was willing to stay overseas. As the senior member of an independent flight echelon that could boast twenty-seven pilots available for one or two combat tours, Miller was all too familiar with the negative effects of breaking up an outfit. In order to prevent history from repeating itself, he launched a campaign, volunteering to remain overseas for an unprecedented fourth combat tour in his attempt to keep the squadron together. He submitted a two-page letter through the chain of command requesting that the squadron be kept intact. To bolster his case, he enclosed a compilation of sixty-four observations and lessons gleaned from Boyington's teachings. Miller urged that by keeping the squadron together, those ideas would be perpetuated. Colonel William G. Manley, the new MAG-11 commander, forwarded the request without comment to Ralph Mitchell at the 1st Marine Air Wing. Along the way a strong endorsement was added by Boyington's greatest supporter, Brig. Gen. James Moore, who underlined his initials boldly on a piece of plain paper: "Keep this combat team intact. JTM. Do not split this group. JTM."

Because a verdict would not be reached for weeks, the Black Sheep could turn their attention to Espiritu's diversions while awaiting their turn for leave in Sydney. Meanwhile they shared the continuing public interest in Greg Boyington's disappearance. The squadron had still been on Vella Lavella when news of his twenty-sixth victory first reached stateside newspapers. Inherent difficulties in sending stories from the South Pacific had delayed the news until January 7 in the *New York Times*. The previous evening, Grace Hallenbeck had learned from the Navy that her son was missing only hours after hearing that he had tied the record. She spoke to reporters from her home in Okanogan, saying, "I'm confident he is all right and he will show up somehow, somewhere." Beyond that, details of his last mission were slow to reach her and other anxious readers. Fred Hampson fired off a story the day after Boyington's disappearance, but it did not run in the *Times* until five days later. A well-crafted piece guaranteed to inspire the public, it included this quote from General Mitchell: "Not only was Boyington of immense value as a pilot but his instructional ability was almost immeasurable. We need men like him to 'read the Bible' to the kids back home who don't know it yet."

Frank Walton was even more dramatic, covering all the angles with a flair that demonstrated his savvy, when he told Hampson, "He may show up or he may not. If he doesn't, you ought to tell the American people they lost about the best and bravest guy that ever came out here to fight for them. The Japs know it already."

Conspicuously absent from these widely syndicated reports and all but a handful of contemporary articles was the nickname "Pappy," probably because the pilots did not use it. Recalled Fred Losch, "I never heard anybody call him Pappy. It was always Greg or Gramps." His statement was echoed by enough squadron mates to rule out use of the nickname among them. It finally appeared in the text of another Fred Hampson story, filed the day after Boyington failed to return, and again in *Time* magazine on January 10.

The origination of the nickname is difficult to ascertain, but it did appear in the Yale "Whiffenpoof" drinking song that the Black Sheep adapted. Fred Hampson, who certainly had the readership to coin the nickname nationwide, reported in a magazine article that the pilots teasingly called Boyington "Grandpappy." The name might have been partially derived from the popular Bureau of Aeronautics newsletter cartoon character Grandpaw Pettibone, a bearded, wizened old aviator who chafed at flying errors and foolish mistakes. Whatever the source, Boyington's nickname appeared in parentheses at first, as in Gregory (Pappy) Boyington. It did not catch on quickly with the Black Sheep.

Two weeks after Boyington went down, the name does not appear in this letter that Frank Walton wrote to his wife on January 18.

> We all miss the skipper but even more important than our personal loss is the loss to combat aviation. Someday I can tell you more, but he was the dean of all combat

pilots. It was a real privilege for me to have been around him. I lived in the same tent with him, put him to bed when he was drunk, hid the bottle when he was sober so he could fly the next day, talked to him for hours on end about flying and home and his 3 children and Warner's Hot Springs and the Flying Tigers. Sometimes he'd wake me up at 1 or 2 in the morning and sit on my cot and talk 'til time to get up—3 or 4. Other pilots used to drop in and sit around the tent just to hear him talk about combat flying and would hang on every word. He taught a lot of boys how to fly, but far more important he taught many of them to fight. They were all green as grass and now they're finished fighting men—22, 23 & 24 years old in time but much older than that in experience and know-how. I've written an official report on Greg's combat tactics which is being printed for distribution to all fighting squadrons throughout the U.S. [The tactics are] as new as were Chennault's in China and they'll save lots of lives and shorten the war. Typical of him and his leadership is the fact that 26 of the 28 pilots in our outfit have been decorated—Air Medal, Distinguished Flying Cross, and Navy Cross. He himself will get the Congressional Medal of Honor and possibly two of them. But to hell with the medals. We loved him and respected him and our boys were all willing to die for and with him—and some of them did, but I'm sure they considered it an honor to do so.

The letter was accurate enough and prophetic. Boyington would receive a Medal of Honor and a Navy Cross, and Walton had indeed assembled (with Henry Miller's help) a lengthy report entitled "The Combat Strategy and Tactics of Major Gregory Boyington, USMCR." Forwarded with Miller's request to keep the squadron intact, it received immediate attention. It went into circulation on January 19 and within weeks had been reprinted in Washington through the Chief of Naval Operations for distribution throughout naval and Marine fighter forces.

After nearly two restful weeks at Turtle Bay, the flight echelon (minus Frank Walton) boarded transports on January 21 for the long-anticipated trip to Sydney. In the Southern Hemisphere it was the middle of summer, and the men enjoyed Australia's beaches this time in addition to Sydney's other splendid offerings. They returned in groups to Espiritu on the last of January and the first of February, then idled for several more weeks while waiting to hear of their fate.

The conclusion was inevitable. Without a squadron number—and with other outfits in need of replacements for their own rotation back to combat—the Black Sheep were split up, just as the Swashbucklers had been four months earlier. In his book Frank Walton hinted that the cause for the breakup was General Moore's transfer to another command. But Walton himself was transferred to the staff of the 1st Marine Air Wing, where Moore was still doing the job he had held for months—assistant wing commander under General Mitchell, who was concurrently serving as ComAirNorSols. Walton's report that the squadron learned of the breakup through the Associated Press in late March was also incorrect.

On March 1 fifteen Black Sheep, including Henry Miller and all of the current aces, were transferred to VMF-211, commanded by Maj. Thomas V. Murto, Jr. Just back from its own trip to Sydney, the squadron whose legacy started on Wake Island was encamped at Turtle Bay and began working up to a return to combat in two weeks. Just before the Wake Avengers (sometimes called the Wake Island Avengers) were scheduled to begin a new combat tour on Bougainville, Mo Fisher fell ill. In taking his place, Fred Losch became part of the single largest contingent of former Sheep to join any one outfit.

From the commencement of VMF-211's combat operations on March 17, there was a noticeable coolness between Murto's pilots and Miller's contingent of former Black Sheep, such that the two halves operated with almost exclusive independence. Individuals coexisted without rancor, and some were friendly, but with rare exceptions their flights were scheduled separately. Early missions from Torokina included barge sweeps and counting Japanese planes on the ground at Rabaul, a measure of how dormant Japanese aviation had become in the region. The only shooting was at ground targets.

The aerial crescendo over Rabaul that finally strangled the once-formidable fortress had come while the former Black Sheep rested on Espiritu. The cost among Corsair squadrons had been frightful. In January and February almost sixty F4Us were lost on combat missions to Rabaul—an average of one plane per day—with thirty-nine of their pilots either dead or missing. Ashmun and Boyington had a lot of company.

On March 19 and 20, the Wake Avengers moved to Green Island, only 115 miles from Rabaul, and continued their mission of besieging the Japanese by interdicting barges and trucks, with some bomber escorts mixed in. For the next five and a half weeks the squadron hunted across New Ireland and northern New Britain, firing at sampans, barges, vehicles, and structures wherever they could find them. The missions were naturally flown at low altitude, where the fighters were vulnerable to AA and small-arms fire. Three F4Us went down on March 28 during a strafing mission against Duke of York Island, in the middle of St. George's Channel. Only one was directly attributed to AA fire (the pilot was rescued); the other two became separated from the rest and were never seen again.

Some of the wildest missions involved shooting trucks as the Marines pitted their six-ton Corsairs against unarmored vehicles, as often as not already abandoned or empty. There was little else to shoot at. John Bolt recalled the challenge that such targets offered.

> We were fanatics at shooting trucks. A truck on a bypassed island probably has no more than a few quarts of gasoline in it, and is hard as hell to burn. We never claimed them unless they burned . . .
>
> We would fly over the coconut groves, which were the primary industry of those islands, it seemed. If the Japanese could get the vehicle off the road and in a coconut grove, you probably couldn't find it. You couldn't shoot at it because you could only see straight down in a coconut grove. Frequently, we would have one guy down low and three guys up and back. He would yell, "truck!" then the others would try to start making a run. It was too late for the spotter to shoot when he saw a truck, but one of the tricks he could use was to fire his guns, not even pointed at the truck. It might startle a driver into thinking he was under fire, and he would jump out of his truck, leaving it in the road.

The squadron continued to fly such missions from Green Island throughout the rest of March and most of April. It was just two days from finishing the tour when Harpo Harper learned that strafing trucks was not risk free. Bolt, Henry Miller, Long Tom Emrich, and several other former Sheep were with Harper on the afternoon of April 24 for a scheduled barge sweep along the coast of New Ireland, but they decided instead to search the Rabaul area. Locating a plantation west of Tobera, they went to work. Most had already expended their ammunition to burn eleven vehicles and a small fuel dump when Burney Tucker spotted one more truck.

Tucker was out of ammunition, but Harper had one gun still working and decided to make a run, calling for Tucker to point it out.

> [Tucker] made a dry run on this truck that was sitting in a small clearing. There were a couple of oil drums beside it. I fired my only gun and missed the truck by about six feet. You could see the slugs cut up the ground alongside the truck. The single gun kicked off to the left. Just as I pulled out, I got hit with a bullet . . . It felt like I'd been hit in the fanny with a four-by-four, and I knew I was in trouble. I pulled up, looked over to my right side, and saw a hole in the canopy where the bullet had come in. I called the guys and told them I had been hit.

One round from a Japanese AA weapon—perhaps on a hilltop or another elevated position—had punctured Harper's bubbletop canopy down low, then passed through his body, collapsing a lung and nicking his spine before punching out the Plexiglas on the other side.

Right away Harper realized that he was in bad shape, and he jettisoned the canopy to prepare for ditching.

> My legs were paralyzed. There were little skids on the floor of the Corsair to put your heels on. My legs were down in the hole between the skids and they weren't moving, and that was pretty disturbing. But my hands and arms were fine and my mind was tolerable, so I turned and headed out to sea intending to ditch in the ocean. I suddenly decided, "If I ditch, I will not survive."
>
> I went into shock right away. I never had much pain, except I couldn't breathe well because of a damaged lung. I had a very shallow breath . . . I just flew along, added power, flew some more and started having blackouts. The instruments would fade and come back, fade and come back. I thought, "If it goes out all the way, I'm done." I took my helmet off and threw it away, trying to get some fresh air on my face from the slipstream. I relaxed, trimmed up the airplane so that I could fly it with a finger, and flew home.

Harper's friends had heard the distress call and joined up as he worked his way back to Green Island, but they could see no evidence of damage because he had jettisoned the canopy. Nor could they discern the nature of his problem via radio after he shucked his helmet. But they could see from his actions that something was very wrong, and they continued to guide him home.

Fortunately enough function returned in Harper's legs to make them useful.

> I was starting to get some feeling back in my legs and I managed to get them up on the rudder pedals. I dropped the gear and made a normal approach. I couldn't control the plane completely and ended up in the weeds off the runway, but I eventually got it stopped without damage. I saw the plane captain standing by the wing with a concerned look on his face. A flight surgeon crawled up and saw that I had blood on my back and said, "We're going to have to get a crane to get him out of here."
>
> I used a lot of profanity. I will never forget it. I said, "Uh, uh, never! I flew this goddamn plane home and I'm not going to sit in this goddamn cockpit and bleed to death while you go looking for a crane. Now you grab hold of me and pull me out of here!"
>
> And they did. They dragged me over the side and carried me to the meat wagon. I passed out on the way and came to two days later.

It took a blood transfusion (which gave him malaria) to get Harper out of danger, but his war was finished. The flight surgeon surmised that he had been shot clean through by a .51-caliber armor-piercing round, leaving what John Bolt later called "a hole in his back where you can put your fist."

Harper was the only member of the Black Sheep contingent to encounter serious trouble in VMF-211, but former

Sheep in other squadrons were even less fortunate. The morning after Harper's encounter, Bill Crocker lost his life in an operational accident on Espiritu Santo. Still attached to the headquarters squadron at MAG-11, he was conducting a proficiency flight in an SBD with a Marine captain at the controls when their plane went down.

Five days later young Bill Hobbs died during a flight that should never have gone up. Several former Black Sheep who had joined VMF-114 when it arrived overseas in March had been based on Green Island for about a month when a predawn mission was scheduled for April 30. The weather was unfit for flying, and Glenn Bowers was among those who protested the order to launch. But their division leader insisted that they fly to log night hours, even though no one could see through the inky blackness. Suffering vertigo, Bowers nearly flew his Corsair into the water. "The worst damn conditions I ever flew in," he remembered. "I looked out the side of the airplane, and cripes, I was practically in the ocean. I could see the white rollers—right there. I had no idea that I was down on the deck like that. Boy, oh boy."

Hobbs and another pilot never returned. Perhaps they were killed by collision or vertigo—or both—but essentially they were victims of a stubborn leader's poor judgment on a flight that had no military value.

The rest of the former Black Sheep finished their combat obligations during what historian Robert Sherrod called "the doldrums of 1944." But for Ned Corman, in VMF-218 on Bougainville, the month of March was far from dull. On the eighth the Japanese launched a counterattack against the American enclave around the three airfields at Torokina, Piva North, and Piva South. Artillery shells, raining onto the strips for two weeks, forced the Marines to evacuate their planes at night and fly them in each day for sorties in their own backyard. In relative terms, it was a brief battle of attrition that the Japanese could not win. Corman recalled, "We organized Jap hunts . . . it was almost like shooting rats."

Rusty March was also at Bougainville, serving for several months on the staff of ComAirNorSols before transferring to VMF-223. He was still there at the end of September, long after the others had fulfilled their combat tours and gone home to the States. His war ended with a serious accident.

On the evening of September 29 he went up for what was supposed to be a routine night proficiency flight, but several factors conspired against him.

> We went out supposedly for an hour's hop at night, and it ended up taking over two hours. I was getting annoyed with the problem because it was a nice moonlit night, and it was really contact flying, not instrument flying. I could see, when I got into the traffic pattern, that guys were dragging out their approaches, and it just annoyed the hell out of me. I had a division to lead by this point, and was going to show them how to shorten up the traffic pattern. The trouble was, when I put my wheels down, I didn't lock them down.

Normally a "wheels watch" officer was on hand to fire a flare if something was amiss, but as Rusty March approached the Marston mat strip at Piva North, no one was on duty. Upon touching down, the wheels folded underneath the Corsair and the aircraft crunched onto its gull wings and propeller. Usually this was satisfactory for a belly landing, but March's Corsair was fitted with a Brewster bomb rack, which quickly snagged in the steel plates of the strip and sent his Corsair out of control.

The rest was a blur. March woke up in the hospital with severe burns.

> I remember the guys telling me afterwards that my plane had slid about halfway down the runway and came to rest in flames, with the nose pointed perpendicular to the runway. Apparently no one had seen me get

> out. I don't know how the hell I got out. I must have instinctively bounced out. The fire truck and the meat wagon pulled up immediately, and I'm told that I was sitting in the flames a few feet behind the plane, trying to beat them out. The shock of the whole thing just blanked that out.

By then, roughly eight months had passed since the Black Sheep disbanded. Rusty March and Harpo Harper were recovering from serious injuries, Bill Hobbs and Bill Crocker were dead from operational accidents, and the rest of the pilots had returned to the States for thirty days of combat leave before reporting to new assignments.

Frank Walton was the lone member still on duty in the Solomons. The months had passed quickly while he participated in some of the last western advances in that part of the South Pacific, including a landing on Emirau on March 20 with the 4th Marines. He set up and directed the intelligence department for a fighter group that moved in after the Seabees built a strip, then was promoted to major and transferred back to Bougainville.

During Walton's service as assistant chief of staff, Intelligence, ComAirNorSols, one of his staff officers was a captain named Joseph R. McCarthy, from Appleton, Wisconsin. "He flew in the back of a dive bomber two or three times and got himself an Air Medal for that," Walton remembered of the man who would earn much greater notoriety in the following decade as a U.S. senator who conducted sensational witch-hunts for Communists among government officials and public figures.

While Walton was overseas, he maintained a cozy dialogue with acquaintances in the press and continued beating a drum for Greg Boyington. Before going ashore at Emirau, he wrote to radio entertainer and *Times* columnist Ed Sullivan in New York. Sullivan eventually ran much of Walton's letter in his "Little Old New York" column, then took the time to send a chatty personal return.

> Back here, we follow such a squadron as your Black Sheep with tremendous interest and pride, because you are our guys. As day after day went by, and Major Boyington kept knocking down those Zeroes [*sic*], we all became official scorekeepers . . . On my CBS radio program, I did a longer story about him and the national reaction was terrific—apparently the whole country had been perched on his wing each time he took off on a new foray . . .

In July, Walton's firsthand account of the squadron and its missing commander (curiously titled "Black Sheep . . . Run!") was published in *Skyways* magazine. Fred Hampson's story, "Boyington, Lost Ace," appeared in *Liberty* that same month. Olga Greenlaw beat them both to the punch with her tale of Boyington's Flying Tiger days in the April *Cosmopolitan,* then a family-oriented news magazine. The public relations department at Chance Vought joined the bandwagon by turning out a full-spread tribute to the missing ace with a title that smacked of finality: "Twenty-six to One!"

The articles sustained public interest in Boyington, who by now was not only a national hero but the recipient of official recognition. Congress took the first step after Ed Sullivan allegedly pointed out on his show that Boyington had never received even an Air Medal, which should have been almost automatically conferred after a pilot scored three victories. On March 15, Boyington was given the permanent rank of first lieutenant under special legislation signed by Franklin Roosevelt. It was essentially a provision on behalf of his dependents, because his temporary rank as a major in the reserves would not yield benefits if he failed to show up after the war. Then the bureaucratic wheels began turning faster, and within a month Roosevelt signed a citation bestowing the Medal of Honor on Boyington. It was a tremendous leap from no recognition to the nation's highest military award for valor.

The newspapers printed anything they could learn about the missing hero, including unsubstantiated rumors. In June the *New York Times* reported that he was alive on an island and being hidden by natives until he could rejoin his squadron. His mother acknowledged the story from her home in Okanogan, saying that she had received it from "a well-known flier who has just returned from the South Pacific." But nothing else developed, and newspaper reporters eventually lost interest. After that, it was up to magazine writers to rehash the known facts.

One small group of pilots took more interest than most in news of Greg Boyington. On the coast of Southern California, thousands of miles from where he disappeared, a new squadron now carried the banner of the Black Sheep.

Reorganized only weeks after Boyington disappeared, the new group was finding the normally friendly skies of the United States to be almost as lethal as the skies over the Solomon Islands.

18

STARTING OVER

The squadron's latest reincarnation, which began inconspicuously in February 1944, bore some resemblance to its original commissioning nineteen months earlier. There were no aircraft in the inventory and only a few people on hand for administrative purposes, a starting point from which the unit would have to acquire pilots and planes.

But there the similarities ended. The global picture had changed dramatically since the summer of 1942 when VMF-214 was commissioned. Back then, Marine Corps aviation was being reconstituted after being knocked silly in the early months of the war, and dusty little Ewa was essentially their foremost air base in the Pacific. A year and a half later, the number of Marine pilots was rapidly approaching ten thousand, and a litany of famous airfields had been opened across the South Pacific: Turtle Bay, Henderson Field, Banika, Munda, Barakoma, Torokina. Now the Solomons were under Allied control and Rabaul would be left to wither.

Although the forces already ringing Rabaul would continue to pound and throttle that dead horse for months to come, the entire scope of the air war was undergoing a major shift to other regions. Senior planners were turning to the Central Pacific, where the islands were too far apart for Marine aviation to contribute much besides rear guardianship. Next would come the Philippines, then the outer islands around Okinawa and the Jimas, and finally the Home Islands of Japan itself.

Marine aviation's role in those campaigns was much in question. The future battles were planned around the mobility of the swift carrier fleets, and Marine pilots were no longer qualifying on carriers as part of their flight training syllabus. The previous summer, when the fight for the Solomons and Rabaul was expected to employ land-based Marine aviation for a year or more, such time-consuming training had been deemed superfluous. It turned out to be a knee-jerk reaction that left a void in employing Marine aviators to their best advantage.

Carrier aviation concerns aside, the Corps was still in a mode of tremendous expansion, commissioning new squadrons almost weekly. When existing units were earmarked for reorganization, experienced pilots were not always immediately available. Such was the case for the new VMF-214. Its first commanding officer, Ranson R. Tilton, was a second lieutenant barely out of flight school. The situation lasted only a few weeks while other fresh-faced pilots reported.

If the new pilots had no aircraft, they could at least appreciate their location at Santa Barbara, California. Officially the squadron was an element of Marine Base Defense Aircraft Group 42 at MCAS (Marine Corps Air Station) Santa Barbara, an odd assortment of permanent buildings and plywood Dallas huts on the site of the municipal airport in Goleta, a few miles up the coast from Santa Barbara's adobe walls and red tile roofs. The Marines made it presentable by maintaining trim green lawns lined with little white fences and painted rocks.

During the weeks that Tilton held his administrative title, he maintained a low profile, and incoming pilots had virtually nothing to do. Twenty-one-year-old Arthur O. Schmagel, fresh from SBD training at Masters Field in Miami, was assigned to VMF-214 instead of a dive-bombing squadron. Searching for his new outfit, he found a sergeant major sitting at a field desk in a plywood hut, the sum total of the squadron. Schmagel asked what he was supposed to do and was told, "Well, you're not going to be doing anything because we don't have our airplanes. Go anywhere you want, just so long as you call in every morning." Not one to look a gift horse in the mouth, Schmagel and a handful of other new arrivals drove to Hollywood and checked into a hotel, then played for days while someone mustered in by phone each morning for the whole bunch.

By the time Maj. Warren H. McPherson arrived as interim commanding officer on March 4, thirty-three officers and twice that number of enlisted men had reported for duty. Immediately they began acquiring Corsairs, mostly FG-1s built under license by Goodyear, with a handful of Brewster-built F3A-1s added later. All were visually identical to the Chance Vought product, although at least one pilot recalled a lack of conformity in their instrumentation.

Test hops of the newly delivered aircraft commenced two days after McPherson's arrival, but a new plane was lost within three weeks. Second Lieutenant Joseph Kuhn, making one of his first hops in an FG-1, was heading back to the field on March 23 with the fuel gauge indicating fifty gallons in the main tank. At that level, the handbook called for placing the fuel switch to reserve, because the engine would not continue to draw below fifty gallons with the selector in "main." But Kuhn forgot, and just short of the field the engine quit. The FG-1 nosed over and cracked up in a drainage ditch, which caused Kuhn to smack his head against the gunsight. After getting a large bandage on his forehead at the dispensary, he sought his fellow lieutenants and found them standing outside a Dallas hut. They had all heard the sirens, and when they saw Kuhn walking under his own power they greeted him warmly. Warren McPherson was less compassionate, popping out of a nearby Dallas hut to growl, "Kuhn, you're in hack for ten days!"

On the same day that Kuhn's punishment period ended, another Corsair was lost during a test hop. Captain Arnot W. Dodds, the nonpilot engineering officer, stuck his head in the ready room door and announced that a pilot was needed to test a new Corsair. Second Lieutenant Glendon L. Alexander, who was playing cards with several other pilots, said, "I'll take it," even though he was not due to fly. He gunned the FG-1 down the strip, but as he left the ground the engine stopped due to complete magneto failure. Although Alexander managed to get the Corsair back on the runway, it overran the end of the strip and tumbled over in the soft ground. A crane lifted the inverted wreckage enough to pull Alexander from underneath, but he died two days later from severe head injuries.

The arrival of an original Black Sheep member within a few more days helped to overcome the early loss. Someone in the Marine hierarchy with an appreciation for continuity sent Maj. Stan Bailey, now twenty-seven, to take permanent command of the squadron. The New Englander's second association with VMF-214 began on April 10 and would last more than a year, overall the longest affiliation of any pilot in the war. He was accompanied by Shirley Bailey, his new bride.

Because the roster was not yet at full strength, one of Bailey's first official acts was a trip to the MAG-42 pilot pool. Twenty-year-old Stanley E. "Red" Free, who had grown up in the little California town of Taft, just across the Sierra Madre mountains, was one of the unassigned pilots lounging at group headquarters when Bailey walked in. The major and Warren McPherson (now the executive officer) began asking questions.

> They wanted to know how many fighter pilots were in the room. Four or five guys held their hands up—Corsair pilots who had been through Jacksonville. "Okay, we'll take you guys," they said. "What do the rest of you clowns do?" Well, we flew SBDs and TBFs.
>
> "Jeez, that's terrible. We need some more fighter pilots. Everybody stand up."
>
> We all stood up, and then Stan Bailey and McPherson,

who were small men, picked me [Free] to become a fighter pilot because I was tall.

Bailey acquired several experienced captains to serve as division leaders by arranging a transfer with VMF-221. Warner O. Chapman, Walter J. Schocker, and Robert M. Jones were veterans of the Solomons with eight Japanese planes among them. Chapman and "Rafe" Schocker had served together in VMF-221 since the early days at Ewa (and sailed on *Nassau* with the original MAG-21 deployment overseas). Chapman had four planes to his credit, including a Zero shot down on April 7 during the big Japanese raid over Guadalcanal, and two Bettys on June 30. Schocker had accounted for two planes during his overseas tour. Jones was not originally in the squadron with them but had gained two victories while flying birdcage Corsairs in VMF-213. Frank P. Barker, Jr., a former torpedo bomber pilot, was the fourth on the roster wearing captain's bars; he was regarded as the most difficult of the division leaders to get along with.

There was but one first lieutenant, twenty-two-year-old Kenneth N. Linder, who had tired of training students at Opa-Locka for eight months and campaigned to get into action.

> The war was going on. I called a friend of the family who was a Colonel in Washington, D.C. at Headquarters and said, "I want to get out of this. I want to go fight!" Oddly enough, he called my mother to make sure it would be all right. Three days later I got orders to Miramar.

In 1944 Marine Corps squadrons were ideally manned with 150 percent of the pilots needed for the assigned aircraft—in this case twenty-four Corsairs. Stan Bailey had a promising mix of seven experienced pilots, but the rest were second lieutenants just out of school, and the beginning of his tenure was troubled by the loss of one within days. Flying with his canopy open, John B. Collins was participating in a gunnery flight over water on April 14 when he shouted on the radio that his life raft was inflating in the cockpit. Whatever caused it to balloon, the result would have been painful as the seat belt tightened across his hips. He began climbing and was passing through five thousand feet when his Corsair suddenly pitched over. Out shot Collins with no parachute; he fell to his death while the life raft fluttered down behind. It was later determined that he released his harness, which allowed the expanding raft to shove the stick forward; the sudden onset of negative g's ejected him. It was a strange coincidence that VMF-214 lost two pilots who fell without parachutes, going back fifteen months to Jerry Reinburg's mishap near Ewa. There was speculation that Collins did not carry a knife, which he could have used to puncture the raft, so ground crews taped a simple shiv to the Corsairs' instrument panels for emergency use.

It was bad enough that three planes and two pilots had already been lost in the first five weeks of flying, but two days later a midair collision occurred during a gunnery hop. This time the Corsairs suffered only minor damage, and for a while the trend appeared to have ended. Six weeks passed without mishap as the pilots flew a steady diet of gunnery hops, formation practice, and night instrument training. They had nearly made it through the month of May when another fatal accident marred the record on the last day. Ervin S. Kindell disappeared during a navigation exercise over the Santa Barbara Channel; he was believed to have flown into the Pacific west of Point Conception.

After that the squadron turned the corner. With twenty-three FG-1As on hand, the Black Sheep accumulated some nineteen hundred flight hours in June, nearly a third of them at night. In addition to routine gunnery and formation hops, training commenced for something relatively new to the fighter community: bombing. Before flying the actual profiles, Stan Bailey gathered all the instructional material he could lay his hands on about glide- and dive-bombing and gave it to his newly arrived ACIO to distribute. With an ante of two Dallas huts and a clerk, 1st Lt. Daniel Rudsen put together a briefing room replete with lounge chairs, magazines, a radio, and a movie projector.

The other notable acquisition in June was a live mascot—the first for VMF-214. A leggy black lamb named Midnite became a fixture around the base, making appearances at intrasquadron softball games and other activities. It was good for publicity. A photograph of Stan Bailey kneeling in front of a Corsair while feeding Midnite from a bottle appeared in the local press, then was featured six months later in a magazine story about the missing Boyington. The little black sheep was also a morale booster, enhancing the enlisted men's solidarity. Their squadron support was evident during a minor accident on June 20, which occurred after Robert Jones, returning from a flight, radioed ahead that only one main wheel had extended. Word spread quickly, and the troops came out to watch as he touched down on the good wheel and held up the Corsair's opposite wing as long as possible. When his airspeed finally bled off, the wing crunched down and slewed the Corsair around in a cloud of dust, but the experienced Jones had done the job with only minimal damage. A spontaneous cheer went up from the enlisted gallery.

June concluded quietly, with only one other incident of minor damage in exchange for the many hundreds of hours flown. Returning from a night hop earlier in the month, twenty-two-year-old John P. Stodd forgot to lower his wheels before landing. The runway officer on duty saw the clean configuration, but his first attempt with the Very pistol misfired. The second attempt was behind Stodd's field of vision, and he bellied in. The sudden stoppage necessitated an engine change and a new prop, but otherwise the Corsair suffered only minor sheet-metal damage.

Inclement weather prevailed during much of July, causing the squadron's flight time to plummet. To make up for the deficit, ground training was intensified. The men spent hours in the Link navigation trainer, in classrooms solving instrument and gunnery problems, or watching instructional movies in what Dan Rudsen liked to call his "situation room." By far the most significant change was the introduction of carrier training. During July the Marine Corps' director of aviation and the commandant himself were engaged in a campaign to send Marine squadrons back to sea, and there were evidently officers at the air group level with the foresight to be prepared. Although VMF-214 was still months away from qualifying, the men began their training with lectures given by a landing signal officer (LSO). The Marines had none of their own, so this one was borrowed from the Navy. His lessons were voluminous, beginning with the dynamics of landing on a moving ship, then covering detailed specifics such as the arm motions he would wave using bright orange "paddles"—the nickname by which all LSOs were invariably called.

Perhaps the LSO's foremost consideration for the Marines when they began flying carrier approaches was the Corsair's limited forward visibility. The advent of safer stall characteristics and the raised seat had improved the F4U's sea legs, but that long nose still ruled out anything resembling a straight-in final approach. Pilots would have to learn to keep their Corsair banked in a continuous left turn and drag it around behind the ship, rolling wings-level just before they crossed the deck and received the "cut" signal. At that point they would chop the throttle and virtually fall the last few feet to an ungentle landing.

Before trying to land aboard a flight deck, the Black Sheep first practiced the rudiments on dry land. The approximate dimensions of a carrier's landing area were outlined on the end of a runway, a low-risk area for pilots to rehearse dozens of approaches. The key was to establish consistent turn points and maintain a steady glide slope.

"Paddles" stood in the same position he would occupy aboard ship (aft, just off the port side of the deck) and used exaggerated motions to guide the pilots onto the designated area. Much like those of a football referee, the LSO's signals told an approaching pilot if he was high, low, slow, fast, left or right of centerline, skidding, or simply okay. As soon as the wheels banged on the strip—the glide slope was deliberately steep—the Corsairs bounded back into the air while the pilots applied power and circled left to perform the maneuver again and again. It was called "bounce drill." The training would occupy a runway for hours, which was impractical within the busy confines of MCAS Santa Barbara, so the decision was made to move the squadron temporarily to a small Army field near Oxnard, California.

The move—no small undertaking with 24 Corsairs, 51 officers, and 275 enlisted men—was accomplished on August 1. Their Army hosts proved accommodating, although the field itelf was described by one pilot as a "bean patch." It was indeed surrounded by hundreds of acres of beans, where pickers endured the constant roar of Corsairs circling just above their heads. Flying commenced within two days, although morning fog precluded bounce drill. The pilots launched instead to fly familiar combat tactics, gunnery hops, and practice bombing, as they had done for the past several months, using Wilson Rock offshore for a target. As their proficiency grew, they became accurate with water-filled practice bombs slung beneath a centerline Brewster rack.

An unexpected invasion began on August 9 when field mice sought refuge inside the buildings and aircraft. Six were discovered drowned in the situation room's coffeepot and another was found crawling about the cockpit of the utility SBD. A four-legged assistant with a reputation as a ferocious mouser was brought in to combat them. She was a Scottie named Angus (Angus Fala McTavish, to be precise), and the pilots were all too happy to move floorboards and furniture "to aid in her ceaseless war against the invaders."

When bounce drill began on August 13, the squadron promptly lost another airplane. Robert K. Hugler's Corsair suffered an engine failure on the downwind leg, but he was able to glide around for an emergency belly landing (why his wheels were up instead of down was not explained). Although the plane needed an overhaul, he was uninjured. Two days later, redheaded Stan Free was in the pattern when his landing gear folded during a bounce, and the Corsair mushed in on its belly. He was not hurt either, but the FG-1's engine, propeller, and undercarriage were damaged.

On the seventeenth a disaster of a different sort befell the squadron. The little black sheep Midnite, which had recently been promoted to corporal, had been given the run of the place, and someone accidentally backed over it with a car. The day after the sheep's demise, another plane was heavily damaged. William A. Nabors got too slow during an approach and stalled, which sent his Corsair into a spin. This was frequently fatal, but Nabors somehow righted the aircraft just above the ground. His sink rate was huge, however; both tires blew on impact with the strip, and the Corsair came to rest on its nose.

Then came another fatal accident, every bit as bizarre as the one that killed John Collins in mid-April. On August 22, Addrian V. Boozer (his friends sometimes laughed that his first initial made him A. Boozer) was on a gunnery hop with Red Free and two others when he started a run on an improved target banner, fitted with weights to let it ride at different angles for high-side or low-side passes.

Boozer, who was flying with an open canopy, somehow collided with the target, as Free later recalled.

> His wingman flew up on him, and told us that he was sitting kind of cocked over. I've always figured that he hit one of those damned weights. The airplane just

> dipped in lazy chandelles, and we were all hollering on the radio, "Get out! Jump out of it!" But at about 5,000 feet the plane just rolled over and did a split-S, straight in. There was just a slick. One guy went low to stay over it, and I went high to get the crash boats. When they got out there we were still overhead, and they recovered very, very little.

Yet another wheels-up landing damaged a Corsair on the twenty-fifth during bounce drill, this time marginally attributed to pilot error on the part of Beverly J. Larche, though an informal board determined that material failure was mostly to blame.

A distraction from the escalating accident rate was fortunately provided by Angus McTavish, whose multiple-kill days were recorded proudly in the war diary. She began with "four casualties in the mice tribe" on the fourteenth and another quadruple event on the twentieth, added triples on the twenty-fourth and twenty-seventh, and finished with two more kills the following day (plus two probables).

Although Angus was a Mouse Ace three times over, her contribution to squadron morale was suddenly overshadowed when a replacement for the dead sheep was acquired on the twenty-ninth. Midnite II, a large, mean-looking ram, immediately established that his appearance matched his nature. A pilot made the mistake of trying to get friendly, then turned his back. Midnite II promptly rammed him from behind.

As the month of August drew to a close, the Black Sheep's training syllabus was recorded as 85 percent complete. Other than carrier qualifications, the only thing left to accomplish was night flying, which commenced late on the thirty-first with navigation hops. From Oxnard they flew three hundred miles north to San Francisco, turned southeast to Fresno, then headed over the dark desert to Mojave before turning west for the final leg over the mountains to Oxnard. After flying above the blackness of the isolated desert east of the mountains, the pilots crossed the San Gabriels to see the dazzling lights in the coastal cities below.

An identical navigation hop the following night, which squeaked into Oxnard just before fog rolled in and closed the field, proved to be the squadron's final training flight there. With bounce drill complete, the Black Sheep moved back to Goleta during the first week of September, then endured a lengthy period of fog and drizzle. The poor weather was not unpleasant for many pilots, for it meant more opportunities to go out on the town. This was another monumental difference between earlier manifestations of VMF-214 and the current roster. Never before had married pilots been able to have their wives nearby, nor had the bachelors been in such close proximity to young ladies, particularly the coeds at the University of California campus in Santa Barbara.

Twenty-three-year-old Albert A. Sibbernsen, who had worked his family's large grain and livestock enterprise in Nebraska before the war, was enjoying a popular nightspot with Ken Linder and several other squadron mates when he met a young coed named Peggy Lindsey. For the midwestern farmer and the city girl from a Los Angeles suburb, it was love at first sight. Art Schmagel met another Santa Barbara student who hailed from Oxnard. Linder's girlfriend, Mickey O'Connor, was a coed from the University of Southern California whom he'd met two years earlier in the desert town of Barstow. It was an exciting wartime period of flying and parties and romance, and more than a few bachelors made a change in their marital status.

During workdays at the air station, little other than ground training could be accomplished until the weather finally broke on September 17. When it did, the pilots tried to recoup hundreds of hours' worth of practice bombing and gunnery flights lost during the first half of the month, but the ensuing weeks brought only on-again, off-again opportunities to fly. By the end of September the Black Sheep had logged only a few hundred hours—just a fourth of what had been planned.

October began with a week of good flying weather, and within a few days the Ordnance Department undertook tests on an aircraft that all hands were eager to observe. An F4U-1C had been acquired from North Island a couple of weeks before, but poor weather had prevented an opportunity to examine its distinctive weapons. Only two hundred of the model, which substituted four long-barreled 20mm automatic cannon for the six machine guns, had been built by Chance Vought. To compare capabilities, the C model and a conventional Corsair were set up to fire into two worn-out Curtiss trainers that were dragged to the rifle range to serve as targets.

The ordnancemen had been unable to obtain explosive shells for the cannons, but the results were impressive even though the standard projectiles passed right through the target. Sizable chunks were shredded from the fuselage of the F4U-1C's target, whereas the other was pocked with much smaller holes. Later the big-gunned Corsair was used for strafing runs. Red Free, who had occasion to try it, reported that the muzzle blast was powerful enough to slow the Corsair, even in a dive.

By early October the training syllabus had entered a holding pattern. The pilots were signed off on field carrier landing practice, bombing, strafing, gunnery, navigation, recognition, parachute dunking, survival, first aid, and a host of lesser requirements. They had to complete the night flying syllabus and were still waiting to carrier qualify, as were several other squadrons. In the meantime, there was little to do but cycle through some of the syllabus again. Despite occasional interruptions due to bad weather, the second lieutenants had accumulated hundreds of Corsair hours during the past seven months. One luxury of the delayed syllabus was extra flight time, which led to improved proficiency and increased confidence.

On Thursday, October 12, four divisions—part of a combined force of fifty Corsairs from several squadrons led by Stan Bailey—launched for a large-scale bombing of Wilson Rock. Six planes carried thousand-pound general-purpose bombs, and the rest made simulated attacks. After proceeding north to Point Conception, the fighter-bombers turned and made their runs. They actually bombed Castle Rock a few miles from Wilson, but the hits were good: three on the rock, three narrowly missing. The pilots soon discovered that the near misses were popular with local commercial fishermen, who bought drinks for the Marines for wiping out some of the sea lions that had been depleting their catch.

As the routine continued, the Black Sheep welcomed diversions. Cross-country flights were regularly scheduled to build up plenty of flight time while providing a change of pace from the local environment. Those from western states took small groups of planes to their hometowns, such as the Saturday in October when Carroll K. "Budd" Faught and Robert Jones flew to Laramie, Wyoming, to spend a night with Faught's family. The closest thing to a cowboy that VMF-214 had ever seen, Faught had ridden the rodeo circuit before the war and once demonstrated his prowess during a rodeo that was visiting Santa Barbara.

Weekends at Santa Barbara offered fun as well, particularly if the Sunday flight schedule called for "division tactics" in the afternoon. This was generally viewed as an excuse to do just about anything, although little of what these hot-blooded fighter pilots did with their two-thousand-horsepower Corsairs was actually legal. Some made sport out of flying down to the seaside amusement park at Long Beach, where they dived at the roller coaster and buzzed passengers at the apex of their already-dizzying ride. From there they tail-chased along the Pacific Coast Highway, Route 101, dropping down to the deck beyond Malibu, reefing Corsairs on wingtips to follow sharp curves, and breaching hills in the face of unsuspecting motorists. At the Seabee base at Port Hueneme, they looked for the flag indicating that the admiral was in; if it flew, it became their racing pylon. Their antics were nothing more than youthful exuberance mixed with impatience. They had gone as far as they could through the syllabus and were restless. Without an enemy to fight, flat-hatting was their way to measure gumption, even when flying over water. As Art Schmagel put it, "You weren't really in the division unless your prop put up a spray."

At the end of October the weather finally improved for night flying, and the Black Sheep logged a hundred hours in two nights, starting right after dinner and flying until nearly time for breakfast. The tempo continued into November but not without risk. On the afternoon of November 2, Bill Nabors ground-looped (the cause was blamed on a jammed throttle) and flipped his Corsair on its back. He escaped with a case of shock plus dirt in his eyes.

Then the rain and fog settled back in, allowing only sporadic periods of flying until the middle of the month. When clear skies returned, the familiar flying activities resumed, until a couple of weddings provided a change in routine. On November 17 Ken Linder and Mickey O'Connor tied the knot, followed by a similar ceremony a week later between Al Sibbernsen and Peggy Lindsey. Art Schmagel and his girlfriend, Margie, decided to wait "until after the Emergency," as folks still referred to the war, but their day would come.

By early December the squadron's future became suddenly clear, dictated by a situation in the far Pacific. Marine aviation was still on hold for carrier qualifications (they were not scheduled to deploy on small-decked CVEs until early 1945), but the onset of macabre suicides of "body-crashing" Japanese pilots had suddenly become widespread and were a major concern for the fast carriers. Five weeks earlier during the Battle of Leyte Gulf, several baby flattops were hit while supporting the landings in the Philippines. On October 29 *Intrepid* became the first of the fast carriers to be hit. The next day her sister ship, *Franklin,* had a thirty-five-foot hole blown in her flight deck and was forced to steam all the way to the West Coast for repairs. Then came hits on the new *Lexington* in early November, followed three weeks later by *Hancock, Essex,* the light carrier *Cabot,* and *Intrepid* again—all four on the same day. None of the big carriers sank, but by the end of November five smaller ships had and twenty-three others were heavily damaged by the terrifying new method that Robert Sherrod defined as "the single most effective air weapon developed by the Japanese in World War II."

The advent of the kamikazes brought pleas for help from the fast carriers, and virtually overnight the decision was made to put Marine fighters aboard for added protection. Concurrently, Marine air groups divided some squadrons into forward and rear echelons. The carriers needed more than a Marine squadron's twenty-four fighters but did not have room for two complete outfits. By creating forward echelons of eighteen aircraft manned at 150 percent (twenty-seven pilots), two squadrons could effectively participate. A side benefit was that squadron commanders could select the most cohesive or suitable group of pilots at their disposal.

In the case of VMF-214, veteran pilots were already established as division leaders. In selecting from among the many second lieutenants, Stan Bailey placed heavy emphasis on personality and compatability as he searched for a mix of pilots who could live and work together within the limited confines of a warship. He finally chose a slightly oversized group of thirty, including himself and the five senior division leaders (Major McPherson and four captains), plus 1st Lt. Ken Linder and twenty-three second lieutenants; thirteen others would have to stay behind. Cutting the latter group was not a simple task. All had hundreds of Corsair hours and most wanted to go, although a few decided they had not joined the Marine Corps to sail with the Navy, which made Bailey's decision easier. Ultimately some highly capable and understandably disappointed aviators were assigned to the rear echelon, soon be transferred to other units.

The squadron was still not ready for carrier qualifications because of a recently added component to the training syllabus. The Marines would deploy with Chance Vought's F4U-1D, the newest model of the Corsair and the first to come factory equipped with "racks and rails" for high-velocity aircraft rockets, or HVARs.* Prior to carrier qualifying, the Black Sheep would train with the rockets in the desert.

On December 5, the pilots of the forward echelon and fifty enlisted men from the Engineering and Ordnance Departments moved to MCAS El Centro on temporary assignment. Located at the extreme southern end of California, El Centro was described as being "about two streets long, just a little tiny town, and there was nothing but desert around." The uninhabited area was ideal for rocket training, and the dry climate ensured plenty of good flying weather. Because of the remote location, there was little for the pilots to do except fly, which was exactly why such training detachments were able to accomplish much in short order.

The Black Sheep, who had flown twenty-two of their own Corsairs to El Centro, commenced an additional round of field carrier landing practice before starting the rocket syllabus. For bounce drill they flew thirty miles east to a dusty outlying strip in the desert, performed their carrier approaches until it was time to refuel at the air station, then returned for more bouncing. The enlisted men sweated to keep the Corsairs flying, and most of the pilots concluded their requisite passes in only three days. In the meantime, training with the five-inch rockets began on December 7.

*The "A" in HVAR has been alternately reported as representing air, aerial, or artillery in various publications. The description comes from Naval Personnel Manual 103-45-13, "Aviation Ordnanceman."

Although the Black Sheep's current Corsairs did not have the factory rails, they were field modified to carry HVARs under the wings. The pilots learned to aim and fire them at horizontal targets on the desert floor while diving at forty-five- to sixty-degree angles. The accurate rockets whooshed away with long fingers of flame and slammed into targets with considerable destruction, leading early observers to name them "Holy Moses," and they gave a Corsair carrying a full load of eight the hitting power of a destroyer's broadside.

By December 11 the entire syllabus of bounce drill and rocket firing had been completed, all with only one plane slightly damaged during a ground loop. The Black Sheep returned to Santa Barbara the next day for more ground training on carrier procedures, which continued for days because there was a huge amount of information to absorb beyond knowing how to land aboard. There were light signals and hand signals used on deck, taxiing procedures, catapult techniques, voice calls when radios could be used and alternate procedures when they could not, and a long list of other lessons.

On the morning of December 16, in the middle of this training, unexpected orders for additional rocket training arrived. The men were watching carrier training films when Stan Bailey was called to hustle the Black Sheep over to the Marine Corps air station at Mojave, where a new kind of rocket had been tested in secrecy. Fortunately the ground crews had been spending the past days preparing the aircraft for carrier qualifications, so all twenty-three Corsairs currently in the inventory were ready to fly. After they took off, the rest of the pilots and some thirty-five enlisted men from Engineering and Ordnance jumped aboard a hastily arranged transport plane to follow.

The Black Sheep found MCAS Mojave to have a lot in common with El Centro. Both were small bases erected near an otherwise-insignificant crossroads in the middle of the

California desert, but in this case the crossroads was located between Rosamond and Tehachapi, on the western fringe of the vast Mojave Desert. Here the Black Sheep were introduced to a large rocket designed for use against capital warships or reinforced-concrete structures. Affectionately dubbed "Tiny Tim," the rocket had an 11.75-inch warhead that held about 150 pounds of TNT, but the extra punch of rocket propulsion gave it the destructive power of a 2,000-pound bomb. Normally the rockets would be mounted on the centerline rack of an F4U-1D (photographs also show them hanging from the inboard pylons), but the Black Sheep made do with a trapeze device on the centerline of their Dash-1As designed to swing the rocket clear of the propeller. Once the rocket had dropped the proper distance, a wire reel ignited the motor. At least one pilot swore he could hear the rocket go off over the sound of his Pratt & Whitney.

Tiny Tims left an impressive trail of smoke, but they were heavy and unpredictable, as Ken Linder learned.

> Boy, when you dropped that thing you went up about a thousand feet. They weren't very accurate: some would go off to the left, some to the right. We weren't essentially trying to hit a target—we were just dropping the damn things to see what would happen.

While at Mojave, the Black Sheep met the pilots of Maj. Charles P. "Pat" Weiland's VMF-452, a squadron commissioned ten months earlier at the desert base. Having undergone training for about as long as VMF-214, the men had been biding their time until the call arrived to go overseas. Now that the kamikazes were causing such a stir in the western Pacific, their time was nigh. The original Black Sheep's "King of the Yamheads," Jim Reames, was now Pat Weiland's flight surgeon. In another coincidence, Pat Weiland and Stan Bailey had been instructors and shared a house together in Pensacola prior to the war. Even with ten thousand pilots, Marine aviation was still in its own small world.

By late afternoon on December 20, the Black Sheep wrapped up their desert training with the Tiny Tims and were back at Goleta. Two days later, the squadron's separation into forward and rear echelons became official with the departure of ten pilots to the Marine detachment at Miramar for reassignment; three remained temporarily in the rear echelon. Just like that, a third of the pilots who had labored for so many months were out of the picture.

Christmas Eve and Christmas Day were quiet at Santa Barbara. The entire forward echelon, save for a flight of thirteen who performed a picturesque flying cross over the city, took advantage of two days of leave. This was not the case for Pat Weiland and VMF-452, who learned on Christmas Day that their remaining syllabus would be accelerated in order for them to join VMF-214 on the fast carrier *Franklin,* where they would integrate with Carrier Air Group 5.

If the Black Sheep already knew of the development, it was not recorded in any of the contemporary logs. Their attention was focused on new airplanes, for the next day brought a belated Christmas present in the form of four fresh F4U-1Ds. The fighters, with more weapons capability than that of their predecessors, were a welcome sight. Perhaps the most striking feature was the paint. Unlike the variegated blue-to-white color scheme that had adorned naval aircraft for many months (it was quick to fade and showed every smear of grease and dirt), the new planes were a businesslike glossy sea blue, so dark that from a distance it appeared almost black.

The Dash-1Ds were factory built as bona fide fighter-bombers, with four launching rails under each wing for HVARs, a centerline point for attaching a variety of stores or weapons, and two additional pylons inboard of the landing gear for Tiny Tims, bombs, external fuel tanks, or napalm. Another improvement was the addition of a small water tank and feeder system for the mighty Pratt & Whitney engine. By banging the throttle past a detent, the pilot could call up roughly two hundred extra horsepower for several minutes. Water injection permitted more fuel–air vapor to be burned without significantly raising the cylinder head temperature, but the 10 percent gain in power was a bonus intended only for combat use because of the water reservoir's limited capacity.

The day after Christmas, a few pilots departed for the naval air station at Santa Rosa, sixty miles north of San Francisco, where the Black Sheep and VMF-452 would soon join them to begin workups with Carrier Air Group 5. The expected transfer of the rest of the echelon was delayed for two days while the Bay Area was closed in by weather, but on December 29 the new Corsairs were ferried up while the remaining personnel arrived by transport. Flying came to a screeching halt, however, as dense fog prevailed for almost two weeks; even the pilots who drove to Naval Air Station, Alameda, to accept fourteen new Corsairs were socked in.

Peggy Sibbernsen, Mickey Linder, and the other young wives of the pilots had no complaints about the weather. Due to a lack of housing in Santa Rosa, several couples had rented cabins some twenty miles north in the Valley of the Moon: Jack London territory. The setting along the Russian River was most romantic, and the poor flying weather gave them a chance to celebrate the New Year with undivided attention. When the weather threatened to improve, Ken Linder joked, "Let's get out the fog machines and keep the planes on the ground!"

But nature finally had its way, and the skies cleared enough by January 11 to bring up the rest of the new Corsairs. The two Marine squadrons brought eighteen planes each and would eventually pare down their rosters to twenty-seven pilots. Unofficially they were formed as

VMF-5 under Stan Bailey's seniority, but few paid attention to the temporary designation and the units operated autonomously. Coordinated workups over the next several days involved strafing, navigation, and simulated attacks. Some took advantage of the time to practice additional field carrier landings after learning that qualifications aboard *Ranger* would begin in a few days.

Indeed the Corsairs were flown down to NAS Alameda on January 16 and hoisted aboard *Ranger,* which was tied up at the carrier pier. The veteran ship—she was called "old" even though she had been commissioned barely a decade earlier—sortied out to sea off the coast of California for carrier landings. She remained within range of alternate airfields in case pilots could not get aboard *Ranger* due to a fouled deck or other emergency. Seas were rough, bringing more than a few Marines the embarrassment of seasickness. The next morning when they arose before dawn to commence their qualifications, it did not help that the wardroom served "the most greasy pork sausages for breakfast." Stomachs tumbled again.

Successful qualification required eight arrested landings on *Ranger*'s deck. The flight deck officer was not concerned with who owned particular Corsairs when he spotted their sequence for takeoff runs, so Marines flew Navy Corsairs and vice versa. Ken Linder, for one, was not happy when his Navy-maintained Corsair with its poorly tuned engine barely pulled him down the flight deck.

After flying off the deck—a new experience for the junior members—the pilots turned left into the traffic pattern and headed downwind, opposite the ship's direction. Roughly abeam the carrier's island they began their approach turn toward the landing area on the flight deck, maintaining a steady left bank so that they could keep the landing area in sight. What no amount of field carrier landing practice could teach them was how to judge the relative motion of the ship itself. The "runway" moved at perhaps twenty-five knots, which created a steady wind along the deck. As the pilots turned in toward the ship, they visually acquired the LSO, who held his large paddles at arm's length and tilted them to mirror the pilot's wings relative to the deck. If an aircraft was out of position for a safe landing, the LSO crisscrossed the wands vigorously in a "waveoff." Otherwise a pilot looked for the "cut" signal as he crossed the deck's threshold with the correct glide slope, pitch angle, and airspeed. When he got the "cut," he chopped the throttle, and his aircraft literally dropped to the deck.

Stan Free's approach procedure was typical.

> I always turned it until the last second, and our LSO, named "Snowflake" Winters, gave me a roger most of the time. He'd slant me into the deck, then would always give me a back slant to tell me to level my wings before my "cut." From the time I'd turn above the plane guard destroyer and the LSO picked me up, it was a piece of cake. You just couldn't fly it in a straight line because you couldn't see over the nose. We'd try to approach at between seventy-three and seventy-five knots. If you were married you got seventy-five, and if you had a kid you got seventy-seven.

Ideally the tail hook snagged one of the dozen arresting cables and hauled the plane to a stop. If the aircraft bounced hard or the hook failed to grab a wire, the aircraft met a series of reinforced cables that were stretched between stanchions to serve as a barricade. Although the array was about four feet high and hopefully prevented runaway planes from hitting other aircraft parked forward, it did not always work out in favor of the errant pilot.

VMF-214's only mishap during qualifications occurred when Joseph E. Stout's F4U floated, clipped the barricade, and flipped onto its back. "We all thought he'd bought it right then," wrote John Stodd, who witnessed the accident from the bridge, "but he walked away with a knot on his head and a missing little finger." Apparently the canopy slammed shut on his finger; doctors closed the wound and he was allowed to finish qualifying.

When *Ranger* returned to Alameda, the planes were off-loaded and Air Group 5 flew back to Santa Rosa to make final preparations for a lengthy ocean deployment aboard the fast carrier *Franklin*. The Black Sheep spent the last days of January stenciling everything with their name and squadron number and packing their gear into steel footlockers. Twenty enlisted men from Engineering and Ordnance traveled to Bremerton Naval Yard in Washington and boarded the carrier as a small advance party to coordinate work and living spaces with the ship's company. During the first two days of February, Stan Bailey made the final cut to twenty-seven pilots; he sent three disappointed pilots to El Centro, where the remnants of the rear echelon had been transferred a few weeks earlier.

At Bremerton, repairs to *Franklin* were nearly complete. Designated CV-13, and affectionately called "Big Ben" by the crew, the carrier was the fifth in a long line of Navy ships named for colonial statesman Benjamin Franklin. Superstition over the hull number was reportedly minimal, even though a kamikaze had punched a big hole in the flight deck on October 30, 1944, killing fifty-six. As *Franklin* prepared to return to the Pacific combat theater, VMF-214's small party of support personnel joined the ship's company of approximately 2,500.

While *Franklin* steamed toward San Francisco on the night of February 1, the commander of Carrier Air Group 5, Comdr. Edwin B. Parker, Jr., launched his entire wing to put on a show for Santa Rosa, flying north to intercept the carrier at sea for a mock attack.

One detail of his operations order seemed simple enough—fighters were to be equipped with belly tanks—but the way it was written created havoc among the Marines. As Warner Chapman remembered it:

We'd all put on belly tanks, but the Navy was either biased or smarter than we and filled theirs up with gas. We were not told to fill them and went out with our tanks empty. The guys began to call in that they were running shy of gas and got permission to peel off and go home, and finally we were down to five Corsairs. I called the Commander and told him I was taking the rest of the Marine fighters in, that we were running low on fuel.

Chapman led his group toward the coast at right angles, but figuring that Santa Rosa was too far south for some to reach safely, he turned north. Having flown with Rafe Schocker to his Northern California hometown during the Christmas holiday, Chapman decided that Arcata was their closest bet. It was night and the weather was turning bad, one of those times when all the gremlins seemed to be out. When Chapman's group reached the coast near Mendocino, the site of an emergency airstrip, he called over the radio for anyone with less than twenty-five minutes of fuel to use the strip. Art Schmagel put down, then passed the long night with a little local help. "Some kid brought out some vension hamburger," he recalled, "and that's what I ate while I guarded my plane all night."

Red Free was able to stay with Chapman, although he had to employ his familiarity with the pilot's manual to squeeze a few minutes out of his dwindling fuel supply.

In the Corsair, minimum rpms was about 1350 to 1400, but the Pratt & Whitney book said that at that rpm you could set maximum manifold pressure. You'd think it would have blown the damn thing up, but that's what the book said, and that's what I did. You'd burn forty-eight gallons an hour, just back to nothing, and that's the only reason I made it.

It was raining, and it was night—a miserable deal. We scattered airplanes all over northern California because we had empty belly tanks. Commander Parker was a little bit pissed at the Marines: "What do you carry belly tanks for, if you don't put fuel in them!"

Although the Black Sheep managed to reach various fields safely, several other planes ditched—an ominous debut for Edwin Parker's new air group. The scattered planes returned to Santa Rosa the next day, and by February 3 the squadron had completed final preparations for boarding *Franklin* at Alameda. Three days of hard work ensued as the airplanes were flown to Alameda, and truckloads of spare parts, tools, administrative supplies, and personal baggage were delivered to the carrier pier. While the ship loaded her air group aboard, the Marines had an opportunity to explore.

Big Ben was impressive. Less than two years old, she was far bigger than the prewar *Ranger* and considerably faster with her four steam turbine–driven screws. The flight deck was comparatively luxurious at 872 feet long by 147 feet at the widest point, though the dimensions would still seem puny when landing aboard. Two sets of twin five-inch AA turrets braced each end of the tall superstructure amidships on the starboard side, and sponsons jutting from the hull supported sets of quadruple 40mm rapid-fire gun mounts. Smaller twin-40mm mounts and light 20mm automatic weapons appeared to be mounted anywhere they would fit. *Franklin* was armed to the teeth, a reassurance after hearing of the terrifying kamikazes.

After boarding the ship by a gangway, the Marines walked onto a designated area that served as the traditional quarterdeck, part of the vast hangar deck. This was essentially *Franklin*'s busiest deck, where work was often conducted twenty-four hours a day. The open-air space began near the bow and extended all the way to the fantail, with room for dozens of aircraft to be parked, repaired, armed, even started and warmed up. Plenty of overhead allowed for the height of the big Corsairs and even Curtiss SB2C dive-bombers with their wings folded steeplelike. Wherever there was space, scores of spare drop tanks and propellers hung from above, though much of that space was festooned with electrical conduits, air ducts, fuel lines, and water and steam lines. Near the fantail, a fully equipped engine shop repaired and maintained a supply of spare radial engines, with room to test them on wheeled stands after they were rebuilt.

The rectangular flight deck was erected like a roof over the huge hangar, and the low-ceilinged gallery deck was sandwiched in between. Here were officers' staterooms, squadron ready rooms, wardrooms, catapult equipment, "admiral's country" (staff offices), and the fighting brain of the ship—the combat information center.

As the Marines ascended steep ladders from the hangar deck to find their ready room, they discovered a labyrinth of shiny linoleum passageways that zigged and zagged around structures—such as the two center-deck aircraft elevators—interrupted every few feet by oval watertight doors. Defining each of the ship's massive frames, these vertical "walls" gave *Franklin* its integral strength by creating compartments that could be sealed off to prevent the spread of flooding or fire. The openings were not tall, enabling doors to be dogged tight, so that walking quickly through dozens of these down the length of the ship took practice. The curved lower sills (called "knee-knockers") and the top arch (lower than an upright man's head) required one to step high and duck low at the same moment every fourth or fifth step, leading to a peculiar gait.

VMF-214's ready room, originally designed for a dive-bomber squadron's separate teams of pilots and enlisted gunners, was spacious. Located amidships on the port side, just aft of the deck-edge elevator, it had an exit onto the catwalk below the flight deck for easy access to aircraft. It was equipped with high-backed chairs built on heavy steel frames to prevent them from sliding. Similar to airline seats, they featured a folding desktop and comfortable cushions. Best of all, they reclined. Pilots traditionally spent most of their nonflying time here, and the chairs served as their office. Any men not asleep in bunk rooms, eating in the wardroom, flying, or using the head utilized this as their communal living room. Here the men smoked, studied, wrote letters, chatted, played acey-deucey, and prepared for flights. Because the latter was the room's intended function, the walls were adorned with chalkboards for briefings and charts for navigation, and the room was connected to the ship's communications: two-way intercom, telephones, teletype machines, the sound-powered talker, and the public address system.

As for living quarters, majors and captains rated a share of various staterooms (Stan Bailey and Pat Weiland had a comfortable two-man room), but the junior officers were jammed into a space just above the fo'c'sle known as "Boystown." Their bunks were stacked three high and were crowded so tightly that only a small locker was available to stow personal belongings. The enlisted men would probably have considered Boystown spacious, crowded as they were on the mess deck, but eventually everyone found a place.

Franklin's departure was set for the afternoon of February 7. The Black Sheep bid heartrending good-byes to wives or girlfriends and made last-minute phone calls to hometown families. Among the married Black Sheep, at least one hugged a protruding belly: 2d Lt. Oscar D. Urbom's wife, Jerry, was seven months pregnant. Several young brides remained in the Valley of the Moon while the men drove down to Alameda, not learning until later—with regret—that they could have boarded *Franklin* to say their farewells and visit the behemoth that would be their husbands' home for a while.

At 1645 that Wednesday afternoon, *Franklin* slipped her moorings at the Alameda pier and was nudged out into San Francisco Bay. Once under way, she steamed past Treasure

Island and turned west by south, passing under the graceful Golden Gate Bridge as many magnificent warships had done before. She was not destined, however, to steam under it again.

19

INFERNO

The Black Sheep had almost six quiet days to settle into the new routine of shipboard life. *Franklin*'s flight deck was crammed with all manner of cargo besides aircraft, making her transit to Pearl Harbor a cruise as far as the squadron was concerned. She tied up at Ford Island at noon on Tuesday, February 13, spent two days off-loading cargo and receiving supplies, then commenced two weeks of operational training for the air group.

The remainder of February turned disastrous. The Marines launched their Corsairs on February 16 to simulate strikes on the carrier, including live strafing against a target sled towed in the ship's wake. Reeled out on several hundred yards of cable, the sled kicked up a rooster tail, an ideal moving target, and the pilots' accuracy could be easily judged by the splashing bullets. Not only did the strafing exercise become a free-for-all this day, something went wrong in Rafe Schocker's division. Second Lieutenants Clare R. Beeler and Herbert D. Scramuzza banged together in midair—some later claimed that elements of VMF-452 dived through them—and both Corsairs plunged into the sea. Only one chute was seen, a streamer; neither body was recovered.

The following day's operations improved only slightly. During an exercise involving navigation away from the ship prior to a practice strike, Frank Barker and Dallas L. Hyatt became separated from the flight and decided to land at an alternate site. Barker managed to make it to the naval air station at Barbers Point, but Hyatt's Corsair developed an oil leak and he was forced to make a belly landing on the big island, Hawaii. He eventually made it back to Oahu, but the aircraft was written off.

Hyatt's news turned even worse. One of his two brothers had already been killed in the war, and now he learned that the other was dead. The armed forces were not without compassion in such situations. After five Sullivan brothers died when their cruiser *Juneau* blew up during the naval battle of Guadalcanal in November 1942, measures were enacted to prevent other families from losing all their sons. Dick Hyatt insisted on remaining with the Black Sheep; Stan Bailey conceded but removed him from the flight schedule.

When *Franklin* returned to Pearl Harbor on February 20 for her final restocking, the Black Sheep flew their planes to Ewa for night field carrier practice. Over the next several days each pilot hopped over to Barbers Point to log five periods of thirty-minute bounce drill in preparation for night qualifying on the carrier. None looked forward to landing on the ship after dark. Since the fiasco over Santa Rosa a few weeks earlier, the Marine contingent had not been in good standing with air group commander Edwin Parker, and the recent rash of accidents was a portent of more trouble. The Black Sheep wrapped up night practice on the twenty-seventh and flew out to trap aboard *Franklin* in bright sunshine the next day, only to encounter another nightmare.

Ralph W. Husted, Jr., made a normal approach to *Franklin,* plopped down his shiny blue Corsair just slightly left of center, and rolled toward the eighth of twelve wires rigged across the broad deck. Two crewmen were so certain of a successful trap that they emerged from the catwalks on either side and ran toward the plane, ready to disengage the tail hook and guide him forward. But as Husted's airplane jerked to a stop, the drop tank mounted on the belly broke loose and skidded through the spinning propeller, splitting open and spraying its contents across the deck. A spark ignited the fuel and the spray became a blowtorch, blown aft by the wind until the searing yellow-white cloud obliterated all but a few feet of the Corsair's wingtips. Husted never got out. Burning fuel flowed across the flight deck, its Douglas fir planks burning so persistently that damage control teams had to struggle for an hour to subdue the blaze. Later that day, Husted's remains were buried at sea. He was only the second of seven Black Sheep killed in the past year whose body was recovered.

A distraught Stan Bailey had called for replacements from the pilot pool less than two weeks earlier, when Beeler and Scramuzza were killed, and now he had to call for a third. First Lieutenant John L. Vandegrift along with second lieutenants Walter C. Berndt and Robert J. McDonnell became the newest Black Sheep.

From the Marines' perspective, the lone bright spot during the operational training period came when Air Group 5's naval squadrons attempted to night-qualify aboard *Franklin*. Pilots in VF-5 (Corsairs), VB-5 (Curtiss SB2C Helldivers), and VT-5 (Grumman TBM Avengers) collectively damaged some twenty-three aircraft, and the Marines' qualification was canceled. The pilots breathed a huge sigh of relief.

Early on the morning of March 3, *Franklin* put to sea again, this time steaming west at high speed for the war zone. During the ten-day transit to Ulithi atoll, in the western Carolines, the Black Sheep acquired sea legs by flying their share of combat air patrols and sub searches. For veteran Marines such as Stan Bailey, Warren McPherson, and others, this was the life. The carrier was luxurious compared to their earlier experience with leaky tents and dismal food in the Solomon Islands. Some grew tired of pineapples at every meal after departing Hawaii, but among those who had seen the worst there were no complaints about the food, or of sleeping on soft mattresses with clean sheets. Only the junior pilots in Boystown were disturbed now that flight operations had resumed: They were directly under an ear-splitting catapult.

The Black Sheep were spared further accidents during the transit, though a few pilots encountered minor difficulties. Ken Linder was repeatedly waved off while trying to land one day, which forced *Franklin* to hold into the wind that much longer—a vulnerability that infuriated *Franklin*'s skipper, Capt. Leslie E. Gehres. Described by one historian as "a pompous martinet," Gehres—a Navy pilot first (like all carrier skippers)—was not thrilled to have Leathernecks aboard his ship. He was already agitated because three Black Sheep had been killed during what should have been routine daylight operations. Linder finally got aboard, but Gehres threatened to put him off at Ulithi. Stan Bailey went to bat for his pilot and Linder made good on the next flight, setting a record for trapping aboard the instant that *Franklin* came into the wind. Nothing more was said. Air group commander Edwin Parker even assigned Linder as the section leader in his own division.

There was a brief scare involving Red Free and his wingman, who returned from a sub search and could not find the ship. Free's description reveals the pressure the Marines were under.

> We went out and did our triangle and came back, and the carrier wasn't where it was supposed to be. Holy mackerel. We started doing a square search, but all of a sudden out of a squall came the carrier. It was where it was supposed to be, but so was that squall. It made me feel awfully good to know that we hadn't screwed up.

On Tuesday morning, March 13, CV-13 steamed into the enormous anchorage at Ulithi atoll. Only two days previously, kamikazes had attacked the facility, one causing a spectacular fire on the fantail of the carrier *Randolph,* the other hitting a small island. But to anyone gazing around the anchorage this day, the attempt must have seemed puny. Stretched across the width of the enormous lagoon like stepping-stones were the long, straight decks of at least fifteen carriers, joined by a hundred or more support vessels to form the largest armada of warships ever assembled. This was Task Force 58, preparing to sortie to the Japanese Home Islands, where the carriers would launch air strikes as a prelude to the invasion of Okinawa.

The day after *Franklin*'s arrival, the sultry voice of Iva Ikuko Toguri came on the radio. Although the American-born graduate of UCLA introduced herself as "your favorite playmate and enemy, Orphan Annie," Toguri was known throughout the Pacific by another name: Tokyo Rose.

Red Free remembered that she had a particular message for them.

> She welcomed the carrier *Franklin* and VMF-214, saying they had lots of kamikazes waiting for us and that kind of crap. She named the squadron and named Major Bailey. It was hard to believe, since we had just come in the evening before. They piped it through the speaker system, and we all looked at each other and said, "What the hell's going on?" It was creepy.

Franklin departed Ulithi that morning as Adm. Marc Mitscher's enormous fleet got under way. Soon after, Warner Chapman's division launched to put on a napalm demonstration for the benefit of Rear Adm. Ralph E. Davison, who was flying his flag from *Franklin*'s yardarm as commander of Task Group 58.2. The Black Sheep had practiced dropping napalm in the desert, but the devilish brew was not altogether trusted. Made from *nap*hthene and *palm*itate (or, in lay terms, a blend of petroleum and soap), napalm was poured into drop tanks. Designed to ignite on contact with the ground, the goo splashed across targets and clung tenaciously, burning whatever it touched. Because any ship captain's worst nightmare was a fire at sea, carrier aircraft were absolutely prohibited from landing aboard with a hung napalm tank.

Chapman recalled:

> We were told to drop on a deserted island, and if we had some difficulty and couldn't get rid of [the napalm], to come back and bail out over the fleet and they would pick us up. Of course, mine didn't come off, so I called to an island where there was a coral strip and told them, "I'm going to come in and bounce it real hard on the runway. If it comes off, it's going to do you no damage, because it will just bounce along the coral and burn, and I'll just keep going out to the carrier."
>
> It did not come off, so I landed, and had to take some time while they removed it. I went out to the ship, and by then the other three planes had already landed. Task Force 58 was en route to Japan and here I was, showing up contrary to the instructions I had. *Franklin* turned into the wind to pick me up and I gave a magnificent exhibition of thoughtful flying. I came in the first time with my flaps up and got a waveoff. I came in the second time with my wheels up and got a waveoff. I was told to land the next time or else land in the water. I came in.

Throughout the daylight hours of the next three days, the Black Sheep participated in constant air and sub patrols that ranged to all points of the compass around the mighty force, logging hour after hour of successful carrier operations. More important, they returned every time to land aboard without incident, finally proving themselves worthy of the decision to send Marine fighters to sea.

On Sunday morning, March 18, *Franklin* steamed at seventeen knots in the upper reaches of the Philippine Sea, approximately 135 miles southeast of Kyushu—southernmost of the main islands in the Japanese home empire. The indispensable combat air patrol (CAP) was launched first, followed by a photo sweep of Kagoshima and Izumi on the western shore. Stan Bailey and four divisions of Black Sheep, who had risen early to brief their first combat mission against the Japanese, now sat inside their Corsairs as the engines warmed. They were hunched in leather flight jackets to ward off the predawn chill of winter on the open ocean.

When their turn to launch arrived, they followed the lighted wands of deck handlers and plane directors. Those aircraft positioned too far forward for deck runs were catapulted; those with room available used the more expedient rolling takeoff. (It took precious time to align a plane on a catapult and connect it to a bridle.) The morning's mission called for Bailey's fighters to sweep the sky before striking Izumi's large airfield, hangars, barracks, and supply dumps. The Corsairs were each fully loaded with HVARs, machine-gun ammunition, and a thousand-pound bomb.

Coasting in over Kagoshima, Stan Bailey found no aerial opposition—the complete opposite of the expected fierce resistance—and turned north toward Izumi, spreading his sixteen fighter-bombers into a line abreast that covered half a mile. The parking apron on Izumi was surprisingly crowded with aircraft. Antiaircraft fire was only moderate, described as "mostly little BBs," which enabled the adrenaline-pumped Marines to aim their rockets at parked planes. For many, it was their first time looking down the barrels of enemy guns as angry puffs of airbursts and glowing balls of tracer snaked toward them. Diving down, they launched salvos from a distance, then got set to pickle their bombs.

Red Free had not dropped many bombs of this type during training, and in the excitement of firing his rockets he forgot about one of the thousand-pounder's features: A small cartridge punched it off the centerline to ensure that it cleared the Corsair's prop. When Free pulled the release handle he smelled smoke and blurted, "I'm hit! I'm hit!" Although Stan Bailey shot back a query to find out who was in trouble, the chagrined lieutenant later admitted: "You talk about the sound of silence; I never said a damn word."

Just as the Corsairs were egressing over the sea, John Stodd's plane was hit squarely in the engine. The war diary blamed a Zeke, but witnesses (including Stodd himself) maintain that ground fire knocked it out. He staggered through the air for several seconds before ditching a thousand yards beyond the beach, then got into his rubber boat and began paddling furiously. The other Black Sheep circled overhead while waiting for the submarine that was hopefully on station as a rescue picket, but within a few minutes an armed sampan headed straight for Stodd. Stan Bailey ordered his men not to strafe it, lest the Japanese capture Stodd anyway and kill him for retribution. Regretfully the Sheep had to depart shortly thereafter; the Corsairs were low on fuel and another wave of carrier aircraft was due to strike in a few minutes. This was of no consolation to Stodd, though their compliance may well have saved his life.

Stan Free later recalled that the men derived some humor from the incident.

> We kidded him about it, and said we flew cover over him, but he said, "You're damn liars. You bastards left immediately; you didn't stay to help me one bit." He was in his little yellow raft, and had a wake behind him like he had a five-horsepower motor on the back.

There was nothing funny, however, about being captured. The patrol boat approached with a machine gun and "about ten guys with rifles" pointed at Stodd, who realized that his combat career had lasted exactly half of a mission. He was plucked from the water and received decent treatment initally (thanks to Stan Bailey's foresight), then was handed over to the Army once ashore. Blindfolded, bound hand and foot, he was tossed into the back of a truck and driven off.

Stodd had the sinking realization during the ride that his captors had likely come from the same air base he had just attacked, and another strike was due at any moment. The truck was probably on a perimeter road when the attack arrived.

> The truck came to a skidding stop, the Japs went over the side and I was left lying in the truck bed. Until then, I had never realized what a noise those HVARs make coming in, but I was consoled by the thought that their targets were on the field and not over here on the road, until it also occurred to me that somebody might decide to strafe the truck and I'd end up getting knocked off by one of my own buddies.

One Japanese, strong or scared or both, picked up Stodd from the truck bed and carried him to the ditch, where they kept their heads down until the strike passed, then they boarded the truck and resumed driving for the rest of the day. After reaching an Army establishment, Stodd was interrogated by a major who was "most gentlemanly." But the next morning he was placed on a train with a warning that his future treatment would not be so congenial. The major was right.

Fifteen Black Sheep returned to *Franklin* from the strike and landed aboard with precision. Chapman trapped first and the rest followed with intervals as tight as twenty seconds, which he knew looked "pretty damn good." The second strike was also successful and the Black Sheep contingent returned intact, but for the day *Franklin* lost four Corsairs with only one Navy pilot rescued.

It was a long night aboard the carrier. No less than a dozen times the public address system blared, "General quarters! General quarters! All hands man your battle stations!" while a loud Klaxon gonged. The pilots reported to the ready room and tried to rest in their recliners until the voice intoned, "Secure from general quarters." They then crawled back to their bunks, only to have the whole scene repeated.

Finally it was time for the predawn fliers to brief the next day's CAP and sub patrols. The other pilots were restless as well. About half the Black Sheep would participate in a predawn fighter sweep that would precede a mass strike on Kure and Kobe harbors, on the main island of Honshu. An hour before daylight on Monday morning, Stan Bailey and his three fighter sweep divisions manned their planes, then watched as deck crewmen moved from plane to plane, signaling for engine starts, until some forty-five Corsairs had rumbled to life. While waiting for cylinder-head temperatures to warm, the pilots maintained their night vision under the soft glow of red instrument lights.

At 0530 *Franklin* had closed to within fifty-five miles of Kyushu as she turned into the wind to launch the patrols and fighter sweep. It has been reported that these Corsairs were armed with Tiny Tims, but such was not the case. The divisions of Black Sheep led by Stan Bailey, Warren McPherson, and Frank Barker were equipped with HVARs. The twelve Corsairs represented nearly all of the squadron's remaining aircraft, now that five of the eighteen hoisted aboard at Alameda had been lost. Second Lieutenant William H. Dancy, Jr., was unable to start his plane and was pushed onto the deck-edge elevator to make room for others to depart. Someone took Dancy's place as the Corsairs roared skyward one by one, but in the darkness no one could tell for certain who it was.

An hour after the first launch, dawn began to materialize into a gray, cloudy day as the main strike prepared for takeoff. Ken Linder, still assigned to group commander Parker's division, manned a Corsair, fitted with HVARs, near the front of the pack. Some of the aircraft behind him were armed with Tiny Tims, others with bombs or a combination of weapons.

Parker, the strike leader, rolled down *Franklin*'s deck a

few minutes before 0700. Normally Linder would have been third in line, but he encountered starter trouble of his own and got shoved onto the deck-edge elevator. Within a minute or two he got the engine started and signaled a director, who guided him out for a deck-run launch. Three or four planes had departed ahead of him, making Linder perhaps the seventh plane airborne. The time was approximately 0705.

Twelve Black Sheep pilots had departed CV-13's deck; fourteen remained on board. Most of those who stayed lounged in the ready room, dressed in flight gear in anticipation of taking off after the first strike returned. Budd Faught, the part-time cowboy from Laramie, stood near a wall chart to study their expected route to the enemy coast. Warner Chapman "flaked out" on his reclining chair, his right leg and arm draped casually across a padded armrest. Bill Dancy came down from the flight deck after failing to get airborne with the fighter sweep. Al Sibbernsen headed down an interior passageway en route from the combat information center. Rafe Schocker slept in; he no longer had a division to lead now that Stodd, Beeler, and Scramuzza were either missing or dead. Art Schmagel dialed the telephone in Boystown and told his wingman, Bob Hugler, to get to the ready room for the next flight's briefing, then Schmagel exited onto the port catwalk to watch the current launch in progress. He always learned something by observing other pilots.

Many of the Black Sheep ordnance and engineering troops stood in line for chow. The task group's radar screens had been empty of bandits since the last secure from general quarters, and the readiness of the ship was slightly relaxed to give the crew an opportunity to eat. Hungry after hours at GQ or preparing aircraft for the day's strikes, the men formed a long line that stretched from the galley up a ladder to the hangar deck and snaked among parked aircraft and bomb carts. Although weapons were usually armed on the flight deck, they were being loaded this morning on the hangar deck as well, with Captain Gehres's authorization. High-octane refueling lines were in use, and the sliding doors of the cavernous hangar bays were open to the outside.

From his spot near the deck-edge elevator, Art Schmagel watched a plane approach *Franklin* from the bow. TBMs from far-off carriers in other task groups were regularly used to drop messages, and this aircraft's approach gave him no cause for concern, at least at first.

> This airplane came from bow to stern below the island, and I said, "message drop my rear end—that's a meatball!" It was a radial-engined Judy. I was standing in the port catwalk opposite our ready room when this thing came roaring down the deck, and all of a sudden the whole world turned to muck. I was on my hands and knees and had to put my hands over my eyes. My God, I was on the barbeque.

The lone Japanese plane was a Yokosuka D4Y Judy dive-bomber, successor to the Val and one of the few single-engine aircraft ever produced in both radial and in-line versions. Detected only seconds before because of conflicting radar blips from *Franklin*'s departing strike, it dived virtually unopposed from a cloud. The sleek bomber—not a suicider, as was frequently reported—released two 250-kilogram bombs as it raced the length of *Franklin*'s deck at mast height.

The ensuing carnage was a dive-bomber's dream. Both bombs struck the deck, one piercing just aft of the forward elevator and detonating inside the busy hangar, the other landing among the planes parked aft. Five Helldivers, fourteen Avengers, and a dozen Corsairs waited with engines idling for their turn to take off. The thirty-one aircraft were fully fueled and armed, some with Tiny Tims. Whether the second bomb exploded among them or had a delayed fuse and passed through to the hangar is uncertain, but the end result was the same.

The horror of the chain reaction that followed could never be adequately described, but anyone who has exploded a large firecracker inside a tin can has a basic idea of the expanding forces that occurred instantaneously within the hangar. Ruptured fuel lines and fuel tanks ignited in sequence, creating a holocaust that raced along the overhead, shot out of the open bays, and spread the length of the hangar in the time it takes to read this sentence. Hardly anyone would have been able to react before being engulfed by searing heat and shock waves. Men standing in line for breakfast, mechanics repairing planes, ordnancemen fitting bombs and rockets—all were immolated where they fell save for a few individuals blown through the openings, and many of those never knew what hit them or were drowned in the cold ocean.

Even with the big doors open, there was far more pressure inside than the overhead structure could withstand. The thirty-two-ton forward elevator burst from its well on a geyser of flame and smoke, then fell back into the hole at a crazy angle. The gallery deck overhead buckled violently upward as though pounded from below by a giant fist.

In the Black Sheep ready room the lounging pilots were caught completely by surprise. The heaving gallery deck crushed several against the overhead and left survivors with grave injuries from the concussion. Warner Chapman's heavy chair protected his torso, but it rammed up and neatly snapped the bones of his draped arm in two places. A chunk of shrapnel broke his dangling right ankle. Budd Faught was standing; his leg bones, absorbing the full impact, shattered below both knees. Bill Dancy likewise suffered two broken legs. The Black Sheep's nonpilot adjutant, Capt. Roger W. Conant, was killed outright. Three pilots were relatively unscathed only because they were not in the ready room—at least not all the way. Al Sibbernsen was on the balls of his feet with his legs flexed, caught literally in the act of stepping through the oval doorway. Rafe Schocker, having slept in, was tumbled from his stateroom bunk. Bob McDonnell, one of the replacement pilots, was also unhurt. Other pilots, Bob Hugler among them, simply disappeared.

A nightmare of darkness and confusion greeted Al Sibbernsen as he gained the ready room. Every light was smashed, and the collapsed overhead had spewed ductwork, piping, wiring, and ceiling material in a jumbled mess. As the dust and smoke settled, he could see through a rent in the deck to the hangar below—a view into hell. Those who could move made their way toward the port catwalk; some, including Faught and Dancy, had to drag themselves. A badly dazed Warner Chapman got to his feet despite his broken ankle. "I wasn't keenly aware of those injuries at that particular moment," he recalled. "I heard people calling for help, and somehow realized that I couldn't help them."

Art Schmagel had not remained on the catwalk for long. Planes on the flight deck had exploded in rapid sequence and sent curtains of fire rolling across the deck. There was little hope for the pilots in them. Many who did escape from cockpits ran blindly into whirling propellers as the planes bounced and burst apart in cartwheeling pieces. Flames cascaded over Schmagel; he dropped to his knees and covered his eyes with unprotected hands. What saved him was the flight gear: a thick rubber Mae West on his torso and one of the newly introduced g suits strapped around his legs. After the flames passed, only the air bladders remained; the rest was charred nylon, which stuck to the remnants of his khaki flight suit. His face and hands were badly burned.

When Schmagel could look up again, he saw that the whole carrier was afire.

> There was no place to go, and the only thing I could see doing was to go overboard. I reached up and grabbed

> a wire and went over the side. I hit the water like a ton of bricks. The next thing I knew I was going down, down, down . . . then there was a realization, like somebody tapped me on the head and said, "You'd better get up if you're ever going to get back to the surface."

Without knowing exactly what happened—he believes that training took over and he yanked on the toggles of his Mae West—Schmagel shot to the surface. It was difficult to swim in the choppy water with the vest inflated as he tried to reach a cork-lined raft. He forever memorized a vivid image of an ordnanceman he knew, sitting astride the raft with his face "just burned black," urging him to swim.

Schmagel finally hooked an arm over the side of the raft, then glanced up in utter surprise as the bow of a destroyer suddenly appeared.

> I could see both sides. It seemed like the bow raised up and came down and hit the raft. I don't know where everybody went, but I went scooting by the starboard side of the destroyer. There was a cargo net down, and I grabbed ahold of that net.

Too weak to climb the net, Schmagel hung on until a burly sailor came over the side, carried him like a sack of wheat, and dumped him onto the deck of the destroyer *Hickox*. Schmagel did not see the badly burned ordnanceman again, but "Tilly" Tilton soon appeared. He may have been on *Franklin*'s catwalk near Schmagel, for the two suffered nearly identical burns.

Warner Chapman and several others reached *Franklin*'s port catwalk, but flames fore and aft eventually forced them over the side. Chappie tried in vain to release the pelican hook on a life-raft container, but he was still too dazed to realize that he was trying with his useless broken arm. For an unknown period of time he remained on the catwalk, later recognizing this as "further evidence that I was in shock." At times the catwalk seemed empty, then someone would drift into his field of vision and jump overboard. Finally his head cleared and he realized that jumping was his only recourse. Although he had never attended preflight survival training, he had heard that the safest way to jump was feet first, with the face covered with one hand and the crotch with the other. "I followed those instructions, but peeked through my fingers and saw that I was falling just absolutely flat," he recalled. "It was a seventy-foot drop and I was waiting for a monumental belly flop."

What Chapman did not realize was that *Franklin* was still moving at some twenty-five knots, and he knifed into the waves like a torpedo. He popped up clear of *Franklin*'s churning propellers, then came upon Al Sibbernsen on the surface nearby, along with a sailor in hysterics. Chapman quieted him by exhaling each breath through the emergency whistle he wore around his neck.

Chapman, who had not been wearing a Mae West when he jumped, orally inflated the bladders of his g suit, which gave him "all the confidence in the world." Sibbernsen then propped him up while he removed his shoes. From the bottoms of the troughs in the choppy seas, they could not see *Franklin,* although its location was clearly marked by the huge pillar of smoke rising into the sky. When they rose to the peaks of the waves, they could see bright flames and flying debris as the carrier's upper decks were ripped apart by explosions.

The men spent twenty-five minutes in the chilly water before the destroyer *Marshall* reached them. Like most of the survivors, too exhausted to move, Chapman could only hook an arm through the ship's cargo net. A sailor jumped in the water and tied a rope around Chapman's waist, then more helping hands pulled him aboard. Al Sibbernsen came up in fairly good shape.

Dozens of explosions shook *Franklin* as bombs and rockets detonated in several places simultaneously. Tiny Tims whooshed spectacularly off the flight deck and into the sea, or cooked off in the hangar and slammed into bulkheads. As they tore through the wreckage, they added to the havoc. The ready ammunition lockers for the five-inch AA turrets and automatic cannons began to erupt. One particularly volcanic blast lifted the 27,000-ton carrier and forcibly spun her to starboard. Captain Gehres had already ordered the main magazines flooded, but most of the electrical panels in the damage control center were knocked out. It was not until later that the magazines were discovered completely dry; the water mains had burst.

The recurrent explosions became ever more perilous for those in the vicinity of the gallery and flight decks, so Budd Faught's escape from the catwalk with two shattered legs was especially harrowing. He was helped by his division leader, Robert Jones, who nine months earlier had stirred the troops with his one-wheel landing at Santa Barbara. Despite burns on his arms and face, Jones inflated Faught's g suit and helped the badly wounded pilot work his way over the side. Faught dangled by an arm from the framework, then dropped into the sea just as an explosion swept the catwalk. Jones vanished.

Faught may have been one of the last Black Sheep into the water. Latched onto a cushion with his legs dangling behind him, he waited for rescue. Although *Franklin* was slowing, it had outdistanced the destroyers that crawled among the flotsam to pick up swimmers. By the time *Marshall* finally reached Faught, it had already hauled more than two hundred survivors out of the water. Bill Dancy was among them. He and Faught were bundled in blankets and rushed to sick bay, where doctors attended to their legs.

Franklin continued to burn and explode as it listed sharply to starboard and lost headway. When her boilers eventually went out, the mighty ship coasted to a stop. She was dead in the water only a few dozen miles from the enemy coast. The cruiser *Santa Fe* came alongside and, in a masterful display of seamanship, Capt. Harold Fitz jammed her bow into *Franklin*'s starboard side. With the two ships stuck fast, Captain Gehres ordered all aviation personnel off his carrier; some eight hundred survivors were transferred onto the cruiser. Rafe Schocker walked to safety, probably accompanied by Bob McDonnell, one of the replacements who had joined at Hawaii.

Seven pilots—Art Schmagel, Ranson Tilton, Budd Faught, Bill Dancy, Warner Chapman, Al Sibbernsen, and John Vandegrift—were pulled from the water, which left five Black Sheep dead or unaccounted for. Robert Jones was listed among the missing, although Budd Faught thought he had disappeared in the catwalk explosion. Dewey Urbom—whose wife, Jerry, was by now eight months pregnant—was seen in the water but never reappeared. He was one among scores who got off the ship but drowned before they could be rescued. No one knew exactly what happened to Dick Hyatt, who had been grounded to prevent his family from losing all three sons, or to Joe Stout, who lost a pinky finger on *Ranger* but still qualified, or to Bob Hugler; they were never found. The toll among the Black Sheep's enlisted men on CV-13 was even worse. In an eerie coincidence, thirteen were listed as killed in action—they were standing in the chow line—and thirteen others were missing.

Ken Linder was lucky to be in the air, and his luck turned even better. After lifting off the flight deck run he turned to port, then proceeded downwind to rendezvous with Commander Parker. As he passed abeam *Franklin* and was climbing through a thousand feet, a Japanese plane suddenly appeared up ahead.

> I charged the guns and started shooting at him. I could see the sparklers hitting him, and the air group commander slid over and shot him a few times. The guy tried to get away. It was a cloudy day, with clouds at maybe fifteen hundred to two thousand feet, and the Jap pulled

up into this little cloud. By this time I was almost flying wing on him—I was right up next to him. I was fascinated; instead of blowing him out of the sky I was flying wing. We got into this cloud and were on our backs. I figured, "Hell, at fifteen hundred feet I'm not going to pull out of it," so I rolled out and watched him come out of the cloud and go straight into the drink.

At this time, neither I nor anybody else in the air knew that the ship had been hit, and we were feeling pretty exuberant because we'd shot down a Jap. We circled around, and there was the ship blowing up. It was a sight to see, blowing like crazy. All the gas lines were flowing, the bays were open, everything was exploding—including those Tiny Tims on the fantail.

Commander Parker gathered the few *Franklin* planes to get aloft, and they joined with other aircraft en route to a strike on Osaka harbor. In the meantime, the Black Sheep on Stan Bailey's earlier fighter sweep, which had encountered little aerial opposition (two fired on a pair of JAAF *Ki*-84 Franks that flashed by, without result), proceeded to strafe and rocket Itami airfield near Osaka.

A few months later Bailey wrote of the attack.

Not one Jap fighter opposed us as we attacked hangars and planes on the ground. We gave the hangars a good working over, damaged about 40 grounded planes and headed for Kobe harbor. A few Zekes jumped us en route. I got two in my sights but my guns refused to fire each time. Before we could square away again, the Japs turned tail and beat it. We went on to the harbor, shot up a freighter and a transport, got in a few rocket hits on other craft, and picked out an airfield on Shikoku Island for our last target. We caught the Nips napping, with planes parked wingtip to wingtip down the runways. It was a perfect setup. We came in at hangar height and opened up with all we had right on down the flight lines.

After firing his rockets, Red Free saw a destroyer steaming into the Inland Sea "just like it was going under the Golden Gate bridge." He turned to strafe it, but the warship began furiously flashing blinker code. After consulting his plotting board, he recognized the code of the day. The American destroyer was racing far into the bay to rescue downed aviators.

Free pulled away just before receiving a radio call.

> Somebody from the Air Group called us and said to break off our attack, conserve fuel and return to Dixie Base, which is what our carrier was called. As we flew out we could see a column of smoke, and when we got there we flew one circle around it. It was listing about fifteen degrees, and burning fuel was pouring out the big opening on the starboard side of the hangar deck—just raw gasoline pouring out like a flaming waterfall.

Stan Bailey and the ten other Black Sheep from the early launch scattered to find friendly decks. Many were accepted by *Hancock,* others by *Yorktown, Wasp,* or *Bunker Hill*. Most of Pat Weiland's pilots from VMF-452 trapped aboard *Hancock,* leaving no room for the ship's own air group. A few Corsairs were shoved overboard, but Weiland and nine of his Marines were welcomed to deliver fighters to *Intrepid* and *Yorktown*.

After the Osaka harbor strike, Ken Linder landed on *Hancock* and reported that he and Commander Parker had together shot down *Franklin*'s attacker. A Marine public relations officer sent the story to the States, where it was widely published, but a minor controversy later developed. Lieutenant (jg) Locke H. Trigg, Jr., from VF-47 on *Bataan,* also claimed to have downed the attacker with his F6F. However, the recorded time was too early (0700), and the aircraft was listed as a Nakajima C6N—used for reconnaissance. Next, Edwin Parker landed aboard the new *Wasp* and claimed to have shot down the Judy three miles from *Franklin* at 0708—the proper distance and time—apparently citing no help on the part of any other pilots, including Linder. The Navy gave him full credit for the kill in VF-86's air combat action report.

Linder was left out, even though he had at least shared in the Judy's destruction and should have been given partial credit. He reported his role, but none of the Black Sheep's records survived aside from the muster rolls, and no official recognition was entered on his behalf. "I know that I was one of the last guys to put bullets into him, and I was over him when he went into the water," he stated later. It was the last time that a Black Sheep pilot's rounds hit a Japanese plane.

For the next two days, a handful of scattered Sheep flew from other decks to provide CAP over *Franklin*'s smoking hulk. It was at first a helpless target that the Japanese were expected to finish off, but she was taken under tow by *Pittsburgh* on the afternoon of the attack, then miraculously worked up steam and retreated from the scene under her own power. Though *Franklin* was considered damaged beyond repair, Gehres ultimately sailed his ship all the way to Brooklyn harbor.

Meanwhile, possessing nothing but the clothes on their backs, the Black Sheep were transferred by breeches buoy to a variety of smaller ships for transit back to Ulithi. They were grateful to be in one piece. Those plucked from the ocean with burns and broken limbs faced painfully challenging days and weeks ahead.

Warner Chapman's broken bones were set aboard *Marshall* about twelve hours after his rescue. The next day he was winched across to *Alaska* in a stretcher, where he was afforded a good view of the burned-out *Franklin*. "From where I was, it appeared that the ship was brand new up to about the hangar deck, but above it was just a tangled mess of rusted wreckage. I didn't realize that fire would cause such rapid rusting."

Alaska, one of only two so-called battle cruisers in the entire fleet, boasted some of the best medical facilities available, including an orthopedic surgeon. But instead of steaming from the combat area, she remained off the Ryukyus to shell Okinawa. From the sick bay located below the number three turret, her patients aboard endured the bombarding.

Budd Faught and Bill Dancy were among the fourteen "bone cases" winched across to *Alaska.* Doctors determined that Faught's left leg was beyond saving; they removed it below the knee and turned under the kneecap to form a natural pad. It healed quickly, and by the time Faught reached Hawaii several weeks later, he was ready for a prosthesis.

After the wounded Marines' conditions stabilized, the men were transferred again by stretcher to a tanker that subsequently passed through a typhoon en route to Ulithi. During the storm a safe broke loose on an upper deck, and the wounded men listened from their bunks as it rumbled back and forth for the next twenty-four hours. After a brief stay on a hospital ship at Ulithi, they were airlifted to Guam, which boasted a large naval hospital. There, Chapman recalled, he could hear the bones in Bill Dancy's legs grinding during his first agonizing attempts to walk. Eventually the orthopedic cases were airlifted to Hawaii for further recuperation in the Aiea Heights hospital.

The burn victims were given syrettes of morphine to reduce their pain. Art Schmagel and Ranson Tilton were initially bandaged "like mummies," their heads and hands completely swathed as they underwent treatment aboard a hospital ship at Ulithi. Some of the burn patients on board began to finagle morphine after the doctors tried to wean them; they were promptly cut off when it became evident that they were gaining dependency on the highly narcotic opium derivative.

By March 23, seventeen healthy Black Sheep pilots had

reached Ulithi aboard several ships and eventually boarded the attack transport *Oneida,* which sailed on the twenty-seventh for Guam. The pilots arrived the following day and caught up with Art Schmagel and Tilly Tilton, who had been flown to the naval hospital for recuperation. Still heavily bandaged, both were undergoing excruciating burn treatment. To prevent infection they received heavy doses of penicillin, injected through thick needles into the buttocks every four hours for days on end. After their muscles toughened, the injections became harder to endure than the burns.

The able-bodied Black Sheep departed Guam on March 31 aboard the baby flattop *Barnes,* where they joined the remnants of Pat Weiland's VMF-452. The small, crowded carrier finally reached Pearl Harbor after a ten-day voyage. By then, Schmagel and Tilton had been airlifted to the Pearl Harbor naval hospital. When *Barnes* docked at Ford Island, they tried to cajole their way aboard, carrying orders for evacuation to the United States. They managed to get approval just before *Barnes* departed the next day for San Francisco. By the time she reached the carrier pier at Alameda on Monday, April 16, all the Marines had been living as vagabonds for a month.

That night, *Franklin*'s survivors held a tremendous party at the Hotel Sir Francis Drake, where they raised drinks to their own good fortune or to fallen friends. Despite spring's chill, most wore a borrowed collection of summer khaki—the only clothes that had been available to them for weeks.

The next day they climbed aboard a dingy troop train for San Diego. They reported to the aviation detachment at Miramar, after which they were bused to MCAS El Centro, VMF-214's new permanent base. For the next few months, the survivors quietly put their lives back together in the remote desolation of the Southern California desert.

Their journey had come full circle, and a misshapen one at that. After training for an entire year—one that saw seven pilots lose their lives—Stan Bailey's fighter squadron completed just one full day of combat. During those few hours off the coast of Japan, one pilot was shot down and captured, and thirty-two officers and men were lost in the conflagration aboard *Franklin*.

Incredibly the Black Sheep were told to keep news of the disaster strictly secret. The information was kept from the public for another month after they reached California. They went about their business, took their thirty days of combat leave, and kept their mouths shut. Even though the mangled carrier reached the Brooklyn Navy Yard on April 28, the news did not break nationwide until radio broadcasts on the evening of May 17. The next day, the stories and photographs of the epic fire were splashed across every major newspaper.

Gazing at the stunning pictures of their own exploding ship for the first time, the survivors realized that their war had ended on that cloudy winter day in the cold Pacific. The war would continue for another three months. But for the incomparable Black Sheep, the fighting was over.

20

THE LAST SHEEP HOME

When at last President Harry Truman officially proclaimed V-J Day on August 15, 1945, the broken bones and painful burns suffered by Black Sheep pilots on *Franklin* were still mending. For two other members of the squadron, a lengthy period of adjustment was about to begin. Both had endured months of depravity and brutality as prisoners of the Japanese, and there was no quick cure for that. Somewhat surprisingly, the one imprisoned for the shortest time was in far worse condition.

That was John Stodd, whose Corsair was shot out from under him five months earlier. On the morning of March 19, as *Franklin* burned, a train took him to what he guessed was the Sasebo prison run by the Kempei Tai, the Gestapo-style military police. Rough interrogations ensued, held inevitably in the middle of the night for several nights running. Between beatings he was kept kneeling on the floor of a foul-smelling, bug-infested cell. His unwashed body was soon crawling with fleas, lice, and crabs; his only source of warmth was the rugged leather flight jacket he had somehow been allowed to hold onto. Interrogators continually reminded him that he could be executed on a whim. One morning they emphasized the point by dragging him to a wall to face a squad of riflemen. The officer in charge walked back to the squad and turned to face Stodd, who wondered why he had not been offered the customary blindfold. The soldiers laughed when the officer pulled out a camera and snapped his picture.

Stodd was placed on another train and delivered to the Tokyo headquarters of the Kempei Tai, where four weeks of interrogations followed. He was aware of other Americans in adjacent cells, though his own cell mates were a Korean civilian and an English-speaking Japanese. Of the latter he wrote, "I asked him what he was in for and he said it was because he had spoken out against the Japanese. I suspected he was a plant."

After a month Stodd was moved again, this time to a smaller Kempei Tai prison near the Imperial Palace, where he was confined in a cramped space with a B-29 navigator named Bill Leslie. They kneeled through interminable hours, only inches apart but prohibited from speaking, always under the watchful eyes of a guard. Their hands were free, however, which allowed the two resilient officers to create their own method of communicating. Facing away from the guard, they picked pieces of straw from their tatami mats and formed alphabets. By pointing surreptitiously at the letters and making slight gestures to signal the ends of words, they could "talk" for hours.

After five days Stodd was moved yet again, this time to a narrow valley twelve miles from the Yokosuka naval base. It was around the end of April or the first of May when he arrived at the Heitei (the Imperial Navy's version of the military police) prison at Ofuna. Here his clothing and body were thoroughly fumigated and he was given his first hot bath. The clothes and even the leather flight jacket were returned, minus the Black Sheep patch.

Stodd was the only Marine in the camp of mostly aviators. During periods when they could mingle, the others pressed him for news of the war, but he had a six-week growth of beard and could offer nothing new. One prisoner had interesting news for Stodd after seeing a guard shining his shoes with the Black Sheep patch. The prisoner informed Stodd that Gregory Boyington was alive and well, having been transferred from Ofuna only a week before. This was confirmed during Stodd's first interrogation with

James K. Sasaki, a law graduate of the University of Southern California who spoke English fluently and talked mostly of Southern California. The prisoners called him "Handsome Harry."

The captives bathed once a week (after the guards were finished with the water) and used a communal head, which led Stodd to call the Heitei prison at Ofuna "a paradise" compared to the filthy Kempei Tai prisons, but he meant it in purely relative terms. Ofuna was an intimidation camp, the guards nothing more than thugs. Camp commander Kango Cho, "a big, sadistic brute," took pleasure in personally administering beatings. The prisoners were starved. Beriberi was common, as was dysentery. "We tried to stay alive on rough low-grade rice or barley and a watery soup of carrot tops, potato peelings and occasionally fish heads and bones," Stodd wrote, but he was soon afflicted with vitamin-deficiency diseases, including beriberi and scurvy.

The war ended just in time for him. In a span of five months he had wasted away to ninety pounds and was too weak to walk. Japan's collapse came just nine days after his twenty-third birthday, but another two weeks passed before the U.S. Navy arrived. Stodd was lifted aboard the hospital ship *Benevolence* in Tokyo Bay on August 29, where two complete blood transfusions, dropped by aircraft, were needed to save him. There was good news about Bill Leslie, his B-29 friend. When the Tokyo prison burned down during a bombing raid, the handcuffed navigator escaped through a flaming wall and found refuge in the Imperial Palace moat. The two men remained close friends throughout their lives.

When Stodd finally reached the States, he was hospitalized in Astoria, Oregon, to recuperate from the ravages of starvation. After six months he finally was able to exercise and he began running to restore his strength, but his full recovery ultimately took a year and several hospital stays.

* * *

In sharp contrast to Stodd's decline in health, Greg Boyington had not only survived twenty months of imprisonment, including thirteen at Ofuna, but was strong enough in April 1945 to complete a five-mile hike, one of two lengthy walks he made while being transferred to Omori prison camp in Tokyo Bay. Situated on a tiny island, Omori was connected to Yokohama by a causeway dredged from the bay. Each day Boyington walked into the city with a work detail to clear heavy rubble from the streets after B-29 raids. In July, according to his autobiography, he began digging air-raid tunnels for twelve hours a day. That it was hard slave labor is not in dispute; the salient point is that Boyington remained healthy enough to work.

By late August, while the terms of Japan's unconditional surrender were being worked out, a small U.S. fleet anchored in Tokyo Bay. From the cruiser *San Juan,* Commodore Roger Simpson and Comdr. Harold E. Stassen reconnoitered the area's prisoner-of-war (POW) camps from a swarm of Higgins landing craft. After seeing the prisoners, the Navy officers claimed, "In general, they were suffering from the worst malnutrition imaginable."

Omori was abandoned to the prisoners on the night of August 27, and food drops began the next day. Rations and supplies stuffed into potentially lethal containers made from fifty-five-gallon drums spilled from the bomb bays of low-flying B-29s. An aerial photographer snapped a picture showing Boyington's name in block letters on a barracks roof. On the twenty-ninth, as Commander Stassen approached the island with his landing craft, scores of joyous prisoners came out to the beach, some leaping into the cold water to swim out to the Higgins boats.

Once the prisoners' euphoria had quieted enough to gather them aboard, they were delivered to *Benevolence* for a delousing and a bath, then a meal. In the wardroom, Boyington sat across from "some poor little starved B-29 pilot" and wolfed down a huge meal, which was later itemized by a reporter from *Time* magazine: eight eggs, two orders of ham, and two helpings of mashed potatoes.

There was a particular reason for Boyington's ability to eat so much while others could not stomach any food. He was not starved. John Stodd, unable to walk after only five months of imprisonment, later explained:

> Boyington doesn't admit it in his "Baa Baa Black Sheep," but he survived at Ofuna only by getting a job as a cook's helper in the *makenai* (kitchen) where he could stay warm, steal food and avoid the guards. It was presumed that Handsome Harry got him the job.

Boyington also didn't report initially his drinking binge on the Japanese New Year. Years after the war, he admitted that he not only kept warm in the kitchen but drank a belly full of sake that night and caroused with his arms around some of the meanest guards. Aboard *Benevolence* he told reporters only about the brutalities he had suffered. News of his recovery was flashed to the States from the communications ship *Ancon,* and appeared in headlines the next day, still August 29 because of the international date line.

After a few days aboard *San Juan,* Boyington was flown by transport to Guam, then to Barbers Point via Kwajalein. A relatively quiet week ensued at MCAS Ewa while doctors poked and prodded, but aside from a physical examination to qualify for promotion he required no hospitalization. After pinning the silver oak leaves of a lieutenant colonel on his collar, he boarded a four-engine transport for the long flight to California. Frank Walton, now a major, had received advance notice of Boyington's arrival and rounded up the Black Sheep on the West Coast; they would greet their long-lost skipper at NAS Alameda.

It was after dark on the evening of September 12 when the transport's engines finally ticked to a stop and the cargo door swung wide. A small boarding platform was rolled in place, and Frank Walton entered the plane to greet his old skipper quietly and prepare him for what lay ahead. On the ramp below, a large crowd of well-wishers, reporters, cameramen, and twenty Black Sheep eagerly awaited. Stan Bailey came from El Centro to join sixteen pilots now serving with other units across the West. Doc Reames was there, as were two ground officers whose claim to the Black Sheep was by association. One was wealthy socialite Art Little, the former rear echelon adjutant, who now lived in the luxurious Plaza Hotel in Los Angeles. The other was Lt. Melanchton P. Paetznick, a Navy chaplain from MAG-11 who had conducted a memorial service for Boyington and George Ashmun on Espiritu Santo a year and a half before.

After a few minutes Boyington emerged onto the platform, grinning hugely at the raucous applause and popping flashbulbs. As he reached the last steps, the former Black Sheep rushed forward and hoisted him on their shoulders. He punched his fist triumphantly skyward. The crowd headed for the terminal, where Boyington was ushered to a chair beside a small table. The room was darkened except for a gooseneck lamp that shined in his face; someone placed a cup of coffee before him. While reporters scribbled furiously and twenty-one Black Sheep leaned on every word, Boyington told the world the details of his final flight and subsequent capture.

Turning back the clock to the fighter sweep over Rabaul, Boyington explained that he and George Ashmun dropped onto half a dozen Zekes at fifteen thousand feet. Boyington opened fire at one of the trailing planes from four hundred yards, and the Zeke went spinning down in flames as Ashmun called, "You got a flamer, Skipper!" Boyington's twenty-sixth victory, visually confirmed by several others, tied the existing record.

Closing fast on the Zekes, Boyington dived past and continued down for another three thousand feet with Ashmun glued to his wing. Finding themselves suddenly overrun by enemy fighters, they immediately began weaving defensively. Within three or four scissor turns, each had shot one Zeke off the other's tail.

Beset by Zekes that riddled his Corsair, Ashmun suddenly straightened out and began gliding toward the water, trailing smoke. Boyington slid in behind and kicked the rudder from side to side, "spraying the Zekes to get them off Ashmun's tail" and finally shooting another of the tormentors down in flames. But Ashmun's plane never waivered, indicating that he was incapacitated or was already dead in the cockpit. All doubts were removed when his Corsair burst into flames and thundered into St. George's Channel.

Now it was Boyington's turn to be pursued, and he dived toward the water. What followed next ranks as one of the most incredible bailouts ever survived.

He was running full bore at perhaps two hundred feet above the water when his main gas tank suddenly erupted in flames. One of the critical design changes on the F4U had been the installation of the huge fuel tank between the engine and the pilot, which placed Boyington just a few feet behind this blazing torch. Other pilots, Capt. James N. Cupp among them, had been grievously burned as a result of main tank fires, but Boyington egressed rapidly.

> When the flames came, I would have climbed to get enough altitude to bail out, but it was too hot. I did all this in a split second. I knew if I kicked that stick forward hard enough, I'd create negative g's, as we called them. Then of course, I only had two hands, so I jerked the rip cord and the safety belt with each hand. I don't know whether the canopy was damaged or not, but if it wasn't, I tore it right off because I kicked so many g's. That was one time I was glad I had short legs.

In other interviews and magazine stories published over the years, Boyington sometimes stated that he rolled the burning Corsair on its back prior to kicking the stick, but from such a low altitude the maneuver would have fired his body straight into the water. If it happened the way he claimed in most versions, there was just enough altitude for the sudden centrifugal force to propel him out of the cockpit. An instant after his chute opened, he slammed into the water. The force crushed his canteen.

As miraculous as his reported bailout had been, the next portion of his story stretched feasibility even further. Initially he described to reporters several injuries, including scalp lacerations and a broken ankle, but by the time he wrote his book the injuries ranged from an ankle "shattered by a twenty-millimeter-cannon shot" to his left ear "almost torn off" to a series of other bullet and shrapnel holes between the extremities. Apparently he received no burns from the fire.

Contact with the cool water revived him, but he soon came under a strafing attack by a flight of Zekes. Of his attempts to evade, Boyington wrote:

> At first I could dive about six feet, but this lessened to four, and gradually I lost so much of my strength that, when the Zeros made their strafing runs at me, I could just barely duck my head under the water. I think they ran out of ammunition, for after a while they left me. Or my efforts in the water became so feeble that maybe they figured they had killed me.

Boyington claimed that, despite such exhaustion, he treaded water for two more hours without any kind of flotation device. His Mae West was full of holes, and he feared inflating the rubber boat in case the Zekes came back. He also claimed that he stripped naked in the water, which would have required shedding his parachute harness before he could remove his fatigues and shoes. Attached to this harness were two bulky packs—one containing the compressed raft with its CO_2 cartridge, the other a jungle survival pack. Both added dead weight throughout the struggle, but he held onto them.

Henry Miller, who gave survival lectures during the war, voiced an opinion based on his experience with water survival training, which was designed to challenge well-rested and healthy pilots.

> We had training of being dropped from about 10 or 15 feet, while wearing a seat pack and full clothing. We were expected to learn how to get out of the seat pack and our shoes, but nothing else. We all had trouble with our shoes, and I cannot imagine getting out of any other clothing.

Survival training was conducted in confined water as opposed to the conditions that Boyington described: "The waves that day in the old South Pacific were about seven feet long."

Obviously at some point Boyington toggled the raft's compressed air cartridge and climbed aboard. Toward evening he was picked up by a Japanese submarine, and rode on the deck virtually naked, still holding his jungle pack, while the sub motored on the surface into Rabaul harbor. There soldiers took over and prodded him on his feet to an IJN headquarters station, where one of his first interrogators was Edward Chikaki "Chicky" Honda, the Hawaiian-born Nisei and former baseball star who had likely been involved in the two-way radio exchanges over Rabaul.

Eventually sent to the dreaded Kempei Tai prison, Boyington suffered treatment that was certainly brutal, including regular beatings with rifle butts, and he was refused all medical attention for many weeks. But this also forces the assumption that his reported injuries—a dangling left ear, a shattered leg, arms and shoulders full of shrapnel, a bullet hole in his left calf, a gash near his groin from an explosive shell—somehow healed by themselves without life-threatening infection or permanent disfigurement. Later photographs, for instance, show a normal-looking ear.

So horrendous were the conditions at the Rabaul prison that only a handful of gaunt creatures lasted the entire war; Boyington lived because he left New Britain altogether, thanks to Chicky Honda. The Nisei was savvy enough to know that the end was near for Rabaul and contrived to escort several prisoners to Tokyo. In mid-February he accompanied Boyington, Marine fighter pilot Maj. Donald Boyle, Australian flight officer Brian Stacy, Army fighter pilot Lt. Charles Taylor, and Navy PBY pilot Lt. John Arbuckle on a twin-engine Betty bound for Truk. Ironically the bomber landed during an American air attack, and the blindfolded prisoners, caught in the open, stumbled into a slit trench. Boyington's description of the incident fits chronologically; the first big carrier raids against Truk occurred on February 16 and 17.

Boyington reported brutal treatment and beatings during the two and a half weeks that the captives were held in Truk.

> They were using baseball bats on us now—and I never knew the old willow could hurt so much without breaking your bones. We lived in tiny cells and they gave us exactly one cup of water a day. We knew we were dying of thirst. On the seventeenth day we were bundled onto a transport and flown to Saipan. We were locked up for a few days, then transferred to Iwo Jima.

After a night on Iwo the prisoners were flown to Yokohama, then moved to the camp at Ofuna.

Sometime prior to the winter of 1944, Boyington was assigned the job of cook's helper. In a magazine article he claimed to have lost seventy pounds as a prisoner, writing that "the scraps of food were getting more and more unpalatable," but he boasted in an interview years later that he was "the best kleptomaniac around" and gained eighty pounds because of the kitchen job. The truth lies somewhere in between. Photographs taken two weeks after his release from Omori show him to be thinner than he was in the Solomons but certainly not emaciated. Compared to John Stodd, who spent a year recovering from starvation and disease, Boyington was in excellent condition.

Now that Boyington was back in the United States, a large cooperative effort got under way to help him celebrate. With contributions from Chance Vought and the War Bond Agency, the Black Sheep secured a banquet room at the St. Francis Hotel in San Francisco. Following dinner, the gathered pilots presented Boyington with a gold watch inscribed, "To Gramps, from his Black Sheep." *Life* magazine published a full spread of photographs on October 1, reportedly their first-ever coverage of a drinking party. One photograph featured Budd Faught, the *Franklin* survivor, back in uniform only six months after the disaster, with Boyington autographing his prosthetic left leg. Though Faught was not one of Boyington's pilots, he had earned as much right as any to be there.

The St. Francis party was only the beginning. For the next two months Boyington was feted in more than twenty different cities during a whirlwind cross-country junket arranged by the Marine Corps. Frank Walton accompanied him as his good manners, alcohol foil, straight man. Despite the potential opportunities for excess, Walton successfully rode herd on Boyington's compulsiveness for most of the tour. They rode by train or aircraft for long journeys, sortied by car for day trips. Boyington gave speeches at exclusive luncheons, spoke again at extravagant dinners. Although the two Marines were provided with a subsistence allowance of seven dollars a day, it was unnecessary wherever they went.

Beginning with their first stop after departing San Francisco, Boyington was overwhelmed with adulation. Near the Seattle garage where he had parked cars three years earlier, an enormous crowd gathered to see him paraded through the city. Bands played, dignitaries crowed, huge banners proclaimed "Welcome Home, Pappy." The nickname was catching on. From there it was on to Okanogan, where a writer for the *Seattle Post-Intelligencer* boasted that all 24,000 inhabitants of the town turned out for the largest parade in the county's history. Boyington enjoyed a brief reunion with his mother and two of his three children (the youngest was still in the custody of his ex-wife's sister), including a hunting trip with Gregory, Jr., then began traveling in earnest. From Seattle, he and Walton flew to Chicago for two days of "chicken and peas and bourbon," then to the nation's capital to prepare for the most important event of all. Harry Truman was going to drape a "posthumous" Medal of Honor around Boyington's neck on Friday, October 5.

Boyington and Walton arrived in Washington at noon on Tuesday with a list of other business to complete first, including two significant events at Marine Corps headquarters. On Thursday they drove down Columbia Pike and entered the Navy Annex, where they were ushered into the commandant's office. There, Gen. Archibald A. Vandegrift presented Boyington with a Navy Cross. Although he had not received so much as an Air Medal during his combat service, he now wore the Navy's highest recognition for valor. Among the ceremony's witnesses were ten other commissioned and enlisted Marines, all of whom would receive a Medal of Honor on the White House lawn.

After the solemn Navy Cross presentation, Boyington and Walton walked to the intelligence department and spent an hour or two quietly absorbed in paperwork that would later have a controversial impact on Marine Corps history. Officially Boyington was still credited with twenty-six victories, though he had been claiming two additional Zekes ever since his release. The overall record no longer concerned him (it had been eclipsed by fighter pilots in the Army and Navy), but the Marine record was still within his grasp. Joe Foss had been given an opportunity to add to his score of twenty-six when he returned to combat but ended up mired in the uneventful last days of Rabaul. Bob Hanson's incredible run also seemed certain to shatter the Marine record, yet he was killed only a month after Boyington was shot down.

Now Boyington stood within headquarters to explain that he shot down two more planes. Perhaps the green light came from Vandegrift himself, but the approving authority is less important than the ultimate result. A written statement and the stroke of a pen were the only requirements necessary to make Boyington's claims official. As the Corps' own aviation historian wrote, "In Washington headquarters there was no attempt at verification; the squadron and group war diaries, when available, were accepted as gospel."

Greg Boyington told his story again—for the record in more ways than one—while Frank Walton boiled it down longhand, just as he had done two years and ten thousand miles ago. Then it was transcribed onto an official Aircraft Action Report, beneath which was typed, "Supplemental Report." Information was entered only into sections that required amendment, such as "Loss or Damage of Own Aircraft," "Personnel Casualties," and "Tactical and Operational Data." In the narrative section the highlights covered George Ashmun's loss (and one victory) and Boyington's two claims and subsequent bailout. When the document was finished, Walton signed as the preparer, then Boyington himself signed as the approving officer. No higher authority was needed, no confirmation sought. Ashmun was dead, so there were no friendly eyewitnesses anyway.

In essence, the Marine Corps allowed a pilot whose career had begun disreputably to walk in the door and declare himself its leading ace. The only reasonable explanation is that the whole country was riding high on the euphoria of victory, and Boyington's miraculous reappearance simply intensified the public's desire to put heroes on pedestals. Boyington, about to wear a Medal of Honor, would sell even more war bonds as the Marine Corps' leading ace. There was also precedent for accepting his claims. The Corps had done it once before when it allowed Boyington's six reported victories as a Flying Tiger without seeking independent confirmation.

As word of Boyington's new score began filtering through the ranks of veteran fighter pilots, some were irritated. The Marine Corps' first ace, Marion Carl, later wrote:

> When Greg came out of captivity in 1945 he had been awarded a "posthumous" Medal of Honor and was proclaimed the Marine Corps' leading ace. The medal was deserved—Greg was a talented aviator and an aggressive combat leader—but I've been rankled by the "top gun" title ever since. Even allowing the two unsubstantiated claims from his last mission, he couldn't match Joe Foss's total or his score in Marine Corps service. To my knowledge, Joe never has made any fuss over the situation—he's too much a gentleman for that—but for the Marine Corps officially to recognize Boyington as its top ace, despite documentation to the contrary, defies all logic. I suspect it's bureaucratic inability to admit such a long-standing error.

Personal opinions aside, the Japanese records provide much stronger evidence that Boyington did not down two additional planes. As of January 3, 1944, only the 204 and 253 Kokutai remained in defense of Rabaul, the 201 Kokutai having been withdrawn to Truk. The 204 Kokutai lost two pilots and the 253 none that day (although one pilot from the latter was wounded). According to American claims, however, a total of ten Navy and Marine fighter pilots, including George Ashmun, were credited with nine aircraft destroyed and three others probably destroyed. Typically, claims were two to three times higher than actual losses, but this was a ratio of greater than four to one. Interestingly, by discounting Boyington's two unconfirmed planes and the one that he asserts Ashmun downed, the net would be six claimed victories against two actual losses—a more consistent excess. The claims for three probables compared to one wounded pilot result in an identical ratio. The Marine Corps did not have access to the Japanese records, of course, but the numerical evidence should not have been necessary. Boyington should not have been allowed to add unconfirmed claims to his record in the first place. Appendix D in this book adjusts his score accordingly.

On Friday, October 5, Lt. Col. Gregory Boyington stood before Harry Truman on the South Lawn of the White House as the newly crowned leading ace of the Marine Corps. He was the first of the day's fourteen Navy and Marine personnel to receive a Medal of Honor. Portions of the citation bear witness that the medal was justly earned: "Consistently outnumbered throughout successive hazardous flights over heavily defended hostile territory . . . daring and courageous persistence . . . a superb airman and determined fighter . . . resourceful leadership . . ."

The White House ceremony was followed by a public rally, with the Medal of Honor recipients seated on a raised platform featuring a huge mocked-up battleship for a backdrop. At thirty-two years of age, Greg Boyington was on top of the world.

He did not take long to fall. Boyington and Walton hopped on a military transport and resumed the war bond tour in New York City. For the next nineteen days they staged from a Waldorf Astoria luxury suite—a tangible realization of Boyington's fame courtesy of *Look* magazine. They traveled by car or train for day trips to speaking engagements and war bond rallies: New Brunswick, New Jersey; Harrisburg and Philadelphia, Pennsylvania; Bridgeport, Connecticut. The latter was an overnight affair hosted by Chance Vought. After touring the enormous Corsair production line, they were wined and dined by some of the pioneers in aviation industry.

But New York was where the trouble began, and her name was Mrs. Lucy Malcolmson. After Boyington sailed aboard *Lurline* in January 1943, Lucy returned to New York and eventually found work at the Music Box Canteen, her lifestyle augmented by a comfortable allowance from her husband, Stewart Malcolmson, now a production manager for General Motors in Australia. When Boyington reached New York he resumed the affair with Lucy, ignoring Frank Walton's open disapproval. Two calendar dates with the scribbled words "save for Lucy" were among the commitments that Walton outlined for Boyington on a sheet of Waldorf Astoria stationery. Others included a visit with George Ashmun's mother, conferences, interviews, photo sessions (one with Boyington drinking a glass of Borden's milk), luncheons, speeches, football games, and parties.

After the couple's lengthy dalliance in New York, the war bond tour resumed in early November and the two men traveled back to the West Coast. They spent several days in Seattle again doing "shows," as Walton called them. "[Boyington's] speech was getting better, getting standardized," Walton remembered. "And I was keeping him sober."

Their final dinner engagement was in Portland, Oregon, where Boyington was scheduled to give a war bond speech to several hundred of the city's most affluent citizens. Exhausted after weeks of watching over him, Walton succumbed to a nap in the bedroom of their two-room suite. Soon he was disturbed by noises. "God Almighty, I woke up and heard this commotion next door. I looked in and there were about ten people in there. Boyington was down on the floor with my bathrobe on, rolling around drunk as a skunk."

Although Walton delayed their appearance as long as he could, Boyington's speech did not go well. He stood at the dais, blinking at the audience, then blurted, "I know what you want me to talk about. You want me to talk about how I shot 'em down; I was flat on my back at 40,000 feet. That's what you want, isn't it? That's what you want! I'm here to sell War Bonds. Buy War Bonds. Why? I don't know, just buy 'em."

Walton recounted:

> This guy put his arm around Boyington's shoulder and said, "We'll have to excuse Colonel Boyington; he's been a prisoner of the Japanese and he's not himself."

After that episode, Walton tried to get Boyington back on an even keel by offering him the spare bedroom in his Los Angeles bungalow. They stayed there for approximately a week while Boyington underwent further evaluation at the Long Beach naval hospital. Walton arranged for a police secretary to come to his house after work and take shorthand while Boyington told his story. "She was getting pages and pages of text," Walton recalled, "and he did pretty good for a while."

One night, Carol Walton introduced Boyington to Frances Baker, a divorced, buxom blonde who had dabbled with acting. It was love at first sight. Shortly thereafter, Greg Boyington and Frank Walton went back on active duty in San Diego. Boyington briefly tried to juggle the situation with Lucy Malcolmson and Frances Baker, but it began to unravel.

Boyington had already discussed marriage with Lucy, who was en route to Reno to receive divorce papers from her husband in Australia. Her hooks were in deep. In the three years since Boyington had arranged for her to handle some of his finances, Lucy had received approximately eighteen thousand dollars of his allotment. More recently in New York, Boyington had negotiated through her a loan for three thousand dollars to purchase a Lincoln Zephyr, which was titled in her name for the trip west.

Totally uncertain of himself, Boyington met Lucy in Reno. They were engaged on New Year's Eve 1945, after which he retreated to San Diego while she waited for Stewart's papers to arrive. In the meantime she gathered reporters and announced their plans to be married in Reno on January 8.

As Frank Walton later recalled, Boyington was at his wit's end.

> Greg was sitting there one night and said, "Gee, Frank, I don't want to marry anybody."
>
> I said, "Greg, you don't have to marry anybody. You're not hooked until you say those words, and if you don't want to marry anybody, just don't answer the phone."
>
> "Well that's what I think I'd better do," he said.

On January 7, responding to direct questions from the press, Boyington denied that he and Lucy Malcolmson were about to marry, which left her "stunned" in Reno.

The following day, he and Frances Baker were married before a justice of the peace in Las Vegas, with Carol Walton as a witness.

The press had a field day, at Boyington's expense. Whereas his status as a great fighter ace had been proclaimed nationwide only weeks earlier, now his name appeared in the tabloids. They feasted on him again the following August, when he took Lucy Malcolmson to court after claiming that she had mishandled the custodial funds intended for his children. He attempted to recover eight thousand dollars, but the contents of his love letters (Lucy had saved every one) were paraded before the public and she won the case, leaving him humiliated. It had taken less than a year to plummet from his pinnacle as a military hero.

Frank Walton was released from active duty and returned to work with the Los Angeles Police Department as a lieutenant, having passed the promotion exam while still overseas. Boyington was ultimately released from active duty on a medical discharge. The newlyweds moved in briefly with the Waltons, but the arrangement was doomed. Carol Walton finally demanded that they leave, after which the two couples were barely on speaking terms.

Almost overnight, Boyington was forgotten. The magazines ignored him after 1946, although his name occasionally appeared in newspapers because of drunk driving charges. One such *New York Times* report in 1951 did not mention his status as leading ace of the Marine Corps, or even that he was an ace at all; he was just another World War II flier.

Seven more years of obscurity followed while Boyington bounced from one menial job to another. With Fran's help he dried out long enough to resume flying and write an autobiography, *Baa Baa Black Sheep,* much of it from the stack of transcripts provided by Frank Walton. It may have been inaccurate in some parts and embellished in others, but his self-deprecating message made the book a huge success. By January 1959 it had already sold 65,000 copies, which prompted *Life* magazine to feature him in a close-up entitled "Bright Days for a 'Bum.'" *Life* borrowed the derogatory term from Boyington's book, his own last word for describing himself.

By then fifteen years had passed since Boyington's brief reign as the dominant Marine Corps fighter pilot of World War II. Of his whole fascinating life, those few months in the South Pacific represented the only time he was in his true element, secure in his role as a warrior and a maverick. His charisma stirred the imagination of millions.

So compelling was his personality that Fred Hampson, once an antagonist, eventually wrote the ultimate compliment:

He would never have done on a magazine cover, yet in the cockpit of a Corsair waiting his turn on the line, with the motor blowing a 2,000 horsepower wind along a fuselage that was greasy and weathered and patched, he looked right. Cocky, homely, steely-eyed. He made you whistle under your breath.

That was Gregory Boyington. Among all of those who flew, fought, and died in Marine Fighting Squadron 214, he was the true black sheep.

EPILOGUE

No pilots have worn the intertwined globe and anchor of the Marine Corps or flown wearing wings of gold with more valor than the men of Marine Fighting Squadron 214 during World War II. A Presidential Unit Citation—the first awarded specifically to a Marine fighter squadron—recognized each of the four Solomon Islands combat tours without naming individuals, thereby acknowledging the enlisted men and journeyman pilots, not just the aces. They were a team, and the citation reflects upon their collective accomplishments.

With the exception of Ken Linder's encounter with the Judy that bombed *Franklin* on March 19, 1945, all of the squadron's air-to-air combats occurred between April 7, 1943, and January 6, 1944. During that nine-month span, the pilots were credited with shooting down or probably destroying 160 planes, although actual Japanese losses were perhaps a third of the total. On the debit side, VMF-214 lost nearly 70 aircraft to all causes during the squadron's thirty-two months of training and operational service, and personnel casualties were high. Of the 132 aviators on the roster, 27 were killed or missing in action; 13 others were wounded, including John Stodd, who was debilitated as a POW. One ground officer was killed aboard *Franklin,* for a total casualty rate of slightly more than 30 percent.

The war indelibly changed the survivors, who went home to lead new lives in a different America, a new superpower. Several stayed in uniform and flew again when new conflicts erupted (John Bolt became the only two-war ace in naval aviation history and the only jet ace in the Marine Corps), and a few even made it through three wars. For a time, Chris Magee lived the life of fighter-pilot-for-hire, flying German-built Messerschmitts during Israel's 1948 war to establish her independence; a decade later he became the only Black Sheep besides Greg Boyington to run afoul of the law. The majority returned to quiet civilian lives, where they played key roles in industry, politics, farming, law, commercial aviation, small businesses, and education.

Boyington eventually settled down, crediting his fourth wife, Josephine, with helping him finally achieve a life of sobriety. Some of his quotes contained herein come from a 1958 speech he gave before a large gathering of Alcoholics Anonymous. He had moments of inspiration—he earned local acclaim for his paintings of desert landscapes—and even attempted a foray into politics.

Fred Losch described the day in 1964 when he and his wife stumbled across Boyington's campaign while they were driving through the California desert.

> Under a couple of palm trees was an old car. On top of it was a big sign that said "Vote for Pappy Boyington," and he was sitting behind a card table. Jean and I stopped, and he was running for state legislator in California, I think it was the 45th district. He probably didn't have $500 for his whole campaign. I mean, literally. You say, "Why the hell was he running?" It wasn't for money, because, cripes, back then they were only making five grand a year. In talking to him, he said, "Somebody's got to do something." He was a patriot. He loved his country. He came in third.

Boyington died on January 11, 1988, at the age of seventy-five. During the few years that this book was in preparation, more than a dozen of his fellow members also succumbed to illness, disease, surgical complications, or natural causes. Three of the aces—Don Fisher, Bill Case, and Chris Magee—died within a few months of one another in 1995.

Of the postwar deaths, none rings of irony like that of Hank Ellis, who survived five days in a tiny raft on the Coral Sea only to drown in a river while fishing. As time continues to take its toll of former members, their memories of awe-inspiring scenes—armadas of ships covering the water, skies filled with hundreds of fighting planes—will go with them. Hopefully, some of those images have been captured within these pages to be preserved awhile longer.

Today the squadron itself remains active—one of only a handful of World War II squadrons still in existence—at MCAS Yuma, Arizona, as VMA-214. The Black Sheep's mission changed to the attack role a few months before John Bolt, by then a lieutenant colonel, began a stint as commanding officer in 1957. At some point, to the disappointment of original members, the central figure in the squadron's insignia evolved from a woebegone sheep to a powerful, charging ram.

The most stunning change is the rising cost of the aircraft. In late 1943, the Navy entered a fixed-price contract with Chance Vought for the purchase of 4,699 F4U Corsairs (including a specified assortment of spare parts and engineering material) for slightly more than $447,513,000, bringing the flyaway cost of each plane to approximately $95,000. Today the replacement cost of a single AV-8B Harrier is more than $23,000,000.

At Yuma, the Black Sheep of VMA-214 have not forgotten their legacy. In establishing a small museum called the "Pappy Room," they have immortalized the man who flew some of those inexpensive piston-engine, partially fabric-covered Corsairs more than half a century earlier, earning a spot as one of the most legendary fighter pilots of all time.

Appendix A

VMF-214 Roster of Pilots and Essential Ground Officers

Name	Service
Alexander, Glendon L.	Santa Barbara, killed accidentally 4/2/44
Alexander, Robert A.	1st Black Sheep tour, killed accidentally 9/30/43
Andre, David C.	Ewa
Ashmun, George M.	1st and 2d Black Sheep tours, MIA 1/3/44
Avey, Fred V.	2d Black Sheep tour
Bailey, Stanley R.	1st Black Sheep tour, Santa Barbara, CV-13
Barker, Frank P., Jr.	Santa Barbara, CV-13
Bartl, Harry R.	2d Black Sheep tour, MIA 12/28/43
Beeler, Clare R.	Santa Barbara, CV-13, killed accidentally 2/16/45
Begert, John F.	1st Black Sheep tour
Bernard, Carol D. C.	Ewa, 1st and 2d Solomons tours
Berndt, Walter C.	CV-13
Blakeslee, Wilbur H.	Ewa, 1st and 2d Solomons tours, MIA 8/6/43
Bolt, John F., Jr.	1st and 2d Black Sheep tours
Bookman, Ralph (USN flight surgeon)	2d Solomons tour
Boozer, Addrian V.	Santa Barbara, killed accidentally 8/22/44

Bourgeois, Henry M.	1st Black Sheep tour
Bowers, Glenn L.	2d Black Sheep tour
Boyington, Gregory	1st and 2d Black Sheep tours, wounded, POW 1/3/44
Bragdon, Robert M.	1st and 2d Black Sheep tours
Britt, George F.	Ewa, 1st Solomons tour
Brown, John S.	2d Black Sheep tour
Brubaker, James E.	2d Black Sheep tour, MIA 12/23/43
Burnett, John R.	Ewa, 1st and 2d Solomons tours
Carnagey, Pierre M.	2d Black Sheep tour, MIA 12/23/43
Carpenter, Vincent W.	Ewa, 1st and 2d Solomons tours
Case, William N.	1st Black Sheep tour
Cassidy, John	Santa Barbara
Cavanagh, Howard L.	Ewa, 1st and 2d Solomons tours
Chapman, Warner O.	Santa Barbara, CV-13, wounded 3/19/45
Chatham, Rufus M., Jr.	2d Black Sheep tour
Collins, John B.	Santa Barbara, killed accidentally 4/14/44
Conant, Roger W. (Adjutant)	CV-13, KIA 3/19/45
Corman, J. Ned	2d Black Sheep tour
Correll, John B.	Ewa
Crocker, William L., Jr.	2d Black Sheep tour
Curran, Hugh J.	2d Solomons tour
Dancy, William H., Jr.	Santa Barbara, CV-13, wounded 3/19/45
Deetz, Lincoln N.	Ewa, 1st and 2d Solomons tours
Detmering, Carl S.	Santa Barbara, CV-13
Dodds, Arnot W. (Engineering)	Santa Barbara
Doswell, Gelon H.	2d Black Sheep tour
Dunbar, Carl O., Jr.	Ewa, 1st and 2d Solomons tours
Dustin, J. Cameron	2d Black Sheep tour, MIA 12/28/43

Eisele, Harold A.	2d Solomons tour
Ellis, Henry A., Jr.	Ewa, 1st and 2d Solomons tours
Emrich, Warren T.	1st and 2d Black Sheep tours
Ewing, Robert T.	1st Black Sheep tour, MIA 9/16/43
Faught, Carroll K.	Santa Barbara, CV-13, wounded 3/19/45
Feigener, Kenneth G.	Santa Barbara, CV-13
Ffoulkes, Bruce J.	Ewa, 2d Black Sheep tour, MIA 12/23/43
Fidler, John L.	Ewa, 1st and 2d Solomons tours
Fisher, Don H.	1st and 2d Black Sheep tours
Folger, Peter (Intelligence)	Ewa, 1st Solomons tour
Free, Stanley E.	Santa Barbara, CV-13
Groover, Denmark, Jr.	1st and 2d Black Sheep tours, wounded 9/23/43
Hanson, Robert M.	2d Solomons tour
Harding, James R.	Santa Barbara, CV-13
Harper, Edwin A.	1st and 2d Black Sheep tours, wounded 10/17/43
Harris, Walter R.	1st Black Sheep tour, MIA 9/27/43
Hatch, Donald (Intelligence)	2d Solomons tour
Haxthausen, Richard L.	Santa Barbara
Hazelwood, Ledyard B.	Ewa, 1st and 2d Solomons tours
Heier, William D.	1st and 2d Black Sheep tours
Hernan, Edwin J., Jr.	2d Solomons tour
Hill, James J.	1st and 2d Black Sheep tours
Hobbs, William H., Jr.	2d Black Sheep tour
Holden, Herbert, Jr.	2d Black Sheep tour
Hollmeyer, Henry W.	Ewa, 1st and 2d Solomons tours
Hoover, Robert T.	Ewa

Hugler, Robert K.	Santa Barbara, CV-13, MIA 3/19/45
Hunter, Ovis D.	2d Solomons tour
Hussey, Wesley E.	Santa Barbara, CV-13
Husted, Ralph W., Jr.	Santa Barbara, CV-13, killed accidentally 2/28/45
Hyatt, Dallas L.	Santa Barbara, CV-13, MIA 3/19/45
Jensen, Alvin J.	Ewa, 1st and 2d Solomons tours
Johnson, Alfred L.	2d Black Sheep tour
Johnson, Harry C.	2d Black Sheep tour
Jones, Robert M.	Santa Barbara, CV-13, MIA 3/19/45
Kindell, Ervin S.	Santa Barbara, killed accidentally 5/31/44
Knipping, Paul A.	2d Solomons tour
Kraft, L. George (USN flight surgeon)	Ewa, 1st Solomons tour
Kuhn, Joseph	Santa Barbara
Lane, Perry T.	2d Black Sheep tour
Lanphier, Charles C.	Ewa, 1st and 2d Solomons tours, died as POW 5/15/44
Larche, Beverly J.	Santa Barbara, CV-13
Linder, Kenneth N.	Santa Barbara, CV-13
Little, Arthur W., Jr. (Adjutant)	Ewa, all South Pacific tours
Losch, Fred S.	2d Black Sheep tour
Magee, Christopher L.	1st and 2d Black Sheep tours
March, Marion J.	2d Black Sheep tour
Marker, Alan D.	2d Black Sheep tour, injured 12/12/43
Matheson, Bruce J.	1st and 2d Black Sheep tours, wounded 10/17/43
McCall, Drury E.	Ewa, 1st and 2d Solomons tours
McCartney, Henry A.	1st Black Sheep tour
McClurg, Robert W.	1st and 2d Black Sheep tours

McDonnell, Robert J.	CV-13
McPherson, Warren H.	Santa Barbara, CV-13
Miller, Harold D.	Santa Barbara, CV-13
Miller, Henry S.	Ewa, 1st and 2d Solomons tours, 2d Black Sheep tour
Moak, David R.	Ewa, 1st and 2d Solomons tours
Moon, Charles G.	Santa Barbara
Moore, Donald J.	1st and 2d Black Sheep tours, MIA 12/28/43
Mullen, Paul A.	1st and 2d Black Sheep tours, wounded 9/23/43
Nabors, William A.	Santa Barbara
O'Dell, Bennie P.	Ewa, 1st and 2d Solomons tours
Olander, Edwin L.	1st and 2d Black Sheep tours
Pace, William H.	Ewa, 1st and 2d Solomons tours, killed accidentally 8/7/43
Peacock, Richard H.	Santa Barbara
Peterson, Phillip A.	Santa Barbara
Petit, Jack W.	Ewa, 1st and 2d Solomons tours
Rankin, David W.	Ewa, 1st and 2d Solomons tours
Ray, Virgil G.	1st and 2d Black Sheep tours, lost in storm 10/13/43
Reames, James M. (USN flight surgeon)	1st and 2d Black Sheep tours
Reinburg, Jeremiah J.	Ewa, killed accidentally 1/12/43
Reynolds, Leon A.	Santa Barbara
Rinabarger, Rolland N.	1st Black Sheep tour, wounded 9/26/43
Rudsen, Daniel (Intelligence)	Santa Barbara
Saulter, William H.	Santa Barbara

Scarborough, Hartwell V.	Ewa, 1st and 2d Solomons tours
Schmagel, Arthur O.	Santa Barbara, CV-13, wounded 3/19/45
Schocker, Walter J.	Santa Barbara, CV-13
Schwarz, Aylward P.	Santa Barbara, CV-13
Scramuzza, Herbert D.	Santa Barbara, CV-13, killed accidentally 2/16/45
Shuman, Perry L.	Ewa
Sibbernsen, Albert A.	Santa Barbara, CV-13
Sigel, Richard A.	Ewa, 1st and 2d Solomons tours
Sims, Sanders S.	1st and 2d Black Sheep tours
Smyth, Gene, Jr.	Santa Barbara
Somers, Charles W.	Ewa
Steed, Harrell	Ewa, 1st Solomons tour, MIA 3/17/43
Stodd, John P.	Santa Barbara, CV-13, POW 3/18/45
Stout, Joseph E.	Santa Barbara, CV-13, MIA 3/19/45
Synar, Stanley T.	2d Solomons tour
Taylor, James G. G.	Ewa, 1st and 2d Solomons tours
Tilton, Ranson R.	Santa Barbara, CV-13, wounded 3/19/45
Tomlinson, Thomas M.	Ewa, 1st and 2d Solomons tours
Tucker, Burney L.	1st and 2d Black Sheep tours
Urbom, Oscar D.	Santa Barbara, CV-13, MIA 3/19/45
Vandegrift, John L.	CV-13
Vetter, Adolph R.	Ewa
Walton, Frank E., Jr. (Intelligence)	1st and 2d Black Sheep tours
White, Philip R.	Ewa
Williams, Otto K.	Ewa, 1st and 2d Solomons tours

Appendix B

VMF-214 Operational and Combat Losses

Date	Type	Bu No.	Cause	Pilot	Injuries
8-28-42	F4F-3		Crashed during maneuvers		None
9-3-42	F4F-3	4031	Crash-landed, surveyed		None
9-4-42	F4F-3	3910	Crash-landed, surveyed		None
9-9-42	F4F-3	4010	Crash-landed, surveyed		None
12-2-42	F4F-3		Wheel failure, water landing	Lt. Vetter	None
1-12-43	F4F-4	11894	Midair, pilot bailed out	Lt. Reinburg	Killed
1-12-43	F4F-4	11895	Midair, pilot bailed out	Lt. Fidler	Rescued, Minor
1-20-43	F4F-4	11897	Ground loop, surveyed	TSgt. Jensen	None
1-21-43	F4F-4	12068	Ground loop, surveyed	Lt. Hoover	None
2-3-43	F4F-4	11898	Spin, pilot bailed out	Lt. Dunbar	Minor
3-14-43	F4F-4	12035	Fuel pump failure, crashed	Capt. Ellis	Rescued, Minor
3-14-43	F4F-4	12068	Fuel starvation, crash-landed	TSgt.Taylor	None
3-17-43	F4F-4		Undetermined, crashed	TSgt. Steed	Missing
4-7-43	F4F-4	11905	Enemy action, pilot bailed out	Capt. Burnett	Minor
4-7-43	F4F-4	11721	Enemy action, crash-landed	Lt. Scarborough	Minor
4-15-43	F4F-4	11941	Engine failure, ditched	Lt. Lanphier	Rescued, None
4-27-43	F4F-4	11777	Engine fire, burned after landing	Lt. McCall	None
7-15-43	F4U-1	17447	Engine fire, pilot bailed out	Lt. Hollmeyer	None

Date	Type	Bu No.	Cause	Pilot	Injuries
7-15-43	F4U-1	02683	Engine failure, ditched	Lt. Tomlinson	Minor
8-1-43	F4U-1	02508	Emergency landing, overturned	Lt. Taylor	None
8-6-43	F4U-1	02485	Engine failure, ditched	Capt. Eisele	Minor
8-6-43	F4U-1	02492	Enemy action	Lt. Blakeslee	Missing
8-7-43	F4U-1	02474	Engine failure, crashed	Maj. Pace	Killed
8-25-43	F4U-1A	18072	Overturned on landing	Lt. Hanson	None
8-28-43	F4U-1	02577	Enemy action or weather	Lt. Lanphier	Died in captivity
9-16-43	F4U-1A	17127	Enemy action	Capt. Ewing	Missing
9-21-43	F4U-1A	17916	Hit tree, pilot bailed out	Lt. Heier	Rescued, None
9-23-43	F4U-1A	55828	Emergency landing, overturned	Lt. Alexander	None
9-23-43	F4U-1		Enemy action, surveyed	Lt. Groover	Serious
9-26-43	F4U-1A	55876	Enemy action, crash-landed	Lt. Rinabarger	Serious
9-27-43	F4U-1A	56016	Enemy action	Lt. Harris	Missing
9-30-43	F4U-1		Shot down by PT boat	Lt. Alexander	Killed
10-13-43	F4U-1A	17679	Undetermined	Lt. Ray	Missing
10-16-43	F4U-1A	17844	Fuel starvation, ditched	Lt. Emrich	Rescued, None
10-17-43	F4U-1A	55889	Enemy action, crash-landed	Lt. Harper	Minor
11-28-43	F4U-1	03803	Fuel starvation, ditched	Lt. Brown	Rescued
12-5-43	F4U-1A	17888	Overturned on landing	Lt. Groover	None
12-12-43	F4U-1A	17840	Overturned on landing	Lt. Marker	Moderate
12-16-43	F4U-1A	17777	Overturned on landing	Lt. Groover	None
12-17-43	F4U-1A	17844	Overturned on landing	Lt. Moore	Moderate
12-23-43	F4U-1	17395	Enemy action	Maj. Carnagey	Missing
12-23-43	F4U-1	17451	Enemy action	Lt. Brubaker	Missing
12-23-43	F4U-1	17443	Enemy action	Lt. Ffoulkes	Missing
12-28-43	F4U-1A	17808	Enemy action	Capt. Dustin	Missing
12-28-43	F4U-1A	17910	Enemy action	Lt. Moore	Missing
12-28-43	F4U-1A	17527	Enemy action	Lt. Bartl	Missing
1-1-44	F4U-1A	17899	Struck by B-24 on ground	Maj. Miller	None
1-3-44	F4U-1A	17915	Enemy action	Maj. Boyington	POW, Survived

Date	Type	Bu No.	Cause	Pilot	Injuries
1-3-44	F4U-1	02723	Enemy action	Capt. Ashmun	Missing
3-23-44	FG-1A	13543	Fuel starvation, crashed	Lt. Kuhn	Minor
4-2-44	FG-1A	13532	Engine failure during takeoff	Lt. Alexander	Died in hospital
4-14-44	FG-1A	13547	Pilot ejected by inflating raft	Lt. Collins	Killed
5-31-44	FG-1A		Failed to return from flight	Lt. Kindell	Missing
8-22-44	FG-1A	13504	Crashed into water	Lt. Boozer	Killed
11-2-44	FG-1A	13521	Overturned on takeoff	Lt. Nabors	Minor
2-16-45	F4U-1D		Midair collision	Lt. Beeler	Killed
2-16-45	F4U-1D		Midair collision	Lt. Scramuzza	Killed
2-17-45	F4U-1D		Wheels-up landing on beach	Lt. Hyatt	None
2-28-45	F4U-1D		Fire during arrested landing	Lt. Husted	Killed
3-18-45	F4U-1D	82368	Enemy AA	Lt. Stodd	POW, Survived
3-19-45	F4U-1D	82403	Fire aboard CV-13		
3-19-45	F4U-1D	82420	Fire aboard CV-13		
3-19-45	F4U-1D	82646	Fire aboard CV-13		
3-19-45	F4U-1D	82683	Fire aboard CV-13		
3-19-45	F4U-1D	82705	Fire aboard CV-13		

Several additional aircraft assigned to VMF-214 were lost in accidents at Turtle Bay. The pilots were assigned to MAG-11 headquarters squadron.

Date	Type	Bu No.	Cause	Pilot	Injuries
10-1-43	F4U-1	02449	Undetermined	Lt. Wolfe	Killed
10-2-43	F4U-1	02329	Undetermined	Maj. Dill	Rescued
10-18-43	F4U-1	17424	Impacted mountain	Lt. McMahan	Killed
10-20-43	F4U-1	02315	Engine failure, pilot bailed out	Lt. Holden	Minor
10-22-43	F4U-1	02608	Crashed into jungle	Lt. Bennett	Killed

Appendix C

The Combat Sorties of Maj. Gregory Boyington, USMCR

FIRST TOUR

Date	Mission	Duration	Claims
9-12-43	Transit to Guadalcanal	0745–1145	
9-12-43	Transit to Banika	1630–1700	
9-14-43	Strike escort	0835–1135	
9-15-43	Photo escort	1015–1255	
9-16-43	Strike escort	1300–1500	4 Hamps, 1 Zeke
9-16-43	Munda to Banika	1710–1755	
9-17-43	Strike escort	0730–0900	
9-18-43	Local patrol	1215–1400	
9-18-43	Local patrol	1730–1845	
9-20-43	Night fighter patrol	0100–0500	
9-21-43	Strafing	0825–1100	
9-21-43	Strafing	1525–1725	
9-23-43	Strike escort	0800–1030	
9-23-43	Scout, strafing	1230–1400	
9-24-43	Transit to Barakoma	1015–1045	
9-24-43	Return to Munda	1700–1730	
9-25-43	Task force cover	0535–0800	
9-25-43	Task force cover	1300–1540	
9-26-43	PV orientation escort	0945–1100	
9-27-43	Strike escort	1105–1330	1 Zeke
9-27-43	Scramble	1700–1900	
9-28-43	Local patrol	1045–1400	
9-28-43	Local patrol	1730–1900	
9-29-43	Scramble	0735–0835	
9-30-43	Task force cover	0545–0830	
10-4-43	Strike escort/Munda	1115–1425	3 Zekes
10-4-43	Return to Banika	1533–1620	
10-11-43	Strike escort	0800–1020	
10-12-43	Fighter sweep	1400–1500	
10-15-43	Strike escort	1045–1320	3 Zekes Probables

Date	Mission	Duration	Claims
10-16-43	Strike escort/sweep	0900–1115	
10-17-43	Fighter sweep	0815–1015	3 Zekes
10-18-43	Strike escort	0900–1145	
10-18-43	Fighter sweep	1530–1745	1 Zeke
10-19-43	Strafing/Barakoma	0450–0645	
10-19-43	Return to Munda	Unknown	
10-21-43	Transit to Barakoma	0700–0730	

SECOND TOUR

Date	Mission	Bu. No.	Duration	Claims
11-28-43	Local patrol	17735	0855–1259	
11-30-43	Local patrol	17735	0908–1315	
12-4-43	Strike escort	17395	0831–1130	
12-4-43	Local patrol	17395	1500–1843	
12-6-43	Strike escort	17452	0845–1219	
12-10-43	Transit to Torokina	17792	0915–1000	
12-10-43	Return to Barakoma	17792	1645–1730	
12-11-43	Local patrol/ Torokina	17395	0450–0915	
12-11-43	Return to Barakoma	17395	1550–1640	
12-12-43	Transit to Munda	17910	1058–1118	
12-12-43	Return to Barakoma	17910	1314–1339	
12-13-43	Transit to Torokina	17527	0510–0557	
12-14-43	Local patrol	17527	0545–0815	
12-14-43	Local patrol	17527	0945–1100	
12-14-43	Local patrol/ Barakoma	17527	1545–1800	
12-16-43	Transit to Munda	17485	1405–1425	
12-16-43	Return to Barakoma	17485	1600–1620	
12-17-43	Transit to Torokina	17395	0510–0620	
12-17-43	Fighter sweep	17395	0900–1205	
12-21-43	Transit to Torokina	17395	0745–0840	
12-21-43	Return to Barakoma	17395	1550–1640	

Date	Mission	Bu. No.	Duration	Claims
12-23-43	Transit to Torokina	17744	0822–0912	
12-23-43	Fighter sweep	17744	1230–1630	4 Zekes
12-27-43	Transit to Torokina	17883	0617–0712	
12-27-43	Fighter sweep	17883	1000–1310	1 Zeke
12-27-43	Return to Barakoma	17883	1515–1615	
12-27-43	Transit to Torokina	17915	1745–1840	
12-28-43	Fighter sweep	17915	0600–0930	Tojo probable
12-29-43	Return to Barakoma	17915	1710–1800	
12-30-43	Transit to Torokina	17915	0659–0800	
12-30-43	Return to Barakoma	17915	1140–1235	
1-2-44	Dumbo escort/ Torokina	02723	0715–0830	
1-2-44	Fighter sweep	17883	1020–1350	
1-2-44	Transit to Torokina	17915	1730–1830	
1-3-44	Fighter sweep	17915	0630–0825*	3 Zekes

The primary sources used to compile this record were the VMF-214 war diary (first tour information) and Henry Miller's meticulous squadron flight log (second tour). To date, no record of specific aircraft for the first tour has been located, but Boyington flew any of a dozen or more different planes, as did the other Black Sheep. Pilots normally maintained their own records in a Navy-issue aviators' flight logbook, but as pilot Bruce Matheson asserts, "It is entirely possible that Boyington didn't even have a flight log with him; certainly I never saw it nor heard him refer to it."

This much is known: Boyington did not fly a personal airplane in combat. On one occasion, on November 26, 1943 (between combat tours), he posed for a photograph taken in a randomly picked Corsair on Espiritu Santo,

*The approximate time he bailed out, allowing ten minutes after initial contact.

hundreds of miles from the combat area. The aircraft was adorned with the name “Lucybelle” and twenty victory flags: fourteen for his victories to date as a Marine, six for his AVG claims. Of the markings, Boyington later said, “We only put them there for publicity purposes. You know, they ran a publicity game out there even during a real war.” Although he did not fly that particular aircraft in combat, entrepreneurs sell “replica” pieces of sheet metal with the markings for hundreds of dollars apiece.

Appendix D

Mulitple-Victory Pilots of VMF-214

Gregory Boyington	23 (3 with the AVG)*
Christopher L. Magee	9
William N. Case	8 (1 with VMF-112)
Alvin J. Jensen	7 (1 with VMF-441)
Robert W. McClurg	7
Paul A. Mullen	6½ (1½ with VMF-122)
John F. Bolt, Jr.	6
Don H. Fisher	6
Henry A. McCartney, Jr.	5 (1 with VMO-251, 3 with VMF-121)
Edwin L. Olander	5
Hartwell V. Scarborough, Jr.	5
William D. Heier	4
Burney L. Tucker	4
Fred V. Avey	3½ (1½ with VMF-213)
John F. Begert	3 (1 with VMF-122)
Bruce J. Matheson	3
Donald J. Moore	3
John R. Burnett	2
Warren T. Emrich	2
Robert M. Hanson	2 (later added 23 with VMF-215)

*The author's figure differs from that in official USMC records. Based on variances among AVG documents, recognition for three aerial victories should have been allowed for Boyington instead of the six claimed. His final two claims in VMF-214, added after the war, were unsubstantiated. Accordingly, his score should be ranked third on the Marine Corps' list behind Joseph J. Foss (26) and Robert M. Hanson (25).

Appendix E

Typical Marine Aviator's Survival Equipment*

Carried on person: Colt .45 automatic in shoulder holster, three clips with seven rounds each, two additional clips on web belt, small sea marker, waterproof matchbox, compass, pocketknife, Ray-Ban sunglasses, sheath knife, canteen, first-aid kit with mirror, strip maps.

Contents of jungle pack: canteen, first-aid kit, poncho, jeep hat, machete (cut down), five pairs wool socks, eight bars D-ration chocolate, sail, mosquito net (head), one pound Australian silver, ID disk, two bottles sperm oil, bottle of oil of citronella, bottle of gun cleaner, can of 3-in-1 oil, bottle of matches, waterproof matchbox with compass cap, pocketknife, sea marker, bottle of vitamin pills, two knife handles, signal flare gun with six rounds, mirror, .45 cleaning rod, sixty rounds .45 ammo, two fishing leaders, fish line, razor blades, three notebooks, six pencils, four strip maps, Rabaul map, four books on jungle edibles, translation reference, Australian government reference, sewing kit.

*As carried by Henry S. Miller in 1943–44.

Appendix F

Text of the Presidential Unit Citation

"For extraordinary heroism in action against enemy Japanese forces at Guadalcanal, April 7, 1943; Munda, July 17 to August 30, 1943; Northern Solomons, September 16 to October 19, 1943; and Vella Lavella and Torokina, December 17, 1943 to January 6, 1944. The first squadron to strafe Kahili, the first to operate from Munda while the field was under heavy enemy artillery fire, and the first to lead a fighter sweep on Rabaul, Marine Fighting Squadron TWO HUNDRED FOURTEEN executed bomber escort missions, strafing attacks, search sweeps and patrol missions. Superbly serviced and maintained by its ground crews despite enemy shellfire and nightly bombing attacks, this unit destroyed or damaged 273 Japanese aircraft during these campaigns and, in some of the most bitterly contested air combats on record, contributed substantially to the establishment of an aerial beachhead over Rabaul and paved the way for Allied bombers to destroy Japanese shipping, supply dumps and shore installations. Frequently outnumbered but never outfought, Marine Fighting Squadron TWO HUNDRED FOURTEEN achieved an outstanding combat record which reflects highest credit upon its skilled pilots, air and ground crews and the United States Naval Service."

For the President,

James Forrestal
Secretary of the Navy

NOTES

The following are abbreviated citations for quoted material and other references. A complete bibliography is provided separately. The bulk of the written documentation came from an eclectic mix of official, semi-official, and private diaries, the most unique among them being a handwritten war diary (HWD) that was hidden from the public for fifty years. Penned by several different hands in an unmarked notebook, the daily entries began with VMF-214's commissioning and continued throughout the second combat tour. The diary was part of an extensive private collection of documents, correspondence, unpublished works, magazine articles, and photographs made available by Frank Walton shortly before his death in 1993. Other diaries used extensively in this work were Henry Miller's *Solomon Islands Diary* (SID), published privately in limited quantity in 1988; the David Rankin diary (DRD) maintained from December 1, 1942, through December 11, 1943; a Flight Operations Summary notebook (FOS) kept by Howard Cavanagh during the first combat tour, and a similar FOS kept by Henry Miller during the second Black Sheep tour. The official typewritten war diaries (WD) and their attached air combat action (ACA) reports for VMF-214 and other USMC squadrons are preserved by the Marine Corps History Center. Comparable USN records are available at the adjacent Naval History Center, located at the Washington Navy Yard. Microfiche copies of the USS *Nassau* war diary and ship's history (SH) are located at the Emil Buehler

Naval Aviation Archives at the National Museum of Naval Aviation in Pensacola, Florida.

Preface

I'm a psychopathic liar: Boyington, quoted in *Air Classics Quarterly Review*.

Introduction

Japanese military philosophy: Nohara, *A6M Zero in Action*, p. 5.

The records were way, way inflated: Walton, oral history.

From the historian's point of view: Olynyk, *USMC Credits*, Introduction.

1 Dark Days

It didn't sit too well: Condon, telephone interview.

We had only about half a dozen, etc.: Ibid.

2 Starting from Scratch

The F2A-3 is not a combat aeroplane: White, statement attached to VMF-221 WD, 6/6/42.

This would be a good time: HWD, 7/18/42.

The Marine Corps expanded so fast: Britt, telephone interview.

Having trouble finding pilots: HWD, 7/30/42.

it was almost impossible: Britt.

off the farm: Cavanagh, telephone interview.

Flight school was one thing, etc.: Ibid.

mad as hell: Taylor, telephone interview.

Britt made it abundantly clear: Ibid.

Let's go for a ride, etc., and details of SNJ mishap: Fidler and Bernard, telephone interviews.

More aircraft would certainly come in handy: HWD, 10/14/42.

Those who were required: Britt.

You fly every day: Taylor.

Great day: HWD, 12/17/42.

It was hotter 'n hell: Fidler.

There were some guys: Ibid.

Most of my gunnery scoring: Britt.

drunken brawls with liquor free: DRD, undated.

After no more than thirty seconds: Britt.

It was just amazing: Fidler.

Bad luck seems to be upon us: HWD, 1/21/43.

they were delighted to have me: Miller, oral history.

Do you know where you are: Taylor.

Plenty of liquor: DRD, undated.

You're not going to be facing amateurs: Taylor.

3 Shellbacks and Submarines

The weather was so warm: Taylor.
every one of those harmonies: Carpenter, telephone interview.
a couple of extra whacks: Britt, correspondence to author.
This procedure was not exactly conducive: SH, p. 8.
I told you so: SID, 3/3/43.
great sighs of relief: SH, p. 8.
The Submarine Plague: Ibid.

4 The Storm before the Calm

mud hole: DRD, undated.
He wasn't much of a drinker: Lanphier, *At All Costs Reach and Destroy,* p. 241.
I was too discouraged: SID, 3/12/43.
tickled to death, etc.: Williams, telephone interview.
real mean: Taylor.
his left wingtip was in my ear: Britt, telephone interview.
guys completely out of control: Fidler.
Good Lord, how long are these engines going to keep running: Britt.
People on Guadalcanal, etc. and details of crash landing.: Taylor.
He was ignored by many: SID, 3/24/43.

5 Cactus

If you go off on your own, etc.: Condon.
beat up: FOS, 3/15/43.
During the time that their tour coincided with ours: Britt.
During the day they were just horrendous: McCall, telephone interview.
We were opening cans of meat: Carpenter.
a hole in the water: Rankin, telephone interview.
He was a fine young man: Britt, correspondence to David J. Ekstrand.
the overtaken pilot was almost instantly killed: SID, 3/19/43.
Though personable, he could not somehow earn the respect: Britt to Ekstrand.
The lights and guns let go: SID, 3/23/43.
The place where he hurt the most: McCall.
A certain squadron personality began to develop: Britt to Ekstrand.
I found quite a few Ivy League guys there: Carpenter.
Nicknames and song titles: Hollmeyer, correspondence to author.
The Seabees saw some of this liquor: McCall.
The calm before the storm: FOS, 3/31/43.
one ground-looped off the runway: SID, 4/1/43.
Our squadron seems plagued: FOS, 4/1/43.
a fine sight sailing westward: SID, 4/5/43.
ass-buster: SID, 4/7/43.
I lost John somewhere near Rendova: Ibid.

6 First Blood

Weather conditions over Guadalcanal: account of James E. Swett in *Aces Against Japan,* p. 94.

just a bunch of screaming and static: Carpenter.

Look at the bogeys: McCall monograph, "VMF-214 on Guadalcanal."

It was a pure overhead: McCall, telephone interview.

flew through the whole pack: SID, 4/7/43.

Four of the Zeros peeled off: Carpenter.

blew a lot of shots away: Ibid.

We just grabbed a few planes: Cavanagh, telephone interview.

It just happened to be there: Ibid.

sieve: McCall, photograph caption.

We looked over toward Tulagi: Williams.

See this smile, Doc: McCall monograph.

Hangovers from the 7th: HWD, 4/9/43.

You've never seen such predawn blackness: Britt, telephone interview.

He was unconscious when I first arrived: SID, 4/13/43.

minor damage: Ibid.

It was still a very informal war: Lanphier, *At All Costs Reach and Destroy,* p. 243.

As our aircraft drifted slowly: Ibid., 243–244.

Tom Lanphier, who was claiming credit: Miller, oral history.

every plane that could carry a rock to drop: Condon.

Bastards kept up all night: DRD, 4/18–19/43.

On the first run last night: SID, 4/19/43.

routine flight, and *no opposition encountered*: WD, multiple entries.

The Horse's F4U-1 model: HWD, 5/5/43.

everyone was quite shaken up: SID, 5/14/43.

dull and uneventful: HWD, 5/14/43.

all possible songs: Ibid.

7 Resting Up, Down Under

It is greatly relieving: SID, 5/16/43.

an excellent movie: SID, 5/18/43.

Takes about two year, details of native canoes: quoted by Rankin, DRD, 5/17/43.

(footnote), *The most useless cuss ever devised*: Mitchell, telephone interview.

Life is beautiful, etc.: HWD, 5/24/3.

a siege of beautiful women: DRD, 5/26/43.

Arthur Paton's nickname and "The Campaign of 11 Carlisle Road": McCall monograph.

Charlie's term of leave: Lanphier, p. 244.

Systems . . . running on 50 proof: HWD, 6/2/43.

One week in a soft cushioned cinema: DRD, 6/5/43.

Positively the worst drunk I've been on: DRD, 6/14/43.

Today we greet: HWD 6/18/43.

Doc Kraft did more than dispense medicinal brandy: Britt, correspondence to author.

8 "The Ewe Is Mighty Sweet"

They got dirty inside: Williams.

The engine was running so hard: Case, oral history.

Red hot: HWD, 6/19/43.

looking forward to flying it: DRD, 6/20/43.

We could do a lot of things: Taylor.

so that I could see: Williams.

a beautiful plane to fly: Carpenter.

He licked me: SID, 6/23/43.

Bill [Pace] is too inexperienced: SID, 6/18/43.

a beat up hypochondriac: HWD, 6/23/43.

Big fight over Rendova: DRD, 6/19/43.

Oil leaks are the worst difficulty: SID, 7/4/43.

The beer at the O. C. is a godsend: HWD, 6/21/43.

sent most of the boys home tight: DRD, 7/4/43.

the Ewe is mighty sweet: HWD, 7/5/43.

the F4U reacts beautifully: HWD, 7/10/43.

drink, fly and brawl: Eisele, correspondence to author.

He would get me or others to help him: Ibid.

What are you doing here: McClurg, oral history.

He was a real husky boy: Curran, telephone interview.

beat the hell out of a lonely reef: HWD, 7/10/43.

The Quartet was the best: HWD, 7/14/43.

even to the smell of hot metal, etc., and subsequent adventure: Hollmeyer, correspondence to author.

a roundhouse to the left: WD, attached ACA report, 7/18/43.

the guy in the top turret: McCall, telephone interview.

I didn't have a hell of a lot: Synar, telephone interview.

palatial: HWD, 7/21/43.

He would come over when the moon was full: Curran.

9 The Swashbucklers

I'll bet this is one of those famous traps, etc.: Carpenter.

scare the hell out of Jap pilots: Hollmeyer quoted by McCall, insignia monograph.

Being more than a little bit nervous: Taylor.

shot his ass off: Synar.

Hell, this is stupid: Cavanagh.

was able to see clearly the white spinner: WD, attached ACA report, 8/4/43.

The Nips have painted their 0's: HWD, 8/4/43.

crack into the trees at the edge of the shore: WD, attached ACA report, 8/6/43.

I went right down to the deck: Fidler.
I went to the Doc: Ibid.
It is assumed that he made a forced landing: HWD, 8/6/43.
I grabbed the tail of the plane: Eisele.
simple, sincere, and nicely carried out: HWD, 8/8/43.
burning like hell: Ibid.
engine offers many complex difficulties: HWD, 8/9/43.
Part of the afternoon: SID, 8/9/43.
dug in like so many chiggers: Sherrod, *History of USMC Aviation in World War II*, p. 150.
go ahead and shoot your heart out: Taylor.
caught them all square, etc.: Rankin, quoted in WD, attached ACA report, 8/15/43.
If I ever see those two pilots: Hernan, quoted in WD, attached ACA report, 8/15/43.
the first attempt at such a mission: Ibid.
a capable pilot: Britt.
Nips were lobbing shells: DRD, 8/20/43.
those lousy Nips: HWD, 8/20/43.
swinging Jap-like above the bombers: SID, 8/26/43.
one of the great single-handed feats: Sherrod, p. 157.
Jensen came out of it upside down: Ibid.
Let's go! etc., and details of strafing attack: WD, attached ACA report, 8/28/43.
ruining about 3 Bettys: HWD, 8/28/43.
fires blossom at both ends of the runway: WD, attached ACA report, 8/28/43.
Our fingers are crossed, Charlie: HWD, 8/28/43.
bite the air, etc., and *details of prison experience:* quoted by Tom Lanphier, p. 250.
and old beat up crates they were: HWD, 9/3/43.
plenty low despite Sydney's proximity: HWD, 9/4/43.
had accomplished something: SID, 9/16/43.
Tenseness wearing off: HWD, 9/5/43.
witnessed and suffered: HWD, 9/8/43.
madly engaged in the Pursuit of Happiness: HWD, 9/22/943.
Many sad hearts: HWD, 9/29/43.
to find the rape of 214: SID, 9/30/43.

10 "He Could Fly Better Drunk . . ."

Background of Boyington's childhood and early military training: Walton, "Pappy and His Black Sheep."
I don't know why I stayed away from this stuff, etc.: Boyington, public address, 10/25/58.
I wasn't one of those methodical chaps: Ibid.
Among the AVG fliers: Greenlaw, *Cosmopolitan.*

What's the matter, Captain: quoted by Greenlaw.
They had every reason in the world: Boyington, public address.
Not too tall: Greenlaw.
I came out here to fight: quoted by Greenlaw.
T' hell with it, etc.: Ibid.
assistant Secretary of the Navy: Boyington, *Baa Baa Black Sheep*, p. 121.
I was president of the AVG: Howard, quoted by Sherrod, p. xii.
in the middle of February, etc.: Boyington, p. 70.
Boyington and Hill each had one more: Ford, *Flying Tigers*, p. 388.
They had to practice: Condon.
I was finally able to con the poor doc: Boyington, p. 138.
bored to distraction: Ibid., p. 139.
going mentally crazier by the day: Ibid.

11 "Poor Little Lambs"

The rest had never been in an active squadron: Boyington, p. 142.
Hell, they know where they're going: Bourgeois, oral history.
The five guys were smart, and other details of the Bourgeois rescue: Ibid.
You never saw a guy travel so fast, etc.: McCartney, telephone interview.
a lovely convenience for traveling, etc.: Sims, oral history.
I'm probably the only Naval Aviation Cadet, etc.: Case, oral history.
I didn't know this guy Boyington, etc.: Fisher, oral history.
Nicknames: Walton, "Boyington's Black Sheep."
You're never gonna get home kid: McClurg, oral history.
The propeller was doing a good job: Boyington, p. 141.
Operations and training: WD, 9/7–11/43.
Bragdon had to relieve himself: Fisher.
[Boyington] suddenly blew into my tent: Johnson, correspondence to Walton.

12 The Bullets Fly

Somehow, when Boyington arrived: Britt, telephone interview.
He gave us his aggressive combat theories: Bailey, "Battling Black Sheep."
spilled out of the clouds: WD, attached ACA report, 9/16/43.
100+ fighters/bombers: 204 Kokutai log translation by Henry Sakaida.
All I could do was keep spinning my neck: Magee, oral history.
circling hive: WD, attached ACA report, 9/16/43.
went hunting: Ibid.
I was right behind him: Fisher.
a fair day's work: WD, attached ACA report, 9/16/43.
I was scared to death: McClurg.
The first time I saw a meatball: Bolt, oral history.

We timed for his fuel to run out: Groover, telephone interview.

that slowed-down, oil-smeared, and shell-riddled Corsair: Boyington, p. 153.

[Walton] would tend to sort this out: Matheson, oral history.

He was mad as hell: Britt, correspondence to author.

Flies were having a field day: Walton, *Once They Were Eagles*, p. 30.

Off you'd go: Matheson.

I got onto this one Zero: Case.

The Japanese were going into a straight dive, etc.: Magee.

Hell, I don't want any medals: Magee, in *Once They Were Eagles*, p. 35.

There was some kind of boat: Magee, oral history.

Oh God, there goes a plane: Ibid.

One . . . wo . . . en, etc.: Heier, oral history.

just some sort of feeling: Groover.

Rinabarger in particular: WD, 9/23/43.

tracers whistling by his ears: WD, attached ACA report, 9/23/43.

Dive out!: Ibid.

I was settled in on two Zeros: Groover.

the swarm of Zeros: WD, attached ACA report, 9/23/43.

seemed like a heck of a lot of blood: Groover.

I lined it up, etc.: Ibid.

a floating body: WD, 9/23/43.

When you have the GIs: McClurg.

You could get it around your rectum: Walton, oral history.

These pilots kept up a continual chatter: WD, 9/26/43.

beat a steady tattoo: WD, attached ACA report, 9/26/43.

I knew I'd got a hell of a blow: Rinabarger, oral history.

snapped at their heels: WD, attached ACA report, 9/26/43.

Bombs started coming down: Rinabarger.

going straight down the funnel, and Boyington's comment: quoted by Case.

Harris, we've got to go back, etc.: Ibid.

some of the recognition they deserved: Walton, *Once They Were Eagles*, p. 45.

We loved him: Olander, oral history.

Boyington's nicknames: the use of "Greg" and "Gramps" (and the absense of "Pappy") is widely agreed upon by surviving Black Sheep pilots. It was only after the war that "Pappy" became universal; consequently, their use of the nickname is frequent when Black Sheep reminisce.

I'm supposed to be the boss: quoted by Hampson in *Liberty*.

Boyington, Reames, and I: Walton, oral history.

Gee, Frank, when is this all gonna end, etc.: Ibid.

Don't fire until I give the word: Bailey, quoted in WD, 9/30/43.

Hold fire: Tucker, quoted in WD, attached statement, 9/30/43.

The Corsairs were right on the water: Wood, telephone interview.

a black, burned swath: Bailey, WD, attached statement, 9/30/43.

He had an attitude: Hill, telephone interview.
(footnote), *His nerves were shot*: Wood.

13 "Come on Up and Fight!"

Shooting us in as replacements: HWD, 10/1/43.
Wayland Bennett: Miller, oral history.
A gunner had some sort of weapon: Curran.
a million miles away in comfort: Walton, *Once They Were Eagles,* p. 46.
settled back on the Zero's tail: WD, attached ACA report, 10/4/43.
P-38, that's an F4U you're shooting at, etc.: quoted in WD, 10/4/43.
Whenever three or more of them got together: Walton, p. 14.
a real fine fellow: McCartney, telephone interview.
He would mooch it: Bolt, oral history.
A group of us sat with Boyington, etc.: Walton, "Boyington—Tragic Hero."
In the month of October: Boyington, p. 167.
killing many small fish: WD, 10/10/43.
We had a pretty poor opinion of them: Matheson.
We dropped down below the B-24s: Case.
I can't cut it anymore: quoted by Hill, telephone interview.
He wasn't an extrovert: Ibid.
Finally we spotted them: Case.
It is recommended: WD, 10/15/43.
The clouds were way the hell up there: Bolt.
Stick in close: quoted by Bolt.
Nobody shoot: Ibid.
As soon as I hit: Emrich, oral history.
Come on guys, etc.: Bolt.
I was only taken under fire etc.: Ibid.
Contents of message from Halsey: Bolt collection.
This boy was awarded the Navy Cross: Boyington, p. 196.
Sample report data: WD, attached ACA report, 10/17/43.
The 21 Marines had, without single loss: Walton, *Once They Were Eagles,* p. 53.
I picked myself a Zero: Harper, oral history.
Boyington always did a lot of shooting, etc.: Olander, telephone interview.
The bombing was the best: WD, 10/18/43.
You buggers: McClurg.
That's gonna have to be verified: Ibid.
Come on up and fight, etc.: Walton, p. 55–56.
The flight of Marines: Ibid.
He was leading this fighter sweep: Matheson, telephone interview.
He did taunt them: Olander, telephone interview.
Well, they're going to make it easy: quoted by Hill, oral history.
McGhee [sic] *didn't seem to be*: Boyington, p. 191.

On this flight, I ran it to the top: Case.

A few of us were on fighter strip alert: Matheson, oral history.

These men have been in combat: quoted by Walton, "Boyington—Tragic Hero."

Never mind, Doc: quoted by Walton.

I crawled out on my hands and knees: Boyington, public address, 10/25/58.

Hell, Greg, you don't have any shoes on, etc.: quoted by Walton.

Normally you'd be able to see: Magee.

He had heard someone up the line: Ibid.

He was an alcoholic: Matheson.

14 A Little Trouble in Paradise

No flying: WD, 10/22/43.

Quotes and details of fistfight: Walton, "Boyington—Tragic Hero."

My darling little rigger: Walton, correspondence to wife, 11/13/43.

Your readings are worse: Matheson.

prettiest damned wife a man could have: Walton, monograph, "Boyington's Black Sheep."

That did me no good: March, telephone interview.

from his shorts to his shoe tops: Avey, oral history.

Rusty [sic] *is one of those quiet boys*: Walton.

He couldn't hear: Losch, oral history.

Somebody detonated some dynamite: Bowers, oral history.

in a state of shock: Bolt, oral history.

I shot into the planes' armor, etc: Ibid.

for personal or departmental benefits: written statement by Boyington, 11/3/43.

for disobedience of orders: arrest orders via Smoak, 11/20/43.

In the meantime he needed some booze: Bowers.

a brilliant combat record, etc.: Strother, "Combat Efficiency Report," 11/15/43.

You are hereby released: orders via Smoak, 11/27/43.

Doc grabbed me: Rinabarger, oral history.

Major Boyington, your "Skipper": Little, memorandum to rear echelon, 11/27/43.

Boyington was a horror: Olander, oral history.

15 Islands in the Sun

a lovely little island: Walton, *Once They Were Eagles,* p. 79.

great air operations: quoted in Sherrod, p. 189.

Darling Carol: Walton, correspondence to wife, 12/6/43.

I weighed 128 pounds: Losch.

My mother warned me: quoted by Walton, "Boyington's Black Sheep."

Whatever you wanted: Ibid.

Southern lingo: Ibid.

Those that know him: Ibid.
It was just like one big family: Bowers.
These tests illustrated: Bolt, correspondence to author.
the place was a quagmire: Olander, telephone interview.
You must be crazy: quoted by Olander, ibid.
no longer a satisfactory base: quoted in Sherrod, p. 194.
All squadron commanders: Air Operations Barakoma, order posted 12/15/43.
I was just in a state of shock: Marker, oral history.
As it was going over: Groover, telephone interview.
Tojo eats spam: quoted in Sakaida, *Siege of Rabaul,* p. 12.
Come on up and fight! etc: quoted in Sherrod, p. 195.
(footnote) *Seaplanes, subs and destroyers*: Okumiya, USSBS interrogation.
I looked down and saw this Rufe: McClurg, oral history.
They were a vivid California blue: quoted in WD, attached ACA report, 12/17/43.
Major Boyington is of the opinion: WD, 12/17/43.

16 Black Sheep Falling

Destroy enemy aircraft: Air Operations Barakoma, order posted 12/22/43.
This is it, fellows: quoted by McClurg in WD, attached ACA report, 12/23/43.
opened fire at 100 yards: WD, attached ACA report, 12/23/43.
leaving only a big cloud: Ibid.
I was having to do esses, and radio calls with Ffoulkes: Heier, oral history.
On the peace-on-earth, etc.: Boyington, p. 213.
We all want to see you break the record, etc.: quoted by Walton, "Pappy Boyington's Last Flight."
I had just soaped down: Avey, oral history.
He kept going all the way around me: Corman, oral history.
Being greedy: Ibid.
They were firing on the PBY: Magee, oral history.
Nobody could control: Carl, *Pushing the Envelope,* p. 47.
Their air discipline was excellent: Case, oral history.
I got a probable, too: quoted by Hampson, *Liberty*.
Sure I am: Ibid.
Taking the formation: WD, attached ACA report, 12/28/43.
He flew us right up into the sun: Olander, oral history.
roofed in: WD, attached ACA report, 12/28/43.
a terrific rate of climb: Ibid.
to murder the jumping jive: Walton, "Boyington's Black Sheep."
daily fighter sweep jaunts: Boyington, p. 218.
He entered the mess hall: Hampson.

more colorful than just singing and drinking: Matheson, correspondence to author.

A B-24 was coming in: Condon, telephone interview.

I was just flying on his wing: Losch, oral history.

Boyington was throwing oil: Ibid.

[Groover] opened up on one, etc.: Ibid.

He looked upon that trip: Olander.

He stayed up there just to get away, etc.: Condon.

I thought, what the hell am I doing here: Hill, telephone interview.

There was a radio recording hookup: Hampson.

About 50 percent of the formation: WD, attached ACA report, 1/4/44.

Okay, go: quoted by Johnson, oral history.

Of course, this was always the daydream, etc.: Johnson.

17 Black Sheep Scattered

George's death bothered me: Olander.

the hottest place this side of Hell: Reames, correspondence to Walton.

Keep this combat team intact: Moore, undated handwritten endorsement.

I'm confident he is alright: Hallenbeck, quoted in *New York Times*, 1/7/44.

Not only was Boyington of immense value: Mitchell, quoted in *New York Times*, 1/8/44.

He may show up: Walton, quoted in *New York Times*, 1/8/44.

I never heard anybody call him "Pappy": Losch, oral history.

We all miss the skipper: Walton, correspondence to spouse.

We were fanatics: Bolt, oral history.

He made a dry run, etc.: Harper, oral history.

a hole in his back: Bolt.

The worst damn conditions: Bowers, oral history.

the doldrums of 1944: Sherrod, p. 237.

We organized Jap hunts: Corman, oral history.

We went out supposedly for an hour's hop, etc.: March, telephone interview.

He flew in the back of a dive bomber: Walton, oral history.

Back here, we follow such a squadron: Sullivan, correspondence with Walton.

a well-known flier: Hallenbeck, quoted in *New York Times*, 6/11/44.

18 Starting Over

Well, you're not going to be doing anything: quoted by Schmagel, telephone interview.

Kuhn, you're in hack: Ibid.

I'll take it: quoted by Free, telephone interview.

They wanted to know how many: Free.

The war was going on: Linder, telephone interview.

bean patch: Free.
to aid in her ceaseless war: WD, 8/11/45.
His wingman flew up on him: Free.
four casualties in the mice tribe: WD, 8/14/45.
you weren't really in the division: Schmagel.
until after the Emergency: Ibid.
the single most effective air weapon: Sherrod, p. 272.
racks and rails: Matheson, correspondence with author.
about two streets long: Linder.
Boy, when you dropped that thing: Ibid.
Let's get out the fog machines: Mickey Linder, telephone interview.
the most greasy pork sausages: Schmagel.
I always turned it until the last second: Free.
We all though he'd bought it: Stodd, correspondence to Condon.
We'd all put on belly tanks: Chapman, telephone interview.
Some kid brought out some venison: Schmagel.
In the Corsair, minimum rpms: Free.

19 Inferno

a pompous martinet: Reynolds, *The Fighting Lady*, p. 260.
We went out and did our triangle: Free.
your favorite playmate: Quoted by Riblett, *Leatherneck*.
She welcomed the carrier: Free.
We were told to drop: Chapman.
mostly little BBs: Free.
I'm hit, etc.: Ibid.
We kidded him: Ibid.
about ten guys with rifles, etc.: Stodd, correspondence to Condon.
pretty damn good: Chapman.
General quarters and *secure from general quarters*: generic.
flaked out: Chapman.
This airplane came from bow to stern: Schmagel.
I wasn't keenly aware: Chapman.
There was no place to go: Schmagel.
just burned black, etc.: Ibid.
further evidence that I was in shock, etc.: Chapman.
I charged the guns: Linder.
Not one Jap fighter: Bailey, "Battling Black Sheep."
just like it was going under the Golden Gate bridge, etc.: Free.
I know that I was one of the last: Linder.
From where I was, and *bone cases*: Chapman.
like mummies: Schmagel.

20 The Last Sheep Home

Details and quotes of Stodd's imprisonment: Stodd, correspondence to Condon.

In general, they were suffering: quoted in *New York Times*, 8/30/45.
some poor little starved B-29 pilot: Boyington, p. 344
Boyington's breakfast: *Time*, 9/2/45.
Boyington doesn't admit it: Stodd.
Details of Boyington drinking with guards: public address, 10/25/58.
You got a flamer: Quoted in WD, addendum to attached ACA, 10/4/45.
spraying the Zekes: Ibid.
When the flames came: Boyington, public address, 10/6/80.
shattered by a twenty-millimeter, etc.: Boyington, *Baa Baa Black Sheep*, p. 233.
At first I could dive: Ibid., p. 232.
We had training of being dropped: Miller, correspondence to author.
The waves that day: Boyington, p. 233.
Names of prisoners transported to Truk: Sakaida, *Siege of Rabaul*, pp. 93-96.
They were using baseball bats, etc.: Boyington, *True*.
the scraps of food: Ibid.
the best kleptomaniac around: quoted by Lagana, *Cross & Crescent*.
Inscription on wristwatch: *New York Times*, 9/14/45.
chicken and peas and bourbon: McCartney, telephone interview.
In Washington headquarters: Sherrod, p. ix.
When Greg came out of captivity: Carl, p. 48.
Consistently outnumbered, etc.: Medal of Honor citation.
His speech was getting better, etc.: Walton, oral history.
He would never have done on a magazine cover: Hampson.

Epilogue

Under a couple of palm trees: Losch, oral history.

Appendix C

It is entirely possible: Matheson, correspondence to author.
We only put them there for publicity: Boyington, public address, 10/6/80.

SOURCES

Books:

Boyington, Gregory, *Baa Baa Black Sheep*, Putnam, 1958, New York, NY

Carl, Marion E. with Tillman, Barrett, *Pushing the Envelope: The Career of Fighter Ace and Test Pilot Marion Carl*, Naval Institute Press, 1994, Annapolis, MD

Ford, Daniel, *Flying Tigers: Claire Chennault and the American Volunteer Group*, Smithsonian Institution Press, 1991, Washington, DC

Hall, R. Cargill, *Lightning Over Bougainville—The Yamamoto Mission Reconsidered*, Smithsonian Institution Press, 1991, Washington, DC

Hammel, Eric M., *Aces Against Japan—The American Aces Speak*, Presidio Press, 1992, Novato, CA

Hoeling, A. A., *The* Franklin *Comes Home: The Saga of the Most Decorated Ship in Naval History*, Hawthorn Books, 1974, New York, NY

Lundstrom, John B., *The First Team and the Guadalcanal Campaign: Naval Fighter Combat from August to November 1942*, Naval Institute Press, 1994, Annapolis, MD

Mason, Herbert, M., Jr., *The Lafayette Escadrille*, Random House, 1964, New York, NY

Morison, Samuel E., *History of Naval Operations in WW II, Vol.6, Breaking the* Bismarck's *Barrier 22 July 1942–1 May 1944*, Little, Brown & Co.,1962, Boston

Nohara, Shigeru, *A6M Zero in Action*, Squadron Signal Publications, 1983, Carrollton, TX

Olynyk, Frank J., *USMC Credits for the Destruction of Enemy Aircraft in Air-to-Air Combat, World War 2, 1982*, published by the author

Reynolds, Clark G., *The Fighting Lady: The New Yorktown in the Pacific War*, Pictorial Histories, 1986, Missoula, MT

Sakaida, Henry, *The Siege of Rabaul*, Phalanx, 1996, St. Paul, MN

Sherrod, Robert L., *History of Marine Corps Aviation in WW II*, Nautical & Aviation Publishing Co. of America, 1980, Baltimore, MD (Revised ed.)

Special Services Division, Services of Supply, *A Pocket Guide to Australia, War and Navy Departments*, 1943, Washington, DC

Swanborough, Gordon and Bowers, Peter M., *United States Navy Aircraft Since 1911*, Naval Institute Press, 1976, Annapolis, MD

Tillman, Barrett, *The F4U in WW II and Korea*, Naval Institute Press, 1979, Annapolis, MD

———, *Wildcat: The F4F in WW II*, Naval Institute Press, 1991, Annapolis, MD

Walton, Frank E. Jr., *Once They Were Eagles: The Men of the Black Sheep Squadron*, University Press of Kentucky, 1986, Lexington, KY

Weiland, Charles P., *Above and Beyond*, Pacifica Press, 1997, Pacifica, CA

Weintraub, Stanley, *Long Day's Journey Into War: December 7, 1941*, Dutton, 1991, New York, NY

———, *The Last Great Victory: The End of World War II, July/August 1945*, Dutton, 1995, New York, NY

Articles:

Allen, Dub and Johnson, Frank, "Colonel Gregory 'Pappy' Boyington," *Air Classics Quarterly Review*, Winter 1976

Belcher, Michael F., "The Flying Sergeants," *Proceedings*, U.S. Naval Institute, February 1982

Boyington, Gregory, "I'll Buy the Drinks, Boys," *True*, (no citation) circa 1946

Ekstrand, David J., "The Swashbucklers," *Marine Corps Gazette*, Dec. 1989

Greenlaw, Olga, "Pappy," *Cosmopolitan*, April 1944

Hampson, Fred, "Boyington, Lost Ace," *Liberty*, July 1, 1944

Lagana, Gregory M., "Gregory Boyington: Still a Legend, But Never a Hero," *Cross & Crescent*, March 1978

Littrell, Gaither, "Pappy's Blacksheep," *Flying*, December 1944

Riblett, Leonard, "The Rose of UCLA," *Leatherneck*, December 1944

Tillman, Barrett, "Five the Hard Way: Navy and Marine Corps Aces-in-a-Day or: Numbers Do Count," *The Hook*, Fall 1993

Walton, Frank E., Jr., "Baa Baa Black Sheep Is Pulling the Wool Over Our Eyes," *TV Guide*, April 23, 1977

———, "The Combat Strategy and Tactics of Major Gregory Boyington, USMCR," Headquarters, Marine Aircraft, South Pacific, *FMF Intelligence Section*, January 19, 1944

———, "Black Sheep . . . Run!," *Skyways*, July 1944

Unpublished Monographs and Transcripts:

Bailey, Stanley R., *Battling Black Sheep*, circa 1945

Boyington, Gregory, public address, Alcoholics Anonymous, San Francisco, CA, October 25, 1958

———, public address, National Air and Space Museum, Washington, DC, October 6, 1980

Lanphier, Thomas G., Jr., *At All Costs Reach and Destroy*, autobiography

Little, Arthur W., Jr., *Somewhere in the Pacific*, April 22, 1943

McCall, Drury E. *VMF-214 on Guadalcanal*, circa 1943

———, *History of Swashbuckler Insignia*, undated

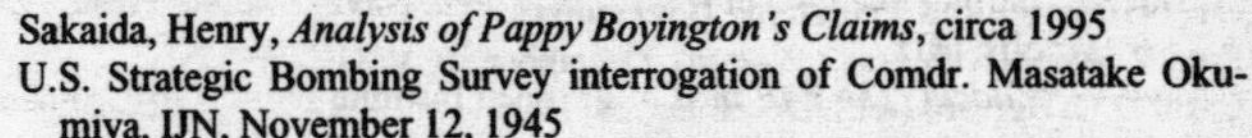

Sakaida, Henry, *Analysis of Pappy Boyington's Claims*, circa 1995

U.S. Strategic Bombing Survey interrogation of Comdr. Masatake Okumiya, IJN, November 12, 1945

Walton, Frank E. Jr., *Boyington's Black Sheep*, circa 1944

———, *Boyington, Tragic Hero*, circa 1977

———, *Pappy and His Black Sheep*, circa 1946

———, *Pappy Boyington's Last Flight*, circa 1977

Official War Diaries, Action Reports, and Unit Histories:

VMF-112, VMF-122, VMF-124, VMF-211, VMF-213, VMF-214, VMF-215, VMF-221,VMSB/VMTB-143

USS *Nassau* (ACV-16)

Ship's History, USS *Nassau*, CVE-16/A12-1 Ser.: 018

Commander, MTB Squadron 6, Ser. 0052, 30 Sept. 1943

11th Air Fleet, 201, 204 and 253 Kokutai, April 1943 to January 1944 (Henry Sakaida collection)

Unofficial Diaries:

VMF-214 handwritten war diary, July 1, 1942 to October 3, 1943

Cavanagh Howard L., Flight Operations Summary notebook, March 15 to April 28, 1943

Miller, Henry S., Flight Operations Summary notebook, November 28, 1943 to January 6, 1944

———, *Solomon Islands Diary*, March 3 to November 13, 1943

Rankin, David W., personal diary, December 1 1942 to December 11, 1943

Correspondence:

John Bolt to author, February 29, 1996

George Britt to David Ekstrand, Sept. 24, 1987

George Britt to author, May 7, 1996

Harold Eisele to author, March 10, 1997

Harry Hollmeyer to author, June 17, 1997, July 10, 1997

Pen Johnson to Frank Walton, May 26, 1986

Bruce Matheson to author, November 27, 1997

Henry Miller to 1st Marine Air Wing, January 12, 1944

Henry Miller to author, October 3, 1997

James Reames to Frank Walton, May 8, 1944

John Stodd to John Condon, May 14, 1994

Ed Sullivan to Frank Walton, March 15, 1944

Frank Walton to wife, November 13, 1943

———, December 6, 1943

———, January 18, 1944

Flight Log Books:

J. F. Bolt, W. N. Case, J. J. Hill, C. L. Magee, B. J. Matheson, D. E. McCall, R. W. McClurg, E. L. Olander, D. W. Rankin, S. S. Sims

Oral Histories and Telephone Interviews:

Fred V. Avey (with Frank Walton), December 10, 1981
Carol D.C. Bernard (tel.), December 28, 1996
John F. Bolt, Jr., November 22, 1991
Henry M. Bourgeois (tel.), March 1, 1996
Glenn L. Bowers, November 30, 1995
George F. Britt (tel.), March 27, 1996
Vincent W. Carpenter (tel.), November 5, 1996
William N. Case, May 12, 1993
Howard E. Cavanagh (tel.), May 20, 1996
Warner O. Chapman (tel.), October 11, 1997
John P. Condon (tel.), July 3, 1996
J. Ned Corman, May 13, 1993
Hugh J. Curran (tel.), March 24, 1997
Warren T. Emrich, May 16, 1993
John L. Fidler (tel.), May 30, 1996
Don H. Fisher, May 15, 1993
Stanley E. Free (tel.), February 20, 1997
Denmark Groover, Jr. (tel.), April 13, 1996
Edwin A. Harper, May 16, 1993
William D. Heier, May 16, 1993
James J. Hill, May 11, 1993 (tel.), August 12, 1997
Herbert Holden, Jr. (tel.), April 7, 1996
Alfred L. Johnson, May 14, 1993
Harry C. Johnson (with Frank Walton), December 16, 1981
Perry T. Lane, May 13, 1993
Kenneth N. Linder (tel.), October 17, 1997
Mickey O. Linder (tel.), October 19, 1997
Frederick S. Losch, May 16, 1993
Christopher L. Magee, May 11, 1993
Marion J. March (tel.), March 2, 1996
Alan D. Marker, May 13, 1993
Bruce. J. Matheson, May 15, 1993
Drury E. McCall (tel.), November 2, 1996
Henry A. McCartney (tel.), March 15, 1996
Robert W. McClurg, May 11, 1993
Henry S. Miller, November 30, 1995
Robert E. Mitchell, September 23, 1997
Edwin L. Olander, May 15, 1993, Aug. 16, 1997 (tel.), September 2, 1997 (tel.)
David W. Rankin (tel.), April 20, 1996
James M. Reames, May 12, 1993
Rinabarger, Rolland N. (with Frank Walton), April 16, 1976
Arthur O. Schmagel (tel.), October 13, 1997
Margaret L. Sibbernsen (tel.), October 16, 1997
Sanders S. Sims, May 13, 1993

Stanley T. Synar (tel.), March 20, 1997
James G. G. Taylor (tel.), May 18, 1996
Frank E. Walton, Jr., May 15, 1993
Otto K. Williams (tel.), April 15, 1996
Leighton C. Wood (tel.), February 25, 1996

INDEX